GLOBALIZATION:
A BIBLIOGRAPHY WITH INDEXES

GLOBALIZATION:
A BIBLIOGRAPHY WITH INDEXES

MARINA ELBAKIDZE (EDITOR)

Nova Science Publishers, Inc.
New York

Senior Editors: Susan Boriotti and Donna Dennis
Coordinating Editor: Tatiana Shohov
Office Manager: Annette Hellinger
Graphics: Wanda Serrano
Editorial Production: Jennifer Vogt, Matthew Kozlowski, Jonathan Rose
and Maya Columbus
Circulation: Ave Maria Gonzalez, Indah Becker, Raymond Davis,
Vladimir Klestov and Jonanthan Roque
Communications and Acquisitions: Serge P. Shohov
Marketing: Cathy DeGregory

Library of Congress Cataloging-in-Publication Data
Available Upon Request

ISBN 1-59033-203-2.

CONTENTS

PREFACE

There are probably few concepts less understood, more cursed and blamed for everything imaginable, and yet perhaps result in so many outstanding developments as globalization. Globalization is the process of denationalization of markets, politics and legal systems, i.e., the rise of the so-called global economy. The consequences of this political and economic restructuring on local economies, human welfare and environment are the subject of vigorous debate among businesses of all sizes, various international organizations, governmental institutions and the academic world. This book gathers the book and journal literature on this controversial subject. Additional access is provided by author, subject and title indexes.

GENERAL BIBLIOGRAPHY

A new ASEAN in a new millennium / Simon
S.C. Tay, Jesus Estanislao, Hadi
Soesastro, editors. Published/Created:
Jakarta, Indonesia: Centre for Strategic
and International Studies; Singapore:
Singapore Institute of International
Affairs, c2000. Related Names: Tay,
Simon. Estanislao, Jesus P. Soesastro,
Hadi. Centre for Strategic and
International Studies. Singapore Institute
of International Affairs. Description: x,
243 p.; 25 cm. ISBN 9798026691
Contents: The relevance of ASEAN, crisis
and change / Simon S.C. Tay and Jesus
Estanislao -- ASEAN's past and the
challenges ahead, aspects of politics and
security / Jusuf Wanandi -- ASEAN in the
past 33 years, lessons for economic
cooperation / Narongchai Akrasanee --
Trade, investment, and interdependence /
Mohamed Ariff -- Southeast Asia,
development, finance, and trade / Jesus
Estanislao -- Challenge for society and
politics / Carolina G. Hernandez --
Globalisation and information and
communications technology, challenges
for ASEAN / Chia Siouw Yue -- New
security issues and their impact on
ASEAN / Kusuma Snitwongse and Suchit
Bunbongkarn -- Institutions and
processes, dilemmas and possibilities /
Simon S.C. Tay -- ASEAN 2030, the long
view / Hadi Soesastro -- ASEAN and the
East Asia, a new religionism? / Simon
S.C. Tay. Notes: Includes bibliographical
references (p. [241]-243).

Aaronson, Susan A. Taking trade to the
streets: the lost history of public efforts to
shape globalization / Susan Ariel
Aaronson; with forewords by Pat Choate
and I.M. Destler. Published/Created: Ann
Arbor: University of Michigan Press,
c2001. Description: xvi, 264 p.; 24 cm.
ISBN 0472112120 (cloth: alk. paper)
Notes: Includes bibliographical references
(p. [237]-252) and index. Subjects:
Canada. Treaties, etc. 1992 Oct. 7.
General Agreement on Tariffs and Trade
(Organization) World Trade Organization.
United States--Commercial policy. Free
trade. Foreign trade regulation.
Globalization. Free trade--United States.
LC Classification: HF1713 .A15 2001
Dewey Class No.: 382 21

Abbott, Jeffrey. Uniting North American
business: NAFTA best practices / Jeffrey
Abbott and Robert T. Moran.
Published/Created: Boston: Butterworth-
Heinemann, 2002. Related Names:
Moran, Robert T., 1938- Description: p.
cm. ISBN 0877193843 (pbk.: alk. paper)
Notes: Includes bibliographical references
and index. Subjects: Canada. Treaties, etc.
1992 Oct. 7. Free trade--North America.
Globalization. Series: Managing cultural
differences series LC Classification:

HF1746 .A23 2002 Dewey Class No.:
382/.917 21

Abdel-Gadir, Faysal Impact of globalization
on small island states: some reflections /
Faysal Abdel-Gadir. Published/Created:
Honolulu, Hawaii: Pacific Islands
Development Program, East-West Center,
1998. Related Names: Pacific Islands
Development Program (East-West Center)
Description: 8 leaves; 28 cm. Subjects:
Globalization--Economic aspects--Islands
of the Pacific. Globalization--Social
aspects--Islands of the Pacific. Islands of
the Pacific--Foreign economic relations.
Islands of the Pacific--Economic
integration. LC Classification: HF1642.55
.A35 1998

Acosta, Nebis. América Latina en el mundo
actual / Nebis Acosta, Olga Arenas.
Published/Created: Maracaibo,
Venezuela: Universidad del Zulia, [1999]
Related Names: Arenas, Olga.
Description: 114 p.: ill.; 22 cm. ISBN
9802327158 Subjects: Latin America--
Foreign economic relations.
Globalization. LC Classification:
HF1480.5 .A26 1999

Activities of foreign affiliates in OECD
countries = Activités des filiales
étrangères dans les pays de l'OCDE.
Published/Created: Paris: OECD, c1997.
Related Names: Organisation for
Economic Co-operation and
Development. Economic Analysis and
Statistics Division. Description: 1 v.: ill.;
28 cm. 1985-94. Notes: "Statistical data."
English and French. "Prepared by the
Economic Analysis and Statistics Division
of the OECD Directorate for Science,
Technology, and Industry."
SERBIB/SERLOC merged record
Subjects: Corporations, Foreign--OECD
countries--Finance--Statistics Periodicals.
Affiliated corporations--OECD countries--
-Finance Statistics--Periodicals.

Investments, Foreign--OECD countries--
Statistics Periodicals. Investments,
Foreign, and employment--OECD
countries Statistics--Periodicals. LC
Classification: HG4538 .A38

Adapting to financial globalisation / edited by
Morten Balling, Eduard H. Hochreiter,
and Elizabeth Hennessy.
Published/Created: London; New York:
Routledge, 2001. Related Names: Balling,
Morten. Hochreiter, Eduard. Hennessy,
Elizabeth. Société universitaire
européenne de recherches financières.
Oesterreichische Nationalbank.
Description: p. cm. ISBN 0415252407
(alk. paper) Notes: Papers presented at a
conference held in Vienna in April 2000
by the Société universitaire européenne de
recherches financières and the Austrian
National Bank. Includes bibliographical
references and index. Subjects:
International finance--Congresses.
Monetary policy--Congresses. Banks and
banking--Congresses. Financial services
industry--Congresses. Globalization--
Economic aspects--Congresses. LC
Classification: HG205 .A3 2001 Dewey
Class No.: 332/.042 21

Adapting to financial globalisation / edited by
Morten Balling, Eduard H. Hochreiter,
and Elizabeth Hennessy.
Published/Created: London; New York:
Routledge, 2001. Related Names: Balling,
Morten. Hochreiter, Eduard. Hennessy,
Elizabeth. Société universitaire
européenne de recherches financières.
Oesterreichische Nationalbank.
Description: p. cm. ISBN 0415252407
(alk. paper) Notes: Papers presented at a
conference held in Vienna in April 2000
by the Société universitaire européenne de
recherches financières and the Austrian
National Bank. Includes bibliographical
references and index. Subjects:
International finance--Congresses.
Monetary policy--Congresses. Banks and

banking--Congresses. Financial services industry--Congresses. Globalization--Economic aspects--Congresses. LC Classification: HG205 .A3 2001 Dewey Class No.: 332/.042 21

Adivasi rights and the law [microform]: workshop in the National Conference on Human Rights, Social Movements, Globalisation, and the Law, Panchagani, 29-30 December, 2000: selected readings / co-organisers, All India Coordinating Forum of Adivasi/Indigenous Peoples, Kalpavriksh, Adivasi Rights Law Network; compiled by Kalpavriksh. Published/Created: [Pune: Kalpavriksh, 2000] Related Names: Kalpavriksh (Organization) Description: 1 v. (unpaged): ill.; 29 cm. Notes: Microfiche. New Delhi: Library of Congress Office; Washington, D.C.: Library of Congress Photoduplication Service, 2001. 2 microfiches. Master microform held by: DLC. Subjects: Adivasis--Legal status, laws, etc.--India. LC Classification: Microfiche 2001/60254 (K)

Adzmi Abdul Wahab, Dato', 1943- Projek kereta nasional: simbol wawasan ke arah 2020 / oleh Dato' Adzmi Abdul Wahab. Published/Created: Shah Alam, Selangor: Antilla, 1995. Description: xxxiv, 224, [2] p.: col. ill.; 27 cm. ISBN 9839901117 Summary: Implementation of national car project towards the 2020 economic globalization of Malaysia. Notes: Includes bibliographical references (p. [225]-[226]) and index. In Malay. Subjects: Automobile industry and trade--Malaysia. LC Classification: HD9710.M32 A39 1995

Africa and the emerging global trade issues: proceedings of an ad hoc experts group meeting on WTO-related issues. Published/Created: [Addis Ababa]: Economic Commission for Africa, [1998?] Related Names: United Nations.

Economic Commission for Africa. Description: iv, 167 p.; 30 cm. Notes: Includes bibliographical references. Subjects: World Trade Organization--Africa--Congresses. Globalization--Economic aspects--Africa--Congresses. Africa--Foreign economic relations--Congresses. Series: Working paper series (United Nations. Economic Commission for Africa) LC Classification: HF1611 .A544 1998

Africa and the multilateral trading system, and the World Trade Organization (WTO): Seattle and beyond. Published/Created: Addis Ababa, Ethiopia: United Nations Economic Commission for Africa, [between 1999 and 2001] Related Names: United Nations. Economic Commission for Africa. Description: xiv, 89 p.; 29 cm. Notes: Includes bibliographical references. Subjects: World Trade Organization--Africa. Globalization--Economic aspects--Africa. Africa--Foreign economic relations. LC Classification: HF1611 .A546 1999

Africa in crisis: new challenges and possibilities / edited by Tunde Zack-Williams, Diane Frost and Alex Thomson. Published/Created: London; Sterling, Va.: Pluto Press, 2001. Related Names: Zack-Williams, Tunde. Frost, Diane, 1962- Thomson, Alex. Description: p. cm. ISBN 0745316484 (hard) 0745316476 (pbk.) Contents: Introduction: Why is Africa in this mess? / Tunde Zack-Williams -- Globalisation, imperialism and exclusion: the case of Sub-Saharan Africa / Ankie Hoogvelt -- Youth, food and peace: a reflection on some African security issues at The Millennium 1 / Paul Richards -- African Renaissance? / Lionel Cliffe -- The colonisation of political consciousness: states and civil society in Africa / Rob Dixon -- The unaccountable state / Bruce Baker -- The US democratic experiment in Ghana / Julie Hearn --

Globalisation and democracy: international donors and civil society in Zimbabwe / Donna Pankhurst -- Misconception about the "World Market": implications for African export policies / H. Laurens van der Laan -- Cotton, food and work: contract farming, food security and the labour market in Northern Mozambique / Claire Melamed -- Continuity and change in French foreign policy toward Africa / Asteris C. Huliaras -- Subaltern terror in Sierra Leone / Jimmy D. Kandeh -- Problems of peace enforcement: lessons to be drawn from multinational peacekeeping operations in on-going conflicts in Africa / Christopher Clapham. Subjects: Africa, Sub-Saharan--Economic conditions. Africa, Sub-Saharan--Foreign economic relations. LC Classification: HC800 .A55335 2001 Dewey Class No.: 330.96 21

Africa on the eve of the 21st century: proceedings of an ALF international conference in Maputo, Mozambique, 9-11 September 1977. Published/Created: Ibadan: Africa Leadership Forum, [1997?] Related Names: Africa Leadership Forum. Description: 191 p.: ill.; 28 cm. Notes: Includes bibliographical references. Subjects: Globalization--Congresses. Africa--Politics and government--1960---Congresses. Africa--Economic conditions--1960---Congresses. LC Classification: DT30.2 .A38 1997 Dewey Class No.: 337.6 21

African democracy in the era of globalisation / edited by Jonathan Hyslop Published/Created: Johannesburg: Witwatersrand University Press, 1999. Related Names: Hyslop, Jonathan. Description: xi, 515 p.; 22 cm. ISBN 1868143317 (pbk.) Notes: Includes index. Bibliography: p. 442-497. Subjects: Democracy--Africa. Africa--Politics and government--1960- LC Classification: JQ1879.A15 A33 1999 Dewey Class No.:

967.03/2 21

African industry 2000: the challenge of going global / United Nations Industrial Development Organization. Published/Created: Vienna: UNIDO, 2000. Related Names: United Nations Industrial Development Organization. Description: xv, 155 p.: tables; 30 cm. ISBN 9211064023 Notes: Includes bibliographical references. Subjects: Industrial statistics--Africa. Globalization--Economic aspects--Africa. Africa--Commerce--Statistics. Africa--Foreign economic relations. LC Classification: HC800 .A5678 2000

Afrikanische Frauen und kulturelle Globalisierung: mit den Beiträgen zur Jahrestagung der Vereinigung von Afrikanisten in Deutschland (VAD), Bayreuth, 8.-10. Oktober 1998 = African women and cultural globalization / herausgegeben von Katharina Städtler, Ursula Trüper. Published/Created: Köln: R. Köppe, c2000. Related Names: Städtler, Katharina. Trüper, Ursula. Vereinigung von Afrikanisten in Deutschland. Jahrestagung (1998: Bayreuth, Germany) Description: 205 p.; 24 cm. ISBN 3896453181 (pbk.) Notes: Includes bibliographical references (p. [197]-205). German, English, and French. Subjects: Women--Africa--Social conditions--Congresses. Globalization--Congresses. LC Classification: HQ1787 .A423 2000

Agricultural globalization, trade, and the environment / edited by Charles B. Moss ... [et al.]. Published/Created: Boston: Kluwer Academic Publishers, c2002. Related Names: Moss, Charles B. (Charles Britt) Description: xxiii, 542 p.: ill.; 25 cm. ISBN 079237472X (alk. paper) Notes: Includes bibliographical references and index. Subjects: Agriculture--Environmental aspects.

Globalization--Environmental aspects. International trade--Environmental aspects. Series: Natural resource management and policy LC Classification: S589.75 .A363 2001 Dewey Class No.: 338.1/873 21

Aguiton, Christophe. Le monde nous appartient / Christophe Aguiton. Published/Created: Paris: Plon, 2001. Description: 251 p.; cm. ISBN 2259193404 Subjects: Labor Unions - Globalization - International Trade.

Ahmadjayadi, Cahyana. Pembinaan kemampuan pengusaha kecil menghadapi era perdagangan bebas / oleh Cahyana Ahmadjayadi. Published/Created: [Jakarta]: Departemen Pertahanan Keamanan RI, Lembaga Ketahanan Nasional, 1997. Description: 1 v. (various foliations): ill.; 29 cm. Summary: Policy for empowering Indonesian small business in the globalization era; paper. Notes: Includes bibliographical references (leaves [1]-[2], 3rd group). LC Classification: MLCME 97/00564 (H)

Aijaz Ahmad. Nationalism & globalisation / by Aijaz Ahmed. Published/Created: Pune: Dept. of Sociology, University of Pune, 2000. Related Names: University of Poona. Dept. of Sociology. Description: 53 p.; 26 cm. Summary: Comprises three lectures delivered by the author at the Dept. of Sociology, University of Poona and a paper written separately. Series: Occasional paper series (University of Poona. Dept. of Sociology); 4.

Aiyar, Swaminathan S. Anklesaria. Towards globalisation: the case for foreign investment / Swaminathan S. Anklesaria Aiyar. Published/Created: New Delhi: Radiant Publishers, 1992. Description: viii, 78 p.; 22 cm. Notes: "Under the auspices of Economic and Scientific Research Foundation." With reference to India. Includes index. Subjects: Investments, Foreign--India. International business enterprises--India. LC Classification: HG5732 .A37 1992

Akami, Tomoko, 1959- Internationalizing the Pacific: the United States, Japan, and the Institute of Pacific Relations in war and peace, 1919-45 / Tokomo Akami. Published/Created: New York: Routledge, 2001. Description: p. cm. ISBN 0415220343 (hc.) Notes: Includes bibliographical references and index. Subjects: Institute of Pacific Relations. Pan-Pacific relations. Globalization--Political aspects. World politics--20th century. Pacific Area--Foreign relations. United States--Foreign relations--20th century. Japan--Foreign relations--20th century. Series: Routledge studies in Asia's transformations; 3 LC Classification: DU29 .A45 2001 Dewey Class No.: 327/.09182/3 21

Albert, Michel. Notre foi dans ce siècle / Michel Albert, Jean Boissonnat, Michel Camdessus. Published/Created: Paris: Arléa, 2001. Related Names: Boissonnat, Jean. Camdessus, Michel. Description: 198 p.; cm. ISBN 2869593603 Subjects: Economics - Finance - Globalization.

Alcaraz, Irving. Bolivia, hora cero / Irving Alcaraz. Edition Information: 1. ed. Published/Created: La Paz: [s.n.], 1999 (La Paz: Editorial Salamandra Srl.) Description: 102 p.; 18 cm. Notes: Cover title. Subjects: Industrial revolution--Bolivia. Bolivia--Economic integration. Globalization. Bolivia--Economic conditions--1982- LC Classification: HC185.I52 A43 1999

Alonso Benito, L. E. (Luis Enrique) Trabajo y ciudadanía: estudios sobre la crisis de la sociedad salarial / Luis Enrique Alonso. Published/Created: Madrid: Editorial Trotta: Fundación 1° de Mayo, 1999.

Description: 281 p.; 23 cm. ISBN 8481643025 Notes: Includes bibliographical references (p. 257-281). Subjects: Working class. Wages. Globalization. Lifestyles. Consumption (Economics) Series: Colección Estructuras y procesos. Serie 1° de mayo

Alonso Piñeiro, Armando. El fraude de la tercera vía / Armando Alonso Piñeiro. Published/Created: Buenos Aires, Argentina: Grupo Editorial Latinoamericano, 2000. Description: 195 p.; 23 cm. ISBN 9506946272 Notes: Includes bibliographical references (p. 187-189) and index. Subjects: International economic relations. Globalization. Economic development-- Social aspects. Democracy. Series: Nuevohacer Colección Estudios políticos y sociales LC Classification: HF1359 .A546 2000

Altman, Dennis. Global sex / Dennis Altman. Published/Created: Chicago: University of Chicago Press, 2001. Description: xii, 216 p.; 23 cm. ISBN 0226016064 (cloth: alk. paper) Notes: Includes bibliographical references (p. 167-204) and index. Subjects: Sex customs. Globalization. LC Classification: HQ16 .A38 2001 Dewey Class No.: 306.7 21

Amable, Bruno. Les Systèmes d'innovation à l'ère de la globalisation / Bruno Amable, Rémi Barré, Robert Boyer. Published/Created: Paris: Economica, c1997. Related Names: Barré, Rémi. Boyer, Robert, 1943- Description: 401 p.; 24 cm. ISBN 2717833323 Notes: Includes bibliographical references (p. [361]-385) and index. Subjects: Technological innovations--Economic aspects. Research, Industrial. Economic development. LC Classification: HC79.T4 A445 1997

Anderson, Walt, 1933- All connected now: life in the first global civilization / Walter Truett Anderson. Published/Created: Boulder, Colo.: Westview Press, 2001. Description: ix, 310 p.; 24 cm. ISBN 0813339375 (alk. paper) Notes: Includes bibliographical references (p. 279-291) and index. Subjects: Civilization, Modern- -1950- Globalization--Social aspects. LC Classification: CB430 .A53 2001 Dewey Class No.: 909.82/5 21

Antisipasi agama terhadap trend globalisasi pembangunan regional dan lokal di Kecamatan Bahorok, Kabupaten Langkat [microform]: laporan penelitian / oleh Soetarman S. ... [et al.]. Published/Created: Jakarta: Departemen Agama R.I., Badan Penelitian dan Pengembangan Agama, Proyek Penelitian Keagamaan, 1992/1993 [i.e. 1993] Related Names: Soetarman. Description: 1 v. (various foliations); 28 cm. Summary: Religious anticipation on effects of globalization in Kecamatan Bahorok, Kabupaten Langkat, Sumatera Utara; research report. Notes: Microfiche. Jakarta: Library of Congress Office; Washington, D.C.: Library of Congress Photoduplication Service, 1997. 2 microfiches; 11 x 15 cm. LC Classification: Microfiche 93/80174 (B)

Antisipasi agama terhadap trend globalisasi pembangunan regional dan lokal di Kecamatan Lubuk Kilangan, Kodya Padang, Propinsi Sumatera Barat [microform]: laporan penelitian / tim peneliti, Nurhayati Djamas ... [et al.]. Published/Created: Jakarta: Departemen Agama R.I., Badan Penelitian dan Pengembangan Agama, Proyek Penelitian Keagamaan, 1992/1993 [i.e. 1993] Related Names: Djamas, Nurhayati. Description: 1 v. (various foliations): map; 28 cm. Summary: Religious anticipation on effects of globalization in Kecamatan Lubuk Kilangan, Kotamadya Padang, Sumatera Barat Province; research report. Notes: Microfiche.

Jakarta: Library of Congress Office; Washington, D.C.: Library of Congress Photoduplication Service, 1994. 3 microfiches; 11 x 15 cm. LC Classification: Microfiche 93/50653 (B)

Antisipasi agama terhadap trend globalisasi pembangunan regional dan lokal t.a. 1992/1993 di Kec. Buduran, Kab. Sidoarjo, Prop. Jawa Timur [microform]: laporan penelitian / oleh Al Humam Mz. ... [et al.]. Published/Created: Jakarta: Departemen Agama RI, Badan Penelitian dan Pengembangan Agama, Proyek Penelitian Keagamaan, 92/93 [i.e. 1992?] Related Names: Al-Human Mz. (Al-Human Munzir) Description: 1 v. (various foliations): maps; 28 cm. Summary: Religious anticipation on effects of globalization in Kecamatan Buduran, Kabupaten Sidoarjo, Jawa Timur Province; research report. Notes: Microfiche. Jakarta: Library of Congress Office; Washington, D.C.: Library of Congress Photoduplication Service, 1994. 4 microfiches; 11 x 15 cm. LC Classification: Microfiche 93/50648 (B)

Antitrust goes global: what future for transatlantic cooperation? / Simon J. Evenett, Alexander Lehmann, Benn Steil, editors. Published/Created: London: Royal Institute of International Affairs; Washington, D.C.: Brookings Institution Press, c2000. Related Names: Evenett, Simon J. Lehmann, Alexander. Steil, Benn. Royal Institute of International Affairs. Brookings Institution. Description: xiii, 206 p.; 24 cm. ISBN 0815725027 (alk. paper) 0815725019 (pbk.: alk. paper) Notes: Includes bibliographical references and index. Subjects: Trade regulation--United States. Antitrust law--United States. Trade regulation--European Union countries. Antitrust law--European Union countries. Globalization. LC Classification: K3850

.A97 2000 Dewey Class No.: 338.8/8 21

Anuário direito e globalização / Programa Interdisciplinar Direito e Globalização, UERJ. Published/Created: Rio de Janerio: Renovar, 1999- Related Names: Universidade do Estado do Rio de Janeiro. Programa Interdisciplinar Direito e Globalização. Description: v.; 23 cm. 1- Notes: Chiefly in Portuguese; some articles in English. Subjects: International law--Periodicals. Law--Periodicals. Globalization--Periodicals. LC Classification: K1 .N9158

Arab business: the globalisation imperative / Ali Al-Shamali & John Denton. Published/Created: London: Kogan page, c2000. Description: vii, 181 p.: ill.; 24 cm. ISBN 0749431385 Notes: "Published in association with The Arab Research Center, Kuwait." Papers presented at the First Annual Middle East Business Conference in Kuwait City. Includes bibliographical references and index. Subjects: Globalization--Economic aspects--Arab countries Congresses. Globalization--Congresses. Arab countries--Foreign economic relations--Congresses. LC Classification: HF1610 .A73 2000

Ardana, Si Putu. Mengembangkan kualitas penduduk melalui jiwa bahari menyongsong era globalisasi / oleh Si Putu Ardana. Published/Created: [Jakarta]: Departemen Pertahanan Keamanan RI, Lembaga Ketahanan Nasional, 1996. Description: vii, 86, [2] leaves; 29 cm. Summary: Development of archipelagic state towards the globalization era in Indonesia; paper. Notes: Includes bibliographical references (leaves [87]-[88]). LC Classification: MLCME 97/00555 (J)

Aristide, Jean-Bertrand. Eyes of the heart: seeking a path for the poor in the age of globalization / Jean-Bertrand Aristide; edited by Laura Flynn. Published/Created: Monroe, ME: Common Courage Press, c2000. Related Names: Flynn, Laura. Description: 89 p.: ill.; 20 cm. ISBN 1567511872 1567511864 (paper) Notes: Includes index. Subjects: Poverty--Haiti. Globalization. Haiti--Economic conditions--1971- LC Classification: HC153.Z9 P613 2000 Dewey Class No.: 330.97294/073 21

Arora, Ashish. Markets for technology: the economics of innovation and corporate strategy / Ashish Arora, Andrea Fosfuri, Alfonso Gambardella. Published/Created: Cambridge, Mass.: MIT Press, 2002. Related Names: Fosfuri, Andrea. Gambardella, Alfonso. Description: p. cm. ISBN 0262011905 Notes: Includes bibliographical references and index. Subjects: High technology industries--Management. Technology--Marketing. License agreements. Technology transfer--Economic aspects. Technological innovations--Economic aspects. Globalization--Economic aspects. Employees--Effect of technological innovations on. LC Classification: HD62.37 .A76 2002 Dewey Class No.: 338/.064 21

Arriola, Aura Marina. Identidad y racismo en este fin de siglo / Aura Marina Arriola. Published/Created: Guatemala: Facultad Latinoamericana de Ciencias Sociales (FLACSO) / Magna Terra Editores, 2001. Description: 152 p.; cm. ISBN 9992266260 Summary: An interpretive study of contemporary social forces in shaping racial and national identities, with focus on frontiers, migration, gender, globalization, regional economies, labor and religion. Includes case study of women in Europe and Tapachula.

Ashcroft, Bill, 1946- Post-colonial transformation / Bill Ashcroft.

Published/Created: New York: Routledge, 2001. Description: p. cm. ISBN 0415238293 (alk. paper) 0415238307 (pbk.: alk. paper) Notes: Includes bibliographical references and index. Subjects: Postcolonialism. Decolonization. Social change. Globalization. LC Classification: JV51 .A75 2001 Dewey Class No.: 325/.3 21

Asheghian, Parviz, 1943- Economic development: a global perspective / Parviz Asheghian. Published/Created: Huntington, N.Y.: Nova Science Publishers, 2001. Description: p. cm. ISBN 1560729430 Notes: Includes bibliographical references and index. Subjects: Economic development. Globalization. LC Classification: HD82 .A695 2001 Dewey Class No.: 338.9 21

Asia-Pacific: security, globalisation, and development / editors, M.L. Sondhi, K.G. Tyagi. Published/Created: New Delhi: Manas Publications, 2001. Related Names: Sondhi, M. L. Tyagi, K. G. (Krishan Gopal), 1942- Indian Council of Social Science Research. International Conference on Asia-Pacific and the Global Order (2000: New Delhi, India) Description: 384 p.; 22 cm. ISBN 8170491290 8170491304 (jacket) Summary: Papers presented at an International Conference on Asia-Pacific and the Global Order from October 2-4, 2000 in New Delhi; organised by Indian Council of Social Science Research on the occasion of its 30th anniversary. Notes: "Indian Council of Social Science Research." Includes bibliographical references and index.

Asien unter Globalisierungsdruck: politische Kulturen zwischen Tradition und Moderne / Günter Schucher [Hrsg.]. Published/Created: Hamburg: Institut für Asienkunde, 2000. Related Names: Schucher, Günter. Description: 148 p.: ill.;

21 cm. ISBN 3889102379 Notes: Includes bibliographical references. Subjects: Globalization. International economic relations. Asia--Politics and government--1945- Asia--Economic conditions--1945- Series: Mitteilungen des Instituts für Asienkunde Hamburg; Nr. 323

Au-delà des délocalisations: globalisation et internationalisation des firmes / sous la direction de Eric Lahille. Published/Created: Paris: Economica, c1995. Related Names: Lahille, Eric. Description: viii, 161 p.: ill.; 24 cm. ISBN 2717829083 Notes: Includes bibliographical references (p. [151]-156). Subjects: Business relocation. Industrial location. International business enterprises. Series: Collection Entreprise et perspectives économiques LC Classification: HD58 .A9 1995

Avila, J. Nelson. Globalización, estado y economía solidaria / J. Nelson Avila. Edition Information: 1a ed. Published/Created: Tegucigalpa: Editorial Guaymuras, 1999. Description: 144 p.; cm. ISBN 999261532X Summary: Analysis of neoliberal economic policies and globalization, calling for an integration of nations like Honduras into the global system. Avila is a professor at UNAH and a functionary of the regional Central American Bank of Economic Integration.

Axtmann, Roland. Liberal democracy into the twenty-first century: globalization, integration, and the nation-state / Roland Axtmann. Published/Created: Manchester; New York: Manchester University Press; New York: Distributed exclusively in the USA by St. Martin's Press, 1996. Description: viii, 198 p.; 24 cm. ISBN 0719043042 0719043050 (pbk) Notes: Includes bibliographical references (p. 171-188) and index. Subjects: Democracy. Liberalism. International

relations--Philosophy. Globalization. Series: Political analyses LC Classification: JC423 .A9 1996

Babb, Sarah L. Managing Mexico: economists from nationalism to neoliberalism / Sarah Babb. Published/Created: Princeton, N.J.: Princeton University Press, 2002. Description: p. cm. ISBN 0691074836 (alk. paper) Notes: Includes bibliographical references and index. Subjects: Economists--Mexico. Economics--Mexico--History--20th century. Globalization. Mexico--Economic policy. LC Classification: HC135 .B214 2002 Dewey Class No.: 338.972 21

Bahasa Indonesia dalam era globalisasi: pemantapan peran bahasa sebagai sarana pembangunan bangsa: risalah Kongres Bahasa Indonesia VII / penyunting, Hasan Alwi, Dendy Sugono, Abdul Rozak Zaidan. Published/Created: Jakarta: Pusat Pembinaan dan Pengembangan Bahasa, Departemen Pendidikan Nasional, 2000. Related Names: Alwi, Hasan. Sugono, Dendy. Zaidan, Abdul Rozak. Pusat Pembinaan dan Pengembangan Bahasa. Description: xiii, 953 p.: ill. (some col.); 25 cm. Summary: Role of Indonesian language in globalization era; proceedings. Notes: Includes bibliographical references. Subjects: Indonesian language--Political aspects--Congresses. Language policy--Indonesia--Congresses. Globalization--Congresses. LC Classification: PL5079 .K64 1998

Baiarkhuu, D. (Dashdorzhiin) The Challenge of globalisation and the shaping of new world order / Dashdorj Bayarkhuu. Published/Created: New Delhi: Rajiv Gandhi Institute for Contemporary Studies, [2000] Related Names: Rajiv Gandhi Institute for Contemporary Studies. Description: 21 p.; 22 cm. Series: RGICS working paper series; 2000, no.

14.

Bailey, Paul. The social and labour impact of globalization in the manufacture of transport equipment: report for discussion at the Tripartite Meeting on the Social and Labour Impact of Globalization in the Manufacture of Transport Equipment, Geneva, 2000 / International Labour Organization, Sectoral Activities Programme. Published/Created: Geneva: International Labour Office, 2000. Related Names: Rai, Pallavi. International Labour Organisation. Sectoral Activities Programme. Tripartite Meeting on the Social and Labour Impact of Globalization in the Manufacture of Transport Equipment (2000: Geneva, Switzerland) Description: viii, 191 p.: ill.; 29 cm. ISBN 9221120325 Notes: "This report ... was prepared by Paul Bailey ... data was collected by Pallavi Rai"--Introd. "TMTE/2000." Includes bibliographical references. Subjects: Foreign trade and employment--Case studies. International division of labor--Case studies. Globalization--Economic aspects--Case studies. Transportation equipment industry--Employees. Automobile industry workers. LC Classification: HD5710.7 .B35 2000

Balam Pereira, Gilberto. Un fantasma recorre el mundo: el depredador más voraz de la historia: [estudio sociologico] / Gilberto Balam. Edition Information: 1. ed. Published/Created: Mérida, Yucatán, México: Maldonado Editores del Mayab, 1999. Description: 180 p., [4] p. of plates: maps: 21 cm. ISBN 9686655069 Notes: Includes bibliographical references. Subjects: Public health--Mexico. Liberalism--Mexico. Globalization. Mexico--Social conditions--1970- Mexico--Economic conditions--1994- Mexico--Environmental conditions. LC Classification: HN113.5 .B35 1999

Dewey Class No.: 306/.0972 21

Balancing democracy / edited by Roland Axtmann. Published/Created: New York: Continuum, 2000. Related Names: Axtmann, Roland Description: p. cm. ISBN 0826450326 0826450318 (pbk.) Notes: Includes bibliographical references and index. Subjects: Democracy. Civil society. Globalization. LC Classification: JC423 .B219 2000 Dewey Class No.: 321.8 21

Balchin, Paul N. Urban economics: a global perspective / Paul N. Balchin, David Isaac, Jean Chen. Published/Created: Houndmills, Basingstoke, Hampshire; New York, N.Y.: PALGRAVE, 2000. Related Names: Isaac, David. Chen, Jean Jinghan. Description: xx, 539 p.: ill., maps; 24 cm. ISBN 0333771281 (pbk.) Notes: Includes bibliographical references and index. Subjects: Urban economics. City planning. Globalization. LC Classification: HT321 .B353 2000 Dewey Class No.: 330.9173/2 21

Baldares Carazo, Thelma. Desafíos de la educación en la globalización: de Maryazul a Maryplata / Thelma Baldares Carazo. Edition Information: 1a ed. Published/Created: Cartago, Costa Rica: Editorial Tecnológico de Costa Rica, 2000. Description: 120 p.; cm. ISBN 9977661197 Summary: A literary examination of globalization in education through the technique of juxtaposing two opposing teachers representing systems of personal motivation and educational ideals as opposed to material acquisition and mercantilism.

Balme, Richard. Les politiques du néo-régionalisme: action collective régionale et globalisation / Richard Balme. Published/Created: Paris: Economica, c1996. Description: 301 p.; 24 cm. ISBN 2717831835 Notes: Includes bibliographical references. Subjects: Regionalism--Europe. Series: Collection Politique comparée LC Classification: JN12 .B35 1996

Bamyeh, Mohammed A. The ends of globalization / Mohammed A. Bamyeh. Published/Created: Minneapolis: University of Minnesota Press, c2000. Description: p. cm. ISBN 0816635927 (HC: acid-free paper) 0816635935 (PB: acid-free paper) Contents: Governmentality and the new global "order" -- The new imperialism: six theses -- The cultural landscape of globalization: historical notes. Notes: Includes bibliographical references and index. Subjects: Globalization. International relations--Philosophy. LC Classification: JZ1318 .B36 2000 Dewey Class No.: 327.1/7 21

Barnes, Justin. Globalisation and change: major trends in the international automotive industry and their likely impact on South African automotive assembly and component manufacturers / Justin Barnes. Published/Created: [Durban]: School of Development Studies (Incorporating the Centre for Social and Development Studies), [1999] Related Names: University of Natal. School of Development Studies. Description: 22 p.: ill.; 21 cm. ISBN 1868403505 (pbk.) Notes: Bibliography: p. 21-22. Subjects: Automobile industry and trade--South Africa. Automobile industry and trade. Series: CSDS working paper; no. 23 LC Classification: HD9710.S72 B372 1999 Dewey Class No.: 338.4/76292/0968 21

Barrett-Lennard, Brian. Anti-globalisation / B. Barrett-Lennard . Published/Created: Mornington, Vic.: Beach Box Books, 2001 Description: 168 p.; 21 cm. ISBN 0958523061 (Pbk) Summary: A powerful and controversial study, elucidating the interconnection between war, politicss,

finance, industry, propaganda, religion and the media and in which globalisation is identified as a front for greed, corporatisation and US imperialism and a smoke-screen for social and environmental destruction. Notes: Includes bibliographical references. Subjects: International economic integration. Globalization--Economic aspects. Globalization--Political aspects. Globalization--Social aspects. LC Classification: HF1418.5 .B37 2001

Barrett-Lennard, Brian. Anti-globalisation / B. Barrett-Lennard . Published/Created: Mornington, Vic.: Beach Box Books, 2001 Description: 168 p.; 21 cm. ISBN 0958523061 (Pbk) Summary: A powerful and controversial study, elucidating the interconnection between war, politicss, finance, industry, propaganda, religion and the media and in which globalisation is identified as a front for greed, corporatisation and US imperialism and a smoke-screen for social and environmental destruction. Notes: Includes bibliographical references. Subjects: International economic integration. Globalization--Economic aspects. Globalization--Political aspects. Globalization--Social aspects. LC Classification: HF1418.5 .B37 2001

Barrillon, Michel. ATTAC, encore un effort pour réguler la mondialisation / Michel Barrillon. Published/Created: Castelnau-le-Lez: Climats, 2001. Description: 217 p.; cm. ISBN 284158190X Subjects: Globalization - Capitalism.

Bayer, József. The impact of globalisation on East-Central Europe / József Bayer. Published/Created: Budapest: Institute for Political Science of the Hungarian Academy of Sciences, 2000. Description: 18 p.; 21 cm. ISBN 9639218456 Notes: Includes bibliographical references (p. 18). Series: Working papers of political science, 1416-8413; 20

Bealey, Frank. Power in business and the state: an historical analysis of its concentration / Frank Bealey. Published/Created: New York: Routledge, 2001. Description: p. cm. ISBN 0415246970 Notes: Includes bibliographical references and index. Subjects: Industrial concentration. State, The. Power (Social sciences) Globalization. Series: Routledge frontiers of political economy; 36 LC Classification: HD2757 .B43 2001 Dewey Class No.: 338.8 21

Beaud, Michel. Le journal du basculement du monde: 2000 / Michel Beaud. Published/Created: Paris: Découverte, 2001. Description: 272 p.; cm. ISBN 2707133973 Subjects: Politico-Socio-Economics - Globalization. Series: Cahiers libres

Becerra, Irma. Educación integrativo reconstructiva: principios de una filosofía social y educativa de la hondureñidad para el fortalecimiento democrático de la autoconciencia ciudadana / Irma Becerra. Edition Information: 1a ed. Published/Created: Tegucigalpa: Baktún Editorial / Fundación Friedrich Ebert, 1999. Description: 250 p.; cm. Summary: A scholarly study of changing concepts and trends in Honduran education in relation to technological innovations, traditional elitism, democratization, traditionalism, the emergence of a "new" national character and the impact of globalization. Series: Colección Materiales de Estudio; no.2

Beck, Ulrich, 1944- What is globalization? / Ulrich Beck; translated by Patrick Camiller. Published/Created: Malden, MA: Polity Press, 2000. Description: p. cm. ISBN 0745621252 (hb.) 0745621260 (pb.) Notes: Includes bibliographical references and index. Subjects:

International economic relations. International relations. Globalization. LC Classification: HF1359 .B413 2000 Dewey Class No.: 337 21

Bello, Walden F. The future in the balance: essays on globalization and resistance / Walden Bello; edited with a preface by Anuradha Mittal. Published/Created: Oakland, CA: Food First Books, 2001. Related Names: Mittal, Anuradha, 1967- Description: p. cm. Notes: Includes bibliographical references and index. Subjects: International economic relations. International business enterprises. Globalization. International trade. International finance. LC Classification: HF1359 .B4325 2001 Dewey Class No.: 337 21

Bende-Nabende, Anthony. Globalisation, fdi, regional integration and sustainable development: theory, evidence and policy / Anthony Bende-Nabende. Published/Created: Burlington, VT: Ashgate, 2002. Description: p. cm. ISBN 0754619370

Benítez, Juan Roberto. Estructura económica y comercio mundial / [Juan Roberto Benítez, Ana María Liberali, Omar Horacio Gejo]. Published/Created: [Buenos Aires]: Ediciones Pharos, [1996] Related Names: Liberali, Ana María. Gejo, Omar Horacio. Description: 158 p.: ill., maps; 20 cm. ISBN 9879532511 Notes: Includes bibliographical references. Subjects: Economic geography. Globalization. Southern Cone of South America--Economic conditions. Argentina--Economic conditions--1983- LC Classification: HF1025 .B44 1996

Bernal-Meza, Raúl, 1950- Sistema mundial y MERCOSUR: globalización, regionalismo y políticas exteriores comparadas / Raúl Bernal-Meza. Edition Information: 1. ed. Published/Created:

Buenos Aires: Universidad Nacional del Centro de la Provincia de Buenos Aires: Nuevohacer, Grupo Editor Latinoamericano, c2000. Description: 480 p.; 23 cm. ISBN 9506946221 Notes: Includes bibliographical references (p. 459-480). Subjects: MERCOSUR (Organization) International economic integration. Globalization. South America--Economic integration. South America--Foreign economic relations. Argentina--Foreign relations--Brazil. Brazil--Foreign relations--Argentina. Series: Colección Estudios internacionales (Buenos Aires, Argentina). LC Classification: HC165+ Dewey Class No.: 337.1/8 21

Bernalt O., Mario. Aquí, sin fronteras?: supranacionalidad, globalización y derecho comunitario en el MERCOSUR / Mario Bernalt O. Published/Created: Asunción, Paraguay: Cromos S.R.L., c1998. Description: 141 p.: col. map; 25 cm. Notes: Includes bibliographical references (p. 127-139). Subjects: MERCOSUR (Organization) International economic integration. Globalization. South America--Economic integration. LC Classification: HC165 .B557 1998

Best practices in international business / [edited by] Michael R. Czinkota, Ilkka A. Ronkainen. Published/Created: Fort Worth: Harcourt College Publishers, c2001. Related Names: Czinkota, Michael R. Ronkainen, Ilkka A. Description: ix, 374 p.: ill.; 24 cm. ISBN 0030287219 Notes: Includes bibliographical references and index. Subjects: International business enterprises--Management. Globalization--Economic aspects. Competition, International. Series: The Harcourt College Publishers series in management LC Classification: HD62.4 .B478 2001 Dewey Class No.: 658/.049 21

Beyond dichotomies: histories, identitities, cultures, and the challenge of globalization / edited by Elisabeth Mudimbe-boyi. Published/Created: Albany: State University of New York Press, 2002. Related Names: Mudimbe-boyi, M. Elisabeth. Description: p. cm. ISBN 0791453839 (alk. paper) 0791453847 (pbk.: alk. paper) Notes: Includes index. Subjects: Globalization. Social sciences. History--Philosophy. Cultural policy. Africa--Civilization--Philosophy. Developing countries--Social conditions. Series: SUNY series, explorations in postcolonial studies LC Classification: D883 .B48 2002 Dewey Class No.: 901 21

Beyond the republic: meeting the global challenges to constitutionalism / editors: Charles Sampford, Tom Round. Published/Created: Leichhardt, NSW: Federation Press, 2001. Related Names: Sampford, C. J. G. (Charles J. G.) Round, Tom. Description: xvii, 344 p.; 25 cm. ISBN 1862873771 Notes: Includes bibliographical references and index. Subjects: Globalization--Australia. Constitutional law--Australia. Australia--Politics and government.

Bhagwati, Jagdish N., 1934- The wind of the hundred days: how Washington mismanaged globalization / Jagdish Bhagwati. Published/Created: Cambridge, Mass.: MIT Press, c2000. Description: xxiii, 383 p.: ill.; 24 cm. ISBN 0262024950 Notes: Includes bibliographical references and index. Subjects: Free trade. Capital movements. Globalization--Economic aspects. Globalization--Social aspects. United States--Foreign economic relations. United States--Commercial policy. LC Classification: HF1455 .B48 2000 Dewey Class No.: 337.73 21

Bieler, Andreas, 1967- Globalisation and enlargement of the European union: Austrian and Swedish social forces in the struggle over membership / Andreas Bieler. Published/Created: London; New York: Routledge, 2000. Description: xii, 196 p.; 24 cm. ISBN 0415213126 (hb: alk. paper) Notes: Includes bibliographical references (p. [169]-191) and index. Subjects: European Union--Austria. European Union--Sweden. Austria--Economic conditions--1945- Sweden--Economic conditions--1945- Series: Routledge/Warwick studies in globalisation; 2 LC Classification: HC240.25.A9 B54 2000 Dewey Class No.: 337.1/42 21

Black women, globalization, and economic justice: studies from Africa and the African diaspora / Filomina Chioma Steady, editor. Published/Created: Rochester, Vt.: Schenkman Books, 2001. Related Names: Steady, Filomina Chioma. Description: p. cm. ISBN 0870470752 Notes: Includes bibliographical references. Subjects: Women--Africa--Social conditions. Women--Africa--Economic conditions. Women, Black--Social conditions. Women, Black--Economic conditions. African diaspora. Globalization--Social aspects. Marginality, Social. LC Classification: HQ1787 .B57 2001 Dewey Class No.: 305.48/896 21

Bodna'r, Judit, 1963- Fin de millénaire Budapest: metamorphoses of urban life / Judit Bodnar. Published/Created: Minneapolis: University of Minnesota Press, c2001. Description: p. cm. ISBN 0816635846 (hard: alk. paper) 0816635854 (pbk.: alk. paper) Contents: Introduction -- Constructing difference: western versus non-western, capitalist versus socialist urban logic -- "he that hath to him shall be given": inequalities of housing privatization -- Inner city doubly renewed: global phenomenon, local accents -- Assembling the square: social transformation in public space and the broken mirage of the second economy -- Globalizing art and consumption: art movies and shopping malls -- Urban texture unraveling: fragmentation of the city -- Conclusion. Notes: Includes bibliographical references and index. Subjects: Cities and towns--Europe, Eastern. Post-communism. Globalization. Budapest (Hungary)--Social conditions. Series: Globalization and community; v. 8 LC Classification: HN420.5.B8 B63 2001 Dewey Class No.: 306/.09439/12 21

Boediono. Indonesia menghadapi ekonomi global / Boediono. Edition Information: Ed. 1., cet. 1. Published/Created: Yogyakarta: BPFE, 2001. Description: viii, 95 p.: ill.; 23 cm. Summary: Economic conditions in Indonesia. Notes: Includes bibliographical references. Subjects: Globalization--Economic aspects--Indonesia. Indonesia--Economic conditions--1997- Series: Seri perekonomian Indonesia; no. 1 LC Classification: HC447 .B64 2001

Böhme, Gottfried, 1951- Die Bildungsfeinde: Einheit auf Irrwegen: Schule in Ost und West / Gottfried Böhme. Edition Information: 1. Aufl. Published/Created: Leipzig: Forum, 1999. Description: 159 p.; 21 cm. ISBN 393180108X Notes: Includes bibliographical references. Subjects: Education--Aims and objectives--Germany (East) Education--Aims and objectives--Germany. Globalization. LC Classification: LA771 .B64 1999

Bonicelli, Tito. Globalización o imperialismo global? / Tito Bonicelli. Published/Created: Lima, Perú: [T. Bonicelli?], 1999. Description: 150 p.; 21 cm. Subjects: International economic integration. Globalization. Imperialism.

Free trade. Capitalism. Peru--Economic conditions--1968- LC Classification: HF1418.5 .B67 1999

Bor, Wout van den, 1949- Rethinking rural human resource management: the impact of globalisation and rural restructuring on rural education and training in Western Europe / W. van den Bor, J.M. Bryden, A.M. Fuller. Published/Created: Wageningen: Agricultural University; Leiden: distribution, Backhuys Publishers, c1997. Related Names: Bryden, J. M. (John M.) Fuller, Anthony M. Description: 214 p.: maps; 24 cm. ISBN 9067545171 Notes: Includes bibliographical references (p. [201]-213). Subjects: Rural development--Europe, Western. Agriculture--Economic aspects--Europe, Western. Agricultural education--Europe, Western. Europe, Western--Rural conditions. Series: Mansholt studies, 1383-6803; 10 LC Classification: HN380.Z9 C633 1997 Dewey Class No.: 307.1/412/094 21

Bor, Wouter van den. Rethinking rural human resource management: the impact of globalisation and rural restructuring on rural education and training in Western Europe / W. van den Bor, J.M. Bryden, A.M. Fuller. Published/Created: Wageningen: Agricultural University; Leiden: Backhuys, c1997. Description: 214 p. ISBN 9067545171 Series: Mansholt studies, 1383-6803; 10

Bourke, Thomas. Japan and the globalisation of European integration / Thomas Bourke. Published/Created: Aldershot, Hants, England: Brookfield, USA: Dartmouth, c1996. Description: vii, 228 p.: ill.; 23 cm. ISBN 1855218348 Notes: "Based on a doctoral thesis at the European University Institute"--Pref. Includes bibliographical references (p. 205-219) and index. Subjects: Investments, Japanese--Europe. Europe--Foreign economic relations--

Japan. Europe--Economic integration. Japan--Foreign economic relations--Europe. LC Classification: HG5422 .B68 1996 Dewey Class No.: 337.4052 21

Bové, José, 1953- La mondialisation en question: José Bové à Maurice. Published/Created: Port Louis, Mauritius: Ldikasyon pu travayer, [2001] Description: 85 p.; 20 cm. Notes: "Public lecture = Konesans pu tu dimunn"--Cover. In French, with some Mauritian French Creole. Subjects: Social problems. Social history--1970- Globalization--Social aspects. Series: Public lecture series (Ledikasyon pu travayer) LC Classification: HN17.5 .B675 2001

Bradford, Colin I. Alternative explanations of the trade-output correlation in the East Asian economies / by Colin I. Bradford Jr. and Naomi Chakwin. Published/Created: Paris: OECD, 1993. Related Names: Chakwin, Naomi. Organisation for Economic Co-operation and Development. Description: 32 p.; 30 cm. Notes: "General distribution. OCDE/GD(93)132." "Produced as part of the research programme on Globalisation and Regionalisation." Includes bibliographical references (p. 27-28) Subjects: Exports--East Asia--Econometric models. Investments--East Asia--Econometric models. Series: Technical papers (Organisation for Economic co-operation and Development. Development Centre); no. 87. LC Classification: HD72 .T43 no. 87

Braithwaite, John. Global business regulation / John Braithwaite, Peter Drahos. Published/Created: Cambridge [England]; New York: Cambridge University Press, 2000. Related Names: Drahos, Peter, 1955- Description: xvii, 704 p.: ill.; 26 cm. ISBN 0521780330 (hardback) 0521784999 (pbk.) Notes: Includes bibliographical references (p. 640-671) and index. Subjects: Commercial law. Foreign trade regulation. International trade. Globalization. LC Classification: K1005 .B73 2000 Dewey Class No.: 346.07 21

Brake, Terence. Managing globally / Terence Brake. Edition Information: 1st American ed. Published/Created: New York, N.Y.: Dorling Kindersley Pub., 2002. Description: p. cm. ISBN 0789484137 (alk. paper) Notes: Includes index. Subjects: International business enterprises--Management. Globalization-- Economic aspects. Competition, International. Series: Essential managers LC Classification: HD62.4 .B72 2002 Dewey Class No.: 658/.049 21

Brandt, Maximiliano, 1962- Cambio de velocidad de desarrollo socioeconómico / Maximiliano Brandt. Edition Information: 1. ed. Published/Created: [San José, Costa Rica]: IMC Editores, 2001. Description: 151 p.; 21 cm. ISBN 9968990116 Notes: Errata sheet inserted. Includes bibliographical references (p. 149-151). Subjects: International economic relations. Globalization. Economic development. LC Classification: HF1359 .B72 2001

Brazilian popular music & globalization / edited by Charles A. Perrone & Christopher Dunn. Published/Created: Gainesville: University Press of Florida, c2001. Related Names: Perrone, Charles A. Dunn, Christopher, 1964- Description: xii, 288 p.: ill.; 24 cm. ISBN 0813018218 (acid-free paper) Notes: Includes bibliographical and discographical references and index. Subjects: Popular music--Brazil--History and criticism. Globalization. LC Classification: ML3487.B7 B76 2001 Dewey Class No.: 781.64/0981 21

Brecher, Jeremy. Globalization from below: the power of solidarity / Jeremy Brecher, Tim Costello, Brendan Smith. Published/Created: Cambridge, Mass.: South End Press, 2000. Related Names: Costello, Tim. Smith, Brendan, 1972- Description: xiv, 164 p.; 22 cm. ISBN 0896086232 (hardcover) 0896086224 (pbk.) Notes: Includes bibliographical references and index. Subjects: Social movements. Globalization. LC Classification: HN59.2 .B74 2000 Dewey Class No.: 303.48/4 21

Brittan, Leon. Globalisation vs. sovereignty?: the European response: the 1997 Rede lecture and related speeches / Leon Brittan. Published/Created: Cambridge, U.K.; New York: Cambridge University Press, 1998. Description: vi, 79 p.; 22 cm. ISBN 0521638844 (pbk.) Notes: Includes bibliographical references. Subjects: European Union. Free trade--Great Britain. Protectionism--Great Britain. Free trade--Europe. Protectionism--Europe. Competition, International. Series: The Rede lecture; 1997 LC Classification: HF2046 .B847 1998

Brody, Betsy Teresa, 1972- Opening the doors: immigration, ethnicity, and globalization in Japan / Betsy Teresa Brody. Published/Created: New York: Routledge, 2001. Description: p. cm. ISBN 0415931924 Notes: Includes bibliographical references and index. Subjects: Aliens--Japan. Immigrants-- Japan. Latin Americans--Japan. Labor policy--Japan. Globalization. Japan-- Ethnic relations. Series: East Asia (New York, N.Y.) LC Classification: DS832.7.A1 B66 2001 Dewey Class No.: 304.8/5208 21

Browne, Stephen. Beyond aid: from patronage to partnership / Stephen Browne. Published/Created: Aldershot, Hants, England; Brookfield, Vt.: Ashgate, c1999.

Description: x, 194 p.: ill.; 23 cm. ISBN 0754611337 Notes: Includes bibliographical references and index. Subjects: Economic assistance--History. Globalization. LC Classification: HC60 .B734 1999 Dewey Class No.: 338.91 21

Brubaker, Pamela, 1946- Globalization at what price?: economic change and daily life / Pamela K. Brubaker. Published/Created: Cleveland, Ohio: Pilgrim Press, 2001. Description: 142 p.; 22 cm. ISBN 0829814388 Notes: Includes bibliographical references and index. Subjects: International economic relations. International economic integration. Globalization--Economic aspects. Globalization--Social aspects. Globalization--Environmental aspects. Globalization--Moral and ethical aspects. Globalization--Religious aspects--Christianity. LC Classification: HF1359 .B77 2001 Dewey Class No.: 337 21

Brunsvick, Yves. Birth of a civilization: the shock of globalization / Yves Brunsvick, André Danzin; with comments by Jacques Delors .... [et al.]; preface by Jean Favier; postscript by Federico Mayor. Published/Created: Paris: Unesco, c1999. Related Names: Danzin, André, 1919- Description: 111 p.; 21 cm. ISBN 9231035037 Notes: Includes bibliographical references. Subjects: International economic relations. Globalization. Series: Challenges series LC Classification: HF1359 .B784 1999 Dewey Class No.: 337 21

Building a world community: globalisation and the common good / edited by Jacques Baudot. Published/Created: Copenhagen: Royal Danish Ministry of Foreign Affairs; Seattle, Wash.: University of Washington Press, c2001. Related Names: Baudot, Jacques. Description: 272 p.; 24 cm. ISBN 0295980990 (alk. paper) Notes: Includes bibliographical references. Subjects: Globalization. International relations. Common good. LC Classification: JZ1318 .B85 2001 Dewey Class No.: 327.1 21

Building a world community: globalisation and the common good / edited by Jacques Baudot. Published/Created: Copenhagen: Royal Danish Ministry of Foreign Affairs; Seattle, Wash.: University of Washington Press, c2001. Related Names: Baudot, Jacques. Description: 272 p.; 24 cm. ISBN 0295980990 (alk. paper) Notes: Includes bibliographical references. Subjects: Globalization. International relations. Common good. LC Classification: JZ1318 .B85 2001 Dewey Class No.: 327.1 21

Building on batik: the globalization of a craft community / edited by Michael Hitchcock, Wiendu Nuryanti. Published/Created: Aldershot, Hants, England; Brookfield, Vt., USA: Ashgate, 2000. Related Names: Hitchcock, Michael. Nuryanti, Wiendu. University of North London. Description: xxxiii, 360 p.: ill.; 23 cm. ISBN 1840149876 Notes: Includes bibliographical references. Subjects: Batik. Globalization. Series: University of North London voices in development management LC Classification: TT852.5 .B83 2000 Dewey Class No.: 338.4/7746662 21

Building women's capacities: interventions in gender transformation / edited by Ranjani K. Murthy. Published/Created: Thousand Oaks, CA: Sage Publications, 2001. Related Names: Murthy, Ranjani K. Description: p. cm. ISBN 0761995331 0761995862 (pbk.) Notes: Includes bibliographical references and index. Subjects: Women in community development--India. Women in economic development--India. Sex role--Government policy--India. Community development personnel--Training of--India. Globalization--Economic aspects--India. Women employees--India--Social conditions. Women employees--India--Economic conditions. LC Classification: HQ1240.5.I4 B85 2001 Dewey Class No.: 305.42/0954 21

Burbach, Roger. Globalization and postmodern politics: from Zapatistas to high tech robber barons / Roger Burbach with Fiona Jeffries and William I. Robinson. Published/Created: London; Sterling, Va.: Pluto Press, 2001. Related Names: Jeffries, Fiona. Robinson, William I. Description: viii, 176 p.; 22 cm. ISBN 0745316506 (hardback) 0745316492 (pbk.) Notes: Includes bibliographical references (p. 162-168) and index. Subjects: Ejército Zapatista de Liberación Nacional (Mexico) Political development. Postmodernism--Political aspects. Government, Resistance to. Elite (Social sciences) Globalization. LC Classification: JC489 .B87 2001 Dewey Class No.: 327.1 21

Búrkun, Mario. Recursos escasos y espacio social: la economía argentina frente a la globalización / Mario E. Burkún. Published/Created: Buenos Aires: Fundación de Relaciones Internacionales, FUNREI, Ediciones Caligraf, c2000. Description: 174 p.: ill.; 21 cm. ISBN 9879453018 Notes: Includes bibliographical references (p. 167-169). Subjects: Budget--Argentina. Argentina--Economic conditions--1983- Globalization--Social aspects--Argentina. Argentina--Appropriations and expenditures. Argentina--Social policy. LC Classification: HJ2075 .B87 2000 Dewey Class No.: 330.982 21

Business and the legal profession in an age of computerization and globalization / editor, C.F.G. Sunaryati Hartono. Published/Created: [Jakarta]: Yayasan Hak Asasi Manusia, Demokrasi dan Supremasi Hukum, 2000. Related Names: Hartono, Sunaryati, 1931- Description:

xvi, 238 p.: ill.; 21 cm. ISBN 9794141224 Notes: Includes bibliographical references. In English, with some articles in Indonesian. Subjects: Practice of law. Practice of law--Indonesia. Globalization. Technology and law LC Classification: K120 .B+

Cable, Vincent. Globalization and global governance / Vincent Cable. Published/Created: London: Royal Institute of International Affairs; London; New York: Pinter, 1999. Description: xvi, 139 p.: ill.; 22 cm. ISBN 1855673509 (hardback) 1855673517 (pbk.) Notes: Includes bibliographical references (p. 131-139). Subjects: Globalization. International cooperation. International economic relations. Series: Chatham House papers (Unnumbered) LC Classification: JZ1318 .C33 1999 Dewey Class No.: 327 21

Calderón G., Fernando. Sociedad y globalización / Fernando Calderón G. Edition Information: 1a.ed. Published/Created: La Paz: PNUD, 1999. Description: 102 p.: ill.; 21 cm. Notes: Includes bibliographical references (p. 99). Subjects: Social change--Bolivia. Civil society--Bolivia. Globalization. Bolivia--Social conditions--1982- Bolivia--Economic conditions--1982- Series: Cuaderno de futuro; 1 LC Classification: HN273.5 .C354 1999 Dewey Class No.: 306/.0984 21

Calleja Pinedo, Margarita. Agricultura de exportación en los tiempos de globalización: el caso de la hortalizas, frutas y flores / Margarita Calleja Pinedo ... [et al.]; coordinadores: Hubert C. Grammont ... [et al.]. Edition Information: 1a ed. Published/Created: Chapingo: Universidad Autónoma de Chapingo, 1999. Description: 378 p.; cm. ISBN 9688845183 Summary: A collection of scholarly articles divided into sections on agricultural exportation and globalization, technological development and the U.S. market, the organization of small producers and the organization and labor of large agricultural exporters.

Callinicos, Alex. Against the third way / Alex Callinicos. Published/Created: Cambridge, U.K.: Polity Press; Malden, MA, USA: Blackwell Publishers, 2001. Description: p. cm. ISBN 0745626742 (HB) 0745626750 (PB) Subjects: International economic relations. Globalization. Capitalism. Socialism. LC Classification: HF1359 .C345 2001 Dewey Class No.: 337 21

Can Japan globalize?: studies on Japan's changing political economy and the process of globalization in honour of Sung-Jo Park / Arne Holzhausen, editor. Published/Created: Heidelberg; New York: Physica-Verlag, c2001. Related Names: Park, Sung-Jo. Holzhausen, Arne, 1967- Description: x, 468 p.: ill.; 24 cm. ISBN 3790813818 Notes: Includes bibliographical references. Subjects: Park, Sung-Jo. Globalization--Economic aspects--Japan. Japan--Economic conditions--1989- Japan--Economic policy--1989- LC Classification: HC462.95 .C36 2001 Dewey Class No.: 330.952 21

Cano Tisnado, Jorge Guillermo. La vida en globo: avatares de la globalización / Jorge Guillermo Cano Tisnado. Edition Information: 1. ed. Published/Created: Culiacán Rosales, Sinaloa: El Colegio de Sinaloa: Centro de Investigaciones y Servicios Educativos, UAS, 1999. Description: 293 p.; 21 cm. ISBN 9687448628 (El Colegio de Sinaloa) 9687636769 (UAS) Notes: Includes bibliographical references (p. 287-293). Subjects: Globalization. International economic relations. LC Classification: HF1359 .C368 1999 Dewey Class No.:

337 21

Capitalism and democracy in the 21st century: proceedings of the International Joseph A. Schumpeter Society Conference, Vienna, 1998 "Capitalism and socialism in the 21st century" / Dennis C. Mueller, Uwe Cantner, editors. Published/Created: New York: Physica-Verlag, 2000. Related Names: Mueller, Dennis C. Cantner, Uwe. Description: p. cm. ISBN 3790813508 (hardcover: acid-free paper) Subjects: Schumpeter, Joseph Alois, 1883-1950 -- Congresses. Capitalism--Congresses. Socialism--Congresses. Democracy--Congresses. Globalization--Economic aspects--Congresses. Twenty-first century--Forecasts--Congresses. Economic development--Moral and ethical aspects Congresses. LC Classification: HB501 .I637 1998 Dewey Class No.: 330.12/2 21

Capitalism without morals?: ethical principles of a global economy. Published/Created: Bad Homburg v.d. Höhe: Herbert Quandt Foundation, 2001. Related Names: Herbert Quandt Stiftung. Description: 97 p.: ill.; 26 cm. ISBN 3000073787 Notes: "November 17-18, 2000." Subjects: Capitalism--Moral and ethical aspects. Economics--Moral and ethical aspects. International trade--Moral and ethical aspects. Globalization--Moral and ethical aspects. Business ethics. Human rights. Series: Sinclair House debate, 1438-7885; 15 LC Classification: HB501 .C24263 2001

Capling, Ann, 1959- Death of distance or tyranny of distance?: the internet, deterritorialisation, and the anti-globalisation movement in Australia / Ann Capling and Kim Richard Nossal. Published/Created: Canberra, Australia: Research School of Pacific and Asian Studies, Australian National University, 2000. Related Names: Nossal, Kim

Richard. Australian National University. Dept. of International Relations. Description: 28 p.; 30 cm. ISBN 0731531086 Notes: "October 2000". Includes bibliographical references (p. 24-28). Subjects: Social movements--Australia. Globalization. Internet--Political aspects--Australia. Series: Working paper (Australian National University. Dept. of International Relations); no. 2000/3.

Capling, Ann, 1959- Death of distance or tyranny of distance?: the internet, deterritorialisation, and the anti-globalisation movement in Australia / Ann Capling and Kim Richard Nossal. Published/Created: Canberra, Australia: Research School of Pacific and Asian Studies, Australian National University, 2000. Related Names: Nossal, Kim Richard. Australian National University. Dept. of International Relations. Description: 28 p.; 30 cm. ISBN 0731531086 Notes: "October 2000". Includes bibliographical references (p. 24-28). Subjects: Social movements--Australia. Globalization. Internet--Political aspects--Australia. Series: Working paper (Australian National University. Dept. of International Relations); no. 2000/3.

Capturing globalization / edited by James H. Mittelman and Norani Othman. Published/Created: New York: Routledge, 2001. Related Names: Mittelman, James H. Norani Othman. Description: p. cm. ISBN 0415257328 (alk. paper) 0415258316 (pbk.: alk. paper) Notes: Includes bibliographical references and index. Subjects: International economic relations. Globalization. Malaysia--Economic conditions. LC Classification: HF1359 .C3689 2001 Dewey Class No.: 337 21

Cardona, Rokael. Ciudadanía en precario: globalización, desigualidad social y pobreza en Rotterdam y San José / Rokael Cardona ... [et al.]. Edition Information: 1a ed. Published/Created: San José: Facultad Latinoamericana de Ciencias Sociales (FLACSO), 2000. Description: 319 p.; cm. ISBN 9977681090 Summary: Four lengthy analytical essays which compare security, globalization, social integration and poverty in San José and Rotterdam during the current wave of neoliberal avarice.

Carias, Marcos. Vara de medir: trivialidades / desproporciones / aire / Marcos Carias. Edition Information: 1a ed. Published/Created: Tegucigalpa: Guardabarranco, 1999. Description: 251 p.; cm. ISBN 9992612053 Summary: A series of philosophical essays on global changes of the post Cold War period, including feminism, revolution and socialism, the empire of new technologies and globalization. Carias in one of Honduras leading intellectuals. Series: Colección Búsqueda Pensamiento Social; no.2

Carmody, Pádraig Risteard. Tearing the social fabric: neoliberalism, deindustrialization, and the crisis of governance in Zimbabwe / Pádraig Carmody. Published/Created: Portsmouth, NH: Heinemann, 2001. Description: xx, 211 p.; 25 cm. ISBN 0325070261 (cloth: alk. paper) Notes: Includes bibliographical references and index. Subjects: Structural adjustment (Economic policy)--Zimbabwe. Globalization. Zimbabwe--Economic conditions--1980- LC Classification: HC910 .C37 2001 Dewey Class No.: 330.96891 21

Carnegie, Charles V., 1952- Postnationalism prefigured: Caribbean borderlands / Charles V. Carnegie. Published/Created: New Brunswick, NJ: Rutgers University

Press, 2002. Description: p. cm. ISBN 0813530547 (alk. paper) 0813530555 (pbk.: alk. paper) Notes: Includes bibliographical references and index. Subjects: Nationalism--Caribbean Area. Blacks--Race identity--Caribbean Area. Group identity--Caribbean Area. Kinship--Caribbean Area. Globalization--Political aspects. Caribbean Area--Race relations. LC Classification: F2176 .C36 2002 Dewey Class No.: 305.8/009729 21

Carranza, Víctor M. Globalización y crisis social en el Perú / Víctor Carranza. Published/Created: Lima, Perú: IFEA, 2000. Description: 155 p.; 23 cm. ISBN 9972623114 Notes: "Este libro corresponde al tomo 121 de la serie Travaux de l'Institut Français d'Études Andines"--verso of t.p. Includes bibliographical references (p. 149-155) Subjects: Globalization. Peru--Social conditions--1968- Peru--Ethnic relations. Peru--Economic conditions--1968- Peru--Politics and government--1980- Series: Travaux de l'Institut français d'études andines; 121. LC Classification: HN343.5 .C37 2000

Cartier, Carolyn L. Globalizing South China / Carolyn L. Cartier. Published/Created: Malden, MA: Blackwell Publishers, 2001. Description: p. cm. ISBN 1557868875 (alk. paper) Notes: Includes bibliographical references and index. Subjects: Globalization--Economic aspects--China, Southeast. Globalization--Social aspects--China, Southeast. China, Southeast--Economic conditions. China, Southeast--Foreign economic relations. China, Southeast--Commerce. Series: RGS-IBG book series LC Classification: HC428 .S74 .C37 2001 Dewey Class No.: 337.51/2 21

Castaño, Sergio Raúl. Orden político y globalización: el estado en la contingencia actual / Sergio Raúl Castaño; prólogo de Héctor H. Hernández.. Published/Created: Buenos Aires: Editorial Abaco de Rodolfo Depalma, 2000. Description: 172 p.; 23 cm. ISBN 9505691467 Notes: Includes bibliographical references (p. [167]-172). Subjects: State, The--Philosophy. Autarchy. Globalization. Common good. LC Classification: JC255 .C32 2000 Dewey Class No.: 320.1 21

Castles, Stephen. Ethnicity and globalization: from migrant worker to transnational citizen / Stephen Castles. Published/Created: London; Thousand Oaks, Calif.: Sage Publications, 2000. Description: x, 228 p.; 25 cm. ISBN 0761956115 0761956123 (pbk.) Notes: Includes bibliographical references (p. [208]-219) and index. Subjects: Emigration and immigration. Ethnicity. Globalization. Multiculturalism. LC Classification: JV6032 .C38 2000 Dewey Class No.: 305.8 21

Castro, Fidel, 1927- Capitalismo actual, características y contradicciones: neoliberalismo y globalización: selección temática, 1991-1998 / Fidel Castro; selección y edición, Iraida Aguirrechu y Nora Madan. Edition Information: 1. ed. Published/Created: La Habana: Editora Política; Melbourne, Australia: Ocean Press, 1999. Related Names: Aguirrechu, Iraida. Madan, Nora. Description: 329 p.; 21 cm. ISBN 9590103146 Subjects: Economic history--1990- Capitalism. Globalization. LC Classification: HC59.15 .C375 1999

Castro, Jorge, doctor. Perón y la globalización: sistema mundial y construcción de poder / Jorge Castro. Edition Information: 1. ed. Published/Created: Buenos Aires, Argentina: Catálogos, 1999. Description: 125 p.; 23 cm. ISBN 9508950692 Notes: Includes bibliographical references. Subjects: Perón, Juan Domingo, 1895-1974 --Political and social views.

Globalization. Series: Colección Segundo centenario LC Classification: F2849.P48 C37 1999

Cause lawyering and the state in a global era / edited by Austin Sarat & Stuart Scheingold. Published/Created: Oxford; New York: Oxford University Press, 2001. Related Names: Sarat, Austin. Scheingold, Stuart A. Description: xi, 417 p.; 24 cm. ISBN 0195141164 (alk. paper) 0195141172 (pbk.) Notes: Includes bibliographical references and index. Subjects: Public interest law. Lawyers. National state. Globalization. Series: Oxford socio-legal studies LC Classification: K118.P82 C38 2001 Dewey Class No.: 340/.115 21

Cécora, James. Cultivating grass-roots for regional development in a globalising economy: innovation and entrepreneurship in organised markets / James Cécora. Published/Created: Aldershot, Hants, England; Brookfield, Vt., USA: Ashgate, c1999. Description: xi, 147 p.: ill.; 23 cm. ISBN 184014856X Notes: Includes bibliographical references (p. 123-147). Subjects: Rural industries. Rural development. Entrepreneurship International economic relations. Globalization. LC Classification: HD2330 .C43 1999 Dewey Class No.: 338.9 21

Cettina, Nathalie. Terrorisme: L'histoire de sa mondialisation / Nathalie Cettina. Published/Created: Paris: Harmattan, 2001. Description: 352 p.; cm. ISBN 2747510840 Subjects: Terrorism - Globalization.

Chaize, Jacques. The quantum leap: tools for managing companies in the new economy / Jacques Chaize; translated by Michael Cain. Published/Created: New York: Plagrave, 2000. Description: xii, 209 p.: ill.; 25 cm. ISBN 0333928989 Notes: Includes bibliographical references (p.

204-205) and index. Subjects: Organizational change. Business enterprises--Technological innovations. Globalization. Corporate culture. LC Classification: HD58.8 .C42413 2000 Dewey Class No.: 658.4/06 21

Challenges of globalisation: the case of Korean investments in the UK: a workshop organised by CIIR, held at CIIR office in London on 28 June 1995. Published/Created: London: Catholic Institute for International Relations, [1996] Related Names: Catholic Institute for International Relations. Description: 17 p.: ill., map; 30 cm. ISBN 185287161X Notes: Cover title. Subjects: Investments, Korean--Great Britain. Series: Reports & briefings (Catholic Institute for International Relations) LC Classification: HG5432 .C48 1996

Challenges of globalization / edited by Bibek Debroy. Published/Created: New Delhi: Konark Publishers, c1998. Related Names: Debroy, Bibek. Rajiv Gandhi Institute for Contemporary Studies. Description: xxii, 492 p.; 23 cm. ISBN 8122005217 (jacket) Summary: Contributed articles. Notes: "In association with Rajiv Gandhi Institute for Contemporary Studies, Rajiv Gandhi Foundation, New Delhi." Includes bibliographical references and index. Subjects: International economic relations. International relations. Globalization. Asia--Economic conditions--1945- LC Classification: HF1359 .C435 1998 Dewey Class No.: 337 21

Challenges to Indian banking: competition, globalisation and financial markets / editor, Narendra Jadhav. Published/Created: Delhi: Macmillan India, 1996. Related Names: Jadhav, Narendra, 1953- Union Bank of India. Conference of Public Sector Bank

Economists (17th: 1994: Goa, India)
Description: xvii, 438 p.: ill.; 24 cm.
Summary: Contributed papers presented
at 17th Bank Economists' Conference at
Goa between 5th and 7th September 1994,
hosted by Union Bank of India as part of
its Platinum Jubilee celebrations. Notes:
"SBN 0333924266." Includes
bibliographical references. Subjects:
Banks and banking--India. India--Foreign
economic relations. LC Classification:
HG3284 .C43 1996

Change the world: an activist's guide to the
globalization movement / edited by Mike
Prokosch and Laura Raymond.
Published/Created: New York: Thunder
Mouth Press/Nation Books, 2001. Related
Names: Prokosch, Mike. Raymond,
Laura. Description: p. cm. ISBN
1560253509 Notes: Includes index.
Subjects: International business
enterprises--Social aspects. Social
movements. Globalization--Social
aspects. LC Classification: HD2755.5
.C457 2001 Dewey Class No.: 337 21

Changing the atmosphere: expert knowledge
and environmental governance / edited by
Clark A. Miller and Paul N. Edwards.
Published/Created: Cambridge, Mass.:
MIT Press, c2001. Related Names: Miller,
Clark A. Edwards, Paul N. Description:
xii, 385 p.: ill.; 24 cm. ISBN 0262133873
(alk. paper) 0262632195 (pbk.: alk. paper)
Notes: Includes bibliographical references
(p. [339]-370) and index. Subjects:
Environmental management. Global
environmental change. Climatic changes--
Environmental aspects. Nature--Effect of
human beings on. Globalization. Series:
Politics, science, and the environment LC
Classification: GE300 .C48 2001 Dewey
Class No.: 551.6 21

Charkiewicz, Eva. Transitions to sustainable
production and consumption: concepts,
policies, and actions / Eva Charkiewicz

with Sander van Bennekom and Alex
Young. Published/Created: The Hague:
Tools for Transition, [2001] Related
Names: Bennekom, Sander van. Young,
Alex. Description: xii, 302 p.; 25 cm.
ISBN 9080634719 Notes: Includes
bibliographical references (p. 274-302).
Subjects: Consumption (Economics)--
Environmental aspects. Production
(Economic theory)--Environmental
aspects. Sustainable development. Green
marketing. Globalization--Environmental
aspects. LC Classification: HC79.C6
C495 2001 Dewey Class No.: 338.9/27 21

Chaves Ortiz, Jorge Arturo. Desarrollo y
cultura / Jorge A. Chaves ... [et al.].
Published/Created: Cobán [Guatemala]:
Ak' Kutan Centro Bartolomé de Las
Casas, 1999. Description: 131 p.: ill.; 21
cm. Notes: Includes bibliographical
references. Subjects: Mayas--Social
conditions. Mayas--Economic conditions.
Mayas--Civil rights. Globalization. Series:
Textos Ak' Kutan; 15 LC Classification:
F1434.2.S62 C53 1999

Cheru, Fantu. African renaissance: roadmaps
to the challenge of globalization / Fantu
Cheru. Published/Created: London; New
York: Zed Books, 2001. Description: p.
cm. ISBN 1842770861 (cased)
184277087X (pbk.) Notes: Includes
bibliographical references and index.
Subjects: Globalization. Africa--
Economic conditions--1960- Africa--
Social conditions--1960- Africa--Politics
and government--1960- LC Classification:
HC800 .C434 2001 Dewey Class No.:
337.6 21

Chonchol, Jacques. Hacia dónde nos lleva la
globalización?: reflexiones para Chile /
Jacques Chonchol. Edition Information: 1.
ed. Published/Created: Santiago: LOM
Ediciones: Universidad Arcis, 1999.
Description: 138 p.; 22 cm. ISBN
9562822230 Notes: Includes

bibliographical references. Subjects: International economic integration. Globalization. Chile--Economic policy. Latin America--Economic policy. Series: Colección Sin norte. Serie Punto de fuga LC Classification: HC192 .C464 1999 Dewey Class No.: 337.83 21

Chossudovsky, Michel. The globalisation of poverty: impacts of IMF and World Bank reforms / Michel Chossudovsky. Published/Created: Penang, Malaysia: Third World Network, c1997. Description: 280 p.: ill.; 22 cm. ISBN 9839747231 Notes: Includes bibliographical references (p. [265]-272) and index. Subjects: International Monetary Fund. World Bank. Poverty. International finance. LC Classification: HC79.P6 C48 1997 Dewey Class No.: 332.1/52 21

Chossudovsky, Michel. The globalisation of poverty: impacts of IMF and World Bank reforms / Michel Chossudovsky. Published/Created: London; Atlantic Highlands, N.J.: Zed Books; Penang, Malaysia: TWN, c1997. Related Names: International Monetary Fund. World Bank. Description: 280 p.; 22 cm. ISBN 1856494012 (hardbound) 1856494020 (pbk.) Notes: Includes bibliographical references (p. [265]-272) and index. Subjects: International Monetary Fund--Developing countries. International Monetary Fund--Europe, Eastern. World Bank--Developing countries. World Bank--Europe, Eastern. Poverty--Developing countries. Poverty--Europe, Eastern. LC Classification: HG3881.5.I58 C47 1997 Dewey Class No.: 339.4/6 20

Cities in a globalizing world: global report on human settlements 2001 / United Nations Centre for Human Settlements (Habitat). Published/Created: London; Sterling, VA: Earthscan Publications, 2001. Related Names: United Nations Centre for Human Settlements. Description: xxxviii, 344 p.: ill., maps; 30 cm. ISBN 1853838055 1853838063 (pbk.: alk. paper) Notes: Includes bibliographical references (p. [236]-251) and index. Subjects: Human settlements. Urbanization. Urban policy. Municipal services. Urban poor. Globalization. Urban Health--trends. Urbanization--trends. Housing--economics. Poverty. Public Policy. Sanitation. Socioeconomic Factors. LC Classification: HT65 .C57 2001 Dewey Class No.: 307.76 21

Cities in transition / guest editor, Deborah Hauptmann; with contributions by Henco Bekkering ... [et al.]; [translation by Lara Schrijver]. Published/Created: Rotterdam: 010 Publishers, 2001. Related Names: Graafland, Ad. Hauptmann, Deborah. Description: 430 p.: ill. (some col.); 24 cm. ISBN 9064504156 (pbk.) Notes: Includes bibliographical references. Subjects: City planning--Netherlands--Rotterdam. City planning--Japan--Tokyo. Urbanization--Netherlands--Rotterdam. Urbanization--Japan--Tokyo. Globalization--Cross-cultural studies. Series: Stylos series

City, space + globalization: an international perspective: proceedings of an international symposium, College of Architecture and Urban Planning, the University of Michigan, February 26-28, 1998 / Hemalata C. Dandekar, editor. Published/Created: Ann Arbor: The College, c1998. Related Names: Dandekar, Hemalata C. University of Michigan. College of Architecture and Urban Planning. Description: viii, 391 p.: ill., maps; 28 cm. ISBN 1891197045 (pbk.) Contents: Global city, local citizenship -- Design, shape and culture: City shape in the twenty-first century. Culture and city shape. East Asia. Middle East. Latin America. USA -- Class, economy and polity: Class and choices.

Public and private roles. Participating in shaping the city. Ways of knowing space. Regional effects. Housing issues and gender. Notes: Includes bibliographical references. Subjects: City planning--Congresses. International relations and culture--Congresses. Cities and towns--Forecasting--Congresses. Twenty-first century--Forecasts--Congresses. Public spaces--Congresses. Space perception--Congresses. Space (Architecture)--Congresses. Architecture--Composition, proportion, etc.--Congresses. Globalization. LC Classification: HT107 .C49 1998 Dewey Class No.: 307.1/216 21

Civil society: creative responses to the challenge of globalization, 3-5 September 1996: proceedings national conference / sponsored by Caucus of Development NGOs ... [ct al.]. Published/Created: Quezon City, Philippines: Center for Alternative Development Initiatives, [1998] Related Names: Caucus of Development NGO Networks. Center for Alternative Development Initiatives (Philippines) Description: 160 p.: ill.; 28 cm. Subjects: Civil society--Philippines--Congresses. Globalization--Congresses. Philippines--Economic policy--Congresses. LC Classification: HC455 .C58 1998

Clapp, Jennifer, 1963- Toxic exports: the transfer of hazardous wastes from rich to poor countries / Jennifer Clapp. Published/Created: Ithaca: Cornell University Press, 2001. Description: xii, 178 p.; 24 cm. ISBN 080143887X (cloth: alk. paper) Notes: Includes bibliographical references and index. Subjects: Hazardous wastes--Developing countries. Hazardous wastes--Transportation. Globalization. LC Classification: TD1045.D44 C58 2001 Dewey Class No.: 363.72/87/091724 21

Clark, Cal, 1945- Globalization's impact on state-local economic development policy / Cal Clark and Robert S. Montjoy. Published/Created: Huntington, N.Y.: Nova Science Publishers, c2001. Related Names: Montjoy, Robert S., 1944- Description: ix, 171 p.: ill.; 26 cm. ISBN 159033017X Notes: Includes bibliographical references and index. Subjects: Globalization--Economic aspects--United States--States. United States--Economic policy--1993-2001. United States--Economic conditions--1981---Regional disparities. LC Classification: HC106.82 .C544 2001 Dewey Class No.: 338.973 21

Clark, Ian, 1949- Globalization and international relations theory / Ian Clark. Published/Created: Oxford; New York: Oxford University Press, 1999. Description: xiv, 197 p.; 25 cm. ISBN 0198782101 (acid-free paper) Notes: Includes bibliographical references (p. [175]-191) and index. Subjects: International relations. World politics. Globalization. LC Classification: JZ1305 .C49 1999 Dewey Class No.: 327.1/01 21

Clark, Robert P., 1940- Global life systems: population, food, and disease in the process of globalization / Robert P. Clark. Published/Created: Lanham, MD: Rowman & Littlefield Publishers, c2000. Description: ix, 351 p.: ill., maps; 23 cm. ISBN 0742500748 (cloth: alk. paper) 0742500756 (pbk.: alk. paper) Notes: Includes bibliographical references and index. Subjects: Human ecology. Globalization. Population. Food supply. Diseases and history. Evolution (Biology) Social evolution. LC Classification: GF50 .C53 2000 Dewey Class No.: 304.2 21

Clash of civilizations, or dialogue of cultures?: papers and interventions of the International Conference on "Clash of Civilizations or Dialouge [sic] of

Cultures," Cairo, 10-12 March 1997 / edited by Fakhry Labib, Nehad Salem. Published/Created: Cairo, Egypt: Afro-Asian Peoples' Solidarity Organization, [between 1997 and 1999] Description: 750 p.; 22 cm. ISBN 977536308X Notes: Includes bibliographical references. Subjects: Civilization, Arab--20th century--Congresses. Civilization, Islamic--Congresses. Civilization, Western--Congresses. East and West--Congresses. Globalization--Congresses. Series: AAPSO publications; 173 LC Classification: DS36.88 .I58 1997

Cochran, Terry, 1955- Twilight of the literary: figures of thought in the age of print / Terry Cochran. Published/Created: Cambridge, Mass.: Harvard University Press, 2001. Description: 288 p.; 25 cm. ISBN 067400454X Notes: Includes bibliographical references (p. 259-281) and index. Subjects: Printing--Social aspects--History. Books--Social aspects--History. Written communication--History. Intellectual life--History. Globalization. LC Classification: Z124 .C66 2001 Dewey Class No.: 302.2/244 21

Cockburn, Alexander. Five days that shook the world: Seattle and beyond / Alexander Cockburn & Jeffrey St. Clair. Published/Created: London; New York: Verso, 2000. Related Names: St. Clair, Jeffrey. Description: 119, [36] p.: ill.; 20 cm. ISBN 185984779X Subjects: World Trade Organization. Globalization. International trade. Riots--Washington--Seattle--History. LC Classification: HF1385 .C63 2000

Cogburn, Derrick L. Globalization and the information economy: challenges and opportunities for Africa / Derrick L. Cogburn and Catherine Nyaki Adeya. Published/Created: [Addis Ababa]: Economic Commission for Africa, [1999] Related Names: Adeya, Catherine Nyaki.

United Nations. Economic Commission for Africa. African Development Forum. Description: iii, 33 p.; 29 cm. Notes: "Theme paper." "E/ECA/ADF/99/7." "September, 1999." "African Development Forum"--Cover. Includes bibliographical references (p. 30-33). Subjects: Information technology--Economic aspects--Africa. Globalization. LC Classification: HC800.Z9 I5536 1999

Cohen, Edward S., 1960- The politics of globalization in the United States / Edward S. Cohen. Published/Created: Washington, D.C.: Georgetown University Press, c2001. Description: x, 214 p.: ill.; 24 cm. ISBN 0878408266 (cloth: alk. paper) 0878408274 (pbk.) Notes: Includes bibliographical references (p. 201-209) and index. Subjects: Globalization. United States--Economic policy--1993-2001. United States--Politics and government--1993-2001. LC Classification: HC106.82 .C64 2001 Dewey Class No.: 337.73 21

Cohen, Elie. L'ordre économique mondial: Essai sur les autorités de régulation / Elie Cohen. Published/Created: Paris: Fayard, 2001. Description: 315 p.; cm. ISBN 2213606994 Subjects: Economics - Globalization.

Cohen, Malcolm S. Global skill shortages: skill shortages around the world / Malcolm S. Cohen and Mahmood A. Zaidi. Published/Created: Cheltenham, UK; Northampton, MA: Edward Elgar, 2002. Related Names: Zaidi, Mahmood A. Description: p. cm. ISBN 1840645202 Notes: Includes index. Subjects: Labor supply. Skilled labor--Supply and demand. Globalization. LC Classification: HD5706 .C59 2002 Dewey Class No.: 331.11/422 21

Coleman, Simon. The globalisation of charismatic Christianity: spreading the gospel of prosperity / Simon Coleman. Published/Created: Cambridge, U.K.; New York: Cambridge University Press, 2000. Description: xii, 264 p.; 23 cm. ISBN 0521660726 (hardback) Notes: Includes bibliographical references (p. 241-258) and index. Subjects: Christianity and culture--Sweden--Uppsala--Case studies. Globalization--Religious aspects--Christianity--Case studies. Faith movement (Hagin)--Sweden--Uppsala--History. Pentecostalism--Sweden--Uppsala--History--20th century. Uppsala (Sweden)--Church history--20th century. Series: Cambridge studies in ideology and religion; 12 LC Classification: BR1018.U66 C65 2000 Dewey Class No.: 306.6/804 21

Coleman, Simon. The globalisation of charismatic Christianity: spreading the gospel of prosperity / Simon Coleman. Published/Created: Cambridge, U.K.; New York: Cambridge University Press, 2000. Description: xii, 264 p.; 23 cm. ISBN 0521660726 (hardback) Notes: Includes bibliographical references (p. 241-258) and index. Subjects: Christianity and culture--Sweden--Uppsala--Case studies. Globalization--Religious aspects--Christianity--Case studies. Faith movement (Hagin)--Sweden--Uppsala--History. Pentecostalism--Sweden--Uppsala--History--20th century. Uppsala (Sweden)--Church history--20th century. Series: Cambridge studies in ideology and religion; 12 LC Classification: BR1018.U66 C65 2000 Dewey Class No.: 306.6/804 21

Coloane, Francisco. Britannia y un general / Juan Francisco Coloane. Edition Information: 1. ed. Published/Created: Santiago [de Chile]: LOM Ediciones, 2000. Description: 253 p.; 21 cm. ISBN 956282280X Notes: Includes bibliographical references (p. 247). Subjects: Pinochet Ugarte, Augusto.

Detention of persons--Great Britain--History--20th century. Criminal jurisdiction. International law. Human rights--Chile--History--20th century. Globalization--Moral and ethical aspects. Chile--Foreign relations. Great Britain--Foreign relations. Series: Colección Septiembre LC Classification: F3101.P56 C65 2000

Colonialism to globalisation, five centuries after Vasco da Gama / [editors], Walter Fernandes, Anupama Dutta. Published/Created: New Delhi: Indian Social Institute, c1999- Related Names: Fernandes, Walter, 1939- Dutta, Anupama. Indian Social Institute. International Conference, Colonialism to Globalisation: Five Centuries after Vasco da Gama (1998: New Delhi, India) Description: v. <1 >; 22 cm. ISBN 8187218118 Summary: Papers presented at the International Conference, Colonialism to Globalisation: Five Centuries after Vasco da Gama, held at Indian Social Institute, New Delhi, Feb. 2- 6, 1998. Subjects: Colonies--History--Congresses. World politics--Congresses. Globalization--Congresses. LC Classification: JV105 .C65 1999 Dewey Class No.: 320.9 21

Colonialism to globalisation, five centuries after Vasco da Gama / [editors], Walter Fernandes, Anupama Dutta. Published/Created: New Delhi: Indian Social Institute, c1999- Related Names: Fernandes, Walter, 1939- Dutta, Anupama. Indian Social Institute. International Conference, Colonialism to Globalisation: Five Centuries after Vasco da Gama (1998: New Delhi, India) Description: v. <1 >; 22 cm. ISBN 8187218118 Summary: Papers presented at the International Conference, Colonialism to Globalisation: Five Centuries after Vasco da Gama, held at Indian Social Institute, New Delhi, Feb. 2-

6, 1998. Subjects: Colonies--History--
Congresses. World politics--Congresses.
Globalization--Congresses. LC
Classification: JV105 .C65 1999 Dewey
Class No.: 320.9 21

Comeliau, Christian. Les impasses de la
modernité: Critique de la marchandisation
du monde / Christian Comeliau.
Published/Created: Paris: Seuil, 2000.
Description: 259 p.; cm. ISBN
2020407604 Subjects: International
economic relations. Globalization. Series:
Economie humaine LC Classification:
HF1359 .C663 2000

Comeliau, Christian. The impasse of
modernity: debating the future of the
global market economy / Christian
Comeliau; translated by Patrick Camiller.
Published/Created: London; New York:
Zed Books, 2001. Description: p. cm.
ISBN 1856499855 (cased) 1856499863
(limp) Notes: Includes bibliographical
references. Subjects: International
economic relations. Globalization. LC
Classification: HF1359 .C66313 2001
Dewey Class No.: 337 21

Comparative education: the dialectic of the
global and the local / edited by Robert F.
Arnove and Carlos Alberto Torres.
Published/Created: Lanham: Rowman &
Littlefield, c1999. Related Names:
Arnove, Robert F. Torres, Carlos Alberto.
Description: vi, 434 p.; 25 cm. ISBN
0847684601 (cloth: alk. paper)
084768461X (pbk.: alk. paper) Notes:
Includes bibliographical references (p.
428-431) and index. Subjects:
Comparative education--Philosophy.
Globalization. LC Classification: LB43
.C68 1999 Dewey Class No.: 370.9 21

Comparative political culture in the age of
globalization: an introductory anthology /
[edited by] Hwa Yol Jung.
Published/Created: Lanham, MD:

Lexington Books, 2001. Related Names:
Jung, Hwa Yol. Description: p. cm. ISBN
0739103172 (cloth: alk. paper)
0739103180 (pbk.: alk. paper) Notes:
Includes bibliographical references and
index. Subjects: Political culture.
Globalization. East and West. Series:
Global encounters LC Classification:
JA75.7 .C65 2001 Dewey Class No.:
306.2 21

Competencia global y cambio tecnológico: un
desafío para la economía española / José
Molero, coordinador. Published/Created:
Madrid: Ediciones Pirámide, c2000.
Related Names: Molero Zayas, José.
Centro Internacional Carlos V.
Description: 349 p.: ill.; 22 cm. ISBN
8436814193 Notes: "Centro Internacional
Carlos V" Includes bibliographical
references. Subjects: Technological
innovations--Economic aspects--Spain.
International business enterprises--
Technological innovations--Spain.
Competition, International. Globalization.
LC Classification: HC390.T4 C66 2000
Dewey Class No.: 338/.064/0946 21

Competition & change. Published/Created:
Newark, NJ: Harwood Academic
Publishers, 1995- Description: v.: ill.; 23-
25 cm. Four issues per v. Some issues
combined. Vol. 1, no. 1 (1995)- Current
Frequency: Irregular ISSN: 1024-5294
Notes: Title from cover. Subjects:
International economic relations--
Periodicals. Competition, International--
Periodicals. Globalization--Periodicals.
World politics--Periodicals. LC
Classification: HF1351 .C65

Competition and regulation: implications of
globalization for Malaysia and Thailand /
Frank Flatters and David Gillen, editors.
Published/Created: Kingston, Ont.: J.D.
International, Queen's University, 1997.
Related Names: Flatters, Frank. Gillen,
David. John Deutsch Institute for the

Study of Economic Policy. International and Development Studies Programs. Description: v, 176 p.: ill.; 23 cm. ISBN 0889117845 Notes: "Conference papers, Bangkok, Thailand, 21-22 March 1997, Kuala Lumpur, Malaysia, 25-26 March 1997." Includes bibliographical references. Subjects: Competition--Government policy--Malaysia--Congresses. Competition--Government policy--Thailand--Congresses. Deregulation--Malaysia--Congresses. Deregulation--Thailand--Congresses. Privatization--Malaysia--Congresses. Privatization--Thailand--Congresses. Globalization--Congresses. Asia, Southeastern--Foreign economic relations Congresses. LC Classification: HF1591 .C65 1997 Dewey Class No.: 338.6/048/09593 21

Compton, Robert W., 1964- East Asian democratization: impact of globalization, culture, and economy / Robert W. Compton, Jr. Published/Created: Westport, Conn.: Praeger, 2000. Description: ix, 208 p.; 24 cm. ISBN 0275964469 (alk. paper) Notes: Includes bibliographical references (p. [191]-203) and index. Subjects: Democratization--East Asia. Globalization. East Asia--Politics and government. LC Classification: JQ1499.A91 C65 2000 Dewey Class No.: 320.95 21

Conert, Hansgeorg. Vom Handelskapital zur Globalisierung: Entwicklung und Kritik der kapitalistischen Ökonomie / Hansgeorg Conert. Edition Information: 1. Aufl. Published/Created: Münster: Westfälisches Dampfboot, 1998. Description: 579 p.; 24 cm. ISBN 3896914286 Notes: Includes bibliographical references (p. 562-579). Subjects: Capitalism--Philosophy. Marxian economic--Philosophy. Globalization--Economic aspects. LC

Classification: HB501 .C7185 1998

Conflictos y comunicación en la globalización / Angel Tello; coautores, Adolfo Negrotto ... [et al.]. Published/Created: Buenos Aires: Facultad de Periodismo y Comunicación Social Universidad Nacional de la Plata, 1999. Related Names: Tello, Angel Pablo, 1947- Negrotto, Adolfo Description: 270 p.; 21 cm. ISBN 9503401615 Notes: Includes bibliographical references. Subjects: Social conflict in mass media. Social conflict. Mass media and war. Terrorism and mass media. Globalization. Ethnic conflict. Communication--Social aspects. Terrorism. Ethnic relations. Chiapas (Mexico)--History--Peasant Uprising, 1994- Series: Ediciones de periodismo y comunicación no. 13 LC Classification: P96.S63 C66 1999 Dewey Class No.: 303.6 21

Connaissance et mondialisation / coordonné par Michel Delapierre, Philippe Moati, El Mouhoub Mouhoud; préface de Marc Humbert. Published/Created: Paris: Economica, 2000. Description: 252 p.; cm. ISBN 2717841261 Subjects: Globalization. Series: Mondialisation

Contemporary problems of international economy / edited by Ewa Oziewicz. Published/Created: Sopot: Institute of Foreign Trade, University of Gda´nsk, 1998. Related Names: Oziewicz, Ewa. Description: 154 p.; 24 cm. ISBN 8386230495 Notes: Includes bibliographical references. Subjects: International economic integration. International economic relations. Globalization. LC Classification: HF1418.5 .C66 1998 Dewey Class No.: 337 21

Contending images of world politics / edited by Greg Fry and Jacinta O'Hagan. Published/Created: Houndmill,

Basingstoke, Hampshire [England]: Macmillan Press; New York: St. Martin's Press, 2000. Related Names: Fry, Greg. O'Hagan, Jacinta. Description: xii, 314 p.; 24 cm. ISBN 0333913752 (cloth) 0333913760 (pbk.) Notes: Includes bibliographical references (p. 272-299) and index. Subjects: International relations. Globalization. World politics--1989- LC Classification: JZ1310 .C66 2000 Dewey Class No.: 327.1 21

Continental shift: globalisation and culture / edited by Elizabeth Jacka. Published/Created: Double Bay, N.S.W.: Local Consumption Publications, c1992. Related Names: Jacka, Elizabeth. Continental Shift Conference (1991: Sydney, N.S.W.) Description: 160 p.: ill.; 21 cm. ISBN 0949793248 Notes: Book derives from papers of the Continental Shift Conference held April 1991. School of Humanities, University of Technology, Sidney gave support in mounting the conference. Includes bibliographical references. Subjects: Communication, International--Congresses. Communication--International cooperation--Congresses. Mass media and technology--Congresses. Mass media and culture--Congresses. LC Classification: P96.I5 C69 1992 Dewey Class No.: 302.2 20

Contro la soluzione politica: note su capitale, stato, rivoluzione nel contesto odierno: appunti e materiali: tre interventi di un compagno prigioniero delle Brigate Rosse, Colonna Walter Alasia. Edition Information: 1. ed. Published/Created: Guasila [Italy]: Arkiviu-Bibrioteka "T. Serra", 1999. Related Names: Alasia, Walter. Description: 266 p.: ill.; 21 cm. Subjects: Capitalism. Globalization. Economic history--1971-1990. Economic history--1991- Italy--Economic conditions--1945- Series: I libri di senza censura; 1 LC Classification: HB501

.C7268 1999

Controversies in white-collar crime / edited by Gary W. Potter. Published/Created: Cincinnati, OH: Anderson Pub., c2002. Related Names: Potter, Gary W. Description: xiv, 262 p.: ill., map; 26 cm. ISBN 1583605142 (pbk.) Notes: Includes bibliographical references (p. 223-251) and index. Subjects: Commercial crimes. White collar crimes. Globalization. Series: Controversies in crime and justice LC Classification: HV6768 .C66 2002 Dewey Class No.: 364.16/8 21

Coping strategies in the North: local practices in the context of global restructuring / MOST. Published/Created: Copenhagen: Nordic Council of Ministers, c1998. Related Names: Unesco. Management of Social Transformations Program. Nordic Council of Ministers. Description: 227 p.: ill., maps; 23 cm. ISBN 9289301619 Notes: "INS 1998:303." Includes bibliographical references. Summary in Norwegian. Subjects: Arctic peoples--Social life and customs. Arctic peoples--Social conditions. Globalization--Arctic regions. LC Classification: GN673 .C69 1998

Cortés Montalvo, Jorge. Economía global, política y medios de comunicación / Jorge Cortés Montalvo. Published/Created: Chihuahua, Chih., México: Universidad Autónoma de Chihuahua: SPAUACH: Doble Hélice, 2000. Description: 230 p.; 21 cm. ISBN 9686331611 Notes: Includes bibliographical references (p. 215-230). Subjects: Mass media--Economic aspects. Globalization. Mass media--Political aspects. Series: Colección Textos universitarios (Universidad Autónoma de Chihuahua); 11. LC Classification: P96.E25 C64 2000 Dewey Class No.: 302.23 21

Courchene, Thomas J. A state of minds: toward a human capital future for Canadians / by Thomas J. Courchene. Published/Created: Montréal: IRPP, c2001. Description: xiv, 323 p.: ill.; 23 cm.; cm. ISBN 0886451884 Notes: Includes bibliographical references (p. 293-305). Subjects: Human capital--Canada. Manpower policy--Canada. Globalization--Economic aspects--Canada. Information society--Canada. Information technology--Social aspects--Canada. LC Classification: HD4904.7 .C674 2001 Dewey Class No.: 331.11/0971 21

Cowen, Tyler. Minerva's owl: sources of creative global culture / Tyler Cowen. Published/Created: Princeton, NJ: Princeton University Press, 2002. Description: p. cm. ISBN 0691090165 (alk. paper) Notes: Includes bibliographical references and index. Subjects: Culture. Globalization. Cultural relations. International relations and culture. LC Classification: HM621 .C69 2002 Dewey Class No.: 306 21

Coyle, Diane. Governing the world economy / Diane Coyle. Published/Created: Malden, Mass.: Polity Press, 2000. Description: 166 p.; 20 cm. ISBN 0745623638 0745623646 (pbk.) Notes: Includes bibliographical references (p. [151]-155) and index. Subjects: Free trade. International finance. Globalization. Series: Themes for the 21st century LC Classification: HF1713 .C695 2000 Dewey Class No.: 382/.71 21

Coyle, Diane. Paradoxes of prosperity: why the new capitalism benefits all / Diane Coyle. Published/Created: New York: Texere, c2001. Description: xix, 316 p.; 24 cm. ISBN 1587990822 Notes: Includes bibliographical references (p. 289-287) and index. Subjects: Capitalism. Globalization. Technological innovations--Social aspects. LC Classification: HB501 .C784 2001 Dewey Class No.: 306.3/42/09049 21

Craig, David, 1961- Familiar medicine: everyday health knowledge and practice in today's Vietnam / David Craig. Published/Created: Honolulu: University of Hawaii Press, 2002. Description: p. cm. ISBN 0824824741 (cloth: alk. paper) Notes: Includes bibliographical references and index. Subjects: Traditional medicine--Vietnam--Red River Delta. Ethnobotany--Vietnam--Red River Delta. Materia medica--Vietnam--Red River Delta. Public health--Vietnam--Red River Delta. Globalization. Red River Delta (Vietnam)--Social life and customs. LC Classification: GN635.V5 C73 2002 Dewey Class No.: 610/.9597 21

Creative destruction: business survival strategies in the global Internet economy / Lee W. McKnight, Paul M. Vaaler, Raul L. Katz, editors. Published/Created: Cambridge, Mass.: MIT Press, 2001. Related Names: McKnight, Lee W. Vaaler, Paul M. Katz, Raul Luciano. Description: p. cm. ISBN 026213389X (hc.: alk. paper) Notes: A collection of 12 papers which "grew out of a March 1999 symposium held at the Fletcher School of Law and Diplomacy, Tufts University. "Creative Destruction -- or Just Destruction? Telecoms in Transition: Survival and Success in the Global Internet Economy" was co-sponsored by the Fletcher School's Hitachi Center for Technology and International Affairs, the Fletcher School's Edward R. Murrow Center for International Information and Communication, and Booz Allen & Hamilton"--P. . Includes bibliographical references and index. Subjects: Technological innovations--Economic aspects--Congresses. Evolutionary economics--Congresses. Organizational change--Congresses. Internet--

Congresses. Globalization--Congresses.
LC Classification: HC79.T4 C74 2001
Dewey Class No.: 658.4/062 21

Critical issues seminar on productivity [sound
recording]. Published/Created: 1989.
Related Names: Bradley, Bill, 1943-
Solow, Robert M. Porter, Michael E.,
1947- Spence, Michael. McElroy, Michael
B., (Michael Bancroft) 1941- Library of
Congress. Description: 4 sound cassettes:
analog. Summary: Noted economists and
other experts discuss the issue of
productivity with a focus on the
economics of productivity. Topics cover
include competition, globalization,
deregulation, the nature of domestic
rivalry, and competitive advantages. This
is the second of four seminars on the
critical issues on productivity. Notes:
Recorded Nov. 27, 1989, at the Library of
Congress, Washington, D.C. Cast: Host,
Sen. Bill Bradley (D-N.J.); speakers:
Robert M. Solow, Michael E. Porter,
Michael Spence, and Michael B.
McElroy. Subjects: Industrial
productivity. Competition. LC
Classification: RYI 3081-RYI 3084

Critical perspectives on globalization and
neoliberalism in the developing countries /
edited by Richard Harris & Melinda J.
Seid. Published/Created: Boston: Brill,
2000. Related Names: Harris, Richard L.
(Richard Legé), 1939- Seid, Melinda.
Description: 183 p.; 24 cm. ISBN
9004118500 Subjects: Free trade--
Developing countries. Globalization--
Developing countries. Liberalism--
Developing countries. Capitalism--
Developing countries. Developing
countries--Dependency on foreign
countries. Series: International studies in
sociology and social anthropology,
00748684; . 79 LC Classification:
HF2580.9 .C75 2000 Dewey Class No.:
337/.09172/6 21

Critical perspectives on internationalisation /
edited by Virpi Havila, Mats Forsgren,
Håkan Håkansson. Edition Information:
1st ed. Published/Created: Amsterdam;
New York: Pergamon, 2002. Related
Names: Havila, Virpi. Forsgren, Mats.
Håkansson, Håkan, 1947- Marcus
Wallenberg Symposium on Critical
Perspectives on Internationalisation
(2000: Uppsala University) Description:
p. cm. ISBN 0080440355 (hardcover)
Notes: "Selected from papers presented at
the 'Marcus Wallenberg Symposium on
Critical Perspectives on
Internationalisation', which took place 10-
11 January, 2000 ... hosted by Uppsala
University, Department of Business
Studies, Sweden"--Pref. Includes indexes.
Subjects: International business
enterprises--Management Congresses.
Globalization--Economic aspects--
Congresses. Competition, International--
Congresses. Series: International business
and management series LC Classification:
HD62.4 .C75 2002 Dewey Class No.:
658/.049 21

Cullmann, Oliver. Die Globalisierung der
Wirtschaft im Lichte der modernen
Arbeitsmarkt- und Beschäftigungstheorie:
Analysen und Befunde / Oliver Cullmann.
Published/Created: Darmstadt: [s.n.];
1998. Description: xv, 227 p.: ill.; 21 cm.
Notes: Thesis (doctoral)--Technische
Universität Darmstadt, 1998. Includes
bibliographical references (p. 183-218).
Subjects: Foreign trade and employment.
Globalization--Economic aspects. Labor
market. Manpower policy. LC
Classification: HD5710.7 .C85 1998

Cultura y carnaval / compiladores, María
Cristina Gálvez V., Jaime Hernán Cabrera
E. Edition Information: 1a ed.
Published/Created: Pasto, Colombia:
Fondo Mixto de Cultura de Nariño: Banco
de la República: Ministerio de Cultura:
Ediciones Unariño, 2000. Related Names:

Gálvez V., María Cristina (Gálvez Vitery) Hernán Cabrera E., Jaime. Description: iv, 154 p.; 22 cm. ISBN 9589479103 Notes: Includes discography (p. 150). Includes bibliographical references (p. 148-149). Subjects: Carnival--Colombia. Carnival--Colombia--Pasto. Globalization. Cultural property. Colombia--Social life and customs. Pasto (Colombia)--Social life and customs. LC Classification: GT4835.A2 C85 2000 Dewey Class No.: 394.25/09861/58 21

Cultura, identidades y ciberespacio / III Congreso Latinoamericano de Humanidades; compiladores, Rocío López Morales, Olmedo España Calderón. Published/Created: Heredia, Costa Rica: Universidad Nacional, 1998. Related Names: López, Rocío. España, Olmedo. Description: 498 p.; 21 cm. ISBN 9968260002 Notes: Includes bibliographical references. Subjects: Humanities--Latin America--Congresses. Cyberspace--Latin America--Congresses. Globalization--Congresses. Education--Latin America--Congresses. Latin America--Civilization--Congresses. LC Classification: F1408.3 .C6718 1997 Dewey Class No.: 980 21

Cusimano, Maryann K. Beyond sovereignty: issues for a global agenda / Maryann K. Cusimano. Published/Created: Boston: Bedford/St. Martins, c2000. Description: xvi, 331 p.; 23 cm. ISBN 1572597518 (pbk.) Notes: Includes bibliographical references. Subjects: Globalization. International cooperation. Sovereignty. LC Classification: JZ1318 .C87 2000 Dewey Class No.: 327 21

Dallmayr, Fred R. (Fred Reinhard), 1928-Achieving our world: toward a global and plural democracy / Fred Dallmayr. Published/Created: Lanham, Md.: Rowman & Littlefield, c2001. Description: xvi, 223 p.; 24 cm. ISBN

0742511847 (alk. paper) 0742511855 (pbk.: alk. paper) Notes: Includes bibliographical references and index. Subjects: Democracy. Human rights. Pluralism (Social sciences) Globalization. Identity (Philosophical concept) LC Classification: JC423 .D277 2001 Dewey Class No.: 321.8 21

Dampak dan implikasi globalisasi terhadap peran petugas pemasyarakatan dan pembinaan warga binaan pemasyarakatan: simposium sehari, 4 Oktober 1996 / kerjasama Universitas HKBP Nommensen ... [et al.]. Published/Created: Pematang Siantar, Sumatera Utara: Yayasan Kebangkitan Hidup Baru, 1998. Related Names: Universitas HKBP Nommensen. Description: xviii, 116 p.; 21 cm. Summary: Impact of globalization on prisons and criminal rehabilitation in Indonesia; proceedings of seminar. Notes: Proceedings of: Simposium Sehari Dampak dan Implikasi Globalisasi Terhadap Peran Petugas Pemasyarakatan dan Pembinaan Warga Binaan Pemasyarakatan. Includes bibliographical references. Subjects: Prisons--Indonesia--Sumatera Utara--v Congresses. Correction personnel--Indonesia--Sumatera Utara Congresses. Criminals--Rehabilitation--Indonesia--Sumatera Utara Congresses. LC Classification: HV9804.S86 D36 1998

Dampak globalisasi informasi dan komunikasi terhadap kehidupan sosial budaya masyarakat Desa Manukasa dan Seloi Malere, Kabupaten Aileu, Propinsi Timor Timur / tim penulis, Emanuel Wahyu Saptomo ... [et al.]; editor, P. Susilo Sastrosuwigyo, Saman, B.A. Published/Created: [Jakarta]: Departemen Pendidikan dan Kebudayaan, Direktorat Jenderal Kebudayaan, Direktorat Sejarah dan Nilai Tradisional, Proyek Pengkajian dan Pembinaan Nilai-Nilai Budaya, 1995/1996 [i.e. 1995] Related Names: Saptomo, Emanuel Wahyu. Sastro

Suwignyo, P. Susilo. Saman. Proyek Pengkajian dan Pembinaan Nilai-Nilai Budaya (Indonesia) Description: xv, 160 p.: ill., maps; 21 cm. Summary: Impact of globalization of information and communication on sociocultural life in Manukasa and Seloi Malere villages, Kabupaten Aileu, Timor Timur Province. Notes: Includes bibliographical references (p. 145-146). Subjects: Communication and culture--Indonesia--Manukasa. Communication and culture--Indonesia--Seloi Malere. Manukasa (Indonesia)--Social conditions. Seloi Malere (Indonesia)--Social conditions. LC Classification: HN710.M34 D36 1995

Dampak globalisasi informasi dan komunikasi terhadap kehidupan sosial budaya masyarakat di daerah Jambi / konsultan, Zuraima Bustamam; tim peneliti/penulis, Eva Zulfita ... [et al.]; editor, Zulyani Hidayat. Published/Created: [Jambi]: Departemen Pendidikan dan Kebudayaan, Bagian Proyek Penelitian, Pengkajian dan Pembinaan Nilai-Nilai Budaya Jambi, 1993/1994 [i.e. 1995] Related Names: Bustaman, Zuraima. Zulfita, Eva. Hidayah, Zulyani. Indonesia. Bagian Proyek Penelitian, Pengkajian dan Pembinaan Nilai-Nilai Budaya Jambi. Description: x, 126 p.: ill., maps; 23 cm. Summary: Impact of communication and information globalization on socio-cultural life in Jambi Province. Notes: Includes bibliographical references (p. 125). Subjects: Communication and culture--Indonesia--Jambi (Province) Jambi (Indonesia: Province)--Social conditions. LC Classification: HN710.J25 D36 1995

Dampak globalisasi informasi dan komunikasi terhadap kehidupan sosial budaya masyarakat di daerah Nusa Tenggara Barat. Published/Created: [Jakarta]: Departemen Pendidikan dan Kebudayaan, [1994] Related Names: Widiani, Baiq

Titiek. Indonesia. Departemen Pendidikan dan Kebudayaan. Description: vii, 145 p.: col. ill., maps; 21 cm. Summary: Impact of communication and information globalization on socio-cultural life in Nusa Tenggara Barat Province. Notes: "Susunan tim peneliti/penulisan ... H. Baiq Titiek Widiani, S.H. ... [et al.]"--P. i. Includes bibliographical references (p. 131-135). Subjects: Communication and culture--Indonesia--Nusa Tenggara Barat. Nusa Tenggara Barat (Indonesia)--Social conditions. LC Classification: HN710.N87 D36 1994

Daniels, John D. Global business: environments and strategies: managing for global competitive advantage / editors, Johan Hough, Ernst W. Neuland; authors, John Daniels, Tim Radebaugh, Ronel Erwee. Published/Created: Oxford; New York: Oxford University Press, 2000. Related Names: Radebaugh, Tim. Erwee, Ronel. Hough, Johan, 1957- Neuland, E. W. (Ernst W.) Description: xviii, 378 p.: ill.; 24 cm. ISBN 0195718526 Notes: Includes bibliographical references and index. Subjects: International business enterprises--Management. Strategic alliances (Business) Globalization--Economic aspects. Competition, International. International business enterprises--Africa, Southern Management. Strategic alliances (Business)--Africa, Southern. Africa, Southern--Foreign economic relations--Africa. Africa--Foreign economic relations--Africa, Southern. LC Classification: HD62.4 .D36 2000 Dewey Class No.: 658/.049 21

Daniels, John D. Globalization and business / John D. Daniels, Lee H. Radebaugh, Daniel P. Sullivan. Edition Information: 1st ed. Published/Created: Upper Saddle River, NJ: Prentice Hall, 2002. Related Names: Radebaugh, Lee H. Sullivan, Daniel P. Daniels, John D. International business. Description: p. cm. ISBN 0130620300 Notes: Based on: International business. 9th ed. c2001. Includes bibliographical references and index. Subjects: International business enterprises. International business enterprises--Management. Globalization. LC Classification: HD2755.5 .D346 2002 Dewey Class No.: 658.1/8 21

Das, Dilip K., 1945- Global trading system at crossroads: a post-Seattle perspective / Dilip K. Das. Published/Created: London; New York: Routledge, 2001. Description: p. cm. ISBN 0415260159 Notes: Includes bibliographical references and index. Subjects: World Trade Organization--Developing countries. Uruguay Round (1987-1994) Free trade. International trade. Globalization--Economic aspects. International economic relations. Series: Routledge studies in the modern world economy; 33 LC Classification: HF1713 .D343 2001 Dewey Class No.: 382 21

Datta, Samar K., 1948- Can globalisation be an unqualified key to success? [microform]: the case of Indian rice / by Samar K. Datta, Sanjeev Kapoor, M.K. Awasthi. Published/Created: Ahmedabad, India: Indian Institute of Management, 1996. Description: 43 p.; 29 cm. Notes: Microfiche. New Delhi: Library of Congress Office; Washington, D.C.: Library of Congress Photoduplication Service, 1996. 1 microfiche Master microform held by: DLC. Series: Working paper (Indian Institute of Management, Ahmedabad); W.P. no. 1292. LC Classification: Microfiche 96/60208 (H)

Davies, Andrew, 1955- Local economies and globalisation. Published/Created: Paris: Organisation for Economic Co-operation and Development, 1995. Related Names: Organisation for Economic Co-operation and Development. Local Economic and Employment Development (Program)

Description: 42 p.; 30 cm. Notes: "This document was prepared by Andrew Davies from written and oral contributions to the conference on "Local Development and Structural Change: a New Perspective on Adjustment and Reform', held in Paris 4 May 1993"--T.p. verso. Includes bibliographical references (p. 40). Subjects: Structural adjustment (Economic policy) Job creation. Community development--Planning. Series: LEED notebook; no. 20 OECD working papers; v. 3, no. 89. LC Classification: HD72 .O38 vol. 3, no. 89

Daya Krishna, 1925- Swadeshi view of globalisation / Daya Krishna. Edition Information: 1st ed. Published/Created: New Delhi: Swadeshi Jagaran Manch, 1994. Description: xxi, 136 p.; 22 cm. Notes: Includes bibliographical references (p. 127-129). Subjects: International economic integration. India--Foreign economic relations. India--Economic policy--1980- LC Classification: HF1590.5.I4 D39 1994

Deacon, Bob. Global social policy: international organizations and the future of welfare / Bob Deacon with Michelle Hulse and Paul Stubbs. Published/Created: London; Thousand Oaks, Calif.: SAGE, 1997. Related Names: Hulse, Michelle. Stubbs, Paul. Description: xiii, 252 p.: ill.; 24 cm. ISBN 0803989539 0803989547 (pbk.) Notes: Includes bibliographical references (p. [222]-243) and index. Subjects: Social policy. International agencies. Non-governmental organizations. Globalization. LC Classification: HN17.5 .D43 1997

Deacon, Bob. Globalization and social policy: the threat to equitable welfare / by Bob Deacon. Published/Created: Geneva, Switzerland: UNRISD 2000. Related Names: United Nations Research Institute for Social Development. Geneva 2000 (2000: Geneva, Switzerland) Description: xiii, 40 p.; 30 cm. ISBN 9290850256 Notes: "February 2000." "Geneva 2000: The next step in social development, 26-30 June 2000"--P. [4] of cover. Includes bibliographical references (p. 34-40). Abstract in English, French and Spanish. Subjects: Social policy. Globalization--Social aspects. Series: Occasional paper (Geneva 2000); 5. LC Classification: HN18 .D4154 2000

Democracy beyond the state?: the European dilemma and the emerging global order / edited by Michael Th. Greven and Louis W. Pauly. Published/Created: Toronto: University of Toronto Press, 2000. Related Names: Greven, Michael Th., 1947- Pauly, Louis W. Description: vii, 191 p.; 23 cm. ISBN 0802083277 Notes: Includes bibliographical references (p. 171-183) and index. Subjects: Democracy--European Union countries. Democracy. Globalization. Démocratie--Pays en voie de développement. Mondialisation (Économie politique) LC Classification: JN40 .D45 2000b Dewey Class No.: 321.8 21

Democracy, citizenship, and the global city / [edited by] Engin F. Isin. Published/Created: New York: Routledge, 2000. Related Names: Isin, Engin F. (Engin Fahri), 1959- Description: p. cm. ISBN 0415216672 0415216680 (pbk.) Notes: Includes bibliographical references and index. Subjects: Municipal government. Cities and towns. Citizenship. Democracy. Globalization. Series: Innis centenary series LC Classification: JS67 .D45 2000 Dewey Class No.: 321.8 21

Democracy, globalisation and transformation in Southern Africa / edited by Linda Freeman. Published/Created: Montreal: Canadian Research Consortium on Southern Africa, 1996. Related Names: Freeman, Linda, 1943- Description: iii, 63 p.; 28 cm. Notes: Includes bibliographical references. Subjects: Africa, Southern--Economic conditions--1975- South Africa--Social conditions--1994- Series: Occasional papers (Canadian Research Consortium on Southern Africa); v. 1. LC Classification: ACQUISITION IN PROCESS (COPIED)

Democratic contracts for sustainable and caring societies: what can churches and Christian communities do? / edited by Lewis S. Mudge & Thomas Wieser. Published/Created: Geneva: WCC Publications, c2000. Related Names: Mudge, Lewis Seymour. Wieser, Thomas. World Council of Churches. W. A. Visser't Hooft Memorial Consultation (4th: 1999: Geneva, Switzerland) Description: viii, 197 p.; 22 cm. ISBN 2825413348 Notes: "The 4th W.A. Visser't Hooft Memorial Consultation was held at the Château de Bossey, near Geneva, Switzerland, from June 1 to 8, 1999. This volume presents the main contributions made for the organization and the debate of the consultation, as well as the final report agreed to by the participants."--P. [vii]. Includes bibliographical references. Subjects: Democracy--Religious aspects--Christianity--Congresses. Globalization--Religious aspects--Christianity Congresses. Christianity and international affairs--Congresses.

Democratization and globalization in Korea: assessments and prospects / edited by Chung-in Moon, Jongryn Mo. Published/Created: Seoul: Yonsei University Press, c1999. Related Names: Moon, Chung-in. Mo, Jongryn, 1961- International Political Science Association. World Congress (17th: 1997: Seoul, Korea) Description: 422 p.: ill.; 23 cm. ISBN 8971414790 Notes: "This volume is the outcome of the conference on 'Democratization and globalization in South Korea' that was held as a part of the 17th World Congress of the International Political Science Association ... in Seoul, Korea on August 19-20, 1997"-- Foreword. Includes bibliographical references and index. Subjects: Democratization--Korea (South)-- Congresses. Globalization--Congresses. Korea (South)--Politics and government-- 1988---Congresses. Korea (South)-- Foreign economic relations--Congresses. Series: Yonsei monograph series on international studies; 4

Demorgon, Jacques. L'interculturation du monde / Jacques Demorgon; préface de Lucette Colin et Remi Hess. Published/Created: Paris: Anthropos, 2000. Description: 166 p.: ill.; 22 cm. ISBN 2717840907 Notes: Includes bibliographical references. Subjects: Information society. Globalization. Multiculturalism. Series: Exploration interculturelle et science sociale LC Classification: HM851 .D47 2000 Dewey Class No.: 303.48/2 21

Demystifying globalization / edited by Colin Hay and David Marsh. Published/Created: Houndmills, Basingstoke, Hampshire: Macmillan Press; New York: St. Martin's Press, 2000. Related Names: Hay, Colin, 1968- Marsh, David, 1946- Description: x, 197 p.: ill.; 23 cm. ISBN 0312230273 (cloth) Notes: Includes bibliographical references and index. Subjects: International cooperation. International relations. Globalization. Series: Globalization and governance LC Classification: JZ1318 .D46 2000 Dewey Class No.: 327.1/7 21

Development strategies for Africa and Asia in the new global structure / editor B. Ramesh Babu. Published/Created: Denver, CO: iAcademic Books, 2001.

Related Names: Babu, B. Ramesh. Description: p. cm. ISBN 1588680371 (paper) Notes: Includes bibliographical references and index. Subjects: Globalization. Africa--Economic policy. Asia--Economic policy. LC Classification: HC800 .D4862 2001 Dewey Class No.: 338.95 21

DeWitt, John, 1934- Early globalization and the economic development of the United States and Brazil / John DeWitt. Published/Created: Westport, Conn.: Praeger, 2002. Description: p. cm. ISBN 0275971996 (alk. paper) Notes: Includes bibliographical references and index. Subjects: Globalization. United States-- Economic conditions. Brazil--Economic conditions. LC Classification: HC103 .D44 2002 Dewey Class No.: 338.981 21

Dezalay, Yves, 1945- The internationalization of palace wars: lawyers, economists, and the contest to transform Latin American states / Yves Dezalay, Bryant G. Garth. Published/Created: Chicago: University of Chicago Press, 2001. Related Names: Garth, Bryant G. Description: p. cm. ISBN 0226144259 (cloth: alk. paper) 0226144267 (pbk.: alk. paper) Notes: Includes bibliographical references and index. Subjects: Globalization. Expertise-- Political aspects--Latin America. Law reform--Latin America. Law and economic development. Latin America-- Foreign relations--United States. United States--Foreign relations--Latin America. Latin America--Politics and government-- 1948-1980. Latin America--Politics and government--1980- Latin America-- Economic policy. Series: The Chicago series in law and society LC Classification: F1418 .D49 2001 Dewey Class No.: 980.03/3 21

Dictionnaire critique de la mondialisation / GERM. Published/Created: Paris: Pré aux clercs, 2001. Description: 423 p.; cm.

ISBN 2842281462 Subjects: Globalization - Economics.

Die Europäische Gemeinschaft in der Welthandelsorganisation: Globalisierung und Weltmarktrecht als Herausforderung für Europa / Peter-Christian Müller-Graff (Hrsg.). Edition Information: 1. Aufl. Published/Created: Baden-Baden: Nomos, 1999/2000 [i.e. 1999?] Related Names: Müller-Graff, Peter-Christian. Description: 245 p.; 23 cm. ISBN 3789064963 (pbk.) Notes: Chiefly rev. papers presented at an interdisciplinary meeting held 1999 in Heidelberg. Includes bibliographical references. One paper in English. Subjects: World Trade Organization. European Union. Globalization. Series: Schriftenreihe des Arbeitskreises Europäische Integration e.V.; Bd. 47 LC Classification: JN30 .E824163 1999 Dewey Class No.: 382/.92 21

Dierckxsens, Wim. The limits of capitalism: an approach to globalization without neoliberalism / Wim Dierckxsens; translated by Jayne Hutchcroft. Published/Created: London; New York: Zed Books; New York: Distributed in the USA exclusively by St. Martin's Press, c2000. Description: x, 170 p.: ill.; 23 cm. ISBN 1856498689 (hb) 1856498697 (pb) Notes: Includes bibliographical references (p. 156-164) and index. Subjects: International economic relations. Globalization. Capitalism. Common good. LC Classification: HF1359 .D53513 2000 Dewey Class No.: 337 21

Dierks, Rosa Gomez. Introduction to globalization: political and economic perspectives for the new century / Rosa Gomez Dierks. Published/Created: Chicago: Burnham, Inc., Publishers, c2001. Description: p. cm. ISBN 083041570X (alk. paper) Notes: Includes bibliographical references and index.

Subjects: Globalization. LC Classification: JZ1318 .D54 2001 Dewey Class No.: 327 21

Diniz, José Janguiê Bezerra. O direito e a justiça do trabalho diante da globalização / José Janguiê Bezerra Diniz; colaborador, André Emmanuel Barreto Campello. Published/Created: São Paulo: Editora LTr, 1999. Related Names: Campello, André Emmanuel Barreto. Description: 260 p.; 23 cm. ISBN 8573226137 Notes: Includes bibliographical references (p. 251-260). Subjects: Brazil. Justiça do Trabalho. Labor laws and legislation-- Brazil. Globalization. LC Classification: KHD1792 .D56 1999

Disability studies today / edited by Colin Barnes, Mike Oliver, and Len Barton. Published/Created: Cambridge, UK: Polity Press in association with Blackwell Publishers, c2002. Related Names: Barnes, Colin. Oliver, Mike. Barton, Len. Description: p. cm. ISBN 0745626564 (hc) 0745626572 (pb) Notes: Includes bibliographical references and index. Subjects: Disability studies. Sociology of disability. People with disabilities LC Classification: HV1568.2 .D595 2002 Dewey Class No.: 305.9/0816 21

Diskurso sa Pilipinismo: pagsilang ng inang bayan / Domingo G. Landicho. Published/Created: Quezon City: University of the Philippines Press, 2001. Description: x, 173 p.; 23 cm. ISBN 9715423167 Summary: Globalization on Philippines culture. Notes: Includes index. In Tagalog.

Distributed work / edited by Pamela Hinds and Sara Kiesler. Published/Created: Cambridge, Mass.: MIT Press, 2002. Related Names: Hinds, Pamela. Kiesler, Sara, 1940- Description: p. cm. ISBN 0262083051 (hc.: alk. paper) Notes: Includes bibliographical references and index. Subjects: Division of labor. International division of labor. Teams in the workplace. Communication in management--Technological innovations. Computer networks. Globalization. LC Classification: HD51 .D57 2002 Dewey Class No.: 658.4/036 21

Diversité des cultures et mondialisation: Au-delà de l'économisme et du culturalisme / Réseau Sud-Nord Cultures et développement, GREL; sous la direction de Henry Panhuys et Hassan Zaoual; avec la participation de Riccardo Petrella, Noël Cannat, Durre Ahmed, ... [et al.]. Published/Created: Paris: Harmattan, 2000. Related Names: Université du littoral Côte d'Opale. GREL (Groupe de recherche sur les économies locales) (Dunkerque) Description: 214 p.; cm. ISBN 2738490786 Subjects: Culture and Globalization.

Dixon, Bill The globalisation of democratic policing: sector policing and zero tolerance in the new South Africa / Bill Dixon. ISBN 0799219894 Series: Occasional paper series

Dolgov, S. I. (Sergei Ivanovich) Globalizatsiia ekonomiki: novoe slovo ili novoe iavlenie / S.I. Dolgov. Published/Created: Moskva: "Ekonomika", 1998. Description: 213, [1] p.; 20 cm. ISBN 5282019264 Notes: Includes bibliographical references (p. 206-[214]). Subjects: Globalization--Economic aspects. International economic relations. International economic integration. Series: Ekonomicheskie problemy na rubezhe vekov LC Classification: HF1359 .D655 1998

Donoso Torres, Roberto. Mito y educación: el impacto de la globalización en la educación en Latinoamérica / Roberto Donoso Torres. Edition Information: 1a ed. Published/Created: Buenos Aires: Espacio, 1999. Description: 250 p.; 23

cm. ISBN 950802092X Notes: Includes bibliographical references (p. [243]-250). Subjects: Education--Latin America. Educational change--Latin America. Globalization--Latin America. Series: Colección Didáctica (Buenos Aires, Argentina) LC Classification: LA541 .D65 1999 Dewey Class No.: 370/.98 21

Doorlopers en breuklijnen: van globalisering, emancipatie en verzet: opstellen aangeboden aan Gerrit Huizer / onder redactie van Paul Hoebink, Detlev Haude, Fons van der Velden. Published/Created: Assen: Van Gorcum, 1999. Related Names: Huizer, Gerrit. Hoebink, Paul. Description: vii, 444 p.: ill.; 24 cm. ISBN 9023235223 (pbk.) Notes: Includes bibliographical references. Subjects: International economic relations. Globalization--Economic aspects. Economic development. LC Classification: HF1359 .D667 1999

Dreiling, Michael C. Solidarity and contention: the politics of security and sustainability in the NAFTA conflict / Michael Dreiling. Published/Created: New York: Garland Pub., 2000. Description: p. cm. ISBN 0815338732 (alk. paper) Notes: Includes bibliographical references and index. Subjects: Canada. Treaties, etc. United States, 1998 Jan. 2. Free trade--United States. Labor movement--United States. Globalization--United States. National security--United States. Series: Garland studies in the history of American labor LC Classification: HF1731 .D74 2000 Dewey Class No.: 382/.917 21

Drobnick, Richard. Economic integration in the Pacific region / by Richard L. Drobnick. Published/Created: Paris: Organisation for Economic Co-operation and Development, 1992. Related Names: Research Programme on Globalisation and Regionalisation. Description: 44 p.;

30 cm. Notes: "General distribution. OCDE/GD(92)79." "Under the direction of Charles Oman. Produced as part of the Research Programme on Globalisation and Regionalisation." Summary in French. Includes bibliographical references (p. 33-36). Subjects: Economic history--1971-1990. Economic history--1990- Pacific Area--Economic integration. Series: Technical papers (Organisation for Economic Co-operation and Development. Development Centre); no. 65. LC Classification: HC681 .D76 1992

Drolshammer, Jens I. The internationalization of the practice of law / edited by Jens Drolshammer & Michael Pfeifer. Published/Created: The Hague; Boston: Kluwer Law International, 2001. Related Names: Pfeifer, Michael, 1947- Description: p. cm. ISBN 9041116206 (hb: acid-free paper) Notes: Includes index. Subjects: Practice of law. Lawyers. Globalization. LC Classification: K120 .D76 2001 Dewey Class No.: 347/.0504 21

Duffield, Mark R. Global governance and the new wars: the merging of development and security / Mark Duffield. Published/Created: New York: Zed Books: St. Martin's Press [distributor], 2001. Description: p. cm. ISBN 1856497488 1856497496 (pbk.) Notes: Includes bibliographical references and index. Subjects: War--Economic aspects--Developing countries. National security--Developing countries. Globalization. LC Classification: HC59.72.D44 D84 2001 Dewey Class No.: 303.6/6 21

Duménil, Gérard. Crise et sortie de crise: ordre et désordres néolibéraux / Gérard Duménil, Dominique Lévy. Published/Created: Paris: Presses universitaires de France, 2000. Related Names: Lévy, Dominique. Description: 286 p.: ill.; 22 cm. ISBN 2130513441

Notes: Includes bibliographical references. Subjects: Economic history--1990- Economic history. Globalization--Economic aspects. Liberalism. Neoclassical school of economics. Depressions--History. Series: Actuel Marx confrontation, 1158-5900 LC Classification: HC59.15 .D86 2000

Dunning, John H. Global capitalism at bay? / John H. Dunning. Published/Created: London; New York: Routledge, 2000. Description: p. cm. ISBN 0415238633 (alk. paper) Notes: Includes bibliographical references and index. Subjects: Capitalism. Globalization. Competition, International. International finance. Economic history--1990- LC Classification: HB501 .D827 2000 Dewey Class No.: 330.12/2 21

Dunning, John H. Globalisation: the challenge for national economic regimes / John H. Dunning. Published/Created: Dublin: Economic and Social Research Institute, [1993] Related Names: Economic and Social Research Institute. Description: ii, 37 p.; 22 cm. ISBN 0707001498 Notes: Bibliography: p. 34-37. Subjects: International business enterprises. International trade. International economic relations. Series: Geary lecture; 24th. LC Classification: HD2755.5 .D864 1993

Duong, Thanh. Hegemonic globalisation: US centrality and global strategy in the emerging world order / Thanh Duong. Published/Created: Burlington, VT: Ashgate, 2002. Description: p. cm. ISBN 0754630137

Dynamics and policy implications of the global reforms at the end of the second millennium / edited by Tukumbi Lumumba-Kasongo. Published/Created: Leiden; Boston: Brill, 2000. Related Names: Lumumba-Kasongo, Tukumbi,

1948- Description: 160 p.; 24 cm. ISBN 9004118470 Notes: Includes bibliographical references and index. Subjects: Policy sciences. Political planning. Globalization. Series: International studies in sociology and social anthropology; v.78 LC Classification: H97 .D93 2000 Dewey Class No.: 320/.6 21

East Asia and globalization / edited by Samuel S. Kim. Published/Created: Lanham, Md.: Rowman & Littlefield Publishers, c2000. Related Names: Kim, Samuel S., 1935- Description: x, 307 p.; 24 cm. ISBN 0742509354 (alk. paper) 0742509362 (pbk.: alk. paper) Notes: Includes bibliographical references and index. Subjects: Globalization. East Asia-- Foreign economic relations. East Asia-- Economic policy. East Asia--Politics and government. Series: Asia in world politics LC Classification: HF1600.5 .E17 2000 Dewey Class No.: 337.5 21

Eatwell, John. Understanding globalisation: the nation-state, democrary, and economic policies in the New epoch essays by John Eatwell, Elizabeth Jelin, Anthony McGrew, and James Rosenau / John Eatwell ... [et al.]. Published/Created: Stockholm: Distributed by Almqvist & Wiksell International, 1998. Description: 100 p. ISBN 9122017828 : LC Classification: ACQUISITION IN PROCESS

EcoNews. U. S. farmland preservation [and] Global sustainable development / director, executive producer, Nancy Pearlman. Published/Created: United States: Educational Communications, Inc., 1990. Related Names: Pearlman, Nancy Sue, 1948- direction, production, editing, host. Educational Communications Collection (Library of Congress) Description: 1 videocassette of 1 (ca. 30 min.): sd. col.; 3/4 in. viewing copy. Contents: Growing concerns: the future of America's farmland / produced by Maguire/Reeder, Ltd.; written by Stacey Berg; photographed by Dennis Reader. Subjects: Farms. Agricultural conservation. Globalization. Sustainable development. LC Classification: VBQ 6803 (viewing copy)

Economic globalisation and the environment / Organisation for Economic Co-operation and Development. Published/Created: Paris: OECD Publications; Washington, D.C.: OECD Washington Center [distributor], c1997. Related Names: Organisation for Economic Co-operation and Development. Description: 88 p.: col. ill.; 23 cm. ISBN 9264155147 Notes: Includes bibliographical references (p. 81- 88). Subjects: Environmental policy. Environmental economics--International cooperation. Environmental pollution-- Economic aspects. Sustainable development. LC Classification: GE170 .E375 1997 Dewey Class No.: 363.7

Economic transition in the Middle East: global challenges and adjustment strategies / edited by Heba Handoussa. Edition Information: 1st. ed. Published/Created: Cairo: The American University in Cairo Press, 1997. Related Names: Handoussa, Heba Ahmad. Description: vii, 275 p.: ill.; 24 cm. ISBN 9774244281 Notes: "Based on papers presented at a conference organized by the Economic Research Forum and held in Rabat in 1995, as well as at an earlier conference organized in 1992 by the American University in Cairo" -- pref. Includes bibliographical references (p. 259-262) and index. Subjects: Globalization--Economic aspects--Middle East--Congresses. Middle East--Economic conditions--Congresses. LC Classification: HC415.15 .E293 1997

Edmunds, June, 1961- Generations, culture and society / June Edmunds and Bryan S.

Turner. Published/Created: Phildelphia, Pa.: Open University, 2002. Related Names: Turner, Bryan S. Description: p. cm. ISBN 0335208525 0335208517 (pbk.) Notes: Includes bibliographical references and index. Subjects: Social change. Globalization--Social aspects. Communication--Social aspects. Culture conflict. Life change events. Generations. LC Classification: HM836 .E368 2002 Dewey Class No.: 303.4 21

Educational restructuring in the context of globalization and national policy / edited by Holger Daun. Published/Created: New York; London: RoutledgeFalmer, 2002. Related Names: Daun, Holger. Description: xxiv, 335 p.; 24 cm. ISBN 0815339410 (HB: alk. paper) Notes: Includes bibliographical references and indexes. Subjects: Education and state--Cross-cultural studies. Educational change--Cross-cultural studies. Globalization--Cross-cultural studies. International economic relations--Cross-cultural studies. Series: Reference books in international education LC Classification: LC71 .E348 2002 Dewey Class No.: 379 21

Edwards, Richard, 1956 July 2- Globalisation and pedagogy: space, place, and identity / Richard Edwards and Robin Usher. Published/Created: London; New York: Routledge, 2000. Related Names: Usher, Robin, 1944- Description: 179 p. 25 cm. ISBN 0415191149 (hard) Notes: Includes bibliographical references (p. [158]-169) and index. Subjects: International education. Internationalism. LC Classification: LC1090 .E33 2000 Dewey Class No.: 370.116 21

Egalitarian politics in the age of globalization / Craig N. Murphy, editor. Published/Created: New York: Palgrave, 2001. Related Names: Murphy, Craig. Description: p. cm. ISBN 0333792408

(cloth) Notes: Includes bibliographical references and index. Subjects: Social movements. Equality. Globalization. Series: Series in international political economy LC Classification: HM881 .E34 2001 Dewey Class No.: 303.48/4 21

Ehrenberg, Johan. Globaliseringsmyten: eller, Hurusom kapitalet skulle frälsa världen / Johan Ehrenberg. Published/Created: Stockholm: Norstedt, c1998. Description: 329 p.; 21 cm. ISBN 9113003712 Subjects: Globalization. Sweden--Economic conditions--1945- LC Classification: HC375 .E38 1998

Ellis, Clarence. The urgency for very small states to articulate specific strategies for globalisation / Clarence Ellis. Published/Created: St. Augustine, Trinidad and Tobago: Caribbean Center for Monetary Studies, [1997?] Related Names: Caribbean Centre for Monetary Studies. Description: 23 p.; 21 cm. ISBN 9766201005 Notes: "This is the revised text of a lecture given on October 28, 1997 at the XXIX Annual Conference of the Caribbean Center for Monetary Studies of the Unversity of the West Indies, St. Augustine, Trinidad and Tobago." Errata slip tipped in. Includes bibliographical references (p. 22-23). Subjects: Caribbean Area--Economic policy. States, Small--Economic conditions. Series: Adlith Brown memorial lecture; 13th LC Classification: HC151 .E52 1997

Ellison, Anthony P. Entrepreneurs and the transformation of the global economy / Anthony P. Ellison. Published/Created: Northampton, MA: Edward Elger Pub., 2002. Description: p. cm. ISBN 1840648198 Notes: Includes bibliographical references and index. Subjects: Deregulation. Entrepreneurship. Deregulation--North America. Entrepreneurship--North America.

Globalization--Economic aspects--North America. Transportation--Deregulation--North America. LC Classification: HD3512 .E45 2002 Dewey Class No.: 338.97/027 21

Ellyard, Peter. Ideas for the new millennium / Peter Ellyard. Published/Created: Carlton, Vic.: Melbourne University Press, 1998. Description: ix, 188 p.; 23 cm. ISBN 0522848192 Notes: Includes bibliographical references (p. 186-188). Subjects: International relations and culture. Globalization. Australia--Foreign relations. LC Classification: JZ1251 .E44 1998 Dewey Class No.: 303.48/2 21

Emadi-Coffin, Barbara, 1951- Rethinking international organization: deregulation and global governance / Barbara Emadi-Coffin. Published/Created: New York: Routledge, 2002. Description: p. cm. ISBN 0415195403 Notes: Includes bibliographical references and index. Subjects: International organization. International economic relations. International business enterprises. International relations. Free ports and zones. Globalization. LC Classification: JZ1308 .E45 2002 Dewey Class No.: 341.2 21

Engelhard, Philippe. La violence de l'histoire: les sociétés contemporaines à l'épreuve du sens / Philippe Engelhard. Published/Created: Paris: Arléa, c2001. Description: 356 p.; 24 cm. ISBN 2869595220 Notes: Includes bibliographical references. Subjects: Globalization--Social aspects. History--Historiography. Violence--Social aspects. World politics--1989- Globalization--Political aspects. Social movements. LC Classification: D2009.+

Entrepreneurship, strategic management, and globalization / edited by D.D. Sharma, S.K. Dhameja, B.R. Gurjar.

Published/Created: Jaipur: Rawat Publications, c1999. Related Names: Sharma, D. D. (Dhruv Dev) Dhameja, S. K. (Suresh K.) Gurjar, B. R. National Seminar on Entrepreneurship, Strategic Management, and Globalization (7th: 1996: Technical Teachers' Training Institute) Description: 285 p.; 23 cm. Summary: Contributed articles presented at the Seventh National Seminar on Entrepreneurship, Strategic Management, and Globalization organized by Technical Teachers' Training Institute, Chandigarh in Dec. 1996. Notes: Includes bibliographical references. Subjects: Entrepreneurship--India. New business enterprises--India--Management. Globalization. LC Classification: HB615 .E63466 1999 Dewey Class No.: 338/.04/0954 21

Environment and global modernity / edited by Gert Spaargaren, Arthur P.J. Mol, and Frederick H. Buttel. Published/Created: London; Thousand Oaks, Calif.: SAGE Publications, 2000. Related Names: Spaargaren, Gert. Mol, A. P. J. Buttel, Frederick H. Description: xii, 257 p.: ill., 24 cm. ISBN 0761967664 0761967672 (pbk.) Notes: "This volume originated out of a conference on 'Social Theory and the Environment' organized under the auspices of the International Sociological Association (ISA) by the Research Group on 'Environment and Society'"--Pref. Includes bibliographical references and index. Subjects: Global environmental change--Congresses. Social change--Congresses. Globalization--Congresses. Series: Sage studies in international sociology; 50 LC Classification: GE149 .E45 2000 Dewey Class No.: 363.7 21

Environmental regulation in the new global economy Published/Created: Northampton, MA Edward Elgar Publishing, 2002. Description: p. cm. ISBN 1840645407 Notes: Papers resulted from a conference held in 1999 at the University of East Anglia. Subjects: Environmental policy--Economic aspects--Europe Congresses. Environmental policy--Economic aspects--Developing countries--Congresses. Environmental law--Compliance costs--Europe--Congresses. Environmental law--Compliance costs--Developing countries Congresses. Factory and trade waste--Environmental aspects--Europe Congresses. Factory and trade waste--Environmental aspects--Developing countries--Congresses. Globalization--Environmental aspects--Europe--Congresses. Globalization--Environmental aspects--Developing countries Congresses. Competition, International--Congresses. LC Classification: HC240.9.E5 E632 2002 Dewey Class No.: 333.7 21

Erasmus: revista para el diálogo intercultural. Published/Created: Río Cuarto, Argentina: Ediciones del ICALA, [1999- Related Names: Fundación ICALA. Description: v.; 22 cm. Año 1, no. 1 (1999)- Current Frequency: Semiannual ISSN: 1514-6049 Notes: Title from cover. Issues also have theme titles. Issued by: Fundación ICALA. Subjects: Catholic Church--Latin America--Periodicals. Postmodernism--Periodicals. Globalization--Periodicals. International relations--Periodicals. Latin America--Civilization--Periodicals. LC Classification: IN PROCESS B831 .E73

Esch, R. F. van (Rob F.) Globalisation and European economies: from Brazilian dialer-squads to Irish teleworkers / R.F. van Esch. Published/Created: The Hague: Ministry of Economic Affairs, Economic Policy Directorate, [1994] Related Names: Netherlands. Directorate for Economic Policy. Description: 27 p.: ill.; 25 cm. Notes: Includes bibliographical references. Subjects: Competition--Europe. Industries--Europe. Competition,

International. Economic history--1990- Series: Discussion paper (Netherlands. Directorate for Economic Policy); 9401. LC Classification: HF1414 .E787 1994

Eschle, Catherine. Global democracy, social movements, and feminism / Catherine Eschle. Published/Created: Boulder, Colo.: Westview Press, 2001. Description: xii, 279 p.; 23 cm. ISBN 0813391490 (alk. paper) Notes: Includes bibliographical references (p. 237-267) and index. Subjects: Democracy. Social movements. Feminism. Globalization. Series: Feminist theory and politics LC Classification: JC423 .E68 2001 Dewey Class No.: 909.82/9 21

Essays in economic globalization, transnational policies, and vulnerability / edited by Alexander Kouzmin and Andrew Hayne. Published/Created: Amsterdam; Washington, DC: IOS Press; Brussels: International Institute of Administrative Sciences, c1999. Related Names: Kouzmin, Alexander. Hayne, Andrew. International Institute of Administrative Sciences. Description: 227 p.: ill.; 25 cm. ISBN 9051995040 Notes: Includes bibliographical references and index. Subjects: International economic relations. International business enterprises--Government policy. Globalization--Economic aspects. Globalization--Political aspects. Globalization--Social aspects. Series: International Institute of Administrative sciences monographs, 1382-4414; v. 9 LC Classification: HF1359 .E83 1999 Dewey Class No.: 337 21

Estado, política y recomposición institucional en el sector rural en América Latina / Concepción Sánchez Quintanar ... [et al.], editores. Edition Information: 1. ed. Published/Created: Texcoco: Colegio de Postgraduados, Instituto de Investigaciones Económicas, Secretaría de

Agricultura, Ganadería y Desarrollo Rural, 2000. Description: 373 p.; cm. ISBN 2688392618 (sic) 9688392618 Summary: Scholarly articles on globalization in Latin America, organized under the areas of globalization and the role of the state, agricultural policies, cases studies in Chile and Brazil, the reorganization of social structures and social actors. Series: Globalización para quién? por un desarrollo global incluyente!. volumen II

Ethics and the future of capitalism / edited by László Zsolnai in cooperation with Wojciech W. Gasparski. Published/Created: New Brunswick, NJ: Transaction Publishers, 2002. Related Names: Zsolnai, László. Gasparski, Wojciech. Description: p. cm. ISBN 0765801205 (cloth: alk. paper) Notes: Against market fundamentalism: "The capitalist threat" reconsidered / George Soros with Andrew Brody ... [et al.] -- Ethics of capitalism / Peter Koslowski -- Misunderstood and abused liberalism / Lubomír Mloch -- Humanizing the economy: on the relationship between the ethics of human rights and economic discourse / Stefano Zamagni -- The possibility of stakeholder capitalism / R. Edward Freeman -- Effectiveness, efficiency, and ethicality in business and management / Wojciech W. Gasparski -- Responsibility and management / László Zsolnai. Includes bibliographical references. Subjects: Capitalism--Moral and ethical aspects. Economics--Moral and ethical aspects. International trade--Moral and ethical aspects. Globalization--Moral and ethical aspects. Business ethics. Human rights. Capitalism--Moral and ethical aspects--Europe, Eastern. Series: Praxiology (New Brunswick, N.J.); v. 9. LC Classification: HB501 .E77695 2002 Dewey Class No.: 330.12/2 21

Europe 2020: adapting to a changing world / [edited by] Otto von der Gablentz ... [et al.]; with contributions by Lynne Chisholm ... [et al.]. Published/Created: Baden-Baden: Nomos, 2000. Related Names: Gablentz, Otto von der. Chisholm, Lynne. Description: 106 p.; 23 cm. ISBN 3789067369 (pbk.) Subjects: European Union--Forecasting. Globalization. Information society. Europe--Foreign economic relations--Forecasting. LC Classification: JN30 .E82433 2000 Dewey Class No.: 303.494 21

European Union and new regionalism: regional actors and global governance in a post-hegemonic era / edited by Mario Telò. Published/Created: Aldershot, England; Burlington, VT: Ashgate, c2001. Related Names: Telò, Mario. Description: 330 p.: maps; 23 cm. ISBN 0754617483 (hard) 0754617491 (pbk.) Notes: Includes bibliographical references (p. 297-321) and index. Subjects: European Union--Congresses. Regionalism--Congresses. Globalization--Congresses. Series: The International political economy of new regionalisms series LC Classification: HC240 .E8557 2001 Dewey Class No.: 337.1/42 21

European working lives: continuities and change in management and industrial relations in France, Scandinavia, and the UK / edited by Steve Jefferys, Frederik Mispelblom Beyer, Christer Thörnqvist. Published/Created: Northampton, MA: Edward Elgar, 2001. Related Names: Jefferys, Steve. Beyer, Frederik Mispelblom, 1950- Thörnqvist, Christer. Description: p. cm. ISBN 1840644761 Notes: Includes bibliographical references and index. Subjects: Labor--Europe. Industrial relations--Europe. Management--Europe. Globalization. LC Classification: HD8374 .E933 2001

Dewey Class No.: 331/.094 21

Evans, Tony, 1944- The politics of human rights: a global perspective / Tony Evans. Published/Created: London; Sterling, Va.: Pluto Press, 2001. Description: 135 p.; 22 cm. ISBN 074531452X (pbk.) 0745314570 (hardback) Notes: Includes bibliographical references (p. 120-130) and index. Subjects: Human rights. Globalization. Series: Human security in the global economy LC Classification: JC571 .E853 2001 Dewey Class No.: 323 21

External and internal constraints on policy making: how autonomous are the states? / edited by John Degnbol-Martinussen. Published/Created: Roskilde, Denmark: International Development Studies, Roskilde University, 1999. Related Names: Degnbol-Martinussen, John. Roskilde universitetscenter. International Development Studies. Description: [x], 219 p.; 26 cm. ISBN 8773494437 Notes: Includes bibliographical references. Subjects: Political planning--Developing countries. Globalization. Developing countries--Economic policy. Series: Occasional paper (Roskilde universitetscenter. International Development Studies); no. 20. LC Classification: HC59.7 .E974 1999

External liberalization, economic performance, and social policy / edited by Lance Taylor. Published/Created: Oxford; New York: Oxford University Press, c2001. Related Names: Taylor, Lance. Description: xiii, 386 p.: ill.; 24 cm. ISBN 0195145461 (alk. paper) Notes: Includes bibliographical references. Subjects: Free trade--Social aspects--Developing countries. Globalization--Economic aspects--Developing countries. Globalization--Social aspects--Developing countries. International economic relations. LC Classification: HF2580.9

.E95 2001 Dewey Class No.: 337 21

Facets of Globalization: international and local dimensions of development / edited by Shahid Yusuf, Simon Evenett, Weiping Wu. Published/Created: Washington, D.C.: World Bank, c2001. Related Names: Yusuf, Shahid, 1949- Evenett, Simon J. Wu, Weiping. Description: xv, 278 p.: ill.; 28 cm. ISBN 082134742X Notes: Includes bibliographical references. Subjects: Urban economics. Economic development. Globalization. Series: World Bank discussion papers; 415. LC Classification: HT321 .F33 2001 Dewey Class No.: 330.9173/2 21

Falk, Richard A. Religion and humane global governance / Richard Falk. Edition Information: 1st ed. Published/Created: New York: Palgrave, 2001. Description: xi, 191 p.; 22 cm. Notes: Includes bibliographical references (p. [167]-185) and index. Subjects: Religion and international affairs. Globalization--Religious aspects. LC Classification: BL65.I55 F35 2001 Dewey Class No.: 291.1/787 21

Felton, John. Global connections: America's role in the 21st century / John Felton. Published/Created: Washington, D.C.: CQ Press, c2001. Description: p. cm. ISBN 1568026544 (alk. paper) Notes: Includes bibliographical references and index. Subjects: World politics--21st century--Encyclopedias. Globalization--Encyclopedias. Twenty-first century--Forecasts--Encyclopedias. United States--Foreign relations--2001---Encyclopedias. LC Classification: E895 .F45 2001 Dewey Class No.: 303.48/273/00112 21

Financial services without borders: how to succeed in professional financial services / Greenwich Associates. Published/Created: New York: J. Wiley, c2001. Related Names: Greenwich Associates (Firm)

Description: xi, 342 p.: ill.; 24 cm. ISBN 047132647X (cloth: alk. paper) Notes: Includes bibliographical references and index. Subjects: Financial services industry. Globalization. Series: Wiley finance series LC Classification: HG173 .F5167 2001 Dewey Class No.: 332.1/068/8 21

Findlay, Mark. The globalisation of crime: understanding transitional relationships in context / Mark Findlay. Published/Created: Cambridge; New York: Cambridge University Press, 1999. Description: x, 243 p.: ill.; 24 cm. ISBN 0521621259 (hardback) Notes: Includes bibliographical references (p. 226-235) and index. Subjects: Criminology. Social change. LC Classification: HV6025 .F46 1999 Dewey Class No.: 364 21

Finn, Ed. Who do we try to rescue today? / by Ed Finn. Published/Created: Ottawa: Canadian Centre for Policy Alternatives, c2000. Related Names: Canadian Centre for Policy Alternatives. Description: iii, 182 p.; 23 cm. ISBN 0886272173 Subjects: Corporations--Political aspects--Canada. Globalization--Economic aspects--Canada. Business and politics--Canada. Democracy--Canada. Free trade--Canada. Canada--Politics and government--1993- Canada--Economic policy--1991- Canada--Social policy. LC Classification: HD2809 .F56 2000

Fishlow, Albert. The United States and the regionalisation of the world economy / by Albert Fishlow and Stephan Haggard. Published/Created: Paris: Organisation for Economic Co-operation and Development; [Washington, D.C.: OECD Publications and Information Centre, distributor], 1992. Related Names: Haggard, Stephan. Research Programme on Globalisation and Regionalisation. Organisation for Economic Co-operation and Development. Description: 48 p.; 27 cm. ISBN 9264136711 : Notes: "April 1992." "Produced as part of the Research Programme on Globalisation and Regionalisation." Includes bibliographical references (p. 35-37). Subjects: International economic integration. International economic relations. International trade. United States--Commerce. Series: Development Centre documents LC Classification: HF3031 .F5 1992 Dewey Class No.: 337.73 20

Flanagan, Stephen J. Challenges of the global century: report of the Project on Globalization and National Security / by Stephen J. Flanagan, Ellen L. Frost, and Richard L. Kugler. Published/Created: Washington, D.C.: Institute for National Strategic Studies, National Defense University, 2001. Related Names: Frost, Ellen L. Kugler, Richard L. National Defense University. Institute for National Strategic Studies. Description: 32 p.: ill.; 28 cm. + 1 computer optical disc (4 3/4 in.) Notes: This report summarizes themes emerging from The Global century: globalization and national security. Accompanied by CD-ROM of The Global Century. CD-ROM can be accessed using Windows 95, Windows NT, Macintosh, and UNIX operating systems. Includes bibliographical references. Subjects: National security--United States. Security, International. Globalization. United States--Foreign relations--1993-2001. LC Classification: UA23 .F53 2001 Dewey Class No.: 355/.033073 21

Flores Olea, Víctor. Crítica de la globalidad: dominación y liberación en nuestro tiempo / Víctor Flores Olea y Abelardo Mariña Flores. Edition Information: 1. ed. Published/Created: México: Fondo de Cultura Económica, 1999. Related Names: Mariña Flores, Abelardo. Description: 598 p.; 23 cm. ISBN 9681659945 Notes: Series title on cover: Política y derecho. Includes

bibliographical references: p. 579-593.
Subjects: Globalization. Liberalism.
International economic relations.
Neoliberalismo. Economía internacional.
Series: Sección de obras de política y
derecho Local Call/Shelving: JZ1318 .F56
1999

Forben, Ako. Globalisation: the African
perspective / [Ako Forben].
Published/Created: Bamenda, Cameroon:
BCC Pub. for the African Centre for the
Humanities, c1995. Description: viii, 102
p.: ill.; 21 cm. Notes: Includes
bibliographical references (p. 95) and
index. Subjects: Africa--Economic
integration. Africa--Foreign economic
relations. Africa--Economic conditions--
1960- Africa--Social conditions--1960-
LC Classification: HC800 .F668 1995
Dewey Class No.: 337.6 21

Formoso, Manuel. Costa Rica en el mundo: los
próximos cincuenta años / Manuel
Formoso. Edition Information: 1a ed.
Published/Created: San José: Editorial
Fundación UNA, 2000. Description: 453
p.; cm. ISBN 996816075x Summary:
Essays on the next half century in Costa
Rica, with focus on education, political
institutions and reform, globalization,
development, technology and quality of
life.

Forrester, Viviane. Une étrange dictature /
Viviane Forrester. Published/Created:
Paris: Fayard, 2000. Description: 223 p.;
22 cm. ISBN 2213602719 Notes: Includes
bibliographical references. Subjects:
International economic relations.
Globalization. Capitalism. LC
Classification: HF1359 .F675 2000
Dewey Class No.: 337 21

Forum on Land, Food Security, and
Agriculture, November 11-12, 1998,
Grand Olympic Hotel, Kuala Lumpur,
Malaysia: an issue forum of the 1998

Asia-Pacific Peoples' Assembly (APPA) /
organised by PAN-AP and ERA
Consumer. Published/Created: [Penang,
Malaysia: Pesticide Action Network Asia
and the Pacific, 1999] Related Names:
Pesticide Action Network (Group). Asia
and the Pacific. ERA Consumer
(Organization) Description: 31 p.: ill.; 29
cm. Notes: Cover title. Subjects: Food
supply--Developing countries--
Congresses. Globalization--Social
aspects--Developing countries
Congresses. LC Classification:
HD9018.D44 F677 1998

Fourçans, André. La mondialisation racontée à
ma fille / André Fourçans.
Published/Created: Paris: Seuil, c2001.
Description: 295 p.; 21 cm. ISBN
2020485990 Notes: Includes
bibliographical references (p. 295-[296]).
Subjects: Globalization. LC
Classification: JZ1318 .F68 2001 Dewey
Class No.: 327 21

Fragmentation: new production patterns in the
world economy / edited by Sven W. Arndt
and Henryk Kierzkowski.
Published/Created: Oxford: Oxford
University Press, 2001. Related Names:
Arndt, Sven W. Kierzkowski, Henryk.
Description: x, 257 p.: ill.; 24 cm. ISBN
019924331X Notes: Includes
bibliographical references and index.
Subjects: International division of labor.
Offshore assembly industry. International
business enterprises. Globalization. LC
Classification: HF1412 .F69 2001 Dewey
Class No.: 338.4/767 21

Frankel, Boris. When the boat comes in:
transforming Australia in the age of
globalisation / Boris Frankel.
Published/Created: Annandale, N.S.W.:
Pluto Press, 2001. Description: ix, 262 p.;
24 cm. ISBN 1864031719 1864031719 :
Notes: Includes index. Includes
bibliographical references: p. 242-256.

Subjects: Globalization. Australia--
Economic conditions--1990- Australia--
Social conditions--1990-

Frankel, Boris. When the boat comes in:
transforming Australia in the age of
globalisation / Boris Frankel.
Published/Created: Annandale, N.S.W.:
Pluto Press, 2001. Description: ix, 262 p.;
24 cm. ISBN 1864031719 1864031719 :
Notes: Includes index. Includes
bibliographical references: p. 242-256.
Subjects: Globalization. Australia--
Economic conditions--1990- Australia--
Social conditions--1990-

Franklin, Sarah, 1960- Global nature, global
culture / Sarah Franklin, Celia Lury and
Jackie Stacey. Published/Created:
London: SAGE, 2000. Related Names:
Lury, Celia. Stacey, Jackie. Description:
x, 246 p., [8] p. of plates: ill. (some col.);
25 cm. ISBN 076196598X 0761965998
(pbk.) Notes: Includes bibliographical
references and index. Subjects: Culture.
Nature. Globalization. Feminist theory.
Culture. Feminist theory. Series: Gender,
theory and culture LC Classification:
HM831 .F73 2000 Dewey Class No.: 306
21

Franzmeyer, Fritz. Der Einfluss ökonomischer
Rahmenbedingungen auf die zukünftige
Sozialpolitik in der EU / Fritz
Franzmeyer. Published/Created: Bonn:
Forschungsinstitut der Friedrich-Ebert-
Stiftung, Abt. Arbeits- und
Sozialforschung, [1998] Description: 44
p.; 30 cm. ISBN 3860776908 Notes:
Includes bibliographical references (p. 41-
44). Subjects: Globalization--Social
aspects--European Union countries. Labor
policy--European Union countries.
European Union countries--Social policy.
European Union countries--Economic
policy. Series: Gesprächskreis Arbeit und
Soziales (Series) LC Classification:

HN373.5 .F735 1998

Frauenpolitische Chancen globaler Politik:
Verhandlungserfahrungen im
internationalen Kontext / Barbara
Holland-Cunz, Uta Ruppert (Hrsg.).
Published/Created: Opladen: Leske +
Budrich, 2000. Related Names: Holland-
Cunz, Barbara, 1957- Ruppert, Uta.
Internationale Konferenz "Global
Governance, Politische
Verhandlungssysteme und Internationale
Frauenpolitik" (1988: Justus-Liebig-
Universität Giessen) Description: 188 p.;
21 cm. ISBN 3810025607 (pbk.) Notes:
Papers presented at the Internationale
Konferenz "Global Governance,
Politische Verhandlungssysteme und
Internationale Frauenpolitik" held Nov.
1998 at the Justus-Liebig Universität
Giessen. Includes bibliographical
references. German and English. Subjects:
International organization--Congresses.
Globalization--Congresses. Feminist
theory--Congresses. Series: Politik und
Geschlecht; Bd. 3. LC Classification:
JZ5566+

Frenkel, Jacob A. Globalization, instability,
and the world financial system / Jacob A.
Frenkel. Published/Created: Bryn Mawr,
Pa.: The American College, c1999.
Description: xi, 34 p.: ill.; 22 cm. Notes:
"Delivered at The American College,
Bryn Mawr, Pennsylvania, on May 4,
1998." Subjects: International finance.
Globalization--Economic aspects.
Financial crises--Asia. Political stability.
Series: The Frank M. Engle lecture; 1998
LC Classification: HG3881 .F733 1999

Fricke, Dietmar. Globalisierung und
Bürgerkriege: eine theoriegeleitete
Analyse von Globalisierungsprozessen
und ihrem Verhältnis zu regionalen
Konflikten / Dietmar Fricke. Edition
Information: 1. Aufl. Published/Created:
Berlin: Köster, c2000. Description: 246

p.; 24 cm. ISBN 3895744107 (pbk.) Notes: Originally presented s the author's thesis (doctoral)--Otto-von-Guericke-Universität Magedburg, 2000, under the Globalisierungsprozesse und ihr Verhältnis zu regionalen Konflikten. Includes bibliographical references (p. 232-246). Subjects: Economic development. Civil war. Globalization. Series: Bewaffnete Konflikte nach dem Ende des Ost-West-Konfliktes; Bd. 8 LC Classification: HD84 .F7195 2000 Dewey Class No.: 303.6/4/09172409049 21

Friedman, Thomas L. The Lexus and the olive tree / Thomas L. Friedman. Edition Information: 1st Anchor Books ed. Published/Created: New York: Anchor Books, c2000. Description: xxii, 490 p.: ill.; 21 cm. ISBN 0385499345 Notes: Originally published: New York: Farrar Straus Giroux, c1999. Includes index. Subjects: International economic relations. Free trade. Capitalism--Social aspects. Technological innovations--Economic aspects. Technological innovations--Social aspects. Intercultural communication. Globalization. United States--Foreign economic relations. LC Classification: HF1359 .F74 2000 Dewey Class No.: 337 21

Friedman, Thomas L. The Lexus and the olive tree / Thomas L. Friedman. Edition Information: Rev. ed. Published/Created: New York: Farrar, Straus, Giroux, 2000. Description: xxi, 469 p.; 24 cm. ISBN 0374185522 (alk. paper) Notes: Includes index. Subjects: International economic relations. Free trade. Capitalism--Social aspects. Technological innovations--Economic aspects. Technological innovations--Social aspects. Intercultural communication. Globalization. United States--Foreign economic relations. LC Classification: HF1359 .F74 2000b Dewey Class No.: 337 21

Friedman, Thomas L. The Lexus and the olive tree / Thomas L. Friedman. Published/Created: Thorndike, Me.: Thorndike Press, 1999. Description: 720 p. (large print); 22 cm. ISBN 0786222395 (lg. print: hc: alk. paper) Notes: Originally published: New York: Farrar Straus Giroux, c1999. Includes index. Subjects: International economic relations. Free trade. Capitalism--Social aspects. Technological innovations--Economic aspects. Technological innovations--Social aspects. Intercultural communication. Globalization. United States--Foreign economic relations. LC Classification: HF1359 .F74 1999b Dewey Class No.: 337 21

Friedman, Thomas L. The Lexus and the olive tree / Thomas L. Friedman. Edition Information: 1st ed. Published/Created: New York: Farrar, Straus, Giroux, 1999. Description: xix, 394 p.: ill.; 24 cm. ISBN 0374192030 (alk. paper) Notes: Includes index. Subjects: International economic relations. Free trade. Capitalism--Social aspects. Technological innovations--Economic aspects. Technological innovations--Social aspects. Intercultural communication. Globalization. United States--Foreign economic relations. LC Classification: HF1359 .F74 1999 Dewey Class No.: 337 21

Fritsch, Winston. Latin America in a changing global environment / by Winston Fritsch. Published/Created: Paris: Organisation for Economic Co-operation and Development, 1992. Related Names: Oman, Charles. Organisation for Economic Co-operation and Development. Development Centre. Description: 36 p.; 30 cm. Notes: "Under the direction of Charles Oman. Produced as part of the research programme on globalisation and regionalisation." On cover: OECD Development Centre. "May 1992"--Cover. "OCDE/GD(92)85."

Subjects: Latin America--Commercial policy. Latin America--Foreign economic relations. Series: Technical papers (Organisation for Economic Co-operation and Development. Development Centre); no. 66. LC Classification: HF1480.5 .F74 1992

From Havana to Seattle and beyond: the quest for free trade and free markets: essays in honour of Frans A. Engering on the occasion of his departure as Director-General for Foreign Economic Relations on June 7th 2000 / Ministry of Economic Affairs of the Netherlands, Directorate-General for Foreign Economic Relations; editorial board, Harry Oldersma ... [et al.]. Published/Created: The Hague: Sdu Publishers, c2000. Related Names: Engering, Frans A. Oldersma, Harry. Netherlands. Directoraat-Generaal voor de Buitenlandse Economische Betrekkingen. Description: 344 p.: ill.; 25 cm. ISBN 9012089158 Notes: Includes bibliographical references. Subjects: Free trade. International trade. Globalization--Economic aspects. Free trade--Netherlands. European Union. Netherlands--Commercial policy. Netherlands--Foreign economic relations. LC Classification: HF1713 .F79 2000 Dewey Class No.: 337 21

Fukasaku, Kiichiro. Economic regionalisation and intra-industry trade: Pacific-Asian perspectives / by Kiichiro Fukasaku; Research Programme on Globalisation and Regionalisation. Published/Created: Paris: OECD, c1992. Related Names: Research Programme on Globalisation and Regionalisation. Description: 64 p.; 30 cm. Notes: Summaries in English and French. "General distribution; OCDE/GD(92)5." "February 1992." Includes bibliographical references (p. 42-47). Subjects: East Asia--Commerce. Asia, Southeastern--Commerce. Pacific Area--Economic integration. Series:

Technical papers (Organisation for Economic Co-operation and Development. Development Centre); no. 53. LC Classification: HF3820.5 .F85 1992

Fungsi perbatasan negara dalam era globalisasi [microform] / oleh kelompok C. Published/Created: [Jakarta]: Departemen Pertahanan Keamanan, Lembaga Ketahanan Nasional, 1994. Related Names: Lembaga Ketahanan Nasional (Indonesia) Description: 55 leaves: maps; 28 cm. Summary: Political function of boundries related to information globalization in Indonesia; paper. Notes: Microfiche. Jakarta: Library of Congress Office; Washington, D.C.: Library of Congress Photoduplication Service, 1996. 1 microfiche; 11 x 15 cm. LC Classification: Microfiche 94/50398 (J)

Gadea, Raúl. Modernización e identidad en el Mercosur / Raúl Gadea. Published/Created: Montevideo: Ediciones de la Banda Oriental, [1999] Description: 142 p.; 22 cm. ISBN 9974100976 Notes: Includes bibliographical references. Subjects: Globalization--Social aspects. Uruguay--Civilization--21st century. South America--Economic integration. Uruguay--Cultural policy. LC Classification: F2729 .G33 1999 Dewey Class No.: 989.506/7 21

Gali budaya sendiri: buku panduan Festival Kesenian Yogyakarta VII, 1995 dan peringatan 50th Indonesia Emas / [tim penulis, M. Adhisupho ... et al.]. Published/Created: [Yogyakarta]: FKY VII, 1995. Related Names: Adhisupho, M. Description: 76 p.: ill.; 28 cm. Summary: Globalization of traditional Indonesian culture; proceedings of a festival. Subjects: Arts--Indonesia--Congresses. LC Classification: NX580.A1 F4 1995

Gallardo, Helio, 1942- Globalización, lucha social, derechos humanos / Helio Gallardo. Edition Information: 1. ed. Published/Created: San José: Ediciones Perro Azul, 1999. Description: 120 p.; 21 cm. ISBN 996898468X Notes: Includes bibliographical references. Subjects: Globalization. Human rights. Democracy--Latin America. Latin America--Social conditions--1982- LC Classification: HN110.5.A8 G29 1999

Galligan, Brian, 1945- Australian citizens and globalisation / Brian Galligan, Winsome Roberts, Gabriella Trifiletti. Published/Created: New York: Cambridge University Press, 2001. Related Names: Roberts, Winsome, 1951- Trifiletti, Gabriella, 1966- Description: p. cm. ISBN 0521811996 0521010896 (pb.) Notes: Includes bibliographical references and index.

García-Ruíz, Jesús. La universidad a las puertas del tercer milenio / Jesús García-Ruíz. Published/Created: Guatemala: Ediciones AMEU, 1998. Description: 151 p.; 21 cm. Summary: An analysis of contemporary systems of higher education, with focus on societal differences, reform in Latin America, recent transformations and the impact of neoliberal globalization. Notes: Includes bibliographical references (p. [149]-151). Subjects: Education, Higher--Aims and objectives--Cross-cultural studies. Education, Higher--Aims and objectives--Guatemala. Education, Higher--Social aspects--Cross-cultural studies. Education, Higher--Social aspects--Guatemala. LC Classification: LB2322.2 .G27 1998

Garza, Gustavo. La globalización en Nuevo León / Gustavo Garza ... [et al.]; coordinadora: Esthela Gutiérrez Garza. Published/Created: Monterrey: Facultad de Filosofía y Letras, Universidad Autónoma de Nuevo León, 1999. Description: 306 p.; cm. ISBN 9686125914 Summary: Seven essays by regional scholars on the globalization of Monterrey, including the region's oligarchy, strategies of production, the "maquila" industries, the labor market, the importance of the current political transition and the city's labor unions.

Gaspar, Karl, 1947- The Lumad's struggle in the face of globalization / Karl M. Gaspar. Edition Information: 1st AFRIM ed. Published/Created: Davao City, Philippines: Alternate Forum for Research in Mindanao, 2000. Related Names: Alternate Forum for Research in Mindanao. Description: xvii, 206 p.: ill., maps; 25 cm. Notes: Includes bibliographical references. Subjects: Indigenous peoples--Philippines--Mindanao Island. Globalization--Economic aspects--Philippines--Mindanao Island. LC Classification: GN671.P5 G37 2000

Gauchon, Pascal. Mondialistes et Français toujours: Le monde, les Etats-Unis et nous / par Pascal Gauchon. Published/Created: Paris: Presses universitaires de France, 2000. Description: 305 p.; cm. ISBN 2130511074 Subjects: Globalization. Series: Major

Gavin, Brigid. The European Union and globalisation: towards global democratic governance / Brigid Gavin. Published/Created: Northampton, MA: Edward Elgar Pub., 2001. Description: p. cm. ISBN 1840640057 Notes: Includes bibliographical references and index. Subjects: World Trade Organization. Globalization--Economic aspects--European Union countries. Free trade--European Union countries. Foreign trade and employment--European Union countries. International finance. International trade--Environmental aspects. Labor laws and legislation,

International. Competition, International. European Union countries--Foreign economic relations. Series: New horizons in international business LC Classification: HF1531 .G38 2001 Dewey Class No.: 337.1/42 21

Gavin, Brigid. The European Union and globalisation: towards global democratic governance / Brigid Gavin. Published/Created: Northampton, MA: Edward Elgar Pub., 2001. Description: p. cm. ISBN 1840640057 Notes: Includes bibliographical references and index. Subjects: World Trade Organization. Globalization--Economic aspects-- European Union countries. Free trade-- European Union countries. Foreign trade and employment--European Union countries. International finance. International trade--Environmental aspects. Labor laws and legislation, International. Competition, International. European Union countries--Foreign economic relations. Series: New horizons in international business LC Classification: HF1531 .G38 2001 Dewey Class No.: 337.1/42 21

Gender, agency, and change: anthropological perspectives / edited by Victoria Ana Goddard. Published/Created: London New York: Routledge, 2000. Related Names: Goddard, Victoria A. Description: xii, 280 p.; 22 cm. ISBN 0415228271 (hb) 041522828X (pbk.) Notes: Includes bibliographical references and index. Subjects: Social change--Cross-cultural studies. Sex role--Cross-cultural studies. Globalization--Cross-cultural studies. LC Classification: GN358 .G45 2000 Dewey Class No.: 303.4 21

George, Victor. Globalization and human welfare / by Vic George and Paul Wilding. Published/Created: New York: Palgrave, 2002. Related Names: Wilding, Paul. Description: p. cm. ISBN

0333915666 0333915674 (alk.) Notes: Includes bibliographical references and index. Subjects: Human services. Social policy. Globalization. LC Classification: HV40 .G455 2002 Dewey Class No.: 361 21

Gerechtigkeit in der sozialen Ordnung: die Tugend der Gerechtigkeit im Zeitalter der Globalisierung / herausgegeben von Rudolf Weiler und Akira Mizunami. Published/Created: Berlin: Duncker & Humblot, c1999. Related Names: Weiler, Rudolf. Mizunami, Akira, 1921- Johannes-Messner-Gesellschaft. Description: 106 p.; 24 cm. ISBN 3428095545 (alk. paper) Notes: Papers presented at the 4th Internationales Symposium der Johannes-Messner-Gesellschaft, held in Brixen on Sept. 16-20, 1997. Includes bibliographical references. Subjects: Social justice--Congresses. Globalization--Congresses. International law--Congresses. Series: Beiträge zur politischen Wissenschaft, 0582-0421; Bd. 105 LC Classification: HM671 .G47 1999

Gerken, Lüder. Der Wettbewerb der Staaten / Lüder Gerken. Published/Created: Tübingen: Mohr Siebeck, c1999. Description: ix, 104 p.; 23 cm. ISBN 3161472810 Notes: Includes bibliographical references (p. 83-104). Subjects: Competition, International. Investments, Foreign. Economic policy. Globalization. Series: Beiträge zur Ordnungstheorie und Ordnungspolitik; 162 LC Classification: HF1414 .G465 1999

Gerontological social work in India: some issues & perspectives / editors, Murli Desai and Siva Raju. Published/Created: New Delhi: B.R. Pub. Corp.: Distributed by BRPC (India), c2000. Related Names: Desai, Murli. Siva Raju, S., 1954. Tata Institute of Social Sciences. National

Seminar on Globalisation and the Ageing: Implications for Gerontological Social Work (1997: Tata Institute of Social Sciences) Description: xiv, 502 p.; 22 cm. ISBN 817646144X Summary: Papers presented at a National Seminar on "Globalisation and Ageing: Implications for Gerontological Social Work", organised by Tata Institute of Social Sciences on Dec. 22-24, 1997. Notes: Includes bibliographical references (p. 427-502). Subjects: Aged--India--Congresses. Social work with the aged--India--Congresses. Public health--India--Congresses. LC Classification: HQ1064.I4 G47 2000

Gibbon, Peter. "Back to the basics" through delocalisation: the Mauritian garment industry at the end of the twentieth century / Peter Gibbon. Published/Created: Copenhagen, Denmark: Centre for Development Research, [2000] Description: 66 p.; 30 cm. Subjects: Clothing trade--Mauritania. Series: CDR working paper; 00.7. CDR working paper. Working paper subseries on globalisation and economic restructuring in Africa; no. 10. LC Classification: HD72 .C38 no. 00.7

Giddens, Anthony. Runaway world: how globalization is reshaping our lives / Anthony Giddens. Published/Created: New York: Routledge, 2000. Description: 124 p.; 21 cm. ISBN 0415927196 (acid-free paper) Notes: Originally published: London: Profile Books, 1999. Includes bibliographical references (p. 101-115) and index. Subjects: Globalization. LC Classification: JZ1318 .G53 2000 Dewey Class No.: 306.2 21

Giddens, Anthony. The third way and its critics / Anthony Giddens. Published/Created: Malden, Mass.: Polity Press, 2000. Description: p. cm. ISBN 0745624499 (hb) 0745624502 (pb) Notes: Includes bibliographical references and index. Subjects: Post-communism. Globalization. Socialism. Welfare state. Right and left (Political science) LC Classification: HX73 .G54 2000 Dewey Class No.: 335 21

Gill, Gerard J. Globalisation and Nepal's agricultural export prospects [microform] / Gerard J. Gill. Published/Created: Kathmandu: Winrock International, Policy Analysis in Agriculture and Related Resource Management, 1997. Related Names: Policy Analysis in Agriculture and Related Resource Management (Program: Nepal) Description: iii, 30 p.: map; 24 cm. Notes: Includes bibliographical references (p. 20-21). Microfiche. New Delhi: Library of Congress Office; Washington, D.C.: Library of Congress Photoduplication Service, 1998. 1 microfiche. Master microform held by: DLC. Subjects: Forestry products industry--Nepal. Food industry and trade--Nepal. Produce trade--Nepal. Series: Research report series (Policy Analysis in Agriculture and Related Resource Management (Program: Nepal); no. 37. LC Classification: Microfiche 98/62613 (H)

Global and European polity?: organisations, policies, contexts / edited by Henri Goverde. Published/Created: Aldershot, Hampshire, England; Burlington, Vt.: Ashgate, c2000. Related Names: Goverde, Henri. Description: xviii, 320 p.: ill.; 23 cm. ISBN 0754612295 Notes: A collection of 17 papers from a conference held as part of the celebrations of the Tenth Anniversary (Second Lustrum) of the Faculty of Policy Sciences at the University of Nijmegen (the Netherlands) in May 1998, and organized by the Nijmegen Cener for Business, Environment, and Government (NICE). Includes bibliographical references and index. Subjects: Globalization--

Congresses. Social structure--Political aspects--Congresses. Organizational behavior--Political aspects--Congresses. International agencies--Political aspects--Congresses. International organization--Political aspects--Congresses. Europe--Politics and government--1989---Congresses. LC Classification: JZ1318 .G555 2000 Dewey Class No.: 341.2 21

Global backlash: citizen initiatives for a just world economy / [edited by] Robin Broad. Published/Created: Lanham, Md.: Rowman & Littlefield Publishers, 2002. Related Names: Broad, Robin. Description: p. cm. ISBN 0742510336 (cloth: alk. paper) 0742510344 (paper: alk. paper) Notes: Includes bibliographical references and index. Subjects: International economic relations. Globalization--Economic aspects. Globalization--Social aspects. Globalization--Environmental aspects. International business enterprises--Management--Citizen participation. Economic policy--Citizen participation. Sustainable development--Citizen participation. Series: New millennium books in international studies LC Classification: HF1359 .G566 2002 Dewey Class No.: 337 21

Global capitalism / edited by Will Hutton and Anthony Giddens. Published/Created: New York: New Press: Distributed by W.W. Norton, 2000. Related Names: Hutton, Will, 1950- Giddens, Anthony. Description: xi, 241 p.; 24 cm. ISBN 1565846486 Notes: Includes bibliographical references and index. Subjects: Capitalism. Globalization. LC Classification: HB501 .G549 2000 Dewey Class No.: 330.12/2 21

Global citizen action / edited by Michael Edwards, John Gaventa. Published/Created: Boulder, Colo.: Lynne Rienner Publishers, 2001. Related Names:

Edwards, Michael, 1957- Gaventa, John, 1949- Description: vii, 328 p. 24 cm. ISBN 1555879683 (alk. paper) 1555879934 (pbk.: alk. paper) Notes: Includes bibliographical references (p. 293-306) and index. Subjects: Political participation. Direct action. Globalization. LC Classification: JF799 .G586 2001 Dewey Class No.: 323/.042 21

Global city-regions: trends, theory, policy / edited by Allen J. Scott. Published/Created: Cambridge, UK New York: Oxford University Press, 2001. Related Names: Scott, Allen John. Description: xv, 467 p.: ill., map; 24 cm. ISBN 0198297998 (acid-free paper) Notes: Includes bibliographical references and index. Subjects: Metropolitan areas. Cities and towns--Growth. Globalization. LC Classification: HT330 .G554 2001 Dewey Class No.: 307.76 21

Global culture: nationalism, globalization, and modernity: a Theory, culture & society special issue / edited by Mike Featherstone. Published/Created: London; Newbury Park: Sage Publications, 1990. Related Names: Featherstone, Mike. Description: 411 p.; 23 cm. ISBN 0803983212 (jkt.) Notes: Published simultaneously as vol. 7, issue 2/3 of Theory, culture & society. Includes bibliographical references. Subjects: Culture. International relations. Nationalism. Globalization. LC Classification: HM101 .G56 1990 Dewey Class No.: 306 20

Global e-commerce and online marketing: watching the evolution / edited by Nikhilesh Dholakia ... [et al.]. Published/Created: Westport, Conn.: Quorum Books, 2001. Related Names: Dholakia, Nikhilesh, 1947- Description: p. cm. ISBN 1567204074 (alk. paper) Notes: Includes bibliographical references and index. Subjects: Electronic commerce.

Internet marketing. Globalization. LC Classification: HF5548.32 .G557 2001 Dewey Class No.: 658.8/4 21

Global financial reform: how? why? when?. Published/Created: Ottawa: North-South Institute, 2000. Related Names: Culpeper, Roy, 1947- Evolution of global financial governance. Kapur, Devesh, 1959- Reforming the international financial system. Description: 93, 81 p.; 23 cm. ISBN 1896770320 Contents: The evolution of global financial governance / Roy Culpeper -- Reforming the international financial system / Devesh Kapur. Notes: Includes bibliographical references. English and French. Subjects: International finance. Financial institutions, International. Globalization. International economic integration. LC Classification: HG3881 .G5745 2000 Dewey Class No.: 332/.042 21

Global food trade and consumer demand for quality / edited by Barry Krissoff, Mary Bohman, and Julie Caswell. Published/Created: New York: Kluwer Academic, 2002. Related Names: Krissoff, Barry. Bohman, Mary. Caswell, Julie A. International Agricultural Trade Research Consortium. Regional Research Project NE-165. Description: p. cm. ISBN 0306467542 Notes: Based on the proceedings of a conference held in June 2000 under the cosponsorship of the International Agricultural Trade Research Consortium and Regional Research Project NE-165: Private strategies, public policies, and food system performance. Includes bibliographical references and index. Subjects: Produce trade-- Government policy. Agriculture-- Economic aspects. Consumption (Economics) Consumer protection. Globalization. LC Classification: HD9000.5 .G583 2002 Dewey Class No.: 382/.456413 21

Global fortune: the stumble and rise of world capitalism / edited by Ian Vásquez. Published/Created: Washington, D.C.: Cato Institute, 2000. Related Names: Vásquez, Ian. Cato Institute. Description: p. cm. ISBN 1882577892 1882577906 Notes: Includes bibliographical references and index. Subjects: International finance. Free enterprise. Capitalism. Economic history--1990- Globalization. LC Classification: HG3881 .G57537 2000 Dewey Class No.: 330.12/2 21

Global governance, regionalism, and the international economy / with contributions from Sergio Arzeni ... [et al.].; Paolo Guerrieri, Hans-Eckart Scharrer, eds. Edition Information: 1 Aufl. Published/Created: Baden-Baden: Nomos, 2000. Related Names: Arzeni, Sergio. Guerrieri, Paolo, 1947- Scharrer, Hans-Eckart. Istituto affari internazionali. HWWA-Institut für Wirtschaftsforschung-Hamburg. Description: 280 p.; 23 cm. ISBN 3789068365 Notes: "This volume contains the proceeding of a conference organised by the Institute of International Affairs (IAI) and the Hamburg Institute of International Economics (HWWA) on 'Global regionalism: economic and institutionalconvergence in European and East Asian regions and the need for new global governance regimes', held in Rome 8-9 February 1999"--Pref. Includes bibliographical references. Subjects: International economic relations-- Congresses. Competition, International-- Congresses. Regionalism--Congresses. International agencies--Congresses. Globalization--Congresses. Series: Veröffentlichungen des HWWA-Institut für Wirtschaftsforschung-Hamburg; Bd. 58. LC Classification: HF1352 .G544 2000 Dewey Class No.: 337 21

Global issues: selections from The CQ researcher. Published/Created:

Washington, D.C.: CQ Press, 2001.
Related Names: Congressional Quarterly,
inc. Description: xiv, 302 p.: ill., maps; 28
cm. ISBN 1568026226 (alk. paper) Notes:
Includes bibliographical references and
index. Subjects: Globalization.
International economic relations. LC
Classification: JZ1318 .G558 2001 Dewey
Class No.: 327 21

Global justice and transnational politics:
essays on the moral and political
challenges of globalization / edited by
Pablo De Greiff and Ciaran Cronin.
Published/Created: Cambridge, Mass.:
MIT Press, 2002. Related Names: De
Greiff, Pablo. Cronin, Ciaran.
Description: p. cm. ISBN 0262042053
(hc.: alk. paper) 0262541335 (pbk.: alk.
paper) Notes: Includes bibliographical
references and index. Subjects: Political
science--Philosophy. Justice. World
politics. Globalization. Series: Studies in
contemporary German social thought LC
Classification: JA71 .G58 2002 Dewey
Class No.: 172/.4 21

Global markets and national interests: the new
geopolitics of energy, capital, and
information / Lincoln P. Bloomfield Jr.,
editor. Published/Created: Washington,
D.C.: CSIS Press, c2001. Related Names:
Bloomfield, Lincoln Palmer, 1920-
Description: p. cm. ISBN 0892064048
(pb: alk. paper) Notes: Includes
bibliographical references and index.
Subjects: Petroleum industry and trade--
Political aspects. Energy industries--
Political aspects. Capital movements--
Political aspects. Globalization. Security,
International. Series: Significant issues
series; v. 23, no. 2 LC Classification:
HD9560.6 .G55 2001 Dewey Class No.:
338.2/7282 21

Global markets: the internationalization of the
sea transport industries since 1850 / edited
by David J. Starkey and Gelina Harlaftis.

Published/Created: St. John's,
Newfoundland: International Maritime
Economic History Association, 1998.
Related Names: Starkey, David J. (David
John), 1954- Harlaftis, Gelina, 1958-
International Maritime Economic History
Association. Description: xvii, 423 p.: ill.,
map; 23 cm. ISBN 096812884X (pbk.)
Notes: Includes bibliographical
references. Subjects: Merchant marine--
History. Merchant marine--Japan--
History. Shipping--History. Shipping--
Japan--History. Globalization--History.
Series: Research in maritime history,
1188-3928; no. 14 LC Classification:
HE735 .G57 1998

Global networks, linked cities / edited by
Saskia Sassen. Published/Created: New
York: Routledge, 2002. Related Names:
Sassen, Saskia. Description: p. cm. ISBN
0415931622 (alk. paper) 0415931630
(pbk.: alk. paper) Notes: Includes
bibliographical references and index.
Subjects: Urban economics--Case studies.
Globalization--Case studies. Computers
and civilization--Case studies.
Information technology--Economic
aspects--Case studies. Business
enterprises--Computer networks--Case
studies. LC Classification: HT321 .G55
2002 Dewey Class No.: 303.48/34 21

Global networks: a journal of transnational
affairs. Published/Created: Oxford, UK;
Malden, MA: Blackwell, [2001-
Description: v.; 25 cm. Vol. 1, no. 1 (Jan.
2001)- Current Frequency: Quarterly
ISSN: 1470-2266 Notes: Title from cover.
Subjects: Globalization--Periodicals.
Internationalism--Periodicals.

Global prescriptions: the production,
exportation, and importation of a new
legal orthodoxy / edited by Yves Dezalay
and Bryant G. Garth. Published/Created:
Ann Arbor: University of Michigan Press,
2002. Related Names: Dezalay, Yves,

1945- Garth, Bryant G. Description: p. cm. ISBN 047211235X (cloth: acid-free paper) Contents: Breaking out: the proliferation of actors in the international system / Anne-Marie Slaughter -- Transnational advocacy networks and the social construction of legal rules / Kathryn Sikkink modern law as a secularized and global model: implications for the sociology of law / Elizabeth Heger Boyle and John W. Meyer -- What institutional regimes for the era of internationalization? / Robert Boyer -- Between liberalism and neoliberalism: law's dilemma in Latin America / Jeremy Adelman and Miguel Angel Centeno -- Legal education and the reproduction of the elite in Japan / Setsuo Miyazawa with Hiroshi Otsuka -- Cultural elements in the practice of law in Mexico: informal networks in a formal system / Larissa Adler Lomnitz and Rodrigo Salazar -- The discovery of law: political consequences in the argentine case / Catalina Smulovitz -- Hybrid(ity) rules: creating local law in a globalized world / Heinz Klug -- Legitimating the new legal orthodoxy / Yves Dezalay and Bryant G. Garth. Notes: Includes bibliographical references and index. Subjects: Law reform. Legal polycentricity. Comparative law. Globalization. Law and economic development. LC Classification: K236 .G59 2002 Dewey Class No.: 340/.2 21

Global production and trade in East Asia / edited by Leonard K. Cheng and Henryk Kierzkowski. Published/Created: Boston: Kluwer Academic, c2001. Related Names: Cheng, Leonard K. (Leonard Kwok-Hon) Kierzkowski, Henryk. Description: xi, 350 p.: ill.; 25 cm. ISBN 0792373308 (alk. paper) Notes: Based largely on papers presented at an international conference held in Hong kong on Oct. 25-27, 1999. Includes bibliographical references and index. Subjects: Free trade--East Asia. Industries--Technological innovations--

Economic aspects East Asia. International division of labor. Globalization--Economic aspects--East Asia. International business enterprises--East Asia. LC Classification: HF2360.5 .G55 2001 Dewey Class No.: 382/.095 21

Global religious movements in regional context / edited by John Wolffe. Published/Created: Burlington, VT: Ashgate, 2002. Related Names: Wolffe, John. Description: p. cm. ISBN 075460747X 0754608190 (pbk.) Notes: Includes bibliographical references and index. Subjects: Religion and sociology--History--20th century. Globalization--Religious aspects--History--20th century. Evangelicalism--History--20th century. S⁻oka Gakkai--History--20th century. Islam--History--20th century. Series: Religion today; v. 4 LC Classification: BL60 .G54 2002 Dewey Class No.: 291.1/71 21

Global repertoires: popular music within and beyond the transnational music industry / edited by Andreas Gebesmair, International Research Institute for Media, Communication, and Cultural Development, Austria and Alfred Smudits, Institute of Music Sociology, Austria. Published/Created: Burlington, VT: Ashgate, 2001. Related Names: Gebesmair, Andreas. Smudits, A. MEDIACULT. Description: p. cm. ISBN 0754605264 (alk. paper) Notes: Contains materials presented at a conference on music and globalization organized by the International Research Institute for Media, Communication and Cultural Development (Mediacult) and held Nov. 4-6, 1999 in Vienna, Austria. Includes bibliographical references. Subjects: Popular music--History and criticism--Congresses. Music trade--Congresses. Globalization--Congresses. Series: Ashgate popular and folk music series LC Classification: ML3470 .G56 2001 Dewey

Class No.: 306.4/84

Global trends and global governance / edited by Paul Kennedy, Dirk Messner and Franz Nuscheler. Published/Created: London; Sterling, Va.: Pluto Press, 2001. Related Names: Kennedy, Paul M., 1945- Messner, Dirk. Nuscheler, Franz. Description: p. cm. ISBN 0745317510 (hardback) 0745317502 (paperback) Contents: Global challenges at the beginning of the twenty-first century / Paul Kennedy -- World society, structures and trends / Dirk Messner -- World economy, structures and trends / Heribert Dieter -- World ecology, structure and trends / Udo Ernst Simonis and Tanja Brühl -- World politics, structures and trends / Dirk Messner and Franz Nuscheler -- Global governance, development, and peace / Franz Nuscheler -- Globalization and global governance: a synopsis. Subjects: Globalization. International organization. LC Classification: JZ1318 .G564 2001 Dewey Class No.: 327 21

Globale Herausforderungen: Diskussionen zur Globaliserung / Peter Schachner-Blazizek, Hrsg. Published/Created: Graz: Leykam, c2000. Related Names: Schachner-Blazizek, Peter. Description: 293 p.; 25 cm. ISBN 3701174229 Subjects: International economic relations--Congresses. Globalization--Congresses. LC Classification: HF1359 .G574 2000

Globalidad, una mirada alternativa / Ricardo Valero, compilador. Edition Information: 1. ed. Published/Created: México: Centro Latinoamericano de la Globalidad: M.A. Porrúa Grupo Editorial, 1999. Related Names: Valero, Ricardo. Description: 254 p.; 21 cm. ISBN 9688429244 Notes: Includes bibliographical references. Subjects: International economic relations--Congresses. Globalization--Congresses. Latin America--Foreign economic relations--Congresses. Series: Colección Las Ciencias sociales LC Classification: HF1480.5 .G566 1999 Dewey Class No.: 337 21

Globalisation and developing countries: proceedings / editors, Kamala Sinha, Pratim K. Dutta. Published/Created: New Delhi: New Age International, c1999. Related Names: Sinha, Kamala. Dutta, Pratim K. Indian Centre for International Co-operation (New Delhi, India). International Conference on "Globalisation and Developing Countries" (1997: New Delhi, India). Description: xxvii, 428 p.: ill. (some col.), map; 24 cm. ISBN 8122412009 Summary: Papers presented at the International Conference on "Globalisation and Developing Countries," held in March 1997 at New Delhi. Notes: "Organised by Indian Centre for International Co-operation, New Delhi, India." Includes bibliographical references. Subjects: Internationa economic relations--Congresses. Developing countries--Foreign economic relations Congresses. Developing countries--Economic conditions--Congresses. Developing countries--Economic policy--Congresses. LC Classification: HF1352 .G56 1999

Globalisation and difference: practical theology in a world context / edited by Paul Ballard and Pam Couture. Published/Created: Fairwater, Cardiff: Cardiff Academic Press, 1999. Related Names: Ballard, Paul H. Couture, Pamela D., 1951- Description: 212 p.; 23 cm. ISBN 1899025111 Notes: Includes bibliographical references. Subjects: Theology, Practical. LC Classification: BV3 .G55 1999 Dewey Class No.: 230/.09 21

Globalisation and dimensions of management in India / edited by Atmanand. Published/Created: Delhi: Shipra, 1997.

Related Names: Atmanand, 1959-
Description: 312 p.; 23 cm. ISBN
8185402930 Summary: Contributed
articles. Notes: Includes bibliographical
references. Subjects: India--Economic
conditions--1947- India--Economic
policy--1980- LC Classification: HC435.2
.G582 1997

Globalisation and economic development:
essays in Honour of J. George
Waardenburg / edited by Servaas Storm,
C.W.M. Naastepad. Published/Created:
Cheltenham, UK; Northampton, MA,
USA: E. Elgar Pub., 2001. Related
Names: Storm, Servaas. Naastepad, C. W.
M., 1961- Description: p. cm. ISBN
1840646934 Notes: Includes
bibliographical references and index.
Subjects: Waardenburg, J. George.
International economic relations.
Globalization. Economic development.
LC Classification: HF1359 .G58177 2001
Dewey Class No.: 338.9 21

Globalisation and economic development:
essays in Honour of J. George
Waardenburg / edited by Servaas Storm,
C.W.M. Naastepad. Published/Created:
Cheltenham, UK; Northampton, MA,
USA: E. Elgar Pub., 2001. Related
Names: Storm, Servaas. Naastepad, C. W.
M., 1961- Description: p. cm. ISBN
1840646934 Notes: Includes
bibliographical references and index.
Subjects: Waardenburg, J. George.
International economic relations.
Globalization. Economic development.
LC Classification: HF1359 .G58177 2001
Dewey Class No.: 338.9 21

Globalisation and environment: preliminary
perspectives / Organisation for Economic
Co-operation and Development.
Published/Created: Paris: OCDE, c1997.
Related Names: Organisation for
Economic Co-operation and
Development. Description: 366 p.: ill.; 27

cm. ISBN 9264155619 Notes: Papers
from a workshop held Jan. 30-31, 1997, in
Vienna, Austria. Includes bibliographical
references. Subjects: Environmental
policy--Economic aspects--International
cooperation--Congresses. Environmental
protection--Economic aspects--
International cooperation--Congresses.
Economic development--Environmental
aspects--International cooperation--
Congresses. Series: OECD proceedings
LC Classification: GE170 .G63 1997
Dewey Class No.: 363.7/0526 21

Globalisation and gender: changing patterns of
women's employment in Bangladesh /
edited by Rehman Sobhan, Nasreen
Khundker. Published/Created: Dhaka:
University Press, 2001. Related Names:
Sobhan, Rehman. Khundker, Nasreen.
Centre for Policy Dialogue (Bangladesh)
Description: xxviii, 276 p.; 22 cm. ISBN
9840515810 Summary: Contributed
articles. Notes: "Centre for Policy
Dialogue." Includes bibliographical
references and index.

Globalisation and human rights in Latin
America / Cynthia Hewitt de Alcántara,
Alberto Minujin, (ed.). Published/Created:
[Bogotá]: UNICEF; [Geneva]: UNRISD,
2000. Related Names: Hewitt de
Alcántara, Cynthia. Minujin Z., Alberto.
Description: 312 p.: ill.; 21 cm. Notes:
Includes bibliographical references.
Subjects: Human rights--Latin America.
Globalization--Social aspects.
International economic relations--Social
aspects. Latin America--Foreign
economic relations.

Globalisation and human rights in Latin
America / Cynthia Hewitt de Alcántara,
Alberto Minujin, (ed.). Published/Created:
[Bogotá]: UNICEF; [Geneva]: UNRISD,
2000. Related Names: Hewitt de
Alcántara, Cynthia. Minujin Z., Alberto.
Description: 312 p.: ill.; 21 cm. Notes:

Includes bibliographical references. Subjects: Human rights--Latin America. Globalization--Social aspects. International economic relations--Social aspects. Latin America--Foreign economic relations.

Globalisation and India: a multi-dimensional perspective / editors, Purusottam Bhattacharya, Ajitava Ray Chaudhuri. Published/Created: New Delhi: Lancers Books, 2000. Related Names: Bhattacharya, Purusottam. Chaudhuri, Ajitava Ray. Description: vi, 189 p.; 22 cm. ISBN 8170950767 Summary: Contributed articles. Notes: Includes bibliographical references and index. Subjects: Globalization. India--Foreign relations. India--Foreign economic relations. LC Classification: DS480.853 .G55 2000 Dewey Class No.: 327.54 21

Globalisation and India: a multi-dimensional perspective / editors, Purusottam Bhattacharya, Ajitava Ray Chaudhuri. Published/Created: New Delhi: Lancers Books, 2000. Related Names: Bhattacharya, Purusottam. Chaudhuri, Ajitava Ray. Description: vi, 189 p.; 22 cm. ISBN 8170950767 Summary: Contributed articles. Notes: Includes bibliographical references and index. Subjects: Globalization. India--Foreign relations. India--Foreign economic relations. LC Classification: DS480.853 .G55 2000 Dewey Class No.: 327.54 21

Globalisation and insecurity: political, economic, and physical challenges / edited by Barbara Harriss-White. Published/Created: New York: Palgrave, 2001. Related Names: Harriss-White, Barbara, 1946- Description: p. cm. ISBN 0333963547 Notes: Includes bibliographical references and index. Subjects: Globalization. Security, International. LC Classification: JZ1318

.G577 2001 Dewey Class No.: 327 21

Globalisation and insecurity: political, economic, and physical challenges / edited by Barbara Harriss-White. Published/Created: New York: Palgrave, 2001. Related Names: Harriss-White, Barbara, 1946- Description: p. cm. ISBN 0333963547 Notes: Includes bibliographical references and index. Subjects: Globalization. Security, International. LC Classification: JZ1318 .G577 2001 Dewey Class No.: 327 21

Globalisation and international competitiveness: Botswana towards 2016: proceedings of the National Business Conference, Best Western Thapama Hotel, Francistown, October 25-27, 1998 / [editor, Keith Jefferis]. Published/Created: Gaborone, Botswana: Botswana Confederation of Commerce, Industry and Manpower, c1999. Related Names: Jefferis, Keith. Botswana Confederation of Commerce, Industry, and Manpower. Description: xiv, 149 p. 30 cm. ISBN 999120282X Notes: Includes bibliographical references (p. 104). Subjects: Competition, International--Congresses. Globalization--Congresses. Botswana--Commercial policy--Congresses. Botswana--Foreign economic relations--Congresses. LC Classification: HF1613.9 .N38 1998 Dewey Class No.: 330.96883 21

Globalisation and international competitiveness: Botswana towards 2016: proceedings of the National Business Conference, Best Western Thapama Hotel, Francistown, October 25-27, 1998 / [editor, Keith Jefferis]. Published/Created: Gaborone, Botswana: Botswana Confederation of Commerce, Industry and Manpower, c1999. Related Names: Jefferis, Keith. Botswana Confederation of Commerce, Industry, and Manpower. Description: xiv, 149 p. 30 cm. ISBN

999120282X Notes: Includes bibliographical references (p. 104). Subjects: Competition, International--Congresses. Globalization--Congresses. Botswana--Commercial policy--Congresses. Botswana--Foreign economic relations--Congresses. LC Classification: HF1613.9 .N38 1998 Dewey Class No.: 330.96883 21

Globalisation and international trade liberalisation: continuity and change / edited by Martin Richardson. Published/Created: Cheltenham [England]; Northampton, MA: E. Elgar, c2000. Related Names: Richardson, Martin, 1960- Description: xvi, 204 p.: ill.; 24 cm. ISBN 1840643501 Notes: Papers from a conference held in Dunedin, New Zealand in July 1999. Includes bibliographical references and index. Subjects: International trade--Congresses. Free trade--Congresses. International economic integration--Congresses. Globalization. LC Classification: HF1372 .G585 2000 Dewey Class No.: 382 21

Globalisation and international trade liberalisation: continuity and change / edited by Martin Richardson. Published/Created: Cheltenham [England]; Northampton, MA: E. Elgar, c2000. Related Names: Richardson, Martin, 1960- Description: xvi, 204 p.: ill.; 24 cm. ISBN 1840643501 Notes: Papers from a conference held in Dunedin, New Zealand in July 1999. Includes bibliographical references and index. Subjects: International trade--Congresses. Free trade--Congresses. International economic integration--Congresses. Globalization. LC Classification: HF1372 .G585 2000 Dewey Class No.: 382 21

Globalisation and linkages to 2020: can poor countries and poor people prosper in the new global age? Published/Created: Paris: OECD, 1997. Related Names: Organisation for Economic Co-operation and Development. Development Co-operation Directorate. Description: 24 p.: ill.; 30 cm. Notes: Cover title. Includes bibliographical references (p. 24). Subjects: International economic relations. Developing countries--Economic conditions. Series: OECD working papers; v. 5, no. 90. LC Classification: HD72 .O38 vol. 5, no. 90

Globalisation and linkages to 2020: challenges and opportunities for OECD countries. Published/Created: Paris: OECD, 1996. Related Names: Organisation for Economic Co-operation and Development. Description: 17 p.; 30 cm. Notes: Cover title. Summary of an international high-level experts meeting held June 17th and 18th 1996. Subjects: International economic relations. OECD countries--Economic policy. OECD countries--Economic conditions. Series: OECD working papers; v. 4, no. 76. LC Classification: HD72 .O38 vol. 4, no. 76

Globalisation and linkages to 2020: challenges and opportunities for OECD countries. Published/Created: Paris: OECD, 1996. Related Names: Organisation for Economic Co-operation and Development. Description: 10 p.; 30 cm. Notes: Cover title. "Progress report to ministers"--P. 3. Subjects: International economic relations. OECD countries--Economic policy. OECD countries--Economic conditions. Series: OECD working papers; v. 4, no. 51. LC Classification: HD72 .O38 vol. 4, no. 51

Globalisation and linkages to 2020: challenges and opportunities for OECD countries: international high-level experts meeting. Published/Created: Paris: OECD, c1996. Related Names: Organisation for Economic Co-operation and

Development. Description: 70 p.: ill.; 27 cm. ISBN 9264153519 Notes: Summary of the discussions, and selection of the papers presented to an international high-level experts meeting held June 17th and 18th 1996. Includes bibliographical references. Subjects: International economic relations. OECD countries--Economic policy. OECD countries--Economic conditions. Series: OECD proceedings LC Classification: HF1359 .G5817 1996

Globalisation and regional integration: their impact on workers and trade unions. Published/Created: Manila: BATU-Project Development Office, <[1994?- > Related Names: Brotherhood of Asian Trade Unionists. Project Development Office. BATU Conference on "Globalisation and Regional Integration" (1994: Bangkok, Thailand) Description: v. <2 >; 23 cm. Notes: Proceedings of: BATU Conference on "Globalisation and Regional Integration." Includes bibliographical references (v. 2, p. 19). Subjects: General Agreement on Tariffs and Trade (Organization) Congresses. Labor unions--Asia--Congresses. Labor unions--Pacific Area--Congresses. Blue collar workers--Asia--Congresses. Blue collar workers--Pacific Area--Congresses. Asia--Economic integration--Congresses. Pacific Area--Economic integration--Congresses. Asia--Foreign economic relations--Congresses. Pacific Area--Foreign economic relations--Congresses. LC Classification: HC412 .G57 1994

Globalisation and SME: globalisation of economic activities and small and medium-sized enterprises (SMEs) development, Finland / Luostarinen ... [et al.] Published/Created: [Helsinki, Finland]: Ministry of Trade and Industry, Business Development Dept.: Painatuskeskus [distributor, 1994] Related Names: Luostarinen, Reijo. Description:

390 p.; 30 cm. ISBN 9514796675 Notes: Includes bibliographical references (p. 382-390). Summary in Finnish. Subjects: Small business--Finland. Small business--Government policy--Finland. Industrial promotion--Finland. Series: Kauppa- ja teollisuusministeriön tutkimuksia ja raportteja; 59. LC Classification: HD2346.F5 G58 1994

Globalisation and SMEs in East Asia / edited by Charles Harvie and Boon-Chye Lee. Published/Created: Northampton, MA: E. Elgar, 2002. Related Names: Harvie, Charles, 1954- Lee, Boon-Chye. Description: p. cm. ISBN 1840643234 Notes: Includes bibliographical references and index. Series: Studies of small and medium size enterprises in East Asia; v. 1

Globalisation and social development: European and Southeast Asian evidence / edited by Ludo Cuyvers. Published/Created: Northampton, MA: Edward Elgar Pub., 2001. Related Names: Cuyvers, L. Description: p. cm. ISBN 1840644680 Notes: Includes index. Subjects: Wages--Asia, Southeastern. Wages--Europe. Globalization. Asia, Southeastern--Social conditions. Asia, Southeastern--Economic conditions. Europe--Social conditions. Europe--Economic conditions--1945- LC Classification: HN690.8.A8 G56 2001 Dewey Class No.: 306/.0959 21

Globalisation and social development: European and Southeast Asian evidence / edited by Ludo Cuyvers. Published/Created: Northampton, MA: Edward Elgar Pub., 2001. Related Names: Cuyvers, L. Description: p. cm. ISBN 1840644680 Notes: Includes index. Subjects: Wages--Asia, Southeastern. Wages--Europe. Globalization. Asia, Southeastern--Social conditions. Asia, Southeastern--Economic conditions. Europe--Social conditions. Europe--

Economic conditions--1945- LC
Classification: HN690.8.A8 G56 2001
Dewey Class No.: 306/.0959 21

Globalisation and the ASEAN public sector /
edited by Sirajuddin H. Salleh and
Ledivina V. Cariño. Published/Created:
Kuala Lumpur, Malaysia: Asian and
Pacific Development Centre, c1995.
Related Names: Sirajuddin H. Salleh.
Cariño, Ledivina V. Asian and Pacific
Development Centre. Description: xiv,
433 p.: ill.; 23 cm. ISBN 9679928470
Contents: Global economic uncertainty
and the ASEAN alliance / Jocelyn C.
Cuaresma -- ASEAN countries' public
sector response to global economic
challenges / Sirajuddin H. Salleh -- The
changing role of ASEAN governments /
Ledivina V. Cariño -- Response of public
administration system of Indonesia to
global challenges / Mustopadidjaja A.R.,
Soewarto, and Mohammad Ikhsari --
Response of public administration system
of Malaysia to global challenges /
Zulkarnain Hj. Awang -- Response of
public administration system of
Philippines to global challenges / Jose N.
Endriga -- Response of public
administration system of Singapore to
global challenges / Tan Peng Chuan --
Response of public administration system
of Thailand to global challenges / Bidhya
Bowornwathana. Notes: Includes
bibliographical references and index.
Subjects: ASEAN. Asia, Southeastern--
Economic policy. LC Classification:
HC441 .G56 1995

Globalisation and the Asia Pacific: contested
territories / edited by Kris Olds ... [et al.].
Published/Created: London; New York:
Routledge, 1999. Related Names: Olds,
Kris, 1961- Description: xii, 293 p.; 24
cm. ISBN 0415199190 (hc: alk. paper)
0415199204 (pbk.: alk. paper) Notes:
From a workshop at the National
University of Singapore, 1997. Includes

bibliographical references and index.
Subjects: Asia--Foreign economic
relations--Pacific Area. Pacific Area--
Foreign economic relations--Asia. Asia--
Commerce--Pacific Area. Pacific Area--
Commerce--Asia. Series: Warwick studies
in globalisation; 1 LC Classification:
HF1583.Z4 P335 1999 Dewey Class No.:
337.509 21

Globalisation and the environment:
perspectives from OECD and dynamic
non-member economies.
Published/Created: Paris, France:
Organisation for Economic Co-operation
and Development, c1998. Related Names:
Chung, Chris. Organisation for Economic
Co-operation and Development.
Environment Directorate. Description:
125 p.: ill.; 28 cm. ISBN 9264160833
Notes: "Edited by Mr. Chris Chung,
OECD Environment Directorate"--P. 3.
Includes bibliographical references.
Subjects: Environmental policy--OECD
countries. International economic
relations--Environmental aspects. Series:
OECD proceedings LC Classification:
GE170 .G64 1998 Dewey Class No.:
363.7/00526 21

Globalisation and the nation-state / edited by
Frans Buelens. Published/Created:
Cheltenham, UK; Northampton, MA:
Edward Elgar Publishing, c1999. Related
Names: Buelens, Frans, 1951- Belgian-
Dutch Association for Institutional and
Political Economy. Description: xi, 185
p.: ill.; 24 cm. ISBN 1840642025 Notes:
Papers presented at a conference
sponsored by the Belgian-Dutch
Association for Institutional and Political
Economy. Includes bibliographical
references and index. Subjects:
International economic relations.
Competition, International. National state.
Economic history--1990- LC
Classification: HF1359 .G5819 1999

Dewey Class No.: 337 21

Globalisation and the post-colonial Africa state / edited by Dani W. Nabudere. Published/Created: Harare, Zimbabwe: AAPS Books, 2000. Related Names: Nabudere, D. Wada. African Association of Political Science. Description: vii, 274 p.; 24 cm. ISBN 0797421106 (pbk.) Notes: "The papers in this volume came out of a conference held in Mauritius (October 2-3rd, 1998) to mark the silver jubilee of the African Association of Political Science"--Cover p. [4]. Includes bibliographical references. Subjects: Democracy--Africa--Congresses. Globalization--Congresses. Africa-- Economic policy--Congresses. LC Classification: HC800 .G5477 2000

Globalisation and the post-colonial Africa state / edited by Dani W. Nabudere. Published/Created: Harare, Zimbabwe: AAPS Books, 2000. Related Names: Nabudere, D. Wada. African Association of Political Science. Description: vii, 274 p.; 24 cm. ISBN 0797421106 (pbk.) Notes: "The papers in this volume came out of a conference held in Mauritius (October 2-3rd, 1998) to mark the silver jubilee of the African Association of Political Science"--Cover p. [4]. Includes bibliographical references. Subjects: Democracy--Africa--Congresses. Globalization--Congresses. Africa-- Economic policy--Congresses. LC Classification: HC800 .G5477 2000

Globalisation and the region: explorations in Punjabi identity / edited and introduced by Pritam Singh and Shinder S. Thandi. Published/Created: Coventry, United Kingdom: Association for Punjab Studies (UK), 1996. Related Names: Pritam Singh, 1932- Thandi, Shinder S. Association for Punjab Studies. Coventry University. Coventry Business School. International Conference on Punjab

Studies (1st: 1994: Coventry University) Description: 416 p.; 24 cm. ISBN 1874699054 Summary: Papers presented at the First International Conference on Punjab Studies organized by the Association for Punjab Studies and Coventry Business School, Coventry University on June 25-26, 1994 at Coventry University. Notes: Includes bibliographical references. Subjects: Punjabis (South Asian people)--Ethnic identity Congresses. LC Classification: DS432.P232 G56 1996 Dewey Class No.: 305.891/42 21

Globalisation and the Third World / edited by Ray Kiely and Phil Marfleet. Published/Created: London; New York: Routledge, 1998. Related Names: Kiely, Ray, 1964- Marfleet, Phil, 1962- Description: vi, 226 p.; 26 cm. ISBN 0415140765 (cloth) 0415140773 (pbk.) Notes: Includes bibliographical references and index. Subjects: Economic development. Developing countries. LC Classification: HD82 .G553 1998 Dewey Class No.: 337/.09172/4 21

Globalisation and trade: implications for exports from marginalised economies / edited by Oliver Morrissey and Igor Filatotchev. Published/Created: London Portland, OR: Frank Cass, 2001. Related Names: Morrissey, Oliver. Filatotchev, Igor. Description: 215 p.: ill.; 22 cm. ISBN 0714651591 (cloth) Notes: "This group of studies first appeared in a special issue ... of The journal of development studies (ISSN 0022-038) 37/2 (December 2000)"--T.p. verso. Includes bibliographical references and index. Subjects: Free trade--Developing countries. Exports--Developing countries. Globalization--Economic aspects-- Developing countries. Developing countries--Commercial policy. Developing countries--Foreign economic relations. LC Classification: HF2580.9

.G58 2001 Dewey Class No.:
382/.6/091724 21

Globalisation and trade: implications for exports from marginalised economies / edited by Oliver Morrissey and Igor Filatotchev. Published/Created: London Portland, OR: Frank Cass, 2001. Related Names: Morrissey, Oliver. Filatotchev, Igor. Description: 215 p.: ill.; 22 cm. ISBN 0714651591 (cloth) Notes: "This group of studies first appeared in a special issue ... of The journal of development studies (ISSN 0022-038) 37/2 (December 2000)"--T.p. verso. Includes bibliographical references and index. Subjects: Free trade--Developing countries. Exports--Developing countries. Globalization--Economic aspects-- Developing countries. Developing countries--Commercial policy. Developing countries--Foreign economic relations. LC Classification: HF2580.9 .G58 2001 Dewey Class No.: 382/.6/091724 21

Globalisation et néolibéralisme dans le Tiers- monde / sous la direction de Firouzeh Nahavandi. Published/Created: Paris: Harmattan, 2000. Related Names: Nahavandi, Firouzeh. Université libre de Bruxelles. Institut de sociologie. Description: 237 p.; 22 cm. ISBN 2738488188 Notes: "Un colloque ... organisé par l'Institut de sociologie de l'Université libre de Bruxelles en décembre 1998"--P. 7. Includes bibliographical references. Subjects: Globalization--Congresses. Liberalism-- Developing countries--Congresses. Developing countries--Economic conditions--Congresses. Series: Bibliothèque du développement LC Classification: JZ1318 .G6784 2000

Globalisation of economy: vision of the future / edited by B. Mohanan. Published/Created: New Delhi: Gyan Pub.

House, 1995. Related Names: Mohanan, B. Description: xiv, 195 p.; 23 cm. ISBN 812120500X Summary: Contributed articles. Notes: Includes bibliographical references and index. Subjects: Free trade- -Government policy--India. Economic development--Social aspects--India. India- -Economic policy--1980- LC Classification: HC435.2 .G583 1995

Globalisation of enterprise, economic activities, present state and perspectives, comparative analyses of Poland and Slovakia: conference papers / editor Jerzy Mika. Published/Created: Katowice: Karol Adamiecki University of Economics, Faculty of Management, 1998. Related Names: Mika, Jerzy. Akademia Ekonomiczna im. Karola Adamieckiego w Katowicach. Description: 104 p.: ill.; 24 cm. ISBN 8387265845 Notes: Includes bibliographical references. Subjects: Industrial management--Poland-- Congresses. Business enterprises--Poland- -Congresses. Industrial management-- Slovakia--Congresses. Business enterprises--Slovakia--Congresses. Globalization--Congresses. LC Classification: HD70.P6 G68 1998

Globalisation of enterprise, economic activities, present state and perspectives, comparative analyses of Poland and Slovakia: conference papers / editor Jerzy Mika. Published/Created: Katowice: Karol Adamiecki University of Economics, Faculty of Management, 1998. Related Names: Mika, Jerzy. Akademia Ekonomiczna im. Karola Adamieckiego w Katowicach. Description: 104 p.: ill.; 24 cm. ISBN 8387265845 Notes: Includes bibliographical references. Subjects: Industrial management--Poland-- Congresses. Business enterprises--Poland- -Congresses. Industrial management-- Slovakia--Congresses. Business enterprises--Slovakia--Congresses. Globalization--Congresses. LC Classification: HD70.P6 G68 1998

Globalisation of Indian financial markets / editors, R.K. Tandon, S.L. Gupta. Edition Information: 1st ed. Published/Created: New Delhi: Anmol Publications, 1995. Related Names: Tandon, R. K. (Rak Kishore) Gupta, S. L. National Seminar on Global Trends in Indian Financial Markets--Thrust and Challenges (1995?: Kurukshetra University) Description: ix, 354 p.; 23 cm. ISBN 8174881255 Summary: Papers presented at the National Seminar on Global Trends in Indian Financial Markets--Thrust and Challenges, organized by the Kurukshetra University. Notes: Includes bibliographical references. Subjects: International finance--Congresses. Capital market--Congresses. Commodity exchanges--Congresses. LC Classification: HG3881 .G5767 1995

Globalisation of industrial activities. Published/Created: Paris: [Organisation for Economic Co-Operation and Development], 1994. Related Names: Organisation for Economic Co-operation and Development. Description: 7 p.; 30 cm. Subjects: International business enterprises. Series: OECD working papers; v. 2, no. 48. LC Classification: HD72 .O38 vol. 2, no. 48

Globalisation of industrial activities: a case study of the clothing industry. Published/Created: Paris: Organisation for Economic Co-operation and Development, 1994. Related Names: Organisation for Economic Co-operation and Development. Description: 53 p.; 30 cm. Notes: Includes bibliographical references. Subjects: Clothing trade. Clothing trade--Government policy. International trade--Case studies. Commercial policy--Case studies. Series:

OECD working papers; v. 2, no. 60. LC Classification: HD72 .O38 vol. 2, no. 60

Globalisation of industrial activities: four case studies: auto parts, chemicals, construction, and semiconductors. Published/Created: Paris: Organisation for Economic Co-operation and Development; [Washington, D.C.: OECD Publications and Information Center, distributor], c1992. Related Names: Organisation for Economic Co-operation and Development. Description: 160 p.; 23 cm. ISBN 9264136274 Notes: Includes bibliographical references. Subjects: International division of labor--Case studies. LC Classification: HF1412 .G55 1992

Globalisation of industry: overview and sector reports. Published/Created: Paris: Organisation for Economic Co-operation and Development; Washington, D.C.: OECD Washington Center,[distributor], c1996. Related Names: Organisation for Economic Co-operation and Development. Description: 355 p.: ill.; 27 cm. ISBN 9264146881 (pbk.) Notes: Published in French under the La mondialisation de l'industrie: vue d'ensemble et rapports sectoriels. Includes bibliographical references. Subjects: International economic relations. International business enterprises. International economic integration. Investments, Foreign. LC Classification: HF1359 .G582 1996

Globalisation of R&D and technology markets: consequences for national innovation policies: proceedings of the international conference on 1 and 2 December 1997 in Bonn, Petersberg, Germany organised by the BMBF and FhG ISI / Frieder Meyer-Krahmer, ed. Published/Created: Heidelberg; New York: Physica-Verlag, c1999. Related Names: Meyer-Krahmer, Frieder.

Germany. Bundesministerium für Bildung, Wissenschaft, Forschung und Technologie. Fraunhofer-Gesellschaft. Fraunhofer-Institut für Systemtechnik und Innovationsforschung. Description: vi, 180 p.: ill.; 24 cm. ISBN 3790811750 (acid-free paper) Notes: Includes bibliographical references. Subjects: Research, Industrial--International cooperation Congresses. Technology--International cooperation--Congresses. Technology and state--Congresses. Technological innovations--Government policy--Congresses. Series: Technology, innovation and policy; 9 LC Classification: HC79.R4 G58 1999 Dewey Class No.: 338.9/26 21

Globalisation of the timber industry in the next millennium: conference proceedings / International Timber Conference '98, Kuala Lumpur, Malaysia, 5-7 March 1998; [jointly organised by Malaysian Timber Industry Board and Malaysian Timber Council]. Published/Created: Kuala Lumpur: The Board, [1998?] Related Names: Lembaga Perindustrian Kayu Malaysia. Malaysian Timber Council. Description: 118 p.: ill.; 27 cm. Notes: Includes bibliographical references. Subjects: Lumber trade--Congresses. Forest products industry--Congresses. LC Classification: HD9750.5 .I542 1998

Globalisation strategies and economic liberalisation / editors, G.S. Batra & Narinder Kaur. Edition Information: 1st ed. Published/Created: New Delhi: Anmol Publications, 1995. Related Names: Batra, G. S. Narinder Kaur. Description: xi, 249 p.; 23 cm. ISBN 8174880224 Summary: In the Indian context; contributed articles. Notes: Includes bibliographical references. Subjects: Free enterprise--India. Liberalism--India. India--Economic policy--1980- 79-13 Series: New economic policies in developing countries

series; 1 LC Classification: HC435.2 .G585 1995

Globalisation, a calculus of inequality: perspectives from the South / edited by Denis Benn, Kenneth Hall. Published/Created: Kingston: Ian Randle Publishers, 2000. Related Names: Benn, Denis. Hall, Kenneth. Description: xxv, 171 p.; 23 cm. ISBN 9766370192 Notes: Includes blbiographical references and index. Subjects: International economic relations. Globalization--Economic aspects--Developing countries. Globalization--Social aspects--Developing countries. Equality. LC Classification: HF1359 .G5814 2000 Dewey Class No.: 337/.09172/4 21

Globalisation, a calculus of inequality: perspectives from the South / edited by Denis Benn, Kenneth Hall. Published/Created: Kingston: Ian Randle Publishers, 2000. Related Names: Benn, Denis. Hall, Kenneth. Description: xxv, 171 p.; 23 cm. ISBN 9766370192 Notes: Includes blbiographical references and index. Subjects: International economic relations. Globalization--Economic aspects--Developing countries. Globalization--Social aspects--Developing countries. Equality. LC Classification: HF1359 .G5814 2000 Dewey Class No.: 337/.09172/4 21

Globalisation, competitiveness, and human security / edited by Cristóbal Kay. Published/Created: London; Portland, OR: F. Cass in association with the European Association of Development Research and Training Institutes (EADI), Geneva, c1997. Related Names: Kay, Cristóbal. Description: 245 p.: ill., map; 22 cm. ISBN 0714643920 (pbk.) Notes: "First appeared in a special issue ... of the European journal of development research, vol. 9, no. 1, June 1997"--T.p. verso. Includes bibliographical references.

Subjects: Economic development--
Research--Developing countries.
Competition, International. Developing
countries--Economic policy. LC
Classification: HD77.5.D44 G58 1997
Dewey Class No.: 338.9/009172/4 21

Globalisation, emerging role of business in
India. Published/Created: New Delhi:
Associated Chambers of Commerce &
Industry of India, 1994. Related Names:
Associated Chambers of Commerce &
Industry of India. Description: 91 p.; 25
cm. Subjects: India--Foreign economic
relations. India--Commercial policy. LC
Classification: HF1589 .G64 1994

Globalisation, migration, and development /
Organisation for Economic Co-operation
and Development. Published/Created:
Paris: OECD, 2000. Related Names:
Organisation for Economic Co-operation
and Development. Conference on
"Globalisation, Migration, and
Development" (1998: Lisbon, Portugal)
Description: 196 p.: ill.; 27 cm. ISBN
9264171665 Notes: "This publication
brings together a selection of the papers
presented at the Conference on
"Globalisation, Migration, and
Development", held in Lisbon on 2 and 3
November 1998"--P. 3. Includes
bibliographical references. Other Edition
Avail.: Mondialisation, migrations et
développement 926427166X Subjects:
International economic integration--
Congresses. Globalization--Congresses.
Emigration and immigration--Congresses.
Economic development--Congresses.
Migration Economic Development Series:
OECD proceedings LC Classification:
HF1418.5 .G573 2000 Dewey Class No.:
337 21

Globalisation, migration, and development /
Organisation for Economic Co-operation
and Development. Published/Created:
Paris: OECD, 2000. Related Names:

Organisation for Economic Co-operation
and Development. Conference on
"Globalisation, Migration, and
Development" (1998: Lisbon, Portugal)
Description: 196 p.: ill.; 27 cm. ISBN
9264171665 Notes: "This publication
brings together a selection of the papers
presented at the Conference on
"Globalisation, Migration, and
Development", held in Lisbon on 2 and 3
November 1998"--P. 3. Includes
bibliographical references. Other Edition
Avail.: Mondialisation, migrations et
développement 926427166X Subjects:
International economic integration--
Congresses. Globalization--Congresses.
Emigration and immigration--Congresses.
Economic development--Congresses.
Migration Economic Development Series:
OECD proceedings LC Classification:
HF1418.5 .G573 2000 Dewey Class No.:
337 21

Globalisation, networking, and small firm
innovation / editor, Dermot P. O'Doherty.
Published/Created: London; Boston:
Graham & Trotman, 1995. Related
Names: O'Doherty, Dermot. Six Countries
Programme on Innovation. Forfás,
Ireland. Description: 320 p.: ill., maps; 24
cm. ISBN 1859660711 1859661890
Notes: "Six Countries Programme on
Innovation and Forfás, Ireland." Includes
bibliographical references. Subjects:
Small business--Technological
innovations--Congresses. International
economic relations--Congresses.
Information networks--Congresses.
International division of labor--
Congresses. LC Classification: HD2341
.G54 1995 Dewey Class No.: 338.6/42 20

Globalisation, spécificités et autonomie:
Approche économique. [Reprend les
contributions au colloque tenu du 11 au 13
décembre 1997, organisé par l'] institut de
recherche économique sur la production et
le développement, IREPD / sous la

coordination de Yves Saillard. Published/Created: Toulouse: Octarès, 1999. Description: 189 p.; cm. ISBN 2906769568 Subjects: Globalization. Series: Colloques, 1159-8719

Globalisation, spécificités et autonomie: Approche économique. [Reprend les contributions au colloque tenu du 11 au 13 décembre 1997, organisé par l'] institut de recherche économique sur la production et le développement, IREPD / sous la coordination de Yves Saillard. Published/Created: Toulouse: Octarès, 1999. Description: 189 p.; cm. ISBN 2906769568 Subjects: Globalization. Series: Colloques, 1159-8719

Globalisation: Australian impacts / edited by Christopher Sheil. Published/Created: Sydney: UNSW Press, 2001. Related Names: Sheil, Christopher. Description: xvi, 312 p.: ill.; 24 cm. ISBN 0868407941 Notes: Includes bibliographical references and index. Bibliography: p. [297]-305. Subjects: International economic relations. International trade. Globalization. Globalization--History. International business enterprises. Australia--Economic conditions--1945- Australia--Social conditions. LC Classification: HF1359 .G58172 2001

Globalisation: Australian impacts / edited by Christopher Sheil. Published/Created: Sydney: UNSW Press, 2001. Related Names: Sheil, Christopher. Description: xvi, 312 p.: ill.; 24 cm. ISBN 0868407941 Notes: Includes bibliographical references and index. Bibliography: p. [297]-305. Subjects: International economic relations. International trade. Globalization. Globalization--History. International business enterprises. Australia--Economic conditions--1945- Australia--Social conditions. LC Classification: HF1359 .G58172 2001

Globalisation: South Asian perspective / editor, Ratnakar Adhikari. Published/Created: Kathmandu: South Asia Watch on Trade, Economics, and Environment, 2000. Related Names: Adhikari, Ratnakar. South Asia Watch on Trade, Economics, and Environment. Description: iv, 45 p.; 23 cm. Summary: Contributed articles. Notes: Includes bibliographical references (p. 44-45). Series: Monograph (South Asia Watch on Trade, Economics, and Environment); 1. LC Classification: HF1359 .G5817255 2000

Globalisation: the perspectives and experiences of the religious traditions of Asia Pacific / edited by Joseph A. Camilleri and Chandra Muzaffar. Published/Created: Petaling Jaya, Selangor Darul Ehsan, Malaysia: International Movement for a Just World, c1998. Related Names: Camilleri, Joseph A., 1944- Chandra Muzaffar, 1947- International Movement for a Just World (Malaysia) Description: 214 p.: ill.; 22 cm. ISBN 9839861093 Notes: Includes bibliographical references. Subjects: Globalization--Religious aspects. Asia--Religion. Pacific Area--Religion. LC Classification: BL1032 .G55 1998 Dewey Class No.: 291.1/787 21

Globalisation: the perspectives and experiences of the religious traditions of Asia Pacific / edited by Joseph A. Camilleri and Chandra Muzaffar. Published/Created: Petaling Jaya, Selangor Darul Ehsan, Malaysia: International Movement for a Just World, c1998. Related Names: Camilleri, Joseph A., 1944- Chandra Muzaffar, 1947- International Movement for a Just World (Malaysia) Description: 214 p.: ill.; 22 cm. ISBN 9839861093 Notes: Includes bibliographical references. Subjects: Globalization--Religious aspects. Asia--Religion. Pacific Area--Religion. LC

Classification: BL1032 .G55 1998 Dewey Class No.: 291.1/787 21

Globalisierung der Weltwirtschaft: Auswahlbibliographie / Wissenschaftliche Dienste des Deutschen Bundestages. Published/Created: Bonn: Die Dienste, 2000. Related Names: Germany. Bundestag. Wissenschaftliche Dienste. Description: 92 p.; 30 cm. Notes: Includes indexes. German and English. Subjects: Economic history--1990---Bibliography. Globalization--Bibliography. Series: Aktuelle Bibliographien der Bibliothek (Germany. Bundestag. Wissenschaftliche Dienste); Nr. 8. LC Classification: Z7164.E2 G585 2000 HC59.15 Dewey Class No.: 016.3309/049 21

Globalisierung: eine Standortbestimmung / Beiträge von Dieter Ruloff ... [et al.]. Published/Created: Chur: Rüegger, 1998. Related Names: Ruloff, Dieter. Schweizerisches Institut für Auslandforschung. Description: 184 p.: ill.; 21 cm. ISBN 3725306060 Notes: At head of Schweizerisches Institut für Auslandforschung. Includes bibliographical references. Chiefly German, 1 article in English. Subjects: International economic relations. International trade. Globalization. Series: Sozialwissenschaftliche Studien des Schweizerischen Instituts für Auslandforschung; n.F., Bd. 27 LC Classification: HF1359 G58174 1998

Globalism and local democracy: challenge and change in Europe and North America / edited by Robin Hambleton, H.V. Savitch and Murray Stewart. Published/Created: New York, N.Y.: Palgrave, 2002. Related Names: Hambleton, Robin. Savitch, H. V. Stewart, Murray. Description: p. cm. ISBN 0333772253 (cloth) Notes: Includes bibliographical references and index. Subjects: Local government--Europe, Western. Local government--North

America. Globalization. Democracy. LC Classification: JS3000 .G58 2002 Dewey Class No.: 320.8/094 21

Globalism, regionalism and nationalism: Asia in search of its role in the twenty-first century / [edited by] Yoshinobu Yamamoto. Published/Created: Oxford, UK; Malden, Mass., USA: Blackwell Publishers, 1999. Related Names: Yamamoto, Yoshinobu. Description: xi, 260 p.: ill.; 25 cm. ISBN 0631214003 Notes: Includes bibliographical references and index. Subjects: Regionalism--Asia. Nationalism--Asia. Globalization. Asia--Foreign relations. Asia--Politics and government--1945- Japan--Foreign relations--1989- Japan--Politics and government--1989- Asia--Foreign relations. Asia--Politics and government--1945- Asia Condiciones económicas.

Globalización neoliberal y neo imperialismo: [selección de artículos]. Edition Information: 1. ed. Published/Created: Santo Domingo, R.D.: Ediciones Caribe Soy, c2000. Description: 132 p.; 21 cm. Subjects: Globalization. Capitalism.

Globalización y comunidades en Centroamérica / Juan Pablo Pérez Sáinz ... [et al.]. Edition Information: 1a ed. Published/Created: San José, Costa Rica: Facultad Latinoamericana de Ciencias Sociales, 2001. Related Names: Pérez Sáinz, Juan Pablo. Description: 280 p.; ill.; 22 cm. ISBN 9977681139 Notes: Includes bibliographical references (p. [275]-280). Subjects: Globalization. Central America--Economic conditions--1979- LC Classification: HC141 .G57 2001

Globalización y libre comercio: memoria del II Seminario de Relaciones Económicas México-Centroamérica, Antigua Guatemala, 15 y 16 de abril. Edition Information: 1. ed. Published/Created:

Ciudad de Guatemala: CIDECA: CALDH; San Salvador, El Salvador: FUNDE; México, D.F.: RMALC, 1999. Related Names: CIDECA. Centro para la Acción Legal en Derechos Humanos. Red Mexicana de Acción Frente al Libre Comercio. Fundación Nacional para el Desarrollo (El Salvador) Description: 159 p.; 21 cm. Notes: Proceedings of conference held in April 1999, organized by Consejo de Investigaciones para el Desarrollo de Centroamérica, Centro para la Acción Legal en Derechos Humanos, Red Mexicana de Acción Frente al Libre Comercio, and Fundación Nacional para el Desarrollo. Subjects: Canada. Treaties, etc. 1992 Oct. 7 --Congresses. Globalization--Congresses. Mexico--Foreign economic relations--Central America Congresses. Central America--Foreign economic relations--Mexico Congresses. Central America--Economic integration--Congresses. Mexico--Economic conditions--1994---Congresses. Central America--Economic conditions--1979---Congresses. LC Classification: HF1482.5.C35 S45 1999

Globalización y políticas sociales en el Perú y España / Tomás Fernández García, Manuel Burgos Cabrejos, coordinadores. Edition Information: [1. ed.] Published/Created: Piura: Asociación Pariñas, 2000. Related Names: Fernández García, Tomás. Burgos Cabrejos, Manuel. Description: 311 p.: maps; 22 cm. Subjects: Globalization. Spain--Social policy. Peru--Social policy. LC Classification: HN583.5 .G56 2000

Globalización y sistemas agroalimentarios: 17 estudios / [revisión de textos, María Bellorín; traducción de textos, Francisco Calvani y Maria Inés Reyes]. Edition Information: 1. ed. Published/Created: Caracas: Fundación Polar, 1999. Related Names: Bellorín, María A. Calvani, Francisco. Reyes, María Inés. Fundación

Polar. Description: 288 p.: ill.; 25 cm. ISBN 9803790021 Notes: Includes bibliographical references. Subjects: Food industry and trade. Globalization. Food supply. Food supply--Latin America. Food industry and trade--Latin America. Series: Sistema alimentario venezolano. Estudios especiales. LC Classification: HD9000.5 .G63 1999

Globalización, América Latina, y la diplomacia de cumbres / Francisco Rojas Aravena, editor. Published/Created: Santiago, Chile: FLACSO-Chile, c1998. Related Names: Rojas Aravena, Francisco. Encuentro Internacional Globalización, América Latina y la Segunda Cumbre de las Américas (1998: Santiago, Chile) Summit of the Americas (2nd: 1998: Santiago, Chile) Description: 572 p.: ill.; 23 cm. ISBN 9562051234 Notes: Papers presented during the Encuentro Internacional Globalización América Latina and the II Cumbre de las Américas, April 18-19, 1998, in Santiago de Chile. Includes bibliographical references. Subjects: Summit of the Americas (2nd: 1998: Santiago, Chile) Globalization--Congresses. Summit meetings--Latin America--Congresses. Latin America--Foreign economic relations--Congresses. Latin America--Economic integration--Congresses. LC Classification: HF1480.5 .G558 1998

Globalización, crisis y desarrollo rural en América Latina: memoria de sesiones plenarias / [coordinadora de la edición, Martha Eloísa Valdivia de Ortega; editores, Juan Pablo de Pina García, Alba González Jácome]. Published/Created: Texcoco, México: Colegio de Postgarduados, Universidad Autónoma Chapingo, 1998. Description: xviii, 233 p.: ill.; 21 cm. ISBN 9688845221 Subjects: Rural development--Latin America--Congresses. Sociology, Rural--Latin America--Congresses.

Globalization--Congresses. Latin America--Economic policy--Congresses. Latin America--Rural conditions--Congresses. LC Classification: HN110.5.Z9 C626317 1998 Dewey Class No.: 307.72/098 21

Globalization / edited by Arjun Appadurai. Published/Created: Durham, NC: Duke University Press, 2001. Related Names: Appadurai, Arjun, 1949- Description: p. cm. ISBN 0822327252 (cloth: alk. paper) 0822327236 (pbk.: alk. paper) Notes: "Public culture books." Parts of the text of this book was originally published in vol. 12, no. 1 and 3 of Public culture. Subjects: Globalization. International relations. LC Classification: JZ1318 .G5787 2001 Dewey Class No.: 303.48/2 21

Globalization / edited by Katrin Sjursen. Published/Created: Bronx, N.Y.: H.W. Wilson Co., 2000. Related Names: Sjursen, Katrin. Description: x, 209 p.; 25 cm. ISBN 0824209869 Notes: Includes bibliographical references (p. 185-186) and index. Subjects: Globalization. International relations. Series: The reference shelf; v. 72, no. 5 LC Classification: JZ1318 .G579 2000 Dewey Class No.: 327.1 21

Globalization and agricultural marketing / edited by Harish Nayyar, P. Ramaswamy. Published/Created: Jaipur: Rawat Publications, c1995. Related Names: Nayyar, Harish. Ramaswamy, P. National Institute of Agricultural Marketing, Jaipur. National Seminar on Globalization and the Changing Dimensions of Agricultural Marketing (1994: Jaipur, India) Description: xii, 337 p.: ill.; 23 cm. Summary: Papers presented to the National Seminar on Globalization and the Changing Dimensions of Agricultural Marketing organized by the National Institute of Agricultural Marketing, Jaipur, 15-16 April 1994. Notes:

"National Institute of Agricultural Marketing, Jaipur." Includes bibliographical references. Subjects: Farm produce--India--Marketing. Free trade--India. India--Economic polity--1980- LC Classification: HD9016.I42 G56 1995

Globalization and agricultural trade policy / edited by Hans J. Michelmann ... [et al.]. Published/Created: Boulder, Co.: Lynne Rienner Publishers, 2001. Related Names: Michelmann, Hans J. Description: x, 357 p.: ill.; 24 cm. ISBN 1555879519 (alk. paper) Notes: Includes bibliographical references (p. 329-334) and index. Subjects: Produce trade--Government policy. Agriculture and state. International economic relations. Globalization. LC Classification: HD9000.6 .G567 2001 Dewey Class No.: 382/.41 21

Globalization and education: integration and contestation across cultures / edited by Nelly P. Stromquist and Karen Monkman. Published/Created: Lanham, Md.: Rowman & Littlefield, c2000. Related Names: Stromquist, Nelly P. Monkman, Karen. Description: xvii, 363 p.; 24 cm. ISBN 0847699188 (cloth: alk. paper) 0847699196 (pbk.: alk. paper) Notes: Includes bibliographical references and index. Subjects: Education--Economic aspects--Cross-cultural studies. Education--Social aspects--Cross-cultural studies. Globalization--Cross-cultural studies. LC Classification: LC65 .G46 2000 Dewey Class No.: 306.43 21

Globalization and integrated area development in European cities / Frank Moulaert in collaboration with Pavlos Delladetsima ... [et al.]. Published/Created: Oxford; New York: Oxford University Press, 2000. Related Names: Moulaert, Frank. Delladetsima, Pavlos. Description: xiv, 159 p.: map; 24 cm. ISBN 0199241139 (alk. paper) Notes: Includes bibliographical references (p. [144]-153) and indexes. Subjects: Economic development projects--Europe--Case studies. Cities and towns--Europe--Case studies. Globalization--Europe--Case studies. Competition, International. Series: Oxford geographical and environmental studies LC Classification: HC240.9.E44 G55 2000 Dewey Class No.: 307.76/094 21

Globalization and its discontents / edited by Stephen McBride and John Wiseman. Published/Created: Houndmills, Basingstoke, Hampshire: Macmillan Press; New York: St. Martin's Press, 2000. Related Names: McBride, Stephen Kenneth. Wiseman, John Richard, 1957- Description: xvi, 237 p.; 23 cm. ISBN 0312229577 (cloth) Notes: Includes bibliographical references and index. Subjects: Globalization. International relations. LC Classification: JZ1318 .G583 2000 Dewey Class No.: 327.1/7 21

Globalization and its victims: as seen by the victims / edited by Michael Amaladoss. Published/Created: Delhi: Vidyajyoti Education & Welfare Society: ISPCK, 1999. Related Names: Amaladoss, M. (Michael), 1936- Vidyajyoti Education & Welfare Society (Delhi, India) I.S.P.C.K. (Organization) International Consultation on Globalization from the Perspective of the Victims of History (1998: Delhi, India) Description: xii, 246 p.; 23 cm. ISBN 8172144806 Summary: Papers presented at the International Consultation on Globalization from the Perspective of the Victims of History held in Delhi, January 18-22, 1998. Notes: Includes bibliographical references. Subjects: Globalization--Congresses. International economic relations--Congresses. Globalization--Social aspects--Developing countries Congresses. LC Classification: JZ1318 .G584 1999 Dewey Class No.: 303.48/2 21

Globalization and labor / edited by Horst Siebert. Published/Created: Tübingen: Mohr Siebeck, c1999. Related Names: Siebert, Horst, 1938- Universität Kiel. Institut für Weltwirtschaft. Kiel Week Conference (1998) Description: viii, 320 p.: ill.; 24 cm. ISBN 3161471830 Notes: "Institut für Weltwirtschaft an der Universität Kiel." Papers and comments presented at the 1998 Kiel Week Conference organized by the Kiel Institute of World Economics. Includes bibliographical references and index. Subjects: Foreign trade and employment--Congresses. International trade--Congresses. Labor--Congresses. Globalization--Congresses. LC Classification: HD5710.7 .G547 1999

Globalization and labour in the Asia Pacific / editors, Chris Rowley, John Benson. Published/Created: London; Portland, OR: Frank Cass, 2000. Related Names: Rowley, Chris, 1959- Benson, John, 1948- Description: p. cm. ISBN 0714650358 (cloth) 0714680893 (pbk.) Notes: "This group of studies first appeared in a special issue of 'Asia Pacific business review, ISSN 1360-2381', vol. 6, nos. 3&4 (Spring/Summer, 2000)"--T.p. verso. Includes bibliographical references and index. Subjects: Foreign trade and employment--Asia. Foreign trade and employment--Pacific Area. Labor market--Asia. Labor market--Pacific Area. Free trade--Asia. Free trade--Pacific Area. Globalization. Series: Studies in Asia Pacific business, 1369-7153 LC Classification: HD5710.75.A78 G58 2000 Dewey Class No.: 331.12/095 21

Globalization and labour markets / edited by David Greenaway and Douglas R. Nelson. Published/Created: Nothampton, MA: Edward Elgar, 2001. Related Names: Greenaway, David. Nelson, Douglas R. Description: p. cm. ISBN 1840641320 Notes: Includes bibliographical references and index. Subjects: Foreign trade and employment. Investments, Foreign and employment. Globalization--Economic aspects. International business enterprises--Employees. International trade--Social aspects. International labor activities. Labor market. Free trade. Series: Globalization of the world economy; 10 LC Classification: HD5710.7 .G5476 2001 Dewey Class No.: 331.1 21

Globalization and marginality in geographical space: political, economic and social issues of development in the new millennium / edited by Heikki Jussila, Roser Majoral, Fernanda Delgado-Cravidão. Published/Created: Aldershot; Burlington, Vt., USA: Ashgate, c2001. Related Names: Jussila, Heikki. Majoral i Moliné, Roser. Cravidão, Fernanda Delgado. International Geographical Union. Description: xix, 304 p.: ill., maps; 23 cm. ISBN 075461476X Notes: Includes bibliographical references. Subjects: Economic development--Congresses. Globalization--Congresses. Marginality, Social--Congresses. Regional disparities--Congresses. Marginal productivity--Congresses. Series: Dynamics of marginal and critical regions LC Classification: HD73 .G59 2001

Globalization and national identities: crisis or opportunity? / edited by Paul Kennedy and Catherine J. Danks. Published/Created: New York: Palgrave, 2001. Related Names: Kennedy, Paul T., 1941- Danks, Catherine J., 1956- Description: xvi, 256 p.; 23 cm. ISBN 0333929632 Notes: Includes bibliographical references (p. 224-240) and index. Subjects: Social change. Globalization. Nationalism. LC Classification: HM836 .G58 2001 Dewey Class No.: 303.4 21

Globalization and Nigeria's economic development: proceedings of the one-day seminar of the Nigerian Economic Society held on 11 February 1999. Published/Created: Ibadan, [Nigeria]: The Society, 1999. Related Names: Nigerian Economic Society. Description: vii, 87 p.; 23 cm. ISBN 9782984604 Notes: Includes bibliographical references. Subjects: Globalization--Congresses. Nigeria--Economic policy--Congresses. LC Classification: HC1055 .G595 1999 Dewey Class No.: 338.9669 21

Globalization and regional dynamics: East Asia and the European Union from the Japanese and the German perspective / Wolfgang Klenner, Hisashi Watanabe, editors. Published/Created: New York: Springer, 2001. Related Names: Klenner, Wolfgang. Watanabe, Hisashi, 1937- Description: p. cm. ISBN 3540425993 (alk. paper) Notes: Papers translated from Japanes and German. Subjects: Globalization--Economic aspects--East Asia. Globalization--Economic aspects--European Union countries. Competition, International. East Asia--Foreign economic relations. European Union countries--Foreign economic relations. East Asia--Economic conditions--20th century. European Union countries--Economic conditions--20th century. LC Classification: HF1600.5. G56 2001 Dewey Class No.: 337.405 21

Globalization and regionalization: challenges for public policy / edited by David B. Audretsch and Charles F. Bonser. Published/Created: Boston: Kluwer Academic Publishers, c2002. Related Names: Audretsch, David B. Bonser, Charles F. Description: 120 p.; 25 cm. ISBN 0792375521 (alk. paper) Notes: Includes bibliographical references. Subjects: Globalization. Regionalism (International organization) LC Classification: JZ1318 .G585 2002 Dewey Class No.: 327.1 21

Globalization and social change / edited by Johannes Dragsbaek Schmidt and Jacques Hersh. Published/Created: London; New York: Routledge, 2000. Related Names: Schmidt, Johannes Dragsbaek, 1960- Hersh, Jacques. Description: p. cm. ISBN 0415241715 (HB) Notes: Includes bibliographical references and index. Subjects: International economic integration. Globalization. Social change. LC Classification: HF1418.5 .G58174 2000 Dewey Class No.: 303.44 21

Globalization and social change in contemporary Japan / edited by J.S. Eades, Tom Gill, Harumi Befu. Published/Created: Melbourne: Trans Pacific Press, 2000. Related Names: Eades, J. S. (Jeremy Seymour), 1945- Gill, Tom, 1960- Befu, Harumi. Description: viii, 295 p.: ill.; 22 cm. ISBN 1876843012 Notes: Includes bibliographical references (p. 245-276) and index. Subjects: Social change--Japan. Globalization--Japan. Japan--Social conditions--1945- Series: Japanese society series, 1443-9670 LC Classification: HN723.5 .G56 2000 Dewey Class No.: 306/.0952 21

Globalization and social movements / edited by Pierre Hamel ... [et al.]. Published/Created: New York: Palgrave, 2001. Related Names: Hamel, Pierre, 1947- Description: p. cm. ISBN 0333725352 Notes: Includes bibliographical references and index. Subjects: Social movements. Globalization. LC Classification: HM881 .G56 2001 Dewey Class No.: 303.48/4 21

Globalization and sport: playing the world / Toby Miller... [et al.]. Published/Created: London: SAGE, 2001. Related Names: Miller, Toby. Description: 160 p.; 24 cm. ISBN 0761959688 0761959696 (pbk.) Notes: Includes bibliographical references and index. Subjects: Globalization.

Sports--Sociological aspects. LC Classification: GV706.5 .G59 2001 Dewey Class No.: 306.4/83 21

Globalization and the environment: risk assessment and the WTO / edited by David Robertson and Aynsley Kellow. Published/Created: Northampton, MA: Edward Elgar Pub., 2001. Related Names: Robertson, David, 1935- Kellow, Aynsley J. (Aynsley John), 1951- Description: p. cm. ISBN 1840645385 Notes: Papers presented at a two-day meeting at the Melbourne Business School in Feb. 1999. Includes bibliographical references and index. Subjects: World Trade Organization. Free trade--Environmental aspects--Congresses. International trade--Environmental aspects--Congresses. Environmental policy--Congresses. Foreign trade regulation--Environmental aspects Congresses. Risk management--Congresses. Globalization--Environmental aspects--Congresses. LC Classification: HF1713 .G563 2000 Dewey Class No.: 333.7 21

Globalization and the European political economy / Steven Weber, editor. Published/Created: New York: Columbia University Press, c2001. Related Names: Weber, Steven. Description: x, 316 p.: ill.; 24 cm. ISBN 0231121482 (cloth: alk. paper) 0231121490 (pbk.: alk. paper) Notes: Includes bibliographical references and index. Subjects: Globalization. Europe--Economic conditions. Europe--Foreign economic relations. LC Classification: HC240 .G535 2001 Dewey Class No.: 337.4 21

Globalization and the small open economy / edited by Daniel Van Den Bulcke and Alain Verbeke. Published/Created: Cheltenham [England]; Northampton, MA: E. Elgar, c2001. Related Names: Bulcke, D. van den. Verbeke, Alain. Dunning, John H. Description: xv, 234 p.:

ill.; 24 cm. ISBN 1840647299 Notes: "This research volume results from a conference at the University of Antwerp, Belgium ... it honoured Professor John H. Dunning"--Pref. Includes bibliographical references and index. Subjects: International economic integration. States, Small--Economic integration--Congresses. States, Small--Economic policy--Congresses. International business enterprises--Congresses. Globalization--Congresses. Series: New horizons in international business LC Classification: HF1418.5 .G58186 2001 Dewey Class No.: 337 21

Globalization and the South / edited by Caroline Thomas and Peter Wilkin. Published/Created: New York: St. Martin's Press, 1997. Related Names: Thomas, Caroline, 1959- Wilkin, Peter, 1963- Description: xii, 235 p.: ill.; 23 cm. ISBN 0333659430 (cloth) 0312175647 (cloth) Notes: Includes bibliographical references and index. Subjects: International economic relations. International relations. Globalization. Southern hemisphere--Foreign economic relations. Series: International political economy series LC Classification: HF1359 .G584 1997 Dewey Class No.: 337.1/1814 21

Globalization and the South Asian State / edited by B. Ramesh Babu. Published/Created: Denver, CO: iAcademic Books, 2000. Related Names: Babu, B. Ramesh. Description: p. cm. ISBN 1588680029 (paper) 1588680037 (library) Notes: Includes bibliographical references and index. Subjects: State, The. Globalization. South Asia--Politics and government. LC Classification: JQ98.A58 G56 2000 Dewey Class No.: 327.54 21

Globalization and the sustainability of cities in the Asia Pacific region / edited by Fu-chen Lo and Peter J. Marcotullio.

Published/Created: New York: United Nations University Press, 2001. Related Names: Lo, Fu-chen. Marcotullio, Peter, 1957- Description: p. cm. ISBN 928081060X (pbk.) Notes: Includes bibliographical references and index. Subjects: Urbanization--East Asia. Urbanization--Pacific Area. Cities and towns--East Asia--Growth. Cities and town--Pacific Area--Growth. Sustainable development--East Asia. Sustainable development--Pacific Area. Globalization. LC Classification: HT384.E18 G56 2001 Dewey Class No.: 307.76/095 21

Globalization and third world socialism: Cuba and Vietnam / edited by Claes Brundenius and John Weeks. Published/Created: Houndmills, Basingstoke, Hampshire; New York, N.Y.: PALGRAVE, 2001. Related Names: Brundenius, Claes, 1938- Weeks, John, 1941- Description: xii, 281 p.: ill.; 23 cm. ISBN 0333800435 (cloth) Notes: Includes bibliographical references (p. 261-276) and index. Subjects: Socialism--Cuba. Socialism--Vietnam. Globalization. Cuba--Economic policy. Vietnam--Economic policy--1975- LC Classification: HC152.5 .G55 2001 Dewey Class No.: 338.9597 21

Globalization in Southeast Asia: local, national and transnational perspectives / edited by Shinji Yamashita and J.S. Eades. Published/Created: New York: Berghahn Books, 2001. Related Names: Yamashita, Shinji. Eades, J. S. (Jeremy Seymour), 1945- Description: p. cm. ISBN 1571812555 (alk. paper) Notes: Includes bibliographical references and index. Subjects: Globalization--Asia, Southeastern. Asia, Southeastern--Civilization. Series: Asian anthropologies LC Classification: DS523.2 .G56 2001 Dewey Class No.: 959 21

Globalization in Southeast Asia: local, national, and transnational perspectives /

edited by Shinji Yamashita and J.S. Eades. Published/Created: New York: Berghahn Books, 2001. Related Names: Yamashita, Shinji. Eades, J. S. (Jeremy Seymour), 1945- Description: p. cm. ISBN 1571812555 (alk. paper) 1571812563 (alk. paper) Notes: "The Japan-Southeast Asia workshop on which this book is based was held in Tokyo on 31 October-1 November 1996"--pref. Subjects: Globalization--Congresses. Asia, Southeastern--Economic integration--Congresses. Asia, Southeastern--Economic conditions--Congresses. Asia, Southeastern--Social conditions--Congresses. LC Classification: HC441 .G565 2001 Dewey Class No.: 337.5 21

Globalization on the line: culture, capital, and citizenship at U.S. borders / edited by Claudia Sadowski-Smith. Published/Created: New York: Palgrave, 2002. Related Names: Sadowski-Smith, Claudia, 1968- Description: p. cm. ISBN 0312294824 0312294832 (pbk.) Notes: Includes bibliographical references and index. Subjects: Globalization. International economic relations. Mexican-American Border Region. United States--Foreign relations--1989- United States--Cultural policy. LC Classification: JZ1318 .G679 2002 Dewey Class No.: 303.48/273071 21

Globalization under threat: the stability of trade policy and multilateral agreements / edited by Zdenek Drabek. Published/Created: Cheltenham, UK; Northampton, MA, USA: Edward Elgar, 2001. Related Names: Drabek, Zdenek. Description: p. cm. ISBN 1840646586 Notes: Includes bibliographical references and index. Subjects: Free trade. International trade. Economic stabilization. Globalization. LC Classification: HF1713 .G564 2001

Dewey Class No.: 382/.3 21

Globalization versus development / edited by Jomo K.S. and Shyamala Nagaraj. Published/Created: Houndmills, Basingstoke, Hampshire; New York: Palgrave, 2001. Related Names: Jomo K. S. (Jomo Kwame Sundaram) Nagaraj, Shyamala. Description: xxvii, 240 p.: ill.; 23 cm. ISBN 0333919653 0333919661 (pbk.) Notes: Rev. papers selected from an international conference on "Globalisation and development: lessons for the Malaysian economy" held in mid-Aug. 1996 in Kuala Lumpur. Includes bibliographical references (p. 225-237) and index. Subjects: International economic integration. Free trade. International finance. Globalization--Economic aspects. Economic development. Globalization--Economic aspects--Developing countries. Series: International political economy series (Palgrave (Firm)) LC Classification: HF1418.5 .G58188 2001 Dewey Class No.: 337 21

Globalization, culture, and women's development / edited by Raj Mohini Sethi. Published/Created: Jaipur: Rawat Publications, c1999. Related Names: Sethi, Raj Mohini, 1940- National Seminar on "Globalization, Culture, and Women's Development" (1999?: Punjab University) Description: 368 p.; 22 cm. Summary: Contributed articles presented at the National Seminar on "Globalization, Culture, and Women's Development", organised by Punjab University with special reference to India. Notes: Includes bibliographical references and index. Subjects: Women--India--Social conditions--Congresses. International relations and culture--Congresses. Globalization--Congresses. Women--India--Economic conditions--Congresses. LC Classification: HQ1742 .G63 1999 Dewey Class No.: 305.42/0954 21

305.42/0954 21

Globalization, employment, and the workplace / edited by Yaw A. Debrah and Ian G. Smith. Published/Created: London; New York: Routledge, 2001. Related Names: Debrah, Yaw A., 1956- Smith, Ian G. Cardiff Business School. Employment Research Unit. Description: p. cm. ISBN 0415252415 (alk. paper) Notes: Papers presented at the 1999 Employment Research Unit conference at the Cardiff Business School. Includes bibliographical references and index. Subjects: Foreign trade and employment--Congresses. Globalization--Economic aspects--Congresses. International business enterprises--Employees--Congresses. International labor activities--Congresses. Labor market--Congresses. Free trade--Congresses. LC Classification: HD5710.7 .G56 2001 Dewey Class No.: 337 21

Globalization, gender, and religion: the politics of implementing women's rights in Catholic and Muslim contexts / edited by Jane H. Bayes and Nayereh Tohidi. Published/Created: New York: Palgrave, 2001. Related Names: Bayes, Jane H., 1939- Tohidi, Nayereh Esfahlani, 1951- Description: p. cm. ISBN 0312228120 0312293690 (pbk.) Notes: Includes bibliographical references and index. Subjects: Women's rights--Cross-cultural studies. Women in the Catholic Church. Women in Islam. Globalization. LC Classification: HQ1236 .G54 2001 Dewey Class No.: 305.42 21

Globalization, growth, and poverty: building an inclusive world economy. Published/Created: Washington, DC: World Bank; New York, N.Y.: Oxford University Press, c2002. Related Names: Collier, Paul Dollar, David. World Bank. Description: xiii, 174 p.: col. ill.; 24 cm. ISBN 0195216083 (OUP) 082135048X (World Bank) Partial Contents: Overview -- The new wave of globalization and its economic effects -- Improving the international architecture for integration -- Strengthening domestic institutions and policies -- Power, culture, and the environment -- An agenda for action. Notes: "This report was prepared under the supervision of Nicolas Stern, Chief Economist and Senior Vice President. It was written by Paul Collier (Director, Development Research Group) and David Dollar (Research Mamager in the Development Research Group" -- xiii "A copublication of the World Bank and Oxford University Press" -- t.p. Includes bibliographical references (p.161-174). Subjects: Poor--Developing countries. Economic development. Poverty--Developing countries Globalization--Economic aspects. International economic integration. Developing countries--Economic policy. Developing countries--Economic conditions. Series: A World Bank policy research report LC Classification: HC59.72.P6 G59 2002

Globalization, institutions and social cohesion: with 19 figures and 29 tables / Felice R. Pizzuti, Maurizio Franzini, editors. Published/Created: New York: Springer, 2000. Related Names: Pizzuti, Felice Roberto. Franzini, M. (Maurizio), 1950- Description: p. cm. ISBN 3540677410 (hardcover alk. paper) Subjects: Globalization. International economic relations. International economic integration. Social change. LC Classification: HF1359 .G586 2000 Dewey Class No.: 337 21

Globalization, power, and democracy / edited by Marc F. Plattner and Aleksander Smolar. Published/Created: Baltimore: Johns Hopkins University Press, c2000. Related Names: Plattner, Marc F., 1945- Smolar, Aleksander. Description: xx, 164 p.; 23 cm. ISBN 0801865689 Notes: Includes bibliographical references and

index. Subjects: Democracy.
Globalization. Post-communism. Series:
A journal of democracy book LC
Classification: JC421 .G59 2000 Dewey
Class No.: 327 21

Globalization, regionalization, and cross-
border regions / edited by Markus
Perkmann and Ngai-Ling Sum.
Published/Created: New York: Palgrave,
2002. Related Names: Perkmann, Markus,
1969- Sum, Ngai-Ling. Description: p.
cm. ISBN 0333919297 (cloth) Notes:
Includes bibliographical references and
index. Subjects: International economic
relations. Regional economics.
Globalization. Series: International
political economy series (Palgrave (Firm))
LC Classification: HF1359 .G58268 2002
Dewey Class No.: 337 21

Globalization: critical reflections / edited by
James H. Mittelman. Published/Created:
Boulder, Colo.: Lynne Rienner Publishers,
1996. Related Names: Mittelman, James
H. Description: xii, 273 p.; 24 cm. ISBN
1555875653 (alk. paper) Notes: Includes
bibliographical references (p. 243-264)
and index. Subjects: International
economic relations. International
relations. Globalization. Series:
International political economy yearbook;
v. 9 LC Classification: HF1410 .I579 vol.
9 HF1359 Dewey Class No.: 337/.05 s
337 20

Globalization: marginalization of dalits,
women & tribals: proceedings of a
workshop on its concept, process &
impact / edited by Rosemary Viswanath
for Solidarity. Published/Created:
Tumkur: Solidarity, 1998. Related Names:
Viswanath, Rosemary. Solidarity
(Organization: Tumkˉur, India)
Workshop on "Globalization: Concept,
Process, and Impact" (1997: Tumkˉur,
India) Description: ix, 69 p.; 29 cm.
Summary: Proceedings of a Workshop on

"Globalization: Concept, Process, and
Impact" held Nov. 28-30, 1997 at
Tumkur, Karnataka. Notes: Includes
bibliographical references. Subjects:
Globalization--Congresses. Marginality,
Social--India--Congresses. Dalits--Social
conditions--Congresses. Women--India--
Social conditions--Congresses. India--
Scheduled tribes--Social conditions--
Congresses. LC Classification: JZ1318
.G5794 1998 Dewey Class No.: 337 21

Globalization: policies, challenges and
responses / edited by Shereen T. Ismael.
Published/Created: Calgary: Detselig
Enterprises, c1999. Related Names:
Ismael, Shereen T. Description: 286 p.:
ill.; 23 cm. ISBN 155059169X Notes:
Selected papers from an international
conference, Globalization: socio-
economic, business and political
dimensions, held at the Eastern
Mediterranean University in the Turkish
Republic of Northern Cyprus. Includes
bibliographical references. Subjects:
International economic relations.
Globalization--Economic aspects.
Globalization--Social aspects. Free trade--
Social aspects--Developing countries. LC
Classification: HF1352 .G574 1999
Dewey Class No.: 337 21

Globalization: reader / edited by John Benyon
and David Dunkerley. Published/Created:
New York: Routledge, 2001. Related
Names: Benyon, John. Dunkerley, David.
Description: p. cm. ISBN 0415929229
(pbk.) Notes: Includes bibliographical
references and index. Subjects:
International economic relations.
Globalization. World politics--1989-
Economic history--1990- LC
Classification: HF1359 .G594 2001
Dewey Class No.: 303.48/2 21

Globalization: the United Nations
development dialogue; finance, trade,
poverty, peace-building / edited by

Isabelle Grunberg, Sarbuland Khan.
Published/Created: Tokyo; New York:
United Nations University Press, c2000.
Related Names: Grunberg, Isabelle. Khan,
Sarbuland. Description: vii, 233 p.; 23 cm.
ISBN 9280810510 Notes: Includes
bibliographical references (219-221) and
index. Subjects: Peace. Globalization.
Developing countries--Foreign economic
relations. Developing countries--
Economic policy. LC Classification:
HF1413 .G585 2000

Globalization: theory and practice / edited by
Eleonore Kofman and Gillian Youngs.
Published/Created: New York: Pinter,
1996. Related Names: Kofman, Eleonore.
Youngs, Gillian, 1956- Description: xii,
339 p.; 24 cm. ISBN 1855673460
(hardback) 1855673479 (pbk.) Notes:
Includes bibliographical references and
index. Subjects: International relations.
Globalization. LC Classification: JX1391
.G528 1996 Dewey Class No.: 320.1/2 20

Globalize this!: the battle against the World
Trade Organization and corporate rule /
edited by Kevin Danaher and Roger
Burbach. Published/Created: Monroe,
Me.: Common Courage Press, c2000.
Related Names: Danaher, Kevin, 1950-
Burbach, Roger. Description: 218 p.; 20
cm. ISBN 1567511961 (pbk.)
156751197X (cloth) Notes: Includes
index. Subjects: World Trade
Organization. International business
enterprises. Free trade--Environmental
aspects. Free trade--Social aspects.
International economic relations
Globalization. Developing countries--
Foreign economic relations. LC
Classification: HF1385 .G58 2000 Dewey
Class No.: 382/.92 21

Globalizing Africa / edited by Malinda Smith.
Published/Created: Trenton, NJ: Africa
World Press, 2000. Related Names:
Smith, Malinda. Description: p. cm. ISBN

0865438692 0865438706 (pbk.) Notes:
Includes bibliographical references and
index. Subjects: Globalization--Africa.
Africa--Politics and government--1960-
Africa--Economic conditions--1960-
Africa--Social conditions--1960- LC
Classification: DT30.5 .G58 2000 Dewey
Class No.: 306/.096 21

Globalizing Europe: deepening integration,
alliance capitalism, and structural
statecraft / edited by Thomas L. Brewer,
Paul A. Brenton, Gavin Boyd.
Published/Created: Northampton, MA:
Edward Elgar Pub., 2002. Related Names:
Brewer, Thomas L., 1941- Brenton, Paul.
Boyd, Gavin. Description: p. cm. ISBN
1840646411 Notes: Includes index.
Subjects: Globalization. European Union
countries--Economic integration.
European Union countries--Economic
policy. Series: New horizons in
international business LC Classification:
HC241 .G57 2002 Dewey Class No.:
337.1/4 21

Globalizing feminist bioethics: crosscultural
perspectives / [edited by] Rosemarie
Tong, with Gwen Anderson, Aida Santos.
Published/Created: Boulder, Colo.:
Westview Press, 2001. Related Names:
Tong, Rosemarie. Anderson, Gwen, R.N.
Santos, Aida F. Description: vii, 368 p.;
23 cm. ISBN 0813366151 Notes: Includes
bibliographical references and index.
Subjects: Bioethics. Feminist ethics.
Globalization. Women's health services--
Moral and ethical aspects. Human
reproductive technology--Moral and
ethical aspects. Research--Moral and
ethical aspects.

Globalizing institutions: case studies in
regulation and innovation / edited by Jane
Jenson, Boaventura de Sousa Santos.
Published/Created: Aldershot, Hampshire;
Burlington, Vt.: Ashgate, c2000. Related
Names: Jenson, Jane. Santos, Boaventura

de Sousa. Description: 284 p.: ill.; 22 cm.
ISBN 0754614042 Notes: Includes
bibliographical references. Subjects:
Globalization--Case studies. Social
change--Case studies. Social institutions--
Case studies. International relations--
Social aspects--Case studies. LC
Classification: JZ1318 .G6795 2000
Dewey Class No.: 303.48/2 21

Globalizing Japan: ethnography of the
Japanese presence in America, Asia, and
Europe / edited by Harumi Befu and
Sylvie Guichard-Auguis.
Published/Created: New York: Routledge,
2001. Related Names: Befu, Harumi.
Guichard-Anguis, Sylvie, 1951-
Description: p. cm. ISBN 0415244129
Notes: Includes bibliographical references
and index. Subjects: Globalization--
Economic aspects--Japan. Globalization--
Social aspects--Japan. Corporations,
Japanese. Japanese--Foreign countries.
Corporate culture--Japan. Japan--Foreign
economic relations. LC Classification:
HF1601 .G56 2001 Dewey Class No.:
337.52 21

Globalizzazione e transizione: dalla
trasformazione interna del capitalismo
mondializzato dell'epoca presente alle
possibili ipotesi di superamento
dell'attuale assetto mondiale: analisi
economica e sociale, discorso politico,
forme culturali / Elmar A[l]tvater ... [et
al.]. Published/Created: Milano: Edizioni
Punto rosso, [1998] Related Names:
Altvater, Elmar. Associazione culturale
punto rosso. Description: v, 267 p.: ill.; 21
cm. Notes: "Atti del Convegno Oltre il
capitale: globalizzazione e transizione,
svoltosi a Milano il 13-14 dicembre 1997,
organizzato dall'Associazione culturale
punto rosso ... [et al.]." Includes
bibliographical references. Subjects:
International economic relations--
Congresses. Globalization--Congresses.
Series: Presente come storia (Edizioni

Punto rosso); 35. LC Classification:
HF1352 .C65 1998

Glucksmann, André. Dostoïevski à Manhattan
/ André Glucksmann. Published/Created:
Paris: Laffont, 2001. Description: 278 p.;
cm. ISBN 2221093216 Subjects:
Philosophy - Globalization - Terrorism -
Nihilism.

Gluckstein, Daniel. Lutte des classes et
mondialisation: le XXe siecle s'achève:
putre'fie', se'nile, parasitaire,
l'impe'rialisme reste une transition--mais
vers quoi? / [Daniel Gluckstein].
Published/Created: Paris: Selio, [1999?]
Description: 511 p.: ill.; 24 cm. ISBN
2906981206 Notes: Includes
bibliographical references. Subjects:
Social conflict. Globalization. Capitalism.
Socialism. LC Classification: HM1121
.G58 1999

God and globalization / edited by Max L.
Stackhouse with Peter Paris.
Published/Created: Harrisburg, Pa.:
Trinity Press International, c2000-c2001
Related Names: Stackhouse, Max L.
Paris, Peter J., 1933- Browning, Don S.
Description: v. <1-2 >; 23 cm. ISBN
156338311X (v. 1) 1563383306 (v. 2)
Notes: Vol. 2 edited by Max L.
Stackhouse with Don S. Browning.
Includes bibliographical references and
index. Subjects: Christian ethics.
Globalization--Moral and ethical aspects.
Globalization--Religious aspects--
Christianity. Series: Theology for the
twenty-first century LC Classification:
BJ1275 .G63 2000 Dewey Class No.:
261.8 21

Going global: the new shape of American
innovation. Published/Created:
Washington, D.C.: Council on
Competitiveness, c1998. Related Names:
Council on Competitiveness (U.S.)
Description: 150 p.: ill. (some col.); 28

cm. ISBN 1889866202 Notes: Includes bibliographical references. Subjects: Technological innovations--Economic aspects--United States. Industrial promotion--United States. Competition, International. Globalization. LC Classification: HC79.T4 G64 1998

Goldmann, Kjell, 1937- Transforming the European nation-state / Kjell Goldmann. Published/Created: London: SAGE, 2001. Description: xiv, 224 p.: ill.; 24 cm. ISBN 076196326X 0761963278 (pbk.) Notes: Includes bibliographical references and index. Subjects: Globalization. Europe--Politics and government--1989- Europe--Politics and government--1989- Series: SAGE politics texts

González Gómez, Carmen Imelda. Cien años de industria en Querétaro / Carmen Imelda González Gómez y Lorena Erika Osorio Franco. Edition Information: 1a ed. Published/Created: Querétaro: Universidad Autónoma de Querétaro / Gobierno del Estado de Querétaro, 2000. Description: 145 p.; cm. ISBN 9688452106 Summary: A history and contemporary analysis of industrial growth in Queretaro during the past century, with focus on transitions from the Porfiriato to the revolution, agricultural and industrial modernization and recent changes accompanying globalization.

Gordon, Philip H., 1962- The French challenge: adapting to globalization / Philip H. Gordon and Sophie Meunier. Published/Created: Washington, D.C.: Brookings Institution Press, c2001. Related Names: Meunier, Sophie. Description: p. cm. ISBN 0815702604 (cloth) 0815702612 (alk. paper) Notes: Includes bibliographical references and index. Subjects: Globalization. France--Foreign economic relations. France--Economic conditions--1995- France--Politics and government--1995- LC

Classification: HF1543 .G67 2001 Dewey Class No.: 337.44 21

Goudzwaard, B. Globalization and the Kingdom of God / Bob Goudzwaard; with responses by Brian Fikkert, Larry Reed, Adolfo García de la Sienra; edited by James W. Skillen. Published/Created: Washington, D.C.: Center for Public Justice; Grand Rapids, Mich.: Baker Books, c2001. Related Names: Fikkert, Brian. Reed, Larry. García de la Sienra, Adolfo. Skillen, James W. Description: 123 p.; 22 cm. ISBN 080106354X (pbk.) Notes: Includes bibliographical references (p. 115-123). Subjects: Globalization--Religious aspects--Christianity. Church and social problems. Series: The Kuyper lecture series LC Classification: JZ1318 .G678 2001 Dewey Class No.: 303.48/2 21

Governance in a globalizing world / Joseph S. Nye, Jr., John D. Donahue, editors. Published/Created: Cambridge, Mass.: Visions of Governance for the 21st Century; Washington, D.C.: Brookings Institution Press, c2000. Related Names: Nye, Joseph S. Donahue, John D. Description: xii, 386 p.: ill.; 24 cm. ISBN 0815764081 (cloth: alk. paper) 0815764073 (pbk : alk. paper) Notes: Includes bibliographical references and index. Subjects: Globalization. State, The. LC Classification: JZ1318 .G68 2000 Dewey Class No.: 327.1/01 21

Governing modern societies / edited by Richard V. Ericson and Nico Stehr. Published/Created: Toronto; Buffalo: University of Toronto Press, c2000. Related Names: Ericson, Richard Victor. Stehr, Nico. Description: vi, 298 p.; 24 cm. ISBN 0802043925 (cloth: acid-free paper) 0802081983 (pbk.: acid-free paper) Notes: Includes bibliographical references. Subjects: Political science. Globalization. Welfare state. Science politique. Series: The Green College thematic lecture series LC Classification: JA66 .G68 2000 Dewey Class No.: 320 21

Government secure intranets / editors, Larry Caffrey, Rogers W'O. Okut-Uma. Published/Created: London: Commonwealth Secretariat, 1999. Related Names: Caffrey, Larry. Okot-Uma, Rogers W'O. Commonwealth Secretariat. Commonwealth Network of Information Technology for Development. International Council for Information Technology in Government Administration. Description: 60 p.; 25 cm. ISBN 0850926114 Notes: On behalf of the Commonwealth Network of Information Technology (COMNET-IT) by the permission of the International Council for Information Technology in Government Administration (ICA). Subjects: Intranets (Computer networks) Electronic government information. Series: Information technology and globalisation series Dewey Class No.: 005.8 21

Govindarajan, Vijay. The quest for global dominance: transforming global presence into global competitive advantage / Vijay Govindarajan, Anil K. Gupta; woreword by C.K. Prahalad. Edition Information: 1st ed. Published/Created: San Francisco: Jossey-Bass, c2001. Related Names: Gupta, Anil K., 1949- Description: xxii, 297 p.: ill.; 24 cm. ISBN 0787957216 (alk. paper) Notes: Includes bibliographical references (p. 261-265) and index. Subjects: International business enterprises--Management. Industrial management. Organizational effectiveness Comparative advantage (International trade) Globalization--Economic aspects. Competition, International. LC Classification: HD62.4 .G68 2001 Dewey Class No.: 658/.049 21

Grady, Patrick. Seattle and beyond: the WTO millennium round / Patrick Grady.

Published/Created: Ottawa: Global Economics: International Trade Policy Consultants, 1999 Related Names: Macmillan, Kathleen, 1956- Description: xvi, 165 p.: ill.; cm. ISBN 0968621007 Notes: Includes bibliographical references (p. [160]-161) and index. Subjects: World Trade Organization. Free trade-- Environmental aspects. Free trade--Social aspects. Foreign trade regulation. Foreign trade and employment. International economic relations Globalization. LC Classification: HF1385 .G73 1999 Dewey Class No.: 382/.92 21

Graham, Edward M. (Edward Montgomery), 1944- Fighting the wrong enemy: antiglobal activists and multinational enterprises / Edward M. Graham Published/Created: Washington, DC: Institute for International Economics, 2000. Description: xvi,234 p.; 23 cm. ISBN 0881322725 (paper) Notes: Includes bibliographical references (p. 213-221) and index. Subjects: International business enterprises--Social aspects. Globalization--Social aspects. Investments, Foreign--Social aspects. Investments, Foreign (International law) Social responsibility of business. Series: Praeger special studies in U.S, economic, social, and political issues LC Classification: HD2755.5 .G722 2000 Dewey Class No.: 332.67/3 21

Graham, Stephen, 1965- Splintering urbanism: networked infrastructures, technological mobilities and the urban condition / Stephen Graham and Simon Marvin. Published/Created: New York: Routledge, 2001. Related Names: Marvin, Simon, 1963- Description: p. cm. ISBN 0415189640 0415189659 (pbk.) Notes: Includes bibliographical references and index. Subjects: Cities and towns. Infrastructure (Economics)--Computer networks. Technology--Social aspects. Globalization. Information society. LC

Classification: HT153 .G72 2001 Dewey Class No.: 307.76 21

Green, Charles (Charles St. Clair) Manufacturing powerlessness in the black diaspora: inner-city youth and the new global frontier / Charles Green. Published/Created: Walnut Creek, CA: AltaMira Press, c2001. Description: xviii, 205 p.; 23 cm. ISBN 0742502686 (alk. paper) 0742502694 (pbk.: alk. paper) Notes: Includes bibliographical references and index. Subjects: Urban youth--United States. Urban youth--Caribbean Area. Urban youth--Africa, East. African diaspora. Inner cities. Globalization--Social aspects. LC Classification: HQ796 .G723 2001 Dewey Class No.: 306.76 21

Gudeman, Stephen. The anthropology of economy: community, market, and culture / Stephen Gudeman. Published/Created: Malden, MA: Blackwell, 2001. Description: p. cm. ISBN 0631225668 (alk. paper) 0631225676 (pbk.: alk. paper) Notes: Includes bibliographical references and index. Subjects: Economic anthropology. Economic history. Globalization--Economic aspects. Capitalism Marginality, Social--Economic aspects. LC Classification: GN448.2 .G827 2001 Dewey Class No.: 306.3 21

Guiding global order: G8 governance in the twenty-first century / edited by John J. Kirton, Joseph P. Daniels, Andreas Freytag. Published/Created: Aldershot, Hampshire, England; Burlington, USA: Ashgate, c2001. Related Names: Kirton, John J. Daniels, Joseph P. Freytag, Andreas. Description: xxiii, 368 p.; 23 cm. ISBN 0754615022 Notes: Includes papers from various meetings. Includes bibliographical references and index. Subjects: Group of Eight (Organization) International economic relations. International trade. International finance.

Globalization--Economic aspects. Series: The G8 and global governance series LC Classification: HF1359 .G846 2001 Dewey Class No.: 337 21

Guillén Villalobos, José. Política indigenista y desarrollo / José Guillén Villalobos. Published/Created: Guatemala: Litografía Comgráfica, 2000. Description: 169 p.; cm. Summary: Analysis of the subordinate position of indigenous groups in Guatemala by leading economist, including the themes of economic integration, language, productive sectors, agricultural production and globalization.

Guillon, Roland. Syndicats et mondialisation: Une stratification de l'action syndicale / Roland Guillon. Published/Created: Paris: L'Harmattan, 2000. Description: 138 p.; cm. ISBN 2738493327 Subjects: Labor Unions - Globalization. Series: Logiques sociales

Gunn, Giles B. Beyond solidarity: pragmatism and difference in a globalized world / Giles Gunn. Published/Created: Chicago: University of Chicago Press, 2001. Description: xxii, 235 p.; 24 cm. ISBN 0226310639 (cloth: alk. paper) 0226310647 (pbk.: alk. paper) Notes: Includes bibliographical references (p. 197-217) and index. Subjects: Ethics. Pragmatism. Globalization--Moral and ethical aspects. LC Classification: BJ1031 .G85 2001 Dewey Class No.: 144/.3 21

Hacisalihoglu, Ya‚sar, 1964- Küreselle‚sme, mekânsal etkileri ve Istanbul / Ya‚sar Hacisalihoglu. Edition Information: 1. basim. Published/Created: Mecidiyeköy, Istanbul: Akademik Düzey Yayinevi, 2000. Description: 240 p.; 20 cm. ISBN 9758542001 Summary: Globalization; effects on; Turkey; social and economic conditions. Series: Bilimsel ara‚stirma; 1

Hadjadj, Bernard. Les parias de la mondialisation: l'Afrique en marge / Bernard Hadjadj; [avec un prologue de Frankétienne] . Published/Created: Paris; Dakar: Présence africaine, 1998. Description: 250 p.: ill., map; 23 cm. ISBN 2708706691 Notes: Includes bibliographical references (p. 219-224). Subjects: Globalization--Africa. Democratization--Bénin. Africa--Economic integration. Africa--Dependency on foreign countries. Africa--Social conditions--1960- LC Classification: HC800 .H33 1998

Halliday, Fred. The world at 2000: perils and promises / Fred Halliday. Published/Created: New York: Palgrave, 2000. Description: p. cm. ISBN 0333945344 0333945352 (pbk.) Notes: Includes bibliographical references and index. Subjects: World politics--21st century. Globalization. Democracy. Security, International. LC Classification: D2003 .H35 2000 Dewey Class No.: 909.83 21

Ham, Peter van, 1963- European integration and the postmodern condition: governance, democracy, identity / Peter van Ham. Published/Created: New York: Routledge, 2001. Description: p. cm. ISBN 0415246997 Notes: Includes bibliographical references and index. Subjects: European Union. Postmodernism--Political aspects. Globalization. Democracy. Series: Routledge advances in European politics LC Classification: JN30 .H35 2001 Dewey Class No.: 341.242/2 21

Hansen, G. Eric. The culture of strangers: globalization, localization, and the phenomenon of exchange / G. Eric Hansen. Published/Created: Lanham, MD: University Press of America, 2002. Description: p. cm. ISBN 0761822054 (pbk.: alk. paper) Notes: Includes bibliographical references and index. Subjects: Culture. Social evolution. Social systems. Exchange. Globalization. LC Classification: HM621 .H36 2002 Dewey Class No.: 306 21

Hansenne, Michel, 1940- Un garde-fou pour la mondialisation: le BIT dans l'après-guerre froide / Michel Hansenne. Published/Created: Gerpinnes [Belgium]: Quorum; Genève: Zoé, c1999. Description: 149 p.; 21 cm. ISBN 2873990716 (Quorum) 2881823661 (Zoé) Subjects: International Labour Office. Globalization. LC Classification: HD7801 .H25 1999

Harvey, Charles. The role of Africa in the global economy: the contribution of regional cooperation, with particular reference to southern Africa / by Charles Harvey. Published/Created: Gaborone, Botswana: Botswana Institute for Development Policy Analysis, [1997] Description: 17 leaves: ill.; 30 cm. Notes: "June 1997." "Paper written at the request of the Vice President and Minister of Finance and Development Planning as background for his speech to a conference organised by Partnership Africa in Sweden in June 1997." Includes bibliographical references (leaves 16-17). Subjects: Globalization--Africa, Southern. Africa, Southern--Economic integration. Series: BIDPA working paper; no. 11 LC Classification: HC900 .H37 1997

Hatzichronoglou, Thomas. Globalisation and competitiveness: relevant indicators. Published/Created: Paris: OECD, 1996. Related Names: Organisation for Economic Co-operation and Development. Description: 61 p.: ill.; 30 cm. Notes: Cover title. Includes bibliographical references (p. 56-60). Summary in English and French. Subjects: Competition, International--Econometric models. Investments,

Foreign--Econometric models. International trade--Econometric models. Series: OECD working papers; v. 4, no. 16. STI working papers; 5. LC Classification: HD72 .O38 vol. 4, no. 16

Haufler, Virginia, 1957- A public role for the private sector: industry self-regulation in a global economy / Virginia Haufler. Published/Created: [Washington, D.C.]: Carnegie Endowment for International Peace, c2000. Description: p. cm. ISBN 0870031767 (pbk.: alk. paper) Notes: Includes bibliographical references and index. Subjects: Social responsibility of business. Business ethics. International business enterprises--Moral and ethical aspects. Corporations--Moral and ethical aspects. International business enterprises--Social aspects. International business enterprises--Environmental aspects. Globalization. Labor laws and legislation. Data protection--Law and legislation. Foreign trade regulation. Environmental law. LC Classification: HD60 .H392 2000 Dewey Class No.: 174/.4 21

Haynes, Jeffrey. Politics in the developing world: a concise introduction / Jeff Haynes. Published/Created: Malden, MA: Blackwell Publishers, 2002. Description: p. cm. ISBN 0631225552 (hbk.) 0631225560 (pbk.) Contents: Politics, economics and societies in the developing world at the new millennium -- Globalisation and international relations -- Economic growth and development -- Democratisation and democracy -- Religious and ethnic conflict -- Human rights -- Women and gender -- Politics of the natural environment. Notes: Includes bibliographical references and index. Subjects: Globalization. Developing countries--Politics and government. LC Classification: JF60 .H385 2002 Dewey Class No.: 909/.097240825 21

Haynes, Jeffrey. Politics in the developing world: a concise introduction / Jeff Haynes. Published/Created: Malden, MA: Blackwell Publishers, 2002. Description: p. cm. ISBN 0631225552 (hbk.) 0631225560 (pbk.) Contents: Politics, economics and societies in the developing world at the new millennium -- Globalisation and international relations -- Economic growth and development -- Democratisation and democracy -- Religious and ethnic conflict -- Human rights -- Women and gender -- Politics of the natural environment. Notes: Includes bibliographical references and index. Subjects: Globalization. Developing countries--Politics and government. LC Classification: JF60 .H385 2002 Dewey Class No.: 909/.097240825 21

Health policy in a globalising world / edited by Kelley Lee, Kent Buse, and Suzanne Fustukian. Published/Created: New York: Cambridge University Press, 2001. Related Names: Lee, Kelley, 1962- Buse, Kent. Fustukian, Suzanne, 1953- Description: p. cm. ISBN 0521804191 052100943X (pb.) Subjects: World health. Globalization--Health aspects. Medical policy. LC Classification: RA441 .H44 2001 Dewey Class No.: 362.1 21

Hellyer, Paul, 1923- Goodbye Canada / Paul T. Hellyer. Published/Created: Toronto: Chimo Media, 2001. Description: x, 206 p.: ill.; 23 cm. ISBN 0969439482 (pbk.) Notes: Includes bibliographical references (p. 199-200) and index. Subjects: Free trade--Canada. Globalization--Economic aspects--Canada. Canada--Economic policy. Canada--Foreign economic relations. Canada--Relations--United States. LC Classification: HC115 .H458 2001

Henderson, J. W. (Jeffrey William), 1947- The globalisation of high technology production: society, space, and semiconductors in the restructuring of the modern world / Jeffrey Henderson; with a foreword by Peter Worsley. Published/Created: London; New York: Routledge, 1989. Description: xxiii, 198 p.: ill.; 23 cm. ISBN 0415031397 Notes: Includes index. Bibliography: p. 176-188. Subjects: Semiconductor industry. Electronic industries. International division of labor. Offshore assembly industry. LC Classification: HD9696.S42 H46 1989 Dewey Class No.: 338.4/762138152 19

Henry, Clement M., 1937- Globalization and the politics of economic development in the Middle East / Clement M. Henry and Robert Springborg. Published/Created: Cambridge, UK; New York, NY, USA: Cambridge University Press, 2001. Related Names: Springborg, Robert. Description: p. cm. ISBN 052162312X 0521626315 (pb.) Notes: Includes bibliographical references. Subjects: Globalization. Middle East--Economic conditions--1979- Middle East--Politics and government--1979- Series: Contemporary Middle East; 1 LC Classification: HC415.15 .H463 2001 Dewey Class No.: 338.956 21

Hernández Angueira, Luisa. Mujeres puertorriqueñas, ''welfare'' y globalización: desconstruyendo el estigma / Luisa Hernández-Angueira Published/Created: Hato Rey, Puerto Rico: Publicaciones Puertorriqueñas, Inc., 2001 Description: xxxiv, 147 p.: ill.; 22 cm. ISBN 1881720330 Notes: Includes bibliographical references (p. 127-147). Subjects: Women--Puerto Rico--Social conditions. Women--Puerto Rico--Economic conditions. Public welfare--Puerto Rico. Puerto Rican families. Puerto Rican women--United States. Women employees--Puerto Rico. Globalization. Series: Colección Temas & temas LC Classification: HQ1522 .H47 2001 Dewey

Class No.: 305.42/097295 21

Herrera Pérez, Octavio. Tamaulipas: los retos del desarrollo / Octavio Herrera Pérez ... [et al.]; coordinadores: Marco Aurelio Navarro y José Luis Pariente. Edition Information: 1a ed. Published/Created: Ciudad Victoria: Universidad Autónoma de Tamaulipas, 2000. Description: 292 p.; cm. Summary: A collection of articles on economic development and challenges in Tamaulipas, with focus on history, land organization, major economic sectors, socio-cultural issues, globalization and sustainable development. Series: Colección Misión XXI

Hills, Jill. The struggle for control of global communication: the formative century / Jill Hills. Published/Created: Urbana: University of Illinois Press, 2002. Description: p. cm. ISBN 0252027574 (alk. paper) Contents: Infrastructure and information in the United States of america -- And Britain, 1840s-1890 -- Following the flag: cable and the British government -- Wireless and the state -- The United States, trade, and communications, 1890s-1917 -- South America: prewar competition in infrastructure and -- Information -- The United States of America: competition for infrastructure -- In the interwar years -- British communications, 1919-40 -- Cultural production and international relations. Notes: Includes bibliographical references and index. Subjects: Telecommunication--History. Globalization--History. Competition, International--History. LC Classification: HE7631 .H543 2002 Dewey Class No.: 384/.09 21

Hines, Colin. Localization: a global manifesto / Colin Hines. Published/Created: London; Sterling, VA: Earthscan, 2000. Description: xiv, 290 p.; 22 cm. ISBN 1853836125 Notes: Includes bibliographical references and index. Subjects: International economic relations. Competition, International. National state. Free trade--Environmental aspects. Free trade--Social aspects. Globalization. LC Classification: HF1359 .H56 2000

Hinkelammert, Franz J. (Franz Josef), 1931- El nihilismo al desnudo: los tiempos de la globalizacio´n / Franz J. Hinkelammert. Edition Information: 1. ed. Published/Created: Santiago: LOM Ediciones, 2001. Description: 297 p.; 22 cm. Notes: Includes bibliographical references. Subjects: Globalization. Latin America--Economic policy. Latin America--Economic conditions--1982- Latin America--Social conditions--1982- Series: Colección Escafandra LC Classification: HC125 .H535 2001

Hiraoka, Leslie S., 1941- Global alliances in the motor vehicle industry / Leslie S. Hiraoka. Published/Created: Westport, Conn.: Quorum Books, 2001. Description: x, 230 p.: ill.; 24 cm. ISBN 1567203469 (alk. paper) Notes: Includes bibliographical references and index. Subjects: Motor vehicle industry-- Mergers. Strategic alliances (Business) Globalization. LC Classification: HD9710.A2 H57 2001 Dewey Class No.: 338.8/87292 21

Histories of the modern Middle East: new directions / [edited by] Israel Gershoni, Hakan Erdem, and Ursula Wokoeck. Published/Created: Boulder, Co.: Lynne Rienner Publishers, 2002. Related Names: Gershoni, I. Erdem, Y. Hakan. Wokoeck, Ursula. Description: p. cm. ISBN 1588260496 (alk. paper) Notes: Includes bibliographical references and index. Subjects: Nationalism--Middle East. National state. Globalization. Historiograpy--Middle East. Middle East- -Historiography. LC Classification:

DS61.6 .H57 2002 Dewey Class No.: 956/.007/2 21

Höffe, Otfried. Demokratie im Zeitalter der Globalisierung / Otfried Höffe. Edition Information: Originalausgabe. Published/Created: München: Beck, 1999. Description: 476 p.; 23 cm. ISBN 3406454240 Notes: Includes bibliographical references (p. [435]-460) and index. Subjects: Democracy. Globalization. LC Classification: JC423 .H738 1999

Hong Kong in transition: the handover years / edited by Robert Ash ... [et al.]. Published/Created: New York: St. Martin's Press, in association with Centre for the Study of Globalisation and Regionalisation, University of Warwick, 2000. Related Names: Ash, Robert F. Description: xx, 327 p.: ill.; 23 cm. ISBN 031223354X (cloth) Notes: Includes bibliographical references and index. Subjects: Hong Kong (China)--Economic conditions. Hong Kong (China)--Politics and government--1997- Hong Kong (China)--Social conditions. LC Classification: HC470.3 .H668 2000 Dewey Class No.: 320.95125/09/049 21

Hoós, János. Globalisation, multinational corporation, and economics / János Hoós. Published/Created: Budapest: Akadémiai Kiadó, c2000. Description: 261 p.: ill.; 24 cm. ISBN 9630577062 Notes: Includes bibliographical references and index. Subjects: International business enterprises. Corporations, Foreign. Globalization. Economic development. Economic policy. LC Classification: HD2755.5 .H655 2000

Hoós, János. Globalisation, multinational corporation, and economics / János Hoós. Published/Created: Budapest: Akadémiai Kiadó, c2000. Description: 261 p.: ill.; 24 cm. ISBN 9630577062 Notes: Includes bibliographical references and index. Subjects: International business enterprises. Corporations, Foreign. Globalization. Economic development. Economic policy. LC Classification: HD2755.5 .H655 2000

Horman, Denis. Mondialisation excluante, nouvelles solidarités: Soumettre ou démettre l'OMC / Denis Horman. Published/Created: Paris: Harmattan; Genève: Centre Europe-Tiers monde; Bruxelles: Groupe de recherche pour une stratégie économique alternative, 2001. Description: 155 p.; cm. ISBN 2747502325 2880530296 Subjects: Globalization - International Market. Series: Alternatives

Horowitz, Leonard G. Death in the air: globalism, terrorism & toxic warfare / Leonard G. Horowitz. Published/Created: Sandpoint, Idaho: Tetrahedron, c2001. Description: xx, 526 p., [16] leaves of plates: ill. (some col.), maps; 24 cm. ISBN 0923550305 Notes: Includes bibliographical references and index. Subjects: Biological warfare World health. Toxins. Poisons. Vaccination--Complications. Birth control. Population policy. Globalization. Propaganda.

Hotz-Hart, Beat. Wissen als Chance: Globalisierung als Herausforderung für die Schweiz / Beat Hotz-Hart, Carsten Küchler. Published/Created: Chur: Rüegger, c1999. Related Names: Küchler, Carsten. Description: 143 p.: ill.; 21 cm. Notes: Includes bibliographical references (p. 133-139). Subjects: Globalization. Switzerland--Economic conditions--1945- Switzerland--Economic policy. Switzerland--Foreign economic relations. LC Classification: HC397 .H728 1999 Dewey Class No.: 337.494 21

Houée, Paul. Le développement local au défi de la mondialisation / Paul Houée; préface de Mamadou Dia. Published/Created: Paris: Harmattan, 2001. Description: 249 p.; cm. ISBN 2747514110 Subjects: Economic Development and Globalization. Series: Questions contemporaines

How might we live?: global ethics in a new century / [edited by Ken Booth, Tim Dunne & Michael Cox]. Published/Created: Cambridge, UK; New York, NY: Cambridge University Press, 2001. Related Names: Booth, Ken, 1943- Dunne, Timothy, 1965- Cox, Michael, 1947- Description: ix, 237 p.; 25 cm. ISBN 0521005205 (paperback) Notes: Includes bibliographical references and index. Subjects: Ethics. Globalization--Moral and ethical aspects. LC Classification: BJ1031 .H78 2001 Dewey Class No.: 172/.4 21

Howell, David, 1936- The edge of now: new questions for democracy in the network age / David Howell. Published/Created: London: Macmillan, c2000. Description: xxiv, 392 p.; 25 cm. ISBN 0333782232 Notes: Includes bibliographical references and index. Subjects: Information technology--Economic aspects. Information technology--Social aspects. Information society. Privatization. Democracy. Globalization. International economic relations. LC Classification: HC79.I55 .H69 2000 Dewey Class No.: 303.48/33 21

Howells, Jeremy, 1956- The globalisation of production and technology / Jeremy Howells and Michelle Wood. Published/Created: London; New York: Belhaven Press; New York: Halsted Press, 1993. Related Names: Wood, Michelle. FAST (Program) Description: viii, 192 p.: ill., maps; 24 cm. ISBN 1852932856 (Uk) 0470221046 (US) Notes: "A report prepared for the Commission of the European Communities, Directorate-

General for Science, Research and Development, as part of the Monitor-FAST Programme (Forecasting and Assessment in the Field of Science and Technology)"--P. opp. t.p. Includes bibliographical references (p. [170]-183) and index. Subjects: International business enterprises. International economic integration. Diffusion of innovations. Research, Industrial. Production management--Technological innovations--Case studies. LC Classification: HD2755.5 .H69 1993 Dewey Class No.: 338.8/8 20

Huerta González, Arturo. La globalización, causa de la crisis asiática y mexicana / Arturo Huerta G. Edition Information: 1. ed. Published/Created: México: Editorial Diana, 1998. Description: xvii, 180 p.: ill.; 21 cm. ISBN 9681331397 Notes: Includes bibliographical references. Subjects: Globalization. International economic relations. Financial crises--Effect of globalization on--Asia, Southeastern. Financial crises--Effect of globalization on--Mexico. Asia, Southeastern--Economic policy. Mexico--Economic policy--1994- LC Classification: HC135 .H848 1998 Dewey Class No.: 330.9/049 21

Human geography: issues for the twenty-first century / edited by Peter Daniels ... [et al.]. Published/Created: Upper Saddle River, NJ: Prentice Hall, 2001. Related Names: Daniels, Peter (Peter W.) Description: p. cm. ISBN 0582367999 Notes: Includes bibliographical references and index. Subjects: Human geography. Human geography--Economic aspects. Globalization--Economic aspects. LC Classification: GF21 .H85 2001 Dewey Class No.: 304.2 21

Human resource implications of globalization and restructuring in commerce: report for discussion at the Tripartite Meeting on the Human Resource Implications of Globalization and Restructuring in Commerce, Geneva, 1999 / International Labour Organization, Sectoral Activities Programme. Published/Created: Geneva: ILO, 1999. Related Names: International Labour Organisation. Sectoral Activities Programme. Tripartite Meeting on the Human Resource Implications of Globalization and Restructuring in Commerce (1999: Geneva, Switzerland) Description: xi, 113 p.: graphs, tables; 30 cm. ISBN 9221117618 Notes: Includes bibliographical references (p. 91). Subjects: International trade. International trade--Social aspects. Consolidation and merger of corporations. Consolidation and merger of corporations--Social aspects. Globalization--Economic aspects. Globalization--Social aspects. Competition. Labor market. Labor supply. LC Classification: HF1371 .H86 1999

Humphrey, John, 1950- Corporate restructuring: Crompton Greaves and the challenge of globalisation / John Humphrey, Raphael Kaplinsky, Prasad V. Saraph, with T.S. Chandrashekhar, Ramesh Datta, Narayan Rangaraj. Published/Created: New Delhi; Thousand Oaks, Calif.: Response Books, 1998. Related Names: Kaplinsky, Raphael. Saraph, Prasad V., 1971- Description: 273 p.: ill.; 25 cm. ISBN 8170367107 (India: HB) 0761992545 (US: HB) Notes: Includes bibliographical references (p. [262]-267) and index. Subjects: Crompton Greaves (Firm)--Reorganization. Corporate reorganizations--India--Case studies. LC Classification: HD2746.55.I4 H86 1998 Dewey Class No.: 658.1/6/0954 21

Hussein Haji Ahmad. Mandat UNESCO dan cabaran globalisasi / Hussein Hj. Ahmad. Published/Created: Kuala Lumpur: Utusan Publications & Distributors, 2001. Description: xxiii, 362 p., [14] p. of plates: ill.; 23 cm. ISBN 9676111279 Summary: Role of Unesco in the development of Malaysia and the globalization. Notes: Includes bibliographical references (p. 345-352). In Malay.

Huws, Ursula. Teleworking and globalisation / Ursula Huws, Nick Jagger, and Siobhan O'Regan. Published/Created: Brighton: Institute for Emploment Studies, 1999. Related Names: Jagger, Nick. O'Regan, S. Description: xiv, 103 p.; 28 cm. ISBN 185184287X Notes: Includes bibliographical references (p. 97-103). Subjects: Telecommuting. Globalization--Economic aspects. Home labor. Series: Report (Institute for Employment Studies); no. 358. LC Classification: HD2336.3 .H88 1999

Huws, Ursula. Teleworking and globalisation / Ursula Huws, Nick Jagger, and Siobhan O'Regan. Published/Created: Brighton: Institute for Emploment Studies, 1999. Related Names: Jagger, Nick. O'Regan, S. Description: xiv, 103 p.; 28 cm. ISBN 185184287X Notes: Includes bibliographical references (p. 97-103). Subjects: Telecommuting. Globalization--Economic aspects. Home labor. Series: Report (Institute for Employment Studies); no. 358. LC Classification: HD2336.3 .H88 1999

Identity in transformation: postmodernity, postcommunism, and globalization / edited by Marian Kempny and Aldona Jawlowska. Published/Created: Westport, Conn.: Praeger, 2002. Related Names: Kempny, Marian. Jawlowska, Aldona. Description: p. cm. ISBN 0275975452 (alk. paper) Notes: Includes bibliographical references and index. Subjects: Group identity--Europe. Identity (Psychology)--Europe. Social change--Europe. Postmodernism--Europe. Post-communism--Europe. Globalization. LC

Classification: HN373.5 I3297 2002 Dewey Class No.: 302.4/094 21

Ietto-Gillies, Grazia. Transnational corporations: fragmentation amidst integration / Grazia Ietto-Gillies. Published/Created: New York: Routledge, 2001. Description: p. cm. ISBN 0415148235 Notes: Includes bibliographical references and index. Subjects: International business enterprises--Management. Business networks. International economic integration. Globalization--Economic aspects. LC Classification: HD62.4 .I39 2001 Dewey Class No.: 658/.049 21

Ife, J. W. (James William), 1946- Community development: community-based alternatives in an age of globalisation / Jim Ife. Edition Information: 2nd ed. Published/Created: Frenchs Forest, NSW: Pearson Education Australia, 2002. Description: xiv, 309 p.: ill.; 24 cm. ISBN 0733999018 Notes: Previous ed.: Longman, 1995. Includes index. Bibliography: p. [291]-302. Subjects: Community development. Community organization. Community development--Citizen participation. Social service--Citizen participation.

Iglesias, Fernando A. República de la tierra: globalización: el fin de las modernidades nacionales / Fernando A. Iglesias. Published/Created: Buenos Aires, Argentina: Colihue, [2000] Description: 443 p.; 22 cm. ISBN 9505811977 Notes: Includes bibliographical references (p. 439-443). Subjects: Globalization World politics--1989- Series: Puñaladas LC Classification: JZ1318 .I45 2000 Dewey Class No.: 303.48/2 21

Iguíñiz, Javier. Caminando por el borde: el Perú en la globalización / Javier Iguíñiz Echeverría. Published/Created: Lima: Instituto Bartolomé de las Casas-Rímac:

CEP, Centro de Estudios y Publicaciones, 1999. Description: 188 p.; 21 cm. ISBN 9972816044 Subjects: Globalization. International economic relations. Peru--Economic conditions--1968- Series: CEP (Series: Lima, Peru); 209. LC Classification: HC227 .I3645 1999

Ihminen ja kulttuuri: suomalainen kansainvälistyvässä maailmassa / [tekijät, Olli Alho ... et al.]. Edition Information: 4. painos. Published/Created: Helsinki: FINTRA, 1996. Related Names: Alho, Olli. Description: 141 p.: ill.; 25 cm. ISBN 9518334552 Notes: Includes bibliographical references. Subjects: National characteristics, Finnish. International relations and culture--Finland. Globalization--Social aspects--Finland. Globalization--Economic aspects--Finland. Finland--Relations--Foreign countries. Series: Fintra-julkaisu, 0786-9517; nro 72 LC Classification: DL1046 .I38 1996

Impact of globalisation [microform]: women, work, living environment, and health. Published/Created: Mumbai: CEHAT, [1999?] Related Names: Centre for Enquiry into Health & Allied Themes (Bombay, India) Description: 153, 10, iv p.; 30 cm. Summary: In the Indian context. Notes: Includes statistical tables. Includes bibliographical references. Microfiche. New Delhi: Library of Congress Office; Washington, D.C.: Library of Congress Photoduplication Service, 2001. 3 microfiches. Master microform held by: DLC. Subjects: Women employees--India. Women--Health and hygiene--India. LC Classification: Microfiche 2001/60213 (H)

In search of boundaries: communication, nation-states and cultural identities / edited by Joseph M. Chan and Bryce T. McIntyre. Published/Created: Westport, CT: Ablex Pub., 2001. Related Names: Chan, Joseph Man. McIntyre, Bryce Telfer. Description: p. cm. ISBN 1567505708 (alk. paper) 1567505716 (pbk.: alk. paper) Notes: Includes bibliographical references. Subjects: Mass media. Group identity. Boundaries. Globalization. Series: Advances in communication and culture LC Classification: HM1206 .I5 2001 Dewey Class No.: 302.23 21

Indian economy after 50 years of independence: experiences and challenges / edited by Debendra Kumar Das. Published/Created: New Delhi: Deep & Deep Publications, c1998. Related Names: Das, Debendra Kumar, 1947- Description: 5 v.; 23 cm. ISBN 8176290564 (set) Summary: Contributed articles. Contents: 1. Globalisation and development -- 2. Trade and development -- 3. Financial sector reforms, tax system, and development -- 4. Social sector and development -- 5. Rural sector and development. Notes: Includes bibliographical references and indexes.

Indigenous cultures in an interconnected world / edited by Clair Smith and Graeme K. Ward. Published/Created: Vancouver: UBC Press, 2000. Related Names: Smith, Claire. Ward, Graeme K. Description: xvii, 230 p.: ill., ports.; 22 cm. ISBN 0774808063 Subjects: Indigenous peoples. Globalization--Social aspects. Autochtones. Mondialisation--Aspect social. LC Classification: GN380 .I52 2000b

Indigenous cultures in an interconnected world / edited by Claire Smith and Graeme K. Ward. Published/Created: St Leonards, N.S.W.: Allen & Unwin, 2000. Related Names: Ward, Graeme, 1943- Smith, Claire, 1957- Description: xvii, 230 p.: ill. , map, ports.; 22 cm. ISBN 186448926X Notes: Includes index. "A collection based on the 1997 Fulbright Symposium of the same name, which brought together indigenous and non-indigenous experts across a range of disciplines and four continents". Bibliography. Subjects: Indigenous peoples--Congresses. Globalization--Congresses. Ethnicity--Congresses. Series: Australian Fulbright papers; no. 5 LC Classification: GN380 .I52 2000 Dewey Class No.: 305.8 21

Individual community nation: fifty years of Australian citizenship / edited by Kim Rubenstein. Published/Created: Melbourne [Australia]; Australian Scholarly Publishing [c2000] Description: xxiv, 194 p.: ill.; 21 cm. ISBN 1875606823 Notes: Includes bibliographical references and index. Subjects: Citizenship. Citizenship--Australia. Citizenship--Social aspects. Civil rights--Australia. Globalization. Nationalism--Australia.

Inequality, globalization, and world politics / edited by Andrew Hurrell and Ngaire Woods. Published/Created: Oxford; New York: Oxford University Press, 1999. Related Names: Hurrell, Andrew. Woods, Ngaire. Description: ix, 353 p.; 23 cm. ISBN 0198295677 (hbk.: alk. paper) 0198295669 (pbk.: alk. paper) Notes: Includes bibliographical references (p. [273]-333) and index. Subjects: International relations. Equality of states. World politics--1989- Globalization. LC Classification: JZ1305 .I54 1999 Dewey Class No.: 327 21

Information sharing between and within governments: study group report / edited by Larry Caffrey. Published/Created: London: Commonwealth Secretariat, 1998. Related Names: Caffrey, Larry. Description: vi, 72 p.: ill.; 24 cm. ISBN 085092555X Notes: Includes bibliographical references. Subjects: Information resources management.

Government information. Series: Information technology & globalisation series. LC Classification: T58.64 .I5337 1998 Dewey Class No.: 352.3/8143 21

Innovation policy in a global economy / edited by Daniele Archibugi, Jeremy Howells and Jonathan Michie. Published/Created: Cambridge, England; New York: Cambridge University Press, 1999. Related Names: Archibugi, Daniele. Howells, Jeremy, 1956- Michie, Jonathan. Description: xvi, 278 p.: ill.; 23 cm. ISBN 0521633613 (pbk.) 0521633273 Subjects: Technological innovations--Economic aspects--Congresses. Technology and state--Congresses. LC Classification: HC79.T4 I5477 1999

International banking in an age of transition: globalisation, automation, banks and their archives / edited by Sara Kinsey and Lucy Newton. Published/Created: Aldershot; Brookfield, VT: Ashgate, c1998. Related Names: Kinsey, Sara, 1969- Newton, Lucy. Description: xii, 196 p.; 24 cm. ISBN 1859283845 (hbk.: acid-free) Notes: Includes index. Subjects: Banks and banking--Europe--History. Banks and banking--Technological innovations. LC Classification: HG2974 .I48 1998 Dewey Class No.: 332.1/094 21

International encyclopedia of the stock market / editor, Michael Sheimo; associate editor, Andreas Loizou; executive editor, Alison Aves; picture editor, Antonia Boström. Published/Created: Chicago: Fitzroy Dearborn Publishers, c1999. Related Names: Sheimo, Michael D., 1944- Loizou, Andreas. Fitzroy Dearborn Publishers. Description: 2 v.: ill.; 29 cm. ISBN 1884964354 Review: "The first major work of its kind to discuss international stock markets, this encyclopedia is essential for anyone interested in investing in today's global markets. Because of the increasing globalization of businesses, American investors can no longer limit themselves to information about the U.S. stock market. These two volumes define over 2,000 terms dealing with the history and practices of international stock markets in industrialized as well as developing countries, and discuss individuals, institutions (such as banks, brokerage and leveraged buyout firms), events, and slang terms relating to stock markets. The readable entries provide accurate, up-to-date information of interest to the burgeoning number of private and professional investors. This work is a valuable addition to school, public, and academic library collections."-- "Outstanding reference sources 2000", American Libraries, May 2000. Comp. by the Reference Sources Committee, RUSA, ALA. Contents: v. 1. A through L -- v. 2. M through Z. Notes: Includes bibliographical references and indexes. Subjects: Stock exchanges-- Encyclopedias. LC Classification: HG4551 .I528 1999 Dewey Class No.: 332.64/2/03 21

International public policy and regionalism at the turn of the century / [edited by] Khosrow Fatemi. Edition Information: 1st ed. Published/Created: Amsterdam; New York: Pergamon, 2001. Related Names: Fatemi, Khosrow. Description: xxiii, 423 p.: ill.; 24 cm. ISBN 0080438857 (hardcover: alk. paper) Notes: Includes bibliographical references and index. Subjects: Policy sciences. Globalization. Series: Series in international business and economics LC Classification: H97 .I579 2001 Dewey Class No.: 320/.6 21

International security in a global age: securing the twenty-first century / edited by Clive Jones and Caroline Kennedy-Pipe. Published/Created: London; Portland, OR: F. Cass, 2000. Related Names: Jones, Clive, 1965- Kennedy-Pipe, Caroline,

1961- Description: xiv, 213 p.; 24 cm. ISBN 0714650617 (cloth) 0714681113 (paper) Notes: Includes bibliographical references (p. [205]-208) and index. Subjects: Security, International. Globalization. LC Classification: JZ5588 .I579 2000 Dewey Class No.: 327.1/72 21

International Seminar the Economic and Financial Imperatives of Globalization: an Islamic response, 8-9 April, 1999: [papers] / organised by Institute of Islamic Understanding. Published/Created: [Kuala Lumpur]: Institute of Islamic Understanding Malaysia, [1999] Description: 1 v. (various foliations); 30 cm. Notes: Cover title. Includes bibliographical references. LC Classification: MLCM 98/00299 (H)

Internationaler Wettbewerb, nationale Sozialpolitik?: wirtschaftsethische und moralökonomische Perspektiven der Globalisierung / herausgegeben von Detlef Aufderheide und Martin Dabrowski; in Verbindung mit Karl Homann ... [et al.]. Published/Created: Berlin: Duncker & Humblot, c2000. Related Names: Aufderheide, Detlef. Dabrowski, Martin, 1965- Homann, Karl. Description: 306 p.: ill.; 24 cm. ISBN 3428098099 (alk. paper) Notes: Papers of a conference held at the Akademie Franz Hitze Haus in Münster, 1999. Includes bibliographical references. Subjects: International economic relations-- Congresses. Globalization--Moral and ethical aspects--Congresses. Social policy--Congresses. Series: Volkswirtschaftliche Schriften, 0505-9372; Heft 500 LC Classification: HF1352 .I62 2000

Internationalization of the economy and environmental policy options / Paul J.J. Welfens, editor. Published/Created: Berlin; New York: Springer, c2001. Related Names: Welfens, Paul J. J.

Description: xiv, 442 p.: ill.; 24 cm. ISBN 3540421742 (alk. paper) Notes: Includes bibliographical references. Subjects: United Nations Framework Convention on Climate Change (1992). Protocols, etc., 1997 Dec. 11. Environmental policy-- Economic aspects. Air pollution. Globalization. LC Classification: HC79.E5 I623 2001 Dewey Class No.: 333.7 21

Iracheta Carroll, Jimena del Carmen. Las grandes ciudades en el contexto de la globalización: el caso de la zona metropolitana del Valle de México / Jimena del Carmen Iracheta Carroll. Edition Information: 1. ed. Published/Created: Toluca: Universidad Autónoma del Estado de México, 2001. Description: 225 p.; cm. ISBN 9688356239 Summary: A scholarly study of the process and impact of globalization on one of the most populated urban centers of Mexico. Series: Tésis Universitarias

Irarrázaval, Diego. Teología en la fe del pueblo / Diego Irarrázaval. Edition Information: 1a ed. Published/Created: San José: Departamento Ecuménico de Investigaciones (DEI), 1999. Description: 323 p.; cm. ISBN 9977831203 Summary: Theological and sociological essays on the role of religion in society, cultural change, globalization, popular movement, women, religious holidays and the ecumenical movement, with focus on Latin America.

Irwin, Douglas A., 1962- Free trade under fire / Douglas A. Irwin. Published/Created: Princeton, NJ: Princeton University Press, 2002. Description: p. cm. ISBN 0691088438 (cl.: alk. paper) Notes: Includes bibliographical references and index. Subjects: Free trade--United States. Globalization. United States--Commercial policy. LC Classification: HF1756 .I68

2002 Dewey Class No.: 382/.71 21

Ishak Shari. Bumi semua manusia: menangani ketidaksetaraan ekonomi dalam arus globalisasi / Ishak Shari. Edition Information: Cet. 1. Published/Created: Bangi: Penerbit Universiti Kebangsaan Malaysia, 1999. Description: 66 p.; 23 cm. ISBN 9679424510 Summary: Developing countries and international economic relations. Notes: Includes bibliographical references (p. [59]-63). In Malay, with summary in English. Subjects: Globalization. International economic relations. Developing countries- -Foreign economic relations. Series: Syarahan perdana. LC Classification: JZ1318 .I84 1999

Issues, challenges, and strategies. Published/Created: Quezon City, Philippines: GABRIELA, [1999] Related Names: Gabriela (Organization: Manila, Philippines) Description: 52 p.; 23 cm. Contents: Building women's unity and solidarity against globalization / Mary John Mananzan -- Strategies of the women's movement in fighting imperialist globalization / Liza Largoza Maza -- Women workers organize and take action against globalization / Nanette Miranda- Tampico -- Peasant women struggles in the Philippines / Carmen Buena and Catarina Estavillo -- Women students live up to a legacy of militant struggle / Maricel Gavina -- The limits of gender mainstreaming / Judy Taguiwalo -- All women unity statement. Notes: "Selected speeches and articles on globalization, Gabriela, March 8, 1999"--Cover. Subjects: Women in politics--Philippines. Globalization. Philippines--Economic conditions--1986- LC Classification: HQ1236.5.P6 I87 1999

Isu-isu pembangunan di awal abad ke-21 / editor, Mohd. Yusof Hussain, Nor Azizan Idris, Lukman Z. Mohamad. Edition

Information: Cet. 1. Published/Created: Bangi: Fakulti Sains Pembangunan, Universiti Kebangsaan Malaysia, 2000. Related Names: Mohd. Yusof Hussain. Nor Azizan Idris. Lukman Z. Mohamad. Description: 176 p.: ill., maps; 23 cm. ISBN 9839152904 Summary: Development issues in Malaysia towards the 21st century; papers of seminar. Notes: Continues: Globalisasi. Includes bibliographical references and index. In Malay. Subjects: Globalization--Economic aspects--Malaysia. Malaysia--Economic policy. Malaysia--Economic conditions. LC Classification: HC445.5 .I854 2000

Jain, Prakash Chandra, 1958- Globalisation and tribal economy / P.C. Jain. Published/Created: Jaipur: Rawat Publications, 2001. Description: 178 p.; 22 cm. ISBN 8170336597 Summary: Field study has been conducted among the tribals of South Rajasthan to link tribal sustenance economy for global exposure. Notes: Includes bibliographical references (p. [171]-174) and index.

Jalfen, Luis Jorge, 1940- Globalización y lógica virtual / Luis Jorge Jalfen. Published/Created: Buenos Aires, Argentina: Ediciones Corregidor, c1998. Description: 171 p.; 20 cm. ISBN 9500511215 Subjects: Social change. Philosophy, Modern. Globalization. Technological innovations. LC Classification: HM621 .J34 1998 Dewey Class No.: 303.4 21

James, Harold. The end of globalization: lessons from the Great Depression / Harold James. Published/Created: Cambridge, Mass.: Harvard University Press, 2001. Description: vi, 260 p.: ill.; 25 cm. ISBN 0674004744 (alk. paper) Notes: Includes bibliographical references (p. 227-254) and index. Subjects: International economic relations. International trade. International finance. Depressions--1929. Financial crises. National state. Globalization--Economic aspects. LC Classification: HF1359 .J36 2001 Dewey Class No.: 337 21

James, Jeffrey. Technology, globalization and poverty / Jeffrey James. Published/Created: Cheltenham, UK; Northampton, MA, USA: E. Elgar Pub., 2002. Description: p. cm. ISBN 1840644842 Notes: Includes bibliographical references an dindex. Subjects: Poverty--Developing countries. Globalization--Economic aspects--Developing countries. Technological innovations--Economic aspects--Developing countries. LC Classification: HC59.72.P6 J36 2002 Dewey Class No.: 337 21

Jha, Avinash. Background to globalisation / Avinash Jha. Published/Created: Mumbai: Centre for Education & Documentation, 2000. Related Names: Centre for Education and Documentation (Bombay, India) Description: 180 p.; 23 cm. Notes: Includes bibliographical references (p. 174-177).

Jhunjhunwala, Bharat. Welfare state and globalization: a critique of Amartya Sen / Bharat Jhunjhunwala. Published/Created: Jaipur: Rawat Publications, c2000. Description: 406 p.; 23 cm. Notes: Includes bibliographical references (p. [392]-399) and index. Subjects: Welfare state. State, The. Globalization. LC Classification: JC479 .J48 2000

Jones, E. L. (Eric Lionel) The record of global economic development / Eric Jones. Published/Created: Northampton, MA: Edward Elgar Pub., 2002. Description: p. cm. ISBN 1840648066 Notes: Includes bibliographical references and index. Subjects: Economic development. Economic development--Social aspects.

Economic development--Environmental aspects. Globalization--Economic aspects. LC Classification: HD75 .J664 2002 Dewey Class No.: 338.9 21

Jones, R. J. Barry. Globalisation and interdependence in the international political economy: rhetoric and reality / R.J. Barry Jones. Published/Created: London; New York: Pinter Publishers; New York: Distributed in the USA & Canada by St. Martin's Press, 1995. Description: vii, 249 p.: ill.; 24 cm. ISBN 1855670577 Notes: Includes bibliographical references (p. [229]-241) and index. Subjects: International trade. International economic relations. LC Classification: HF1379 .J66 1995 Dewey Class No.: 337 20

Jones, Ronald Winthrop, 1931- Globalization and the theory of input trade / Ronald W. Jones. Published/Created: Cambridge, Mass.: MIT Press, c2000. Description: x, 177 p.: ill.; 21 cm. ISBN 026210086X (alk. paper) Notes: Includes bibliographical references (p. [163]-170) and index. Subjects: International trade. Globalization. Input-output analysis. Factor proportions. Heckscher-Ohlin principle. Series: The Ohlin lectures; 8 LC Classification: HF1379 .J664 2000 Dewey Class No.: 382 21

Junk APEC [videorecording]. Published/Created: [Diliman, Quezon City: AsiaVisions Media Foundation?, 1997?] Description: 1 videocassette of 1 (VHS): sd., col.; 1/2 in. viewing copy. Summary: A Philippine video documentary on the people struggle against APEC and globalization. LC Classification: VAG 7957 (viewing copy)

Kankwenda Mbaya. Marabouts ou marchands du développement en Afrique? / Mbaya Kankwenda; préface de Samir Amin. Published/Created: Paris; Montréal:

L'Harmattan, c2000. Related Names: Amin, Samir. Description: 319 p.; 22 cm. ISBN 2738492193 Notes: Includes bibliographical references (p. 311-314). Subjects: Capitalism--Africa. Economic assistance--Africa. Globalization--Africa. Africa--Economic conditions--1960- Africa--Economic policy. Series: Collection Economie et innovation LC Classification: HC800 .K358 2000

Kasper, Wolfgang. Building prosperity: Australia's future as a global player / Wolfgang Kasper. Published/Created: St Leonards, N.S.W.: Centre for Independent Studies, 2000. Related Names: Centre for Independent Studies (N.S.W.) Description: xxv, 118 p.: 24 cm. ISBN 1864320532 (pbk.) Summary: The author argues that periods of plenty are the best time to prepare for eventualities by cutting back on unnecessary government activity and placing economic freedom on more solid foundations. He warns that the present phase of high worldwide economic growth is likely to peter out before too long. Notes: Includes index. Bibliography. Subjects: Economic forecasting--Australia. Globalization. Australia--Economic conditions. Australia--Economic policy. Australia--Foreign economic relations. LC Classification: HC605 .K3293 2000 Dewey Class No.: 330.994 21

Katsioloudes, Marios I. Global strategic planning: cultural perspectives for profit and nonprofit organizations / Marios I. Katsioloudes. Published/Created: Boston: Butterworth-Heinemann, 2002. Description: p. cm. ISBN 075067413X (alk. paper) Notes: Includes bibliographical references and index. Subjects: Strategic planning. Nonprofit organizations. Globalization. LC Classification: HD30.28 .K3755 2002 Dewey Class No.: 658.4/012 21

Keet, Dot. Globalisation and regionalisation: contradictory tendencies, counteractive tactics, or strategic possibilities? / Dot Keet. Published/Created: Braamfontein: Foundation for Global Dialogue, [1999] Description: 42 p.; 30 cm. ISBN 1919697381 Notes: "April 1999." Includes bibliographical references (p. 40-42). Subjects: International economic integration. Globalization. Regionalism. Series: FGD occasional paper; no. 18 LC Classification: HF1418.5 .K44 1999 Dewey Class No.: 337 21

Keet, Dot. Globalisation and regionalisation: contradictory tendencies, counteractive tactics, or strategic possibilities? / Dot Keet. Published/Created: Braamfontein: Foundation for Global Dialogue, [1999] Description: 42 p.; 30 cm. ISBN 1919697381 Notes: "April 1999." Includes bibliographical references (p. 40-42). Subjects: International economic integration. Globalization. Regionalism. Series: FGD occasional paper; no. 18 LC Classification: HF1418.5 .K44 1999 Dewey Class No.: 337 21

Keet, Dot. Integrating the world community: political challenges and opportunities for developing countries / Dot Keet. Published/Created: Bellville, South Africa: Centre for Southern African Studies, 1998. Description: 52 p.: ill.; 25 cm. ISBN 1868084140 Notes: Includes bibliographical references (p. 46-48). Subjects: International economic integration. Globalization. World politics--1989- Developing countries--Foreign relations. Series: Southern African perspectives; no. 70 LC Classification: HF1418.5 .K443 1998

Kelley-Lainé, Kathleen. Contes cruels de la mondialisation / Kathleen Kelley-Lainé, Dominique Rousset. Published/Created: Paris: Bayard, 2001. Related Names: Rousset, Dominique. Description: 139 p.;

cm. ISBN 2227137835 Subjects: Globalization - Essay.

Kelly, Paul, 1947- Paradise divided: the changes, the challenges, the choices for Australia / Paul Kelly. Published/Created: St Leonards, N.S.W.: Allen & Unwin, 2000. Description: viii, 296 p.; 23 cm. ISBN 1865082910 Notes: Includes index. Subjects: Globalization. Australia--Politics and government--1990- Australia--Social conditions--1990- LC Classification: IN PROCESS

Kelsey, Jane. Reclaiming the future: New Zealand and the global economy / Jane Kelsey. Published/Created: Wellington: Bridget Williams Books, 1999. Description: 430 p.: ill.; 23 cm. ISBN 1877242012 Notes: Includes bibliographical references (p. [417]-424) and index. Subjects: International economic relations. Globalization--Economic aspects--New Zealand. New Zealand--Foreign economic relations. LC Classification: HF1642.5 .K45 1999 Dewey Class No.: 337.93 21

Kennes, Walter, 1949- Small developing countries and global markets: competing in the big league / Walter Kennes. Published/Created: New York: St. Martin's Press, 2000. Description: xii, 201 p.; 23 cm. ISBN 0312233582 (cloth) Notes: Includes bibliographical references (p. 188-194) and index. Subjects: States, Small--Economic integration. Globalization. International economic integration. Developing countries--Economic integration. LC Classification: HC59.7 .K386 2000 Dewey Class No.: 337.1/724 21

Kerr, D. J. C. (Duncan James Colquhoun) Elect the ambassador!: building democracy in a globalised world / Duncan Kerr. Published/Created: Annandale, N.S.W.: Pluto Press, 2001. Description:

ix, 194 p.; 22 cm. ISBN 1864031328
Notes: Includes bibliographical references
(p. 182-185) and index. Subjects:
Democracy. Globalization. International
economic relations--Social aspects.
International finance--Social aspects.

Keyman, Emin Fuat. Globalization, state,
identity/difference: toward a critical social
theory of international relations / E. Fuat
Keyman. Published/Created: Atlantic
Highlands, N.J.: Humanities Press, 1997.
Description: ix, 224 p.; 24 cm. ISBN
0391039954 (cloth) 0391039962 (pbk.)
Notes: Includes bibliographical references
and index. Subjects: International
relations--Philosophy. Critical theory.
Globalization. LC Classification: JZ1251
.K49 1997 Dewey Class No.: 327 20

Keynes, uncertainty and the global economy:
beyond Keynes volume two / edited by
Sheila Dow and John Hillard.
Published/Created: Cheltenham, UK;
Northampton, MA, USA: E. Elgar Pub.,
2002. Related Names: Dow, Sheila C.
Hillard, John, 1946- Description: p. cm.
ISBN 1858987970 Notes: "In association
with the Post-Keynesian Economics Study
Group." Includes bibliographical
references and index. Subjects: Keynes,
John Maynard, 1883-1946. Keynesian
economics. Macroeconomics.
Microeconomics. Economic policy.
Economic history--20th century.
Economic forecasting. Uncertainty.
Competition. Labor economics.
International finance. Globalization--
Economic aspects. LC Classification:
HB99.7.K38 K485 2002 Dewey Class
No.: 330.1 21

Khan, Azizur Rahman. Inequality and poverty
in China in the age of globalization /
Azizur Rahman Khan, Carl Riskin.
Published/Created: Oxford; New York:
Oxford University Press, c2001. Related
Names: Riskin, Carl. Description: xi, 184

p.: ill.; 25 cm. ISBN 0195136497 (alk.
paper) Notes: Includes bibliographical
references (p. 175-179) and index.
Subjects: Poverty--China. Equality--
China. Globalization. LC Classification:
HC430.P6 K45 2001 Dewey Class No.:
339.5/0951 21

Khor, Kok Peng. Krisis ekonomi Asia Timur:
komentar dan analisis / Khor Kok Peng.
Published/Created: Pulau Pinang,
Malaysia: Persatuan Pengguna Pulau
Pinang, [1998?] Description: 90 p.: ill.; 19
cm. Summary: Globalization and the
economic crises in Asia; collection of
articles. Notes: In Malay. Subjects:
Financial crises--Asia. Globalization.
Asia--Foreign economic relations. LC
Classification: HB3808 .K56 1998

Khor, Kok Peng. The global South: a blueprint
for action / Martin Khor.
Published/Created: New York: Zed
Books: Distributed in the United States by
Palgrave, 2001. Description: p. cm. ISBN
1842770543 1842770551 Notes: Includes
bibliographical references and index.
Subjects: International economic
relations. Globalization. Developing
countries--Foreign economic relations.
Series: Global issues series (New York,
N.Y.: 1999) LC Classification: HF1413
.K454 2001 Dewey Class No.:
337/.09172/4 21

Kim, T`ae-won, 1953- Han'guk hyondae
munhwa ui hyangbang: 1985-yon ihu /
Kim T`ae-won chium. Edition
Information: Ch`op`an.
Published/Created: Soul-si: Hyondae
Mihaksa, 2000. Description: 476 p.: ill.;
23 cm. ISBN 8977271495 Notes: Includes
index. Subjects: Arts--Korea (South)--
History. International relations and
culture--Korea (South) Globalization.
Series: Munhwa pip`yongson; 12 LC
Classification: NX584.6.A1 K58 2000

Kitching, G. N. Seeking social justice through globalization: escaping a nationalist perspective / Gavin Kitching. Published/Created: University Park, Pa.: Pennsylvania State University Press, 2001. Description: xv, 339 p.; 24 cm. ISBN 0271021624 Notes: Includes bibliographical references (p. 323-333) and index. Subjects: Social justice. Globalization. LC Classification: HM671 .K57 2001 Dewey Class No.: 303.3/72 21

Klug, Heinz, 1957- Constituting democracy: law, globalism, and South Africa's political reconstruction / Heinz Klug. Published/Created: Cambridge, UK; New York: Cambridge University Press, 2000. Description: xi, 270 p.; 24 cm. ISBN 0521781132 (hardback) 0521786436 (pbk.) Notes: Includes bibliographical references (p. 224-259) and index. Subjects: Constitutional history--South Africa. Apartheid--South Africa. Democracy. Globalization. Series: Cambridge studies in law and society LC Classification: KTL2101 .K59 2000 Dewey Class No.: 340/.115/0968 21

Knauder, Stefanie, 1937- Globalization, urban progress, urban problems, rural disadvantages: evidence from Mozambique / Stefanie Knauder. Published/Created: Aldershot, Hampshire, England; Burlington, Vt., USA: Ashgate, c2000. Description: xviii, 329 p.: ill., maps; 23 cm. ISBN 1840148438 Notes: Includes bibliographical references (p. 269-289). Subjects: Poverty--Mozambique. Globalization--Economic aspects--Mozambique. Urbanization--Mozambique. Mozambique--Economic conditions--1975- Mozambique--Rural conditions. LC Classification: HC890 .K57 2000

Kneschaurek, Francesco. Weltwirtschaft im Umbruch: Probleme, Analysen, Perspektiven / Francesco Kneschaurek.
Published/Created: Zu¨rich: Verlag Neue Zürcher Zeitung, c1999. Description: 286 p.: ill.; 23 cm. ISBN 3858237647 Notes: Includes bibliographical references (p. 267-286). Subjects: International economic relations. International trade. Globalization. LC Classification: HF1359 .K58 1999

Kohler, Gernot. Global keynesianism: critique of unequal exchange, global exploitation and global neoliberalism, theory of world income, productivity, growth and employment, critique of the social and economic development of Europe / Gernot Köhler and Arno Tausch. Published/Created: Huntington, NY: Nova Science Publishers, 2001. Related Names: Tausch, Arno, 1951- Description: p. cm. ISBN 1590330021 Notes: Includes bibliographical references and index. Subjects: International economic relations. Globalization--Economic aspects. International trade. Commercial policy. Economic policy. Economic development. Keynesian economics. European Union countries--Foreign economic relations. European Union countries--Commercial policy European Union countries--Economic policy. LC Classification: HF1359 .K592 2001 Dewey Class No.: 338.94 21

Kokkinos, Theodore. Economic structure-functionalism in European unification and globalization of the economies / Theodore Kokkinos; [English translation, John Davis]. Published/Created: Frankfurt am Main; New York: Peter Lang, 2000. Description: xiii, 218 p.; 21 cm. ISBN 0820447889 (U.S.) Notes: Includes bibliographical references (p. [197]-208) and index. Subjects: Financial crises--Europe. Globalization. Economics. Europe--Economic integration. LC Classification: HC240 .K72258 2000 Dewey Class No.: 337.1/4 21

Kolodko, Grzegorz W. Globalization and catching-up in transition economics / Grzegorz W. Kolodko. Published/Created: Rochester, NY: University of Rochester Press, 2002. Description: p. cm. ISBN 158046050X (alk. paper) Notes: Includes bibliographical references and index. Subjects: Globalization--Economic aspects. Post-communism--Europe, Eastern Post-communism--Former Soviet republics. Europe, Eastern--Economic conditions--1989- Former Soviet republics--Economic conditions. Series: Rochester studies in Central Europe, 1528-4808 LC Classification: HC244 .K6316 2002 Dewey Class No.: 338.947 21

Kresl, Peter Karl. France encounters globalization / Peter Karl Kresl, Sylvain Gallais. Published/Created: Cheltenham [England]; Northampton, MA: Edward Elgar Pub., 2002. Related Names: Gallais, Sylvain. Description: p. cm. ISBN 1840645423 Notes: Includes bibliographical references and index. Subjects: Globalization. France--Economic conditions--1945- France--Economic policy--1945- France--Foreign economic relations. LC Classification: HC276.2 .K73 2002 Dewey Class No.: 337.44 21

Kunczik, Michael, 1946- Media giants: ownership concentration and globalisation / Michael Kunczik. Published/Created: Bonn: Friedrich-Ebert-Stiftung, c1997. Related Names: Simon, Diet. Friedrich-Ebert-Stiftung. Abteilung Internationale Entwicklungszusammenarbeit. Description: 213 p.: ill.; 22 cm. Notes: "Communication manual"--Cover. "Published by the Division for International Development Cooperation of Friedrich-Ebert-Stiftung (FES)--T.p. verso. Includes bibliographical references (p. 203-213). "Translated from the German by Diet Simon"--T.p. verso.

Subjects: Mass media--Ownership. Communication, International. Mass media and culture. LC Classification: P96.E25 K86 1997 Dewey Class No.: 302.23 21

Küreselle,sme, sivil toplum ve Islam: Türkiye üzerine yansimalar / derleyenler, E. Fuat Keyman, A. Ya,sar Saribay. Edition Information: 1. baski. Published/Created: Kizilay, Ankara: Vadi Yayinlari, 1998. Related Names: Keyman, Emin Fuat. Saribay, Ali Ya,sar, 1952- Description: 274 p.; 20 cm. ISBN 9757726834 Notes: "90"--T.p. verso. Includes bibliographical references. Subjects: Globalization, civil society and Islam; Turkey Series: Toplum dizisi (Vadi Yayinlari (Firm)); 34. LC Classification: MLCSN 2001/01185 (H)

Kurien, John. Small-scale fisheries in the context of globalisation [microform] / John Kurien. Published/Created: Thiruvananthapuram, India: Centre for Development Studies, 1998. Related Names: Centre for Development Studies (Trivandrum, India) Description: 44 p.; 21 cm. Summary: In the Asian context; revised version of a keynote paper presented at a conference. Notes: Includes bibliographical references (p. 36-40). Microfiche. New Delhi: Library of Congress Office; Washington, D.C.: Library of Congress Photoduplication Service, 2001. 1 microfiche. Master microform held by: DLC. Subjects: Small-scale fisheries--Asia. Fishery industry--Asia. Series: Working paper (Centre for Development Studies (Trivandrum, India)); no. 289. LC Classification: Microfiche 2001/60437 (S)

Kurisaki, Yoshiko. The changing role of telecommunications in the economy: globalisation and its impact on national telecommunication policy / [by Yoshiko Kurisaki]. Published/Created: Paris: Organisation for Economic Co-operation and Development, 1995. Related Names: Organisation for Economic Co-operation and Development. Description: 71 p.: ill.; 30 cm. Notes: Includes bibliographical references (p. 67-71). Subjects: Telecommunication policy. Telecommunication--International cooperation. Investments, Foreign. Series: OECD working papers; v. 3, no. 79. LC Classification: HD72 .O38 vol. 3, no. 79

La colonialidad del saber: eurocentrismo y ciencias sociales: perspectivas latinoamericanas / Edgardo Lander, compilador; Santiago Castro-Go´mez ... [et al., autores]. Edition Information: 1. ed. Published/Created: Buenos Aires: Consejo Latinoamericano de Ciencias Sociales-CLACSO; [Caracas, Venezuela]: UNESCO, Unidad Regional de Ciencias Sociales y Humanas para América Latina y el Caribe, 2000. Related Names: Lander, Edgardo. Castro-Gómez, Santiago, 1958- Description: 246 p., [1] folded leaves of plates: ill., maps (one col.); 22 cm. ISBN 9509231517 Notes: Selected and revised papers originally given at a simposium held during the World Congress of Sociology, in Montreal, July 24 - Aug ?, 1998. Includes bibliographical references. Subjects: Social sciences Philosophy-- Congresses. Social sciences--Latin America--Congresses. Social sciences-- Caribbean Area--Congresses. Eurocentrism--Congresses. Postcolonialism--Congresses. Globalization--Congresses. LC Classification: H61 .C515 2000

La globalisation du religieux / AFSR; sous la direction de Jean-Pierre Bastian, Françoise Champion et Kathy Rousselet. Published/Created: Paris: Harmattan, c2001. Description: 282 p.; cm. ISBN 2747502376 Subjects: Religion - Globalization. Series: Religion et sciences humaines

La globalisation du religieux / AFSR; sous la direction de Jean-Pierre Bastian, Françoise Champion et Kathy Rousselet. Published/Created: Paris: Harmattan, c2001. Description: 282 p.; cm. ISBN 2747502376 Subjects: Religion - Globalization. Series: Religion et sciences humaines

La pensée comptable: Etat, néolibéralisme, nouvelle gestion publique / sous la direction de Marc Hufty. Published/Created: Paris: Presses Universitaires de France, 1998. Related Names: Hufty, Marc. Description: 256 p.: ill.; 23 cm. ISBN 2882470282 Notes: Includes bibliographical references. Subjects: Public administration. Globalization. Series: Nouveaux cahiers de l'Institut universitaire d'études du développement Collection Enjeux (Presses universitaires de France); 8. LC Classification: JF1352 .P45 1998

La revista: arte / cultura. Nos.01 (1999), 2 (enero-marzo 2000) / editor: Gustavo García González. Published/Created: Guatemala: La Revista, 1999. Related Names: La ERvista. Description: 72-76 p.; cm. Current Frequency: quarterly Summary: New Guatemalan journal of art and literature. Articles include the historic center of Guatemala, urban nomads, the works of Cesar Brañas, Central American art and globalization, the music of Bob Marley and poetry and short stories by national artists. Notes: Description based on: número 2 - enero, febrero, marzo 2000.

La Rivière, Franck de. Mondialisme: un défi pour les Français / Franck de La Rivière. Published/Created: Paris, France: G. de Bouillon, c1999. Description: 399 p.: ill.; 22 cm. ISBN 2841910822 Notes: Includes bibliographical references. Subjects: World politics--1945- Globalization. France--Foreign relations--20th century.

Geopolitics. LC Classification: D840 .L274 1999 Dewey Class No.: 909.82/5 21

La Salle, Jean de. La prospérité viendra demain de l'économie locale: de la mondialisation aux racines territoriales de l'économie et de la monnaie / Jean de La Salle; préface de Gilbert Blardone. Published/Created: Paris: Harmattan, c2000. Description: 237 p.: ill., maps; 24 cm. ISBN 2738491715 Notes: Includes bibliographical references (p. 235-236). Subjects: Globalization--Economic aspects--France. Regional planning--France. Community development--France. Globalization--Regional disparities. France--Economic policy--1995- LC Classification: HC276.4 .L37 2000

Labor and capital in the age of globalization: the labor process and the changing nature of work in the global economy / edited by Berch Berberoglu. Published/Created: Lanham, MD: Rowman & Littlefield, c2002. Related Names: Berberoglu, Berch. Description: ix, 221 p.; 24 cm. ISBN 0742516601 (cloth: alk. paper) 074251661X (pbk.: alk. paper) Notes: Includes bibliographical references (p. 95-207) and index. Subjects: Labor--United States. Labor movement--United States. Working class--United States. Capitalism--United States. Globalization--Economic aspects--United States. Social conflict--United States. Marxian economics. LC Classification: HD8072.5 .L27 2002 Dewey Class No.: 331/.0973 21

Labour, environment, and globalisation: social clause in multilateral trade agreements: a southern response / editors, J. John and Anuradha M. Chenoy. Published/Created: New Delhi: New Age International (P) Ltd. Publishers, c1996. Related Names: John, J. Chenoy, Anuradha M. Centre for Education and Communication (New Delhi, India) Description: viii, 188 p.; 25 cm. ISBN 8122409679 Summary: Contributed articles. Notes: "Centre for Education and Communication." Includes bibliographical references and index. Subjects: Uruguay Round (1987-1994) World Trade Organization. Foreign trade and employment--India. Labor laws and legislation--India. Labor laws and legislation, International. Free trade--Environmental aspects. India--Foreign economic relations. India--Commercial treaties--Social aspects. LC Classification: HF1589 .L33 1996 Dewey Class No.: 331.1 21

Laïdi, Zaki. La gauche à venir: Politique et mondialisation / Zaki Laïdi. Published/Created: La Tour d'Aigues: Aube, 2001. Description: 149 p.; cm. ISBN 2876786737 Subjects: Political Science - Left and Globalization. Series: Monde en cours

Laird, John. Money politics, globalisation, and crisis: the case of Thailand / John Laird. Published/Created: Singapore: Graham Brash, c2000. Description: xii, 463 p.; 20 cm. ISBN 9812180761 Subjects: Sustainable development--Thailand. Thailand--Economic conditions--1986- Thailand--Economic policy--1986- Thailand--Politics and government--1988- LC Classification: HC445 .L32 2000 Dewey Class No.: 320/.6/09593 21

Lal, Deepak. Culture, democracy, and development / by Deepak Lal. Published/Created: New Delhi: National Council of Applied Economic Research, 1999. Related Names: Mohan, Rakesh. Dutta, Bhaskar. Madan, T. N. National Council of Applied Economic Research. Description: 41 p.; 24 cm. ISBN 8185877521 Summary: With reference to India. Notes: "Chairperson: Rakesh Mohan; discussants: Bhaskar Dutta, T.N. Madan." Includes bibliographical references (p. 30). Subjects: International

economic relations. Globalization--
Economic aspects--India. Globalization--
Social aspects--India. Democracy--India.
India--Civilization--Foreign influences.
Series: Golden jubilee seminar series; 5th
lecture LC Classification: HF1352 .L35
1999

Lamfalussy, Alexandre. Financial crises in
emerging markets: an essay on financial
globalisation and fragility / Alexandre
Lamfalussy. Published/Created: New
Haven, [Conn.]: Yale University Press,
c2000. Description: xx, 199 p.: ill.; 22 cm.
ISBN 0300082304 (alk. paper) Notes:
Includes bibliographical references (p.
183-184) and index. Subjects: Business
cycles. Financial crises. Series: Henry L.
Stimson lectures, Yale University. LC
Classification: HB3711 .L24 2000 Dewey
Class No.: 332 21

Landau, Alice. Redrawing the global
economy: elements of integration and
fragmentation / Alice Landau.
Published/Created: Houndmills,
Basingstoke, Hampshire; New York:
Palgrave, 2001. Description: xv, 277 p.:
ill.; 23 cm. ISBN 0333802403 Notes:
Includes bibliographical references (p.
250-270) and index. Subjects:
International economic integration.
Regional economics. Globalization. LC
Classification: HF1418.5 .L36 2001
Dewey Class No.: 337 21

Lane, Jan-Erik. Government and the economy:
a global perspective / Jan-Erik Lane and
Svante Ersson. Published/Created: New
York: Continuum, 2001. Related Names:
Ersson, Svante O. Description: p. cm.
ISBN 0826454917 0826454925 Notes:
Includes bibliographical references and
index. Subjects: Economic policy--Case
studies. Economic development--Case
studies. Mixed economy--Case studies.
Globalization--Case studies. LC
Classification: HD87 .L374 2001 Dewey

Class No.: 338.9 21

Lange, Niels. Globalisierung und regionaler
Nationalismus: Schottland und Quebec im
Zeitalter der Denationalisierung / Niels
Lange. Edition Information: 1. Aufl.
Published/Created: Baden-Baden: Nomos,
2000. Description: 230 p.: ill.; 23 cm.
ISBN 3789066486 Notes: Includes
bibliographical references (p. 209-230).
Subjects: Privatization--Québec
(Province) Privatization--Scotland.
Decentralization in government--Québec
(Province) Decntralization in government-
-Scotland. Globalization. LC
Classification: HD4010.Q4 L36 2000

Langhorne, Richard, 1940- The coming of
globalization: its evolution and
contemporary consequences / Richard
Langhorne. Published/Created:
Houndmills, Basingstoke, Hampshire,
London; New York: Palgrave, 2001.
Description: xv, 155 p.; 23 cm. ISBN
0333917774 0333947185 (pbk.) Notes:
Includes bibliographical references (p.
151-152) and index. Subjects:
Globalization. LC Classification: JZ1318
.L36 2001 Dewey Class No.: 303.4 21

Lankoski, Leena. Economic globalisation and
the environment / Leena Lankoski, Jussi
Lankoski. Published/Created: Helsinki:
Ministry of the Environment, 1999.
Related Names: Lankoski, Jussi.
Description: 66 p.: ill.; 30 cm. ISBN
9521105461 Notes: Includes
bibliographical references. Summary in
Finnish and Swedish. Subjects:
Environmental policy. Environmental
economics--International cooperation.
Environmental pollution--Economic
aspects. Sustainable development. Series:
Suomen ympäristö; 336. LC
Classification: GE170 .L36 1999 Dewey
Class No.: 363.7 21

Lanusse, Federico, 1952- Color profundo: caminando por los márgenes de la globalización / Federico Lanusse. Published/Created: Buenos Aires: Francotirador Ediciones, c1999. Description: 179 p.: ill.; 23 cm. ISBN 9508502444 Subjects: Lanusse, Federico, 1952- Globalization--Social aspects--South America. Globalization--Economic aspects--South America. South America--Description and travel. South America--Social conditions. South America--Civilization--Foreign influences. LC Classification: F2225 .L36 1999 Dewey Class No.: 980.03/9 21

Larsen, Marianne Nylandsted. Zimbabwean cotton sector liberalisation: a case of successful private coordination? / Marianne Nylandsted Larsen. Published/Created: Copenhagen, Denmark: Centre for Development Research, [2001] Description: 28 p.; 30 cm. Subjects: Cotton trade--Zimbabwe, Series: CDR working paper; 01.1. CDR working paper. Working paper subseries on globalisation and economic restructuring in Africa; no. 11. LC Classification: HD72 .C38 no. 01.1

Larsson, Tomas, 1966- The race to the top: the real story of globalization / by Tomas Larsson. Published/Created: Washington, D.C.: CATO, 2001. Description: p. cm. ISBN 1930865147 (cloth) 1930865155 (pbk.) Notes: "A revision and expansion of the book originally published by Timbro in Swedish as Världens Klassresa (1999)"--Introd. Includes bibliographical references and index. Subjects: International trade--Social aspects. International trade--Effect of technological innovations on. Free trade--Social aspects--Developing countries. Globalization--Economic aspects--Developing countries. Globalization--Social aspects--Developing countries. International economic relations. LC

Classification: HF1379 .L37 2001 Dewey Class No.: 337 21

Laszlo, Ervin, 1932- Macroshift: navigating the transformation to a sustainable world / Ervin Laszlo; foreword by Arthur C. Clarke. Edition Information: 1st ed. Published/Created: San Francisco: Berrett-Koehler Publishers, c2001. Related Names: Club of Budapest. Description: xvii, 218 p.; 24 cm. ISBN 1576751635 Notes: "The official report of the Club of Budapest." Includes bibliographical references (p. [195]-198) and index. Subjects: Sustainable development--Mathematical models. Globalization. LC Classification: HC79.E5 L375 2001 Dewey Class No.: 306.3 21

Latin America: its future in the global economy / edited by Patricia Gray Rich. Published/Created: New York: Palgrave, 2001. Related Names: Rich, Patricia Gray. Description: p. cm. ISBN 0333929012 Notes: Includes bibliographical references and index. Subjects: World Trade Organization--Latin America. Globalization. Latin America--Foreign economic relations. Latin America--Economic integration. LC Classification: HF1480.5 .L3852 2001 Dewey Class No.: 337.8 21

Latin American perspectives on globalization: ethics, politics, and alternative visions / edited by Mario Sáenz. Published/Created: Lanham, Md.: Rowman & Littlefield Publishers, c2002. Related Names: Sáenz, Mario, 1956- Description: p. cm. ISBN 0742507769 (cloth: alk. paper) 0742507777 (pbk.: alk. paper) Contents: The world is no longer broad but continues being alien: the end of modernity and the transformation of cultures in times of globalization -- The ethics of globalization and the globalization of ethics --

Transnationalization, state, and political power -- Globalization and latinidad -- Going home: Tununa Mercado's en estado de memoria -- Globalization, philosophy, and Latin America -- Globalization: competition within a cooperative framework -- A global democratic order: a normative proposal -- Latin American feminism in the face of the new challenges of globalization -- Feminism and globalization processes in Latin America -- Latin American liberation theology, globalization and historical projects -- Theses for the comprehension and practice of interculturality as an alternative to globalization. Notes: Includes bibliographical references and index. Subjects: Globalization. Latin America--Foreign relations. Latin America--Politics and government--1980- LC Classification: JZ1318 .L38 2002 Dewey Class No.: 327/.098 21

Le bateau ivre de la mondialisation: Escales au sein du village planétaire / sous la direction de Arnaud Zacharie ct Eric Toussaint. Published/Created: Paris: Syllepse; Bruxelles: Comité pour l'annulation de la dette du tiers monde, 2000. Description: 263 p.; cm. ISBN 2913165346 2960025407 Subjects: Globalization.

Leclerc, Gérard, 1943- La mondialisation culturelle: les civilisations à l'épreuve / Gérard Leclerc. Published/Created: Paris: Presses universitaires de France, 2000. Description: vi, 486 p.; 22 cm. ISBN 2130506410 Notes: Includes bibliographical references (p. [479]-486). Subjects: East and West. Globalization. Acculturation. Series: Sociologie d'aujourd'hui LC Classification: CB251 .L37 2000 Dewey Class No.: 909.82 21

Lee, James R., 1951- Exploring the gaps: vital links between trade, environment, and culture / James R. Lee. Published/Created:

West Hartford, CT: Kumarian Press, 2000. Description: xvi, 249 p.: ill.; 23 cm. ISBN 1565491157 (cloth) 1565491149 (pbk.) Notes: Includes bibliographical references (p. [239]-240) and index. Subjects: International trade-- Environmental aspects--Case studies. International trade--Social aspects--Case studies. International trade--Cross-cultural studies. International trade--Effect of technological innovations on--Case studies. Globalization--Cross-cultural studies. LC Classification: HF1379 .L44 2000 Dewey Class No.: 382 21

Leigh, Michael B. Unity in diversity: globalisation, democracy, and cultural vitality / Michael Leigh. Published/Created: Kota Samarahan, Sarawak, Malaysia: Institute of East Asian Studies, Universiti Malaysia Sarawak, [1998?] Related Names: Universiti Malaysia Sarawak. Institute of East Asian Studies. Description: 17 leaves; 31 cm. Notes: Includes bibliographical references (leaves 14-16). Subjects: Multiculturalism. Globalization. Democracy. Multiculturalism--Malaysia-- Sarawak. Series: IEAS working papers LC Classification: HM1271 .L45 1998

Leigh, Michael B. Unity in diversity: globalisation, democracy, and cultural vitality / Michael Leigh. Published/Created: Kota Samarahan, Sarawak, Malaysia: Institute of East Asian Studies, Universiti Malaysia Sarawak, [1998?] Related Names: Universiti Malaysia Sarawak. Institute of East Asian Studies. Description: 17 leaves; 31 cm. Notes: Includes bibliographical references (leaves 14-16). Subjects: Multiculturalism. Globalization. Democracy. Multiculturalism--Malaysia-- Sarawak. Series: IEAS working papers LC Classification: HM1271 .L45 1998

Les jeunes et le savoir: Perspectives internationales / sous la direction de Bernard Charlot; [contributions] Elisabeth Bautier, Jean-Yves Rochex, Ahmed Chabchoub, ... [et al.]. Published/Created: Paris: Anthropos, 2001. Description: 168 p.; cm. ISBN 271784192X Subjects: Education - Globalization of Knowledge. Series: Education

Les mondialisations: Gouffre ou tremplin / coordination Michel Van Cromphaut; préface de Jacques Lesourne. Published/Created: Paris: Harmattan, 2001. Description: 279 p.; cm. ISBN 2747512991 Subjects: Globalization. Series: Economie et innovation

Les nouvelles logiques du développement: globalisation versus localisation / [éditeurs] Lahsen Abdelmalki, Claude Courlet. Published/Created: Paris: L'Harmattan, c1996. Related Names: Abdelmalki, Lahsen, 1957- Courlet, Claude. Description: 415 p.; 22 cm. ISBN 2738440126 Notes: Includes bibliographical references. Subjects: Industrial location--Developing countries. Regional planning--Developing countries. Developing countries--Economic conditions. Series: Collection "Logiques économiques" Logiques économiques. LC Classification: HC59.7 .N679 1996

Levitt, Peggy, 1957- The transnational villagers / Peggy Levitt. Published/Created: Berkeley: University of California Press, c2001. Description: x, 281 p.: maps; 24 cm. ISBN 0520228111 (cloth: alk. paper) 0520228138 (pbk.) Notes: Includes bibliographical references (p. 249-269) and index. Subjects: Dominicans (Dominican Republic)--Massachusetts--Boston. Globalization. Transnationalism. Emigrant remittances--Dominican Republic--Miraflores. Miraflores (Dominican Republic)--Emigration and immigration. Boston (Mass.)--Emigration and immigration. LC Classification: JV7395 .L48 2001 Dewey Class No.: 304.8/744610729373 21

Lewellen, Ted C., 1940- The anthropology of globalization: cultural anthropology enters the 21st century / Ted C. Lewellen. Published/Created: Westport, CT: Bergin & Garvey, 2002. Description: p. cm. ISBN 0897897382 (alk. paper) 0897897404 (pbk.: alk. paper) Notes: Includes bibliographical references and index. Subjects: Anthropology. Globalization. LC Classification: GN27 .L65 2002 Dewey Class No.: 306 21

Lewis, Howard, 1948- Why global integration matters most! / Howard Lewis, III, J. David Richardson. Published/Created: Washington, DC: Institute for International Economics, 2001. Related Names: Richardson, J. David. Description: p. cm. ISBN 0881322989 Notes: "September 2001." Includes bibliographical references and index. Subjects: International economic integration. Globalization--Economic aspects--United States. Globalization--Social aspects--United States. United States--Economic policy--1993-2001. LC Classification: HF1418.5 .L49 2001 Dewey Class No.: 337.1 21

Liberalisation and globalisation of Indian economy / edited by K.R. Gupta. Published/Created: New Delhi: Atlantic Publishers and Distributors, c1995-2000. Related Names: Gupta, Kulwant Rai, 1933- Description: 4 v.; 22 cm. ISBN 8171569633 (set) Summary: Contributed articles. Notes: Includes bibliographical references. Subjects: Economic development--Social aspects--India. India--Economic policy--1980- Free trade--Government policy--India. LC Classification: HC435.2 .L52 1995

Licence to kill: how the unholy trinity-- the World Bank, the International Monetary Fund, and the World Trade Organisation-- are killing livelihoods, environment, and democracy in India / [compiled.by] Vandana Shiva ... [et al.]. Published/Created: New Delhi: Research Foundation for Science, Technology, and Ecology, 2000. Related Names: Shiva, Vandana. Research Foundation for Science, Technology, and Ecology (New Delhi, India) Description: 85 p.: ill.; 29 cm. Subjects: Financial institutions, International. Globalization--Economic aspects--India. Globalization--Social aspects--India. LC Classification: HG3881 .L483 2000

Lincoln, Edward J. Japan's rapidly emerging strategy toward Asia / by Edward J. Lincoln. Published/Created: Paris: Organisation for Economic Co-operation and Development, 1992. Description: 55 p.: ill.; 30 cm. Notes: "Under the direction of Charles Oman. Produced as part of the Research Programme on Globalisation and Regionalisation." "General distribution code/GD(92)59." Summary also in French. Includes bibliographical references (p. 39-47). Subjects: Japan-- Foreign economic relations--Asia, Southeastern. Asia, Southeastern--Foreign economic relations--Japan. Japan--Foreign economic relations--East Asia. East Asia-- Foreign economic relations--Japan. Series: Technical papers (Organisation for Economic Co-operation and Development. Development Centre); no. 58. LC Classification: HF1602.15.A75 L56 1992 Dewey Class No.: 337.52059 20

Lindenberg, Marc. Going global: transforming relief and development NGOs / Marc Lindenberg and Coralie Bryant. Published/Created: Bloomfield, CT: Kumarian Press, 2001. Related Names: Bryant, Coralie. Description: xiv, 270 p.: ill.; 23 cm. ISBN 1565491351 (pbk.: alk. paper) 156549136X (cloth: alk. paper) Notes: Includes bibliographical references and index. Subjects: International relief. Non-governmental organizations. Globalization. LC Classification: HV544.5 .L56 2001 Dewey Class No.: 361.2/6 21

Lindsey, Brink. Against the dead hand: the uncertain struggle for global capitalism / Brink Lindsey. Published/Created: New York: Wiley, c2002. Description: xii, 336 p.; 24 cm. ISBN 0471442771 (cloth: alk. paper) Notes: Includes bibliographical references and index. Subjects: International economic relations. Globalization. Capitalism. Economic policy. LC Classification: HF1359 .L555 2002 Dewey Class No.: 337 21

Links von Nord und Süd: chilenisch-deutsche Ortsbestimmungen im Neoliberalismus / Olaf Kaltmeier, Michael Ramminger (Hrsg.). Published/Created: Münster: LIT, [1999] Related Names: Kaltmeier, Olaf, 1970- Ramminger, Michael, 1960- Description: 224 p.; 21 cm. ISBN 3825844897 Notes: Includes bibliographical references. Subjects: Liberalism--Chile--Congresses. Globalization--Congresses. Series: Kontroversen; Bd. 11 LC Classification: JC574.2.C5 L556 1999 Dewey Class No.: 320.51/3/0983 21

Lisichkin, V. A. (Vladimir Aleksandrovich) Global'naia imperiia zla / V.A Lisichkin, L.A. Shelepin. Published/Created: Moskva: Krymskii most-9D: Forum, 2001. Related Names: Shelepin, L. A. Description: 445 p.; 21 cm. ISBN 5897470332 Notes: "Novaia geopoliticheskaia rasstanovka sil"--P. 1 of cover. Includes bibliographical references (p. 424-438). Subjects: Globalization. Geopolitics. Economic history--1990- United States--Social conditions--1980-

Russia (Federation)--Social conditions--1991- Series: Seriia "Velikoe protivostoianie". LC Classification: HC59.15 .L57 2001

Local dynamics in an era of globalization: 21st century catalysts for development / edited by Shahid Yusuf, Weiping Wu, and Simon Evenett. Published/Created: New York, N.Y.: Oxford University Press, 2000. Related Names: Yusuf, Shahid, 1949- Wu, Weiping. Evenett, Simon J. Description: vii, 179 p.: ill., maps; 28 cm. ISBN 0195215974 Notes: "Published for the World Bank." Includes bibliographical references. Subjects: Economic development. Globalization. Decentralization in government. Urbanization. LC Classification: HD75 .L63 2000 Dewey Class No.: 338.9 21

Local matters: perspectives on the globalisation of technology / edited by John Phillimore. Published/Created: Murdoch, W.A.: Institute for Science and Technology Policy, Murdoch University, 1995. Related Names: Phillimore, John. Description: xii, 186 p.: ill.; 21 cm. ISBN 0869054112 Notes: Includes bibliographical references. Subjects: Technology and state--Australia. Research, Industrial--Australia. Technology--International cooperation. Science and state--Australia. LC Classification: T29.A1 L63 1995 Dewey Class No.: 338.99406 21

Loewendahl, Henry. Bargaining with multinationals: the investment of Siemens and Nissan in north-east England / Henry Bernard Loewendahl. Published/Created: Houndmills, Basingstoke, Hampshire; New York: Palgrave, 2001. Description: xviii, 431 p.; 23 cm. ISBN 0333948130 Notes: Includes bibliographical references (p. 371-412) and index. Subjects: International business enterprises--Great Britain. International business enterprises--England--Case studies. Investments, Foreign--Great Britain. International business enterprises--Government policy Great Britain. Globalization--Economic aspects--Great Britain. LC Classification: HD2845 .L628 2001 Dewey Class No.: 332.67/3/09428 21

López, Ernesto, 1947- Globalización y democracia / Ernesto López. Published/Created: Buenos Aires: Pagina/12: Red de Editoriales de Universidades Nacionales, [1998?] Description: 92 p.; 19 cm. ISBN 9875031135 Subjects: Globalization. Democracy--Latin America. Political culture--Latin America. Series: Papeles de investigación; 2 LC Classification: JZ1318 .L66 1998 Dewey Class No.: 320.98 21

Lorenzo Palomera, Julio Gerardo. Ensayando a ensayar: ensayos académicos universitarios / Julio Gerardo Lorenzo Palomera ... [et al.]. Published/Created: Ciudad Victoria: Universidad Autónoma de Tamaulipas, 1999. Description: 294 p.; cm. Summary: A collection of prize-winning selections in a university competition for essays. Topics include alternative and creative education, research in the social sciences, education and globalization, the nature of the city and didactic disputes. Series: Ensayos Académicos Universitarios

Louie, Miriam Ching Yoon. Sweatshop warriors: immigrant women workers take on the global factory / Miriam Ching Yoon Louie. Published/Created: Cambridge, Mass.: South End Press, c2001. Description: x, 306 p.: ill.; 23 cm. ISBN 0896086399 (cloth) 0896086380 (pbk.) Notes: Includes bibliographical references (p. 257-294) and index. Subjects: Women alien labor--United States--Interviews. Sweatshops--United States. Foreign trade and employment--

United States. International division of labor. Globalization--Economic aspects. LC Classification: HD6057.5.U5 L68 2001 Dewey Class No.: 331.4/086/24 21

Luard, Evan, 1926- The globalization of politics: the changed focus of political action in the modern world / Evan Luard. Published/Created: New York: New York University Press, 1990. Description: xii, 195 p.; 23 cm. ISBN 0814750478 : Notes: Includes bibliographical references and index. Subjects: International relations. World politics--1945- International economic relations. Globalization. LC Classification: JX1391 .L83 1990 Dewey Class No.: 327.1/1 20

Luard, Evan, 1926- The globalization of politics: the changed focus of political action in the modern world / Evan Luard. Published/Created: Houndmills, Basingstoke, Hampshire: Macmillan, 1990. Description: xii, 195 p.; 23 cm. ISBN 0333521315 0333521323 Notes: Includes bibliographical references and index. Subjects: International relations. World politics--1945- International economic relations. Internationalism. Globalization. LC Classification: JX1391 .L83 1990b

Lubbers, R. F. M. Revitalizing liberal values in a globalizing world / Ruud Lubbers. Published/Created: Toronto; Buffalo: Published in association with Victoria University by University of Toronto Press, c1999. Description: x, 46 p.: ill.; 19 cm. ISBN 0802083676 (pbk.) Notes: Includes bibliographical references. Subjects: Liberalism. Globalization. Libéralisme. Series: Senator Keith Davey lecture series. LC Classification: JC574 .L83 1999 Dewey Class No.: 320.51 21

Lubritz, Stefan, 1964- Internationale strategische Allianzen mittelständischer Unternehmen: eine theoretische und empirische Analyse / Stefan Lubritz. Published/Created: Frankfurt am Main; New York: Lang, c1998. Description: xx, 284, xxi-liv p.: ill.; 21 cm. ISBN 3631329822 (acid-free paper) Notes: Originally presented as the author's thesis (doctoral)--Universität Saarbrücken, 1996. Includes bibliographical references (p. xxi-liv). Subjects: Strategic alliances (Business) Small business. International trade. Globalization. Series: Europäische Hochschulschriften. Reihe V, Volks- und Betriebswirtschaft; Bd. 2318. LC Classification: HD69.S8 L83 1998 Dewey Class No.: 338.8/8 21

L'université dans la tourmente / sous la direction de Anne-Marie Dillens. Published/Created: Bruxelles: Facultés universitaires Saint-Louis, 2000. Related Names: Dillens, Anne-Marie. Description: 221 p.; 23 cm. ISBN 2802801376 (pbk.) Notes: Includes bibliographical references. Subjects: Education, Higher--Social aspects--Europe. Education, Higher--Aims and objectives--Europe. Globalization. Series: Publications des Facultés universitaires Saint-Louis; 85 LC Classification: LC191.98.E85 U55 2000

Machbares Denken: Wege aus dem Scherbenhaufen / Egon Bahr ... [et al.]. Published/Created: Wuppertal: Hammer, c1999. Related Names: Bahr, Egon, 1922- Description: 108 p.; 21 cm. ISBN 3872948210 (pbk.) Notes: Includes bibliographical references. Subjects: Globalization. Ecology--Europe. Europe--Politics and government--1989- Series: Wuppertaler Gesellschaftsbilder; Nr. 1 LC Classification: D2003 .M33 1999 Dewey Class No.: 940.55/9 21

Mahathir bin Mohamad, 1925- Globalisation, smart partnership and government: selected speeches / by Mahathir Mohamad; edited by Hashim Makaruddin. Published/Created: Subang Jaya, Selangor

Darul Ehsan, Malaysia: Published by Pelanduk Publications for the Prime Minister's Office of Malaysia, Putrajaya, Malaysia, c2000. Related Names: Hashim Makaruddin. Description: 216 p.; 22 cm. Notes: On t.p.: "Volume 2." Includes index. Subjects: Globalization--Economic aspects--Malaysia. Business and politics--Malaysia. Malaysia--Foreign economic relations. Malaysia--Economic policy. LC Classification: HF1352+

Mahathir bin Mohamad, 1925- Globalisation, smart partnership and government: selected speeches / by Mahathir Mohamad; edited by Hashim Makaruddin. Published/Created: Subang Jaya, Selangor Darul Ehsan, Malaysia: Published by Pelanduk Publications for the Prime Minister's Office of Malaysia, Putrajaya, Malaysia, c2000. Related Names: Hashim Makaruddin. Description: 216 p.; 22 cm. Notes: On t.p.: "Volume 2." Includes index. Subjects: Globalization--Economic aspects--Malaysia. Business and politics--Malaysia. Malaysia--Foreign economic relations. Malaysia--Economic policy. LC Classification: HF1352+

Mahé, Serge. Propriété et mondialisation / Serge Mahé. Published/Created: Paris: Harmattan, 1999. Description: 191 p.; 22 cm. ISBN 2738481647 Subjects: Property. Globalization. Property--France. Series: Collection Questions contemporaines LC Classification: HB701 .M32 1999

Maîtriser la mondialisation: la régulation sociale internationale / sous la direction de Pierre de Senarclens. Published/Created: [Paris]: Presses de sciences PO, c2000. Related Names: Senarclens, Pierre de. Description: 243 p.; 22 cm. ISBN 2724608348 Notes: Includes bibliographical references (p. [242]-243). Subjects: International economic relations. Globalization--Social aspects.

Globalization--Economic aspects. LC Classification: HF1359 .M354 2000 Dewey Class No.: 337 21

Makarychev, A. S. (Andrei Stanislavovich) Islands of globalization: regional Russia and the outside world / by Andrei S. Makarychev. Published/Created: Zurich: Center for Security Studies and Conflict Research, [2000] Related Names: Eidgenössische Technische Hochschule Zürich. Forschungsstelle für Sicherheitspolitik und Konfliktanalyse. Russian Study Group. Description: 58 p.; 30 cm. Notes: "August 2000"--Cover. "Project organized by the Russian Study Group at the Center for Security Studies and Conflict Research ... Eidgenössische Technische Hochschule Zürich."--Cover. Also available via the World Wide Web. Includes bibliographical references. Subjects: Regionalism--Russia (Federation) Globalization. Russia (Federation)--Politics and government--1991- Series: Working paper (Regionalization of Russian Foreign and Security Policy (Zurich, Switzerland)); no. 2.

Management and international business issues in Jordan / Hamed El-Said, Kip Becker, editors. Published/Created: New York: International Business Press, c2001. Related Names: El-Said, Hamed. Becker, Kip. Description: xvi, 198 p.: 22 cm. ISBN 0789014459 (hard: alk. paper) 0789014467 (pbk.: alk. paper) Notes: "Co-published simultaneously as Journal of transnational management development, volume 6, numbers 1/2 2001." Includes bibliographical references and index. Subjects: Management--Jordan. Industrial management--Jordan. International business enterprises--Jordan--Management. Globalization--Economic aspects--Jordan. Globalization--Social aspects--Jordan. LC Classification: HD70.J6 M36 2001 Dewey Class No.:

658/.049/095695 21

Managerial challenges: insights on reforms, socio-economic development, and globalisation. Published/Created: Chennai: M.K. Raju Consultants, 1999. Related Names: M.K. Raju Consultants (Madras, India) Description: xii, 323 p.: ill.; 23 cm. Summary: In the Indian context. Notes: "25 years, 1974-1999"-- Cover. Includes statistical tables. Subjects: Globalization. India--Economic policy--1980- India--Economic conditions--1947- India--social conditions--1947- LC Classification: HC435.2 . M3346 1999

Managerial challenges: insights on reforms, socio-economic development, and globalisation. Published/Created: Chennai: M.K. Raju Consultants, 1999. Related Names: M.K. Raju Consultants (Madras, India) Description: xii, 323 p.: ill.; 23 cm. Summary: In the Indian context. Notes: "25 years, 1974-1999"-- Cover. Includes statistical tables. Subjects: Globalization. India--Economic policy--1980- India--Economic conditions--1947- India--social conditions--1947- LC Classification: HC435.2 . M3346 1999

Managing migration: time for a new international regime? / edited by Bimal Ghosh. Published/Created: Oxford [England]: Oxford University Press, 2000. Related Names: Ghosh, Bimal. Description: xiii, 258 p.; 24 cm. ISBN 0198297645 Notes: Includes bibliographical references and index. Subjects: Emigration and immigration-- Government policy. Emigration and immigration--International cooperation. Globalization. LC Classification: JV6038 .M35 2000 Dewey Class No.: 325 21

Mandaville, Peter G., 1971- Transnational Muslim politics: reimagining the umma /

Peter G. Mandaville. Published/Created: New York: Routledge, 2001. Description: p. cm. ISBN 0415246946 Notes: Originally presented as the author's thesis (doctoral--University of Kent). Includes bibliographical references and index. Subjects: Islam and politics. Globalization--Religious aspects--Islam. Islam and state. Ummah (Islam) Series: Transnationalism. Routledge research in transnationalism; 2 LC Classification: JC49 .M26 2001 Dewey Class No.: 320.5/5 21

Mandelbaum, Jean. La victoire de la Chine: L'occident piégé par la mondialisation / Jean Mandelbaum, Daniel Haber. Published/Created: Paris: Descartes, 2001. Related Names: Haber, Daniel. Description: 134 p.; cm. ISBN 2844460305 Subjects: China - Economics - Globalization.

Mandle, Jay R. Globalization and the poor / Jay R. Mandle. Published/Created: New York, NY: Cambridge University Press, 2002. Description: p. cm. ISBN 0521815045 (hardback) 0521893526 (pbk.) Notes: Includes bibliographical references and index. Subjects: International economic relations. Globalization--Economic aspects. Poverty--Government policy. LC Classification: HF1359 .M356 2002 Dewey Class No.: 337 21

Many globalizations: cultural diversity in the contemporary world / Tomatsu Aoki ... [et al.].; edited by Peter L. Berger and Samuel P. Huntington. Published/Created: New York: Oxford University Press, 2002. Related Names: Aoki, Tomatsu. Berger, Peter L. Huntington, Samuel P. Description: p. cm. ISBN 0195151461 (alk. paper) Notes: Includes bibliographical references and index. Subjects: Culture. Globalization. LC Classification: HM621 .M36 2002 Dewey

Class No.: 306 21

Market killing: what the free market does and what social scientists can do about it / edited by Greg Philo and David Miller. Published/Created: New York: Longman 2001. Related Names: Philo, Greg. Miller, David, 1964- Description: xvii, 262 p.; 24 cm. ISBN 058238236X (paper: alk. paper) Notes: Includes bibliographical references and index. Subjects: Free enterprise--Social aspects. Values. International economic relations. Globalization. LC Classification: HB95 .M364 2001 Dewey Class No.: 337 21

Mar-Molinero, Clare, 1948- The politics of language in the Spanish-speaking world: from colonisation to globalisation / Clare Mar-Molinero. Published/Created: London: New York: Routledge, 2000. Description: xiii, 242 p.; 24 cm. ISBN 0415156548 0415156556 (pbk.) Notes: Includes bibliographical references (p. [218]-230) and index. Subjects: Language and languages--Political aspects. Spanish language--Political aspects. Language and education. Language planning. Nationalism. Series: The Politics of language LC Classification: P119.3 .M36 2000 Dewey Class No.: 460/.9/0904 21

Martin, Hervé René. La mondialisation racontée à ceux qui la subissent / Hervé René Martin. Published/Created: Castelnau-le-Lez: Climats, c1999. Description: 173 p.; 18 cm. ISBN 2841581284 Notes: Includes bibliographical references. Subjects: Economic history--1990- Globalization. LC Classification: HC59.15 .M36 1999

Martínez Gutiérrez, Enrique. Dimensiones de la integración europea y americana / Enrique Martínez Gutiérrez ... [et al.]; compiladores: Carlos Molina del Pozo y Jaime Delgado Rojas. Edition Information: 1a ed. Published/Created:

Heredia: Facultad de Ciencias Sociales UNA, 2000. Description: 305 p.; cm. ISBN 9968994707 Summary: Eight scholarly essays on regional economic and political integration relative to the European community, including security and defense, globalization, MERCOSUR, the business sector in Central America and sustainable development.

Mathew, Grace. Towards enriching years: a programme for the elderly by the Family Welfare Agency / Grace Mathew, in collaboration with Gita Shah and Rosamma Veedon. Published/Created: Mumbai: Tata Institute of Social Sciences, [1997?] Related Names: Shah, Gita. Veedon, Rosamma. Tata Institute of Social Sciences. National Seminar on "Globalisation and the Ageing: Implications for Gerontological Social Work (1997: Tata Institute of Social Sciences) Description: 75 p., [4] p. of plates: col. ill.; 23 cm. Notes: "Originally presented at the National Seminar on "Globalisation and the Ageing: Implications for Gerontological Social Work" organised by the Tata Institute of Social Sciences and the Family Welfare Agency, Mumbai, December 22-24, 1997." Includes bibliographical references (p. [69]-70). Subjects: Social work with the aged--India. Gerontology--India. Aged--Services for--India. Aged--India--Family relationships. Aged--Care--India. LC Classification: HV1464.I52 M37 1997 Dewey Class No.: 362.6/0954 21

McAleese, Dermot. Economics for business: competition, macro-stability, and globalisation / Dermot McAleese. Edition Information: 2nd ed. Published/Created: Harlow, England; New York: Financial Times, Prentice Hall, 2001. Description: xxi, 649 p.: ill.; 24 cm. ISBN 0273646222 (alk. paper) Notes: Includes bibliographical references and index. Subjects: Managerial economics. LC

Classification: HD30.22 .M29 2001
Dewey Class No.: 330/.024/658 21

McAuley, Andrew. International marketing: consuming globally, thinking locally / Andrew McAuley. Published/Created: New York: Wiley, 2001. Description: p. cm. ISBN 0471897442 Notes: Includes bibliographical references and index. Subjects: Export marketing. International economic relations. Globalization. LC Classification: HF1416 .M345 2001 Dewey Class No.: 658.8/48 21

McCall, Morgan W. Developing global executives: the lessons of international experience / Morgan W. McCall, Jr., George P. Hollenbeck. Published/Created: Boston: Harvard Business School Press, 2002. Related Names: Hollenbeck, George P. Description: p. cm. ISBN 1578513367 (alk. paper) Notes: Includes index. Subjects: Executives--Training of. Executive ability. Globalization. Industrial management. LC Classification: HD30.4 .M42 2002 Dewey Class No.: 658.4/07124 21

McCormick, Dorothy, 1941- Globalization and regionalisation of Kenya's foreign trade and production / Dorothy McCormick & Poul Ove Pedersen. Published/Created: Copenhagen, Denmark: Centre for Development Research, in cooperation with Institute of Development Studies, University of Nairobi, 1999. Related Names: Pedersen, Poul O. Description: 40 p.: ill.; 30 cm. Notes: "Working paper subseries on globalisation and economic restructuring in Africa no. vi." Includes bibliographical references. Subjects: Kenya--Commerce. Series: CDR working paper, 0904-4701; 99.8 LC Classification: HD72 .C38 no. 99.8

McGrew, Anthony G. Global politics: globalization and the nation-state / Anthony G. McGrew, Paul G. Lewis, et al. Published/Created: Cambridge [England]: Polity Press; Oxford [England]; Cambridge, MA, USA: Blackwell Publishers, 1992. Related Names: Lewis, Paul G., 1945- Description: 337 p.: ill., map; 26 cm. ISBN 0745607551 (alk. paper) 074560756X (pbk.: alk. paper) Notes: "Revised versions of papers originally published as part of the teaching package for Global Politics"--Pref. Includes bibliographical references and index. Subjects: International relations. National state. World politics--1989- Globalization. LC Classification: JX1395 .M347 1992 Dewey Class No.: 327/.09/048 20

McLean, Martin. Educational traditions compared: content, teaching, and learning in industrialised countries / Martin McLean. Published/Created: London: D. Fulton, 1995. Description: vi, 202 p.; 23 cm. Notes: Includes bibliographical references (p. [181]-193) and index. Subjects: Comparative education. Education--Curricula--Cross-cultural studies. Globalization. LC Classification: LB43 .M38 1995 Dewey Class No.: 370/.9 21

McMurray, Christine. Diseases of globalization: socioeconomic transitions and health / Christine McMurray and Roy Smith. Published/Created: Sterling, VA: Earthscan Publications, 2001. Related Names: Smith, Roy (Roy Hugh), 1956- Description: p. cm. ISBN 1853837105 (hardcover) 1853837113 (pbk.) Notes: Includes bibliographical references and index. Subjects: Health transition. World health. Globalization--Health aspects. Public health--Mongolia. Public health--Uzbekistan. Public health--Marshall Islands. LC Classification: RA441 .M43 2001 Dewey Class No.: 362.1 21

McNiven, James D. Atlantic Canada and the future: trends, challenges and opportunities / submitted to Atlantic Canada Opportunities Agency; submitted by J.D. McNiven, J.E. Plumstead, B.R. Russell. Published/Created: [Ottawa]: The Agency, 1997. Related Names: Plumstead, J. E. (Janice E.) Russell, B. R. (Brian R.) Atlantic Canada Opportunities Agency. Description: 51 p.; 28 cm. ISBN 0662274407 Notes: Cover title. Subjects: Technological innovations--Economic aspects--Canada. Economic forecasting--Atlantic Provinces. Globalization. Atlantic Provinces--Economic conditions. Atlantic Provinces--Economic policy. LC Classification: HC117.A88 M37 1997 Govt. Doc. No.: C89-4/52-1997E

Meanings of globalisation: Indian and French perspective / edited by Rama S. Melkote. Published/Created: New Delhi: Sterling Publishers, c2001. Related Names: Melkote, Rama S. Description: xxiv, 272 p.; 23 cm. ISBN 8120723759 Notes: Includes bibliographical references.

Measures of the transnationalization of economic activity / [prepared by Robert E. Lipsey with assistance of Ewa Wojas and Li Xu]; United Nations Conference on Trade and Development. Published/Created: New York: United Nations, 2001. Related Names: Lipsey, Robert E. Wojas, Ewa. Xu, Li. United Nations Conference on Trade and Development. Description: xi, 93 p.; 30 cm. ISBN 9211125111 Notes: Includes bibliographical references. Subjects: Globalization--Economic aspects--Statistical methods. International trade--Statistical methods. International business enterprises--Statistical methods. Economic indicators. LC Classification: HF1016 .M43 2001

Measuring globalisation: the role of multinationals in OECD economies = Mesurer la mondialisation: le poids des multinationales dans les économies de

l'OCDE / Organisation for Economic Co-operation and Development. Edition Information: 1999 ed. Published/Created: Paris: Organisation for Economic Co-operation and Development, 1999. Related Names: Organisation for Economic Co-operation and Development. Economic Analysis and Statistics Division. Organisation for Economic Co-operation and Development. Working Party on Industrial Statistics Description: 306 p.: ill.; 28 cm. ISBN 926405877X Notes: "This publication is the first to present statistical data on the share of OECD economies controlled by multinationals. It has been prepared by the Economic Analysis and Statistics Division of the OECD Directorate for Science, Technology and Industry, under the auspices of the Working Party on Industrial Statistics of the Industry Committee (Expert Group on Globalisation)"--P. 3. Text in English and French Subjects: International business enterprises--OECD countries Statistics International economic integration--Statistics Globalization--Statistics. Industrial statistics--OECD countries. Industrial surveys--OECD countries. Series: OECD statistics LC Classification: HD2755.5 M47 1999 Dewey Class No.: 338.8/89171/3 21

Measuring globalisation: the role of multinationals in OECD economies = Mesurer la mondialisation: le poids des multinationales dans les économies de l'OCDE / Organisation for Economic Co-operation and Development. Edition Information: 1999 ed. Published/Created: Paris: Organisation for Economic Co-operation and Development, 1999. Related Names: Organisation for Economic Co-operation and Development. Economic Analysis and Statistics Division. Organisation for Economic Co-operation and

Development. Working Party on Industrial Statistics Description: 306 p.: ill.; 28 cm. ISBN 926405877X Notes: "This publication is the first to present statistical data on the share of OECD economies controlled by multinationals. It has been prepared by the Economic Analysis and Statistics Division of the OECD Directorate for Science, Technology and Industry, under the auspices of the Working Party on Industrial Statistics of the Industry Committee (Expert Group on Globalisation)"--P. 3. Text in English and French Subjects: International business enterprises--OECD countries Statistics International economic integration--Statistics Globalization--Statistics. Industrial statistics--OECD countries. Industrial surveys--OECD countries. Series: OECD statistics LC Classification: HD2755.5 M47 1999 Dewey Class No.: 338.8/89171/3 21

Mehta, Vasant P. FERA, Indian reforms, globalisation (FIRG) / Vasant P. Mehta. Edition Information: 1st ed. Published/Created: Bombay: Snow White Publications, 1994. Description: xxi, 921 p.; 25 cm. ISBN 8185561117 : Summary: Pleads for the abolition of the Foreign Exchange Regulation Act, 1973. Notes: Spine FIRG. Includes index. Subjects: Foreign exchange--Law and legislation--India. LC Classification: KNS2772 .M44 1994 Dewey Class No.: 343.54/032 345.40332 20

Meier, Bernd, 1944- Mobile Wirtschaft--immobile Gesellschaft: gesellschaftspolitische Konsequenzen der Globalisierung / Bernd Meier. Published/Created: Köln: Deutscher Instituts-Verlag, c1999. Description: 288 p.: ill.; 19 cm. ISBN 3602144860 Notes: Includes bibliographical references (p. 266-287). Subjects: Globalization. Social change--Germany. Germany--Economic

conditions--1990- LC Classification: HC286.8 .M45 1999

Meier, Bernd, 1944- Technischer Fortschritt und Mobilität: neue Herausforderungen durch die Globalisierung / Bernd Meier. Published/Created: Köln: DTV, c1997. Description: 56 p.: ill.; 21 cm. ISBN 3602240614 Notes: Includes bibliographical references (p. 53-55). Subjects: Technological innovations. International economic integration. Globalization. Series: Beiträge zur Wirtschafts- und Sozialpolitik; 239. LC Classification: HC79.T4 M426 1997 Dewey Class No.: 337.1 21

Mejía A., Carlos. Globalización, trabajo e identidad sindical en el Perú / Carlos Mejía A. Published/Created: [Lima: Instituto de Defensa Legal, 1999]. Description: 31 p.; 21 cm. Subjects: Labor unions--Peru. International economic relations. Globalization.

Memoria del xi Congreso de Economistas de América Central y el Caribe: Tecucigalpa, M.D.C., Honduras, C.A., 23, 24 y 25 de septiembre de 1998. Published/Created: Tegucigalpa, M.D.C., Honduras, C.A.: Colegio Hondureño de Economistas, [1999]. Description: 587 p.: ill. ISBN 9992662301 Notes: Includes bibliographical references. Subjects: Economic development--Caribbean Area--Congresses. Agriculture and state--Caribbean Area--Congresses. Globalization--Congresses. Caribbean Area--Economic conditions--Congresses. Caribbean Area--Economic integration--Congresses.

Mencía Bárcenas, Olga Iris. La máscara del despojo / Olga Iris Mencía Bárcenas. Edition Information: 1a ed. Published/Created: Tegucigalpa: Guardabarranco, 1999. Description: 74 p.; cm. ISBN 999262017X Summary:

Socioeconomic and political essays critical of Honduras' subordinate role in a world of globalization and transnational ascendancy.

Methfessel, Klaus. Der Preis der Gleichheit: wie Deutschland die Chancen der Globalisierung verspielt / Klaus Methfessel, Jörg M. Winterberg. Published/Created: Düsseldorf: Econ, c1998. Related Names: Winterberg, Jörg M., 1963- Description: 287 p.; 22 cm. ISBN 3430156610 Notes: Includes bibliographical references (p. 263-273) and indexes. Subjects: Globalization. International economic relations. Competition, International. Germany--Foreign economic relations. LC Classification: HF1545 .M45 1998 Dewey Class No.: 337.43 21

Michalet, Charles Albert. La séduction des nations, ou, comment attirer les investissements / Charles-Albert Michalet. Published/Created: Paris: Economica, 1999. Description: 134 p.; 24 cm. ISBN 2717839240 Notes: Includes bibliographical references. Subjects: Investments, Foreign. International business enterprises. Industrial promotion. Globalization. Investissements étrangers. Concurrence internationale. Mondialisation (économie politique). LC Classification: HG4538 .M415 1999

Michel, Joachim. Globalization and labor: bibliography of German and English language literature / compiled by Joachim Michel. Published/Created: Kiel: Bibliothek des Instituts für Weltwirtschaft, 1998. Description: 150 p.; 30 cm. Notes: Includes index. Subjects: Labor--Bibliography. Globalization--Bibliography. Series: Kieler Bibliographien zu aktuellen ökonomischen Themen; Bd. 17 LC Classification: Z7164.L1 M6175 1998

HD4901

Micklethwait, John. A future perfect: the challenge and hidden promise of globalization / John Micklethwait and Adrian Wooldridge. Edition Information: 1st ed. Published/Created: New York: Crown Business, c2000. Related Names: Wooldridge, Adrian. Description: xxix, 386 p.; 24 cm. ISBN 0812930967 (alk. paper) Notes: Includes bibliographical references (p. 361-368) and index. Subjects: Globalization. International economic relations. LC Classification: JZ1318 .M53 2000 Dewey Class No.: 303.48/2 21

Mies, Maria. Globalisierung von unten: der Kampf gegen die Herrschaft der Konzerne / Maria Mies. Published/Created: Hamburg: Rotbuch, c2001. Description: 254 p.; 21 cm. ISBN 3434530843 (pbk.) Notes: Includes bibliographical references (p. 221-226). Subjects: International economic relations. Globalization--Social aspects. Protest movements. LC Classification: HF1359 .M54 2001

Migration, globalisation, and human security / edited by David T. Graham and Nana K. Poku. Published/Created: London; New York: Routledge, 2000. Related Names: Graham, David T., 1953- Poku, Nana, 1971- Description: x, 222 p.; 24 cm. ISBN 0415184363 Notes: Includes bibliographical references and index. Subjects: Emigration and immigration--Political aspects. National security. Series: Routledge research in population and migration; 2 LC Classification: JV6255 .M54 2000 Dewey Class No.: 325/.09/049 21

Mills, Greg, Dr. The wired model: South Africa, foreign policy, and globalisation / Greg Mills. Edition Information: 1st ed. Published/Created: Cape Town: Tafelberg: South African Institute of

International Affairs, 2000. Related Names: South African Institute of International Affairs. Description: 368 p.; 22 cm. ISBN 0624039218 Notes: Includes bibliographical references and index. Subjects: Globalization. South Africa-- Foreign relations--1994- South Africa-- Foreign economic relations. LC Classification: DT1971 .M55 2000 Dewey Class No.: 327.68 21

Mills, Greg, Dr. The wired model: South Africa, foreign policy, and globalisation / Greg Mills. Edition Information: 1st ed. Published/Created: Cape Town: Tafelberg: South African Institute of International Affairs, 2000. Related Names: South African Institute of International Affairs. Description: 368 p.; 22 cm. ISBN 0624039218 Notes: Includes bibliographical references and index. Subjects: Globalization. South Africa-- Foreign relations--1994- South Africa-- Foreign economic relations. LC Classification: DT1971 .M55 2000 Dewey Class No.: 327.68 21

Minority nationalism and the changing international order / edited by Michael Keating and John McGarry. Published/Created: Oxford; New York: Oxford University Press, 2001. Related Names: Keating, Michael, 1950- McGarry, John. Description: viii, 366 p.: ill., maps; 24 cm. ISBN 0199242143 (alk. paper) Notes: Includes bibliographical references and index. Subjects: Nationalism. Minorities--Political activity. Globalization. European Union. LC Classification: JC312 .M56 2001 Dewey Class No.: 320.54/08 21

Mittelman, James H. The globalization syndrome: transformation and resistance / James H. Mittelman. Published/Created: Princeton, N.J.: Princeton University Press, 2000. Description: xvi, 286 p.; 24 cm. ISBN 0691009872 (cloth: alk. paper)

0691009880 (pbk.: alk. paper) Notes: Includes bibliographical references (p. [253]-275) and index. Subjects: International economic relations. International relations. Globalization. LC Classification: HF1359 .M58 2000 Dewey Class No.: 337 21

Mkandawire, P. Thandika. Globalization and social development after Copenhagen: premises, promises, and policies / by Thandika Mkandawire and Virginia Rodríguez. Published/Created: Geneva: United Nations Research Institute for Social Development, [2000] Related Names: Rodríguez, Virginia. United Nations Research Institute for Social Development. Geneva 2000 (2000: Geneva, Switzerland) Description: x, 33 p.: ill.; 30 cm. ISBN 9290850337 Notes: "Geneva 2000: the next step in social development"--Cover. "May 2000." Includes bibliographical references (p. 30-33). Summaries in English, French, and Spanish. Subjects: Economic development--Social aspects--Congresses. Globalization--Economic aspects-- Congresses. Globalization--Social aspects--Congresses. Globalization-- Economic aspects--Developing countries Congresses. Globalization--Social aspects--Developing countries Congresses. Developing countries-- Economic conditions--Congresses. Series: Occasional paper (Geneva 2000); 10. LC Classification: HD73 .M53 2000

Moe-Lobeda, Cynthia, 1954- Healing a broken world: globalization and God / Cynthia D. Moe-Lobeda. Published/Created: Minneapolis, Minn.: Fortress Press, 2002. Description: p. cm. ISBN 0800632508 (alk. paper) Notes: Includes bibliographical references and index. Subjects: Globalization--Religious aspects--Christianity. Economics-- Religious aspects--Christianity. Globalization--Moral and ethical aspects.

Economics--Moral and ethical aspects. Christian ethics--Lutheran authors. LC Classification: BR115.E3 M64 2002 Dewey Class No.: 261.8/5 21

Mol, A. P. J. Globalization and environmental reform: the ecological modernization of the global economy / Arthur P.J. Mol. Published/Created: Cambridge, Mass.: MIT Press, 2001. Description: p. cm. ISBN 0262133954 (hc.: alk. paper) Notes: Includes bibliographical references and index. Subjects: Sustainable development. Environmental policy. Environmental degradation. Globalization. LC Classification: HC79.E5 .M64 2001 Dewey Class No.: 333.7 21

Mondialisation capitaliste et dominations impériales: Seattle, Porto Alegre, Gênes / dossier préparé par Christophe Aguiton et Daniel Bensaïd; [Christophe Aguiton, Sophie Zafari, Josep-Maria Atentas... et al.]. Published/Created: Paris: Textuel, 2001. Description: 186 p.; cm. ISBN 284597034X Subjects: Globalization. Series: Contretemps; no. 2

Mondialisation et régulations: Europe et Japon face à la singularité américaine / sous la direction de Robert Boyer et Pierre-François Souyri. Published/Created: Paris: Découverte, 2001. Description: 179 p.; cm. ISBN 2707135429 Subjects: Globalization. Series: Textes à l'appui. Economie

Mondialisation et sociétés multiculturelles: l'incertain du futur / sous la direction de Marina Ricciardelli, Sabine Urban, Kostas Nanopoulos. Edition Information: 1re éd. Published/Created: Paris: Presses universitaires de France, 2000. Related Names: Ricciardelli, M. (Marina) Urban, Sabine M.-L. Nanopoulos, Kostas. Description: 424 p.; 22 cm. ISBN 2130500404 Notes: Includes bibliographical references. Subjects:

Globalization--Forecasting. LC Classification: IN PROCESS

Mondialisation: les mots et les choses / GEMDEV; coordonné par Michel Beaud ... [et al.]. Published/Created: Paris: Karthala, c1999. Related Names: Beaud, Michel. GEMDEV (Group) Description: 358 p.; 24 cm. ISBN 2865379574 Notes: At foot of Groupe mondialisation du GEMDEV. Includes bibliographical references and index. Subjects: International economic relations. Globalization. Series: Hommes et sociétés LC Classification: HF1359 .M665 1999

Mora A., Jorge A. Universidad y sociedad en el siglo XXI / Jorge Mora Alfaro. Edition Information: 1a ed. Published/Created: Heredia: Editorial Universidad Nacional, 2000. Description: 170 p.; 21 cm. ISBN 9977651957 Summary: An analysis of contemporary higher education in Costa Rica by sociologist and rector of the national university during 1995-2000. Includes sections on the political and educational impact of globalization, human development, cooperativism and new trends. Notes: Includes bibliographical references. Subjects: Education, Higher--Costa Rica. Universities and colleges--Costa Rica. LC Classification: LA448 .M67 2000 Dewey Class No.: 378.7286 21

Moran, Albert. Copycat television: globalisation, program formats, and cultural identity / Albert Moran. Published/Created: Luton, Bedfordshire, U.K.: University of Luton Press, c1998. Description: xi, 204 p.: ill., ports. 24 cm. ISBN 1860205372 (pbk) Notes: Includes bibliographical references (p. 179-196) and indexes. Subjects: Television programs--Europe. Television programs--Australia. LC Classification: PN1992.3.E78 M67 1998 Dewey Class

No.: 791.45/75/094 21

Moreau Defarges, Philippe. Les relations internationales dans le monde d'aujourd'hui: entre globalisation et fragmentation / Philippe Moreau Defarges. Edition Information: 4e éd. actualisée et aug. Published/Created: Paris: Editions S.T.H., 1992. Description: 474 p.: map; 24 cm. ISBN 2903463182 : Notes: Includes bibliographical references (p. [461]-470). Subjects: International relations. World politics--1945- Series: Collection "Les Grands actuels", 1152-0000 LC Classification: JX1391 .M59 1992

Morris, Mike, 1949- Globalisation and the restructuring of Durban's industry / Mike Morris, Justin Barnes, Nikki Dunne. Published/Created: Durban: School of Development Studies (incorporating the Centre for Social & Development Studies), University of Natal, 1998. Related Names: Barnes, Justin. Dunne, Nikki. University of Natal. School of Development Studies. Description: 37 p.; 21 cm. ISBN 186840286X (pbk.) Notes: Bibliography: p. 34-37. Subjects: Manufacturing industries--South Africa--Durban. Manufacturing industries--Government policy--South Africa. Industrial policy--South Africa. Free trade--South Africa. Competition, International. Globalization. Series: CSDS working paper; no. 18 LC Classification: HD9737.S63 D87 1998 Dewey Class No.: 338.09684/55 21

Morris, Mike, 1949- Globalisation and the restructuring of Durban's industry / Mike Morris, Justin Barnes, Nikki Dunne. Published/Created: Durban: School of Development Studies (incorporating the Centre for Social & Development Studies), University of Natal, 1998. Related Names: Barnes, Justin. Dunne, Nikki. University of Natal. School of Development Studies. Description: 37 p.; 21 cm. ISBN 186840286X (pbk.) Notes: Bibliography: p. 34-37. Subjects: Manufacturing industries--South Africa--Durban. Manufacturing industries--Government policy--South Africa. Industrial policy--South Africa. Free trade--South Africa. Competition, International. Globalization. Series: CSDS working paper; no. 18 LC Classification: HD9737.S63 D87 1998 Dewey Class No.: 338.09684/55 21

Morrison, Janet. The international environment of business: diversity and the global economy / Janet Morrison. Published/Created: New York: Palgrave, 2002. Description: p. cm. ISBN 0333921445 0333921453 (pbk.) Notes: Includes bibliographical references and index. Subjects: International economic relations. International business enterprises. International trade. Globalization--Economic aspects. Competition, International. LC Classification: HF1359 .M672 2002 Dewey Class No.: 337 21

Morshidi Sirat. Globalisation of economic activity and Third World cities: a case study of Kuala Lumpur / Morshidi Sirat, Suriati Ghazali. Published/Created: Kuala Lumpur: Utusan Publications & Distributors, 1999. Related Names: Suriati Ghazali. Description: 122 p.: ill., maps; 23 cm. ISBN 9676109045 Notes: "Bibliography on Kuala Lumpur and globalisation": p. 94-122. Includes bibliographical references (p. 84-93). Subjects: Urbanization--Malaysia--Kuala Lumpur. Kuala Lumpur (Malaysia)--Economic conditions. LC Classification: HT395.G7 M67 1999

Mosler, David, 1941- Global America: imposing liberalism on a recalcitrant world / David Mosler and Bob Catley. Published/Created: Westport, Conn.:

Praeger, 2000. Related Names: Catley, Robert. Description: xiv, 225 p.; 24 cm. ISBN 0275966623 (alk. paper) Notes: Includes bibliographical references (p. [213]-215) and index. Subjects: Globalization. International economic relations. United States--Foreign relations--1993-2001. LC Classification: JZ1480 .M67 2000 Dewey Class No.: 327.73/009 21

Moving mountains: communities confront mining and globalisation / Geoff Evans, James Goodman, Nina Lansbury, editors. Published/Created: Sydney, N.S.W.: Mineral Policy Institute and Otford Press, 2001. Related Names: Goodman, James, 1965- Evans, Geoff (Geoffrey Russell), 1952- Lansbury, Nina. Description: xxiii, 284 p.: ill.; 21 cm. ISBN 1876928492 Notes: Includes index. Subjects: Mineral industries--Australia. Mining corporations--Papua New Guinea. Mining corporations--Australia. Mineral industries--Canada. Mineral industries--Papua New Guinea. Mining corporations--Philippines. Mineral industries--Asia. Mining corporations--Canada. Globalization. Series: Contemporary Otford series

Moving mountains: communities confront mining and globalisation / Geoff Evans, James Goodman, Nina Lansbury, editors. Published/Created: Sydney, N.S.W.: Mineral Policy Institute and Otford Press, 2001. Related Names: Goodman, James, 1965- Evans, Geoff (Geoffrey Russell), 1952- Lansbury, Nina. Description: xxiii, 284 p.: ill.; 21 cm. ISBN 1876928492 Notes: Includes index. Subjects: Mineral industries--Australia. Mining corporations--Papua New Guinea. Mining corporations--Australia. Mineral industries--Canada. Mineral industries--Papua New Guinea. Mining corporations--Philippines. Mineral industries--Asia. Mining corporations--Canada.

Globalization. Series: Contemporary Otford series

Müftüoglu, Riza. Küreselle‚sme ve Türkiye / Riza Müftüoglu. Published/Created: Ankara: [s.n.], 1995 (Ankara: Grafiker) Description: iv, 74 p.: ill.; 20 cm. Notes: Includes bibliographical references (p. 74). Subjects: Globalization--Economic aspects--Turkey. Turkey--Economic integration. LC Classification: MLCSN 2001/01444 (J)

Müller, Hans-Erich, 1945- Neue Managementkonzepte: Trends und Erfahrungen = Nowe koncepcje w zarzadzaniu: trendy i do´swiadczenia / Hans-Erich Müller. Published/Created: Pozna´n: Wydawn. Wyzszej Szkoly Bankowej, 1997. Description: 36 p.: ill.; 24 cm. Notes: Includes bibliographical references. German and Polish. Subjects: Management--Employee participation. Management. Globalization. Competition, International. Series: Wyklady otwarte Wyzszej Szkoly Bankowej w Poznaniu; zesz. 3. LC Classification: HD5650 .M755 1997

Multinational firms and impacts on employment, trade, and technology: new perspectives for a new century / edited by Robert E. Lipsey and Jean-Louis Mucchielli. Published/Created: London; New York: Routledge, 2001. Related Names: Lipsey, Robert E. Mucchielli, Jean Louis. Description: p. cm. ISBN 0415270537 (alk. paper) Notes: "This book is the first volume of a collection selected papers from a conference held in la Sorbonne, Paris, June 17-18, 1999"-- Acknowledgments. Includes bibliographical references and index. Subjects: Foreign trade and employment--Congresses. International business enterprises--Congresses. Investments, Foreign--Congresses. International division of labor--Congresses.

Employees--Effect of technological innovations on Congresses. Unemployment--Congresses. Labor economics--Congresses. Industrial policy--Congresses. Economic policy--Congresses. Full employment policies--Congresses. Globalization--Economic aspects--Congresses. Series: Studies in global competition; v. 11 LC Classification: HD5710.7 .M85 2001 Dewey Class No.: 338.8/8 21

Multinationals in a new era: international strategy and management / edited by James H. Taggart, Maureen Berry, and Michael McDermott. Published/Created: New York: Palgrave, 2001. Related Names: Taggart, J. H. (James H.), 1943- Berry, Maureen. McDermott, Michael C. Academy of International Business. UK Chapter. Conference (27th: 2000?: University of Strathclyde) Description: p. cm. ISBN 033396389X (cloth) Notes: Papers from the 27th Annual Conference of the UK Chapter of the Academy of International Business hosted by the University of Strathclyde in 2000? Includes bibliographical references and index. Subjects: International business enterprises--Management Congresses. Globalization--Economic aspects--Congresses. Series: Academy of International Business (Series) (Palgrave (Firm)) LC Classification: HD62.4 .M844 2001 Dewey Class No.: 658/.049 21

Munck, Ronaldo. Globalisation and labour: the new great transformation / Ronaldo Munck. Published/Created: New York, N.Y.: Zed Books, 2002. Description: p. cm. ISBN 1842770705 (cased) 1842770713 (limp) Notes: Includes bibliographical references and index. Subjects: International labor activities. Globalization. LC Classification: HD6475.A1 M86 2002 Dewey Class No.: 331 21

Munck, Ronaldo. Globalisation and labour: the new great transformation / Ronaldo Munck. Published/Created: New York, N.Y.: Zed Books, 2002. Description: p. cm. ISBN 1842770705 (cased) 1842770713 (limp) Notes: Includes bibliographical references and index. Subjects: International labor activities. Globalization. LC Classification: HD6475.A1 M86 2002 Dewey Class No.: 331 21

Murden, Simon. Islam, the Middle East, and the new global hegemony / Simon Murden. Published/Created: Boulder, Colo.: Lynne Rienner Publishers, 2002. Description: p.; cm. ISBN 1588260593 (alk. paper) Notes: Includes bibliographical references and index. Subjects: Islam and politics--Middle East. Globalization. Liberalism. Middle East--Politics and government--1945- LC Classification: DS63.1 M84 2002 Dewey Class No.: 327/.0917/671 21

Murillo Rodríguez, Carlos. Comercio y ambiente: ensayos críticos / Carlos Murillo Rodríguez. Edition Information: 1a ed. Published/Created: Heredia: Editorial Fundación UNA, 2000. Description: 192 p.; cm. ISBN 9968140791 Summary: A scholarly analysis of globalization and sustainable development in Central and Latin America.

Murtha, Thomas P. Managing new industry creation: global knowledge formation and entrepreneurship in high technology / Thomas P. Murtha, Stefanie Ann Lenway, and Jeffrey A. Hart. Published/Created: Stanford, Calif.: Stanford University Press, c2001. Related Names: Lenway, Stefanie Ann. Hart, Jeffrey A. Description: xvi, 269 p.; 24 cm. ISBN 0804742286 (alk. paper) 0804742464 (pbk.) Notes: Series statement on jacket. Includes bibliographical references (p.

249-254) and index. Subjects: New
products--Management. New products--
Marketing. High technology industries--
Management. Technology transfer.
Globalization--Economic aspects. Series:
[Stanford business books] LC
Classification: HF5415.153 .M87 2001
Dewey Class No.: 658.5/75 21

Mussali Galante, Rina. El desencuentro
americano: México y Estados Unidos en
la globalización / Rina Mussali Galante.
Published/Created: México, D.F.: Instituto
Mora, 2000. Description: 249 p.; 21 cm.
ISBN 9706840303 Notes: Includes
bibliographical references (p. 229-249).
Subjects: Globalization. Mexico--Foreign
economic relations--United States. United
States--Foreign economic relations--
Mexico.

Nana-Sinkam, Samuel. Le Cameroun dans la
globalisation: conditions et prémisses
pour un développement durable et
équitable / Samuel C. Nana-Sinkam.
Published/Created: Yaoundé: Editions
CLE, 1999. Description: 203 p.; 21 cm.
Notes: Includes bibliographical references
(p. 197-199). Subjects: International
economic relations. Globalization.
Cameroon--Economic policy. LC
Classification: HC995 .N34 1999

Nana-Sinkam, Samuel. Le Cameroun dans la
globalisation: conditions et prémisses
pour un développement durable et
équitable / Samuel C. Nana-Sinkam.
Published/Created: Yaoundé: Editions
CLE, 1999. Description: 203 p.; 21 cm.
Notes: Includes bibliographical references
(p. 197-199). Subjects: International
economic relations. Globalization.
Cameroon--Economic policy. LC
Classification: HC995 .N34 1999

Narula, Rajneesh, 1963- Multinational
investment and economic structure:
globalisation and competitiveness /

Rajneesh Narula. Published/Created:
London; New York: Routledge, 1996.
Description: xviii, 217 p.: ill.; 24 cm.
ISBN 0415130131 (hb.: alk. paper) Notes:
Includes bibliographical references (p.
198-208) and index. Subjects:
Investments, Foreign--Developing
countries. International business
enterprises--Finance. Series: Routledge
studies in international business and the
world economy, 1359-7930; 4 LC
Classification: HG5993 .N33 1996 Dewey
Class No.: 332.6/73 20

Nasir. Dampak globalisasi informasi dan
komunikasi terhadap kehidupan sosial
budaya generasi muda di Kelurahan
Cililitan, D.K.I. Jakarta / tim
peneliti/penulis, Abd. Nasir, Hendrika
T.S.; editor, A.S. Nasution.
Published/Created: [Jakarta]: Departemen
Pendidikan dan Kebudayaan, Bagian
Proyek Pengkajian dan Pembinaan Nilai-
Nilai Budaya Daerah Khusus Ibukota
Jakarta, 1994/1995 [i.e. 1994] Related
Names: Hendrika. Indonesia. Bagian
Proyek Pengkajian dan Pembinaan Nilai-
Nilai Budaya Daerah Khusus Ibukota
Jakarta. Description: viii, 78 p.: ill.; 24
cm. Summary: Impact of information and
communication globalization on
sociocultural life of the young generation
in Cililitan, Daerah Khusus Ibukota
Jakarta. Notes: Includes bibliographical
references (p. 67). Subjects: Mass media
and youth--Indonesia--Cililitan (Jakarta)
Communication and culture--Indonesia--
Cililitan (Jakarta) Communication--Social
aspects--Indonesia--Cililitan (Jakarta)
Cililitan (Jakarta, Indonesia)--Intellectual
life. LC Classification: HQ799.2.M35
N37 1994

Nationaler Staat und internationale Wirtschaft:
Anmerkungen zum Thema Globalisierung
/ Andreas Busch und Thomas Plümper
(Hrsg.). Published/Created: Baden-Baden:
Nomos, 1999. Related Names: Busch,

Andreas, 1962- Plümper, Thomas.
Description: xi, 367 p.: ill.; 23 cm. ISBN
3789060933 Notes: Includes
bibliographical references. Subjects:
International economic relations. State,
The. Globalization. LC Classification:
HF1359 .N379 1999

Nationalism and globalisation: east and west /
edited by Leo Suryadinata.
Published/Created: Singapore: Institute of
Southeast Asian Studies, c2000. Related
Names: Suryadinata, Leo. Institute of
Southeast Asian Studies. Description: xii,
366 p.; 24 cm. ISBN 9812300732 (pbk.)
9812300783 (hard) Notes: Includes
bibliographical references and index.

Nations et mondialisation / Gérard Lafay ... [et
al.]; préface de Erik Izraelewicz.
Published/Created: Paris: Economica,
1999. Related Names: Lafay, Gérard.
Description: 410 p.: col. ill.; 24 cm. ISBN
2717838600 Notes: Includes
bibliographical references (p. [385]-388).
Subjects: International economic
relations. Competition, International.
Globalization. LC Classification: HF1359
.N383 1999

Nations under siege: globalization and
nationalism in Asia / edited by Roy Starrs.
Published/Created: New York: Palgrave,
2002. Related Names: Starrs, Roy, 1946-
Description: p. cm. ISBN 0312294107
Notes: Includes index. Subjects:
Nationalism--Asia--History.
Globalization. Asia--Politics and
government. Ethnicity--Asia. Asia--Ethnic
relations. LC Classification: DS33.3
.N385 2002 Dewey Class No.: 320.54/095
21

Nelson Avila, Jorge Globalización, Estado y
economía solidaria / J. Nelson Avila.
Edition Information: 1. ed.
Published/Created: Tegucigalpa,
Honduras: Editorial Guaymuras, 1999.

Description: 144 p. ISBN 999261532X
Notes: Includes bibliographical
references. Subjects: Globalization.
International economic integration.
Honduras--Economic policy. Series:
Colección Códices

Nercessian, Andy. Postmodernism and
globalization in ethnomusicology: an
epistemological problem / Andy
Nercessian. Published/Created: Lanham,
Md.: Scarecrow Press, 2002. Description:
p. cm. ISBN 0810841223 (cloth: alk.
paper) Notes: Includes bibliographical
references (p.) and index. Subjects:
Ethnomusicology. Postmodernism.
Globalization. LC Classification: ML3798
.N46 2002 Dewey Class No.: 780/.89 21

Nevile, Ann. Policy choices in a globalized
world / Ann Nevile. Published/Created:
Huntington, NY: Nova Science, 2002.
Description: p. cm. ISBN 1590331958
Notes: Includes index. Subjects: Japan--
Economic policy--1989- International
economic relations. Globalization.
Australia--Economic policy. LC
Classification: HC605 .N442 2002 Dewey
Class No.: 338.994 21

New dimensions in global business:
perspective 2001 / edited by B.
Bhattacharyya, Amit Gupta. Edition
Information: 1st ed. Published/Created:
New Delhi: Excel Books, 1998. Related
Names: Bhattacharyya, B. (Bisweswar)
Gupta, Amit. Indian Institute of Foreign
Trade. Jagan Institute of Management
Studies. Description: 334 p.: ill.; 25 cm.
ISBN 8174461299 Summary: Papers
presented at a conference jointly
organized by Indian Institute of Foreign
Trade, and Jagan Institute of Management
Studies, on 27 September, 1997. Notes:
Includes statistical tables. Includes
bibliographical references. Subjects:
International economic relations--
Congresses. Globalization--Economic

aspects--India--Congresses. India--
Commercial policy--Congresses. India--
Economic conditions--1947---Congresses.
LC Classification: HF1352 .N43 1998

New directions in global economic
governance: managing globalisation in the
twenty-first century / edited by John J.
Kirton, George M. Von Furstenberg.
Published/Created: Aldershot, Hants,
England; Burlington, USA: Ashgate,
c2001. Related Names: Kirton, John J.
Von Furstenberg, George M., 1941-
Description: xxv, 364 p.; 23 cm. ISBN
0754616983 Notes: Includes selected
papers from varius conferences. Includes
bibliographical references (p. 329-347)
and index. Subjects: International
economic relations. Technological
innovations--Economic aspects. Free
trade. International finance. Globalization-
-Economic aspects. Series: The G8 and
global governance series LC
Classification: HF1359 .N468 2001
Dewey Class No.: 337 21

New directions in global economic
governance: managing globalisation in the
twenty-first century / edited by John J.
Kirton, George M. Von Furstenberg.
Published/Created: Aldershot, Hants,
England; Burlington, USA: Ashgate,
c2001. Related Names: Kirton, John J.
Von Furstenberg, George M., 1941-
Description: xxv, 364 p.; 23 cm. ISBN
0754616983 Notes: Includes selected
papers from varius conferences. Includes
bibliographical references (p. 329-347)
and index. Subjects: International
economic relations. Technological
innovations--Economic aspects. Free
trade. International finance. Globalization-
-Economic aspects. Series: The G8 and
global governance series LC
Classification: HF1359 .N468 2001
Dewey Class No.: 337 21

New regional development paradigms / edited
by Asfaw Kumssa ... [et al.]; foreword by
Yo Kimura. Published/Created: Westport,
Conn.: Greenwood Press, 2001- Related
Names: Kumssa, Asfaw. Description: v.
<1-2 >: ill., maps; 25 cm. ISBN
0313319170 (set: alk. paper) 0313317658
(v. 1: alk. paper) 0313317666 (v. 2: alk.
paper) 0313317674 (v. 3: alk. paper)
0313317682 (v. 4: alk. paper) Notes:
"Published in cooperation with the United
Nations and the United Nations Centre for
Regional Development." Includes
bibliographical references and indexes.
Subjects: Regional planning--Developing
countries. Globalization. Sustainable
development. Series: Contributions in
economics and economic history, 0084-
9235; no. 225 LC Classification:
HT395.D44 N48 2001 Dewey Class No.:
338.9 21

New worlds, new lives: globalization and
people of Japanese descent in the
Americas and from Latin America in
Japan / edited by Lane Ryo Hirabayashi,
Akemi Kikumura-Yano, James A.
Hirabayashi. Published/Created: Stanford,
California: Stanford University Press,
2002. Related Names: Hirabayashi, Lane
Ryo. Kikumura-Yano, Akemi.
Hirabayashi, James A. Description: p. cm.
ISBN 0804744610 (cloth: alk. paper)
0804744629 (paper: alk. paper) Notes:
Includes bibliographical references and
index. Subjects: Japanese--Ethnic
identity--America. Japanese--America--
History. Japanese--America--Social
conditions. Globalization--Social aspects.
America--Ethnic relations. Japan--
Relations--America. America--Relations--
Japan. Series: Asian America LC
Classification: E29.J3 N49 2002 Dewey
Class No.: 305.895/607 21

Newman, Nathan, 1966- Net loss: Internet
prophets, private profits, and the costs to
community / Nathan Newman.

Published/Created: University Park, Pa.: Pennsylvania State University Press, 2002. Description: p. cm. ISBN 0271022043 (cloth: alk. paper) 0271022051 (pbk.: alk. paper) Notes: Includes bibliographical references and index. Subjects: Internet industry--Government policy--United States. Internet--Government policy--United States. Industrial promotion--United States--Regional disparities Case studies. Computer industry--California--Santa Clara Valley (Santa Clara County) Computer industry--Developing countries. International division of labor. Globalization--Economic aspects--United States. United States--Economic conditions--1981---Regional disparities. LC Classification: HD9696.8.U62 N48 2002 Dewey Class No.: 338.4/7004678/0973 21

Newman, Otto. The promise of the third way: globalization and social justice / Otto Newman and Richard de Zoysa. Published/Created: Houndmills, Basingstoke, Hampshire; New York: Palgrave, 2001. Related Names: De Zoysa, Richard, 1944- Description: xiii, 255 p.; 23 cm. ISBN 0333792858 Notes: Includes bibliographical references (p. 243-249) and index. Subjects: Mixed economy. Globalization. Post-communism. Social justice. LC Classification: HB90 .N484 2001 Dewey Class No.: 337 21

News in a globalized society / edited by Stig Hjarvard. Published/Created: Göteborg: NORDICOM, c2001. Related Names: Hjarvard, Stig. Description: 236 p.; 25 cm. ISBN 9189471059 Contents: News media and the globalization of the public sphere / Stig Hjarvard -- Global news research and complex citizenship / Daniel Biltereyst -- International communication theory in transition / Ingrid Volkmer -- Media imperialism revisited / Chris A.

Paterson -- Why virtuality can be good for democracy / Klaus Bruhn Jensen -- The effect of globalization on media structures and norms / Hans-Henrik Holm -- Transnational politics and news production / Tore Slaatta -- Striving for credibility / Norbert Wildermuth -- Frames in television news / Claes de Vreese -- Globalisation of war news / Stig A. Nohrstedt & Rune Ottosen -- An "Insight" into CNN's coverage of NATO's Firts War / Daya Kishan Thussu. Notes: Includes bibliographical references. Subjects: Broadcast journalism. LC Classification: PN4784.B75 N49 2001 Dewey Class No.: 302.23 21

Ngwane, Trevor. The World movement against neo-liberal globalisation and resistance in South Africa / Trevor Ngwane. Published/Created: Port Louis, Mauritius: Ledikasyon pu travayer, [2001] Description: 53 p.; 20 cm. ISBN 999033336X Notes: Includes bibliographical references (p. 18-19). English and Mauritian French Creole. Series: Public lecture series (Ledikasyon pu travayer)

Nineteenth National District Development Conference: "human resource development (HRD): key to growth, development, and globalisation of the economy": Boipuso Conference Centre, Gaborone, 23rd-27th November 1998 / [prepared by Buchilan for Department of District Administration, Ministry of Local Government, Lands and Housing]. Published/Created: [Gaborone]: The Department, [1999] Related Names: Buchiplan. Botswana. Dept. of District Administration. Description: xi, 286 p.: ill.; 30 cm. Notes: "May 1999." Includes bibliographical references. Subjects: Personnel management--Botswana--Congresses. Globalization--Botswana--Congresses. Botswana--Economic policy--Congresses. LC Classification:

HF5549.2.B55 N38 1998 Dewey Class
No.: 331.11/096883 21

Nineteenth National District Development
Conference: "human resource
development (HRD): key to growth,
development, and globalisation of the
economy": Boipuso Conference Centre,
Gaborone, 23rd-27th November 1998 /
[prepared by Buchilan for Department of
District Administration, Ministry of Local
Government, Lands and Housing].
Published/Created: [Gaborone]: The
Department, [1999] Related Names:
Buchiplan. Botswana. Dept. of District
Administration. Description: xi, 286 p.:
ill.; 30 cm. Notes: "May 1999." Includes
bibliographical references. Subjects:
Personnel management--Botswana--
Congresses. Globalization--Botswana--
Congresses. Botswana--Economic policy-
-Congresses. LC Classification:
HF5549.2.B55 N38 1998 Dewey Class
No.: 331.11/096883 21

Ninsin, Kwame Akon, 1938- Globalisation
and the future of Africa / Kwame A.
Ninsin. Published/Created: [Harare]:
African Association of Political Science,
2000. Related Names: African Futures
Network of Centres of Excellence.
African Association of Political Science.
Description: 35 p.; 24 cm. Notes:
"Submitted to the African Futures
Network of Centres of Excellence by the
African Association of Political Science"-
-Acknowledgements. Includes
bibliographical references (p. 30-33).
Series: Occasional paper series (African
Association of Political Science); v. 4, no.
1.

Nirwhono, Lego. Kerjasama pelaku ekonomi
pada era globalisasi / oleh Lego
Nirwhono. Published/Created: [Jakarta]:
Departemen Pertahanan Keamanan RI,
Lembaga Ketahanan Nasional, 1997.
Description: xi, 46 leaves: ill.; 28 cm.

Summary: Economic cooperation
globalization among ASEAN countries;
paper. Notes: Includes bibliographical
references (leaves 45-46). LC
Classification: MLCME 98/00132 (H)

Nixon, Bruce. Global forces: a guide for
enlightened leaders: what companies and
individuals can do / Bruce Nixon.
Published/Created: Chalford,
Gloucestershire: Management Books
2000, 2000. Description: 259 p.; 21 cm.
ISBN 1852523530 (pbk.) Notes: Includes
bibliographical references (p. 247-250)
and index. Subjects: Organizational
change. Organizational behavior.
Leadership. International business
enterprises--Social aspects. Globalization-
-Social aspects. LC Classification:
HD58.8 .N577 2000

Non-state actors and authority in the global
system / edited by Richard A. Higgott,
Geoffrey R.D. Underhill, and Andreas
Bieler. Published/Created: London; New
York: Routledge, 2000. Related Names:
Higgott, Richard A. Underhill, Geoffrey
R. D. Bieler, Andreas, 1967- Description:
xvii, 301 p.: ill.; 25 cm. ISBN
0415220858 (hbk.: alk. paper) Notes:
Includes bibliographical references and
index. Subjects: International economic
relations. International economic
integration. International business
enterprises. Non-governmental
organizations. Series: Routledge/Warwick
studies in globalisation; 1 LC
Classification: HF1359 .N662 2000
Dewey Class No.: 337 21

Non-state actors in world politics / edited by
Daphne Josselin and William Wallace.
Published/Created: New York: Palgrave,
2001. Related Names: Josselin, Daphne.
Wallace, William. Description: p. cm.
ISBN 0333961250 (cloth) 033396814X
(pbk.) Notes: Includes bibliographical
references and index. Subjects:

International relations. Globalization. Non-governmental organizations. LC Classification: JZ1305 .N66 2001 Dewey Class No.: 327 21

Nunnenkamp, Peter. Globalisation of production and markets / Peter Nunnenkamp, Erich Gundlach, Jamuna P. Agarwal. Published/Created: Tübingen: J.C.B. Mohr, c1994. Related Names: Gundlach, Erich. Agarwal, Jamuna P. (Jamuna Prasad) Description: xii, 187 p.: ill.; 24 cm. ISBN 3161462807 Notes: Includes bibliographical references (p. 175-187). Subjects: International division of labor. International economic relations. International business enterprises. Series: Kieler Studien, 0340-6989; 262 LC Classification: HF1412 .N86 1994

Nyahoho, Emmanuel. Le marché culturel à l'ère de la mondialisation / Emmanuel Nyahoho. Published/Created: Sainte-Foy, Québec, Canada: Presses de l'Université du Québec, 2001. Description: xiv, 220 p.; 23 cm. ISBN 2760511286 Notes: Includes bibliographical references (p. [211]-220). Subjects: Culture--Economic aspects. Cultural property--Protection International relations and culture. International trade. Globalization--Social aspects. LC Classification: HM621+

Nye, Joseph S. The Paradox of American power: why the world's only superpower can't go it alone / Joseph S. Nye, Jr. Published/Created: New York: Oxford University Press, 2001. Description: p. cm. ISBN 0195150880 Notes: Includes index. Subjects: Power (Social sciences)--United States. International cooperation. Globalization. Information technology--Political aspects--United States. United States--Foreign relations--Philosophy. United States--Relations--Philosophy. United States--Foreign relations--2001-LC Classification: E183.7 .N94 2001

Dewey Class No.: 327.73 21

O'Connor, David E. (David Edward) Demystifying the global economy: a guide for students / David E. O'Connor. Published/Created: Westport, CT: Greenwood Press, 2002. Description: p. cm. ISBN 0313318638 (alk. paper) Notes: Includes bibliographical references and index. Subjects: Economic history--20th century. Globalization. LC Classification: HC54 .O26 2002 Dewey Class No.: 337 21

Olds, Kris, 1961- Globalization and urban change: capital, culture, and Pacific Rim mega-projects / Kris Olds. Published/Created: Oxford; New York: Oxford University Press, 2001. Description: xvii, 311 p.: ill.; 24 cm. ISBN 0198233612 Notes: Includes bibliographical references (p. [266]-301) and index. Subjects: Urban economics. City planning. Globalization. Series: Oxford geographical and environmental studies LC Classification: HT321 .O53 2001 Dewey Class No.: 307.76 21

Oliveira, Miguel Darcy de. Cidadania e globalização: a política externa brasileira e as ONGs / Miguel Darcy de Oliveira. Published/Created: Brasília, DF: Instituto Rio Branco: Fundação Alexandre Gusmão: Centro de Estudos Estratégicos, 1999. Description: 143 p.; 21 cm. Notes: Includes bibliographical references (p. [140]-143). Subjects: Non-governmental organizations. Non-governmental organizations--Brazil. Human rights. Human rights--Brazil. Women's rights Women's rights--Brazil. Globalization. Brazil--Foreign relations--1985- Series: Coleção Curso de Altos Estudos do Instituto Rio Branco LC Classification: F2538.3 .O454 1999

Oman, Charles. Globalisation and regionalisation: the challenge for developing countries / by Charles Oman. Published/Created: Paris, France: Development Centre of the Organisation for Economic Co-operation and Development, c1994. Description: 138 p.; 23 cm. ISBN 9264141065 (pbk.) Notes: Includes bibliographical references (p. 131-138). Subjects: International economic integration. Developing countries--Economic policy. Developing countries--Economic integration. Series: Development Centre studies LC Classification: HC59.7 .O428 1994

On biocultural diversity: linking language, knowledge, and the environment / edited by Luisa Maffi. Published/Created: Washington, [D.C.]: Smithsonian Institution Press, c2001. Related Names: Maffi, Luisa. Description: xxi, 578 p.: ill., maps; 24 cm. ISBN 156098905X (alk. paper) 1560989300 (paper: alk. paper) Notes: Includes bibliographical references and index. Subjects: Ethnoscience. Language attrition. Biological diversity conservation. Pluralism (Social sciences) Nature--Effect of human beings on. Globalization. LC Classification: GN476 .O5 2001 Dewey Class No.: 306.44 21

Onimode, Bade. Africa in the world of the 21st century / Bade Onimode. Published/Created: Ibadan: Ibadan University Press, 2000. Description: xxiv, 318 p.; 22 cm. ISBN 9781212705 Notes: Includes bibliographical references (p. [293]-305) and indexes. Subjects: Globalization. Africa--Economic conditions--1960- LC Classification: HC800 .O545 2000

Ooi, Su-Mei. Globalisation and security: the role of international financial institutions in Pacific Asian security / Ooi Su-Mei. Published/Created: Baden-Baden: Nomos, 2001. Description: 144 p.: ill.; 23 cm. ISBN 3789072591 (pbk.) Notes: Includes bibliographical references (p. 139-142).

Subjects: Financial institutions, International--Pacific Area. Financial institutions, International--Asia. Economic security--Pacific Area. Economic security--Asia. Globalization. Series: Aktuelle Materialien zur internationalen Politik; Bd. 64 LC Classification: HG3881 .O575 2001

Ooi, Su-Mei. Globalisation and security: the role of international financial institutions in Pacific Asian security / Ooi Su-Mei. Published/Created: Baden-Baden: Nomos, 2001. Description: 144 p.: ill.; 23 cm. ISBN 3789072591 (pbk.) Notes: Includes bibliographical references (p. 139-142). Subjects: Financial institutions, International--Pacific Area. Financial institutions, International--Asia. Economic security--Pacific Area. Economic security--Asia. Globalization. Series: Aktuelle Materialien zur internationalen Politik; Bd. 64 LC Classification: HG3881 .O575 2001

Organising labour in globalising Asia / edited by Jane Hutchison and Andrew Brown Published/Created: New York: Routledge, 2001. Related Names: Hutchison, Jane, 1954- Brown, Andrew, 1953- Description: p. cm. ISBN 0415250595 0415250609 (pbk.) Notes: Includes bibliographical references and index. Subjects: Labor movement--Asia. Globalization. Series: New rich in Asia LC Classification: HD8653.5 .O74 2001 Dewey Class No.: 331.88/095 21

Ortiz, Gonzalo. En el alba del milenio: globalización y medios de comunicación en América Latina / Gonzalo Ortiz Crespo. Published/Created: Quito, Ecuador: Corporación Editora Nacional, 1999. Description: 276 p.; 21 cm. ISBN 9978842624 Notes: Includes bibliographical references (p. [263]-269) Subjects: Mass media--Social aspects-- Latin America. Globalization. Series:

Biblioteca de ciencias sociales (Quito, Ecuador); v. 50. LC Classification: HN110.5.Z9 M36 1999

Oum, Tae Hoon. Globalization and strategic alliances: the case of the airline industry / Tae Hoon Oum, Jong-Hun Park, and Anming Zhang. Edition Information: 1st ed. Published/Created: New York: Pergamon, 2000. Related Names: Park, Jong-Hun. Zhang, Anming. Description: xxii, 229 p. p.: ill.; 24 cm. ISBN 0080435963 Notes: Includes bibliographical references (p. 213-223) and index. Subjects: Airlines. Strategic alliances (Business) Globalization. LC Classification: HE9780 .O96 2000 Dewey Class No.: 658/.044 21

Owolabi, E. A. Globalisation, liberalisation and the risk of marginalisation of Nigeria / by E.A. Owolabi. Published/Created: [Abuja, Nigeria]: Central Bank of Nigeria, [1998] Description: 2, 38 p.; 25 cm. Notes: "February 3, 1998." Includes bibliographical references (p. 37). Subjects: Competition, International. Nigeria--Foreign economic relations. Nigeria--Economic conditions. Series: Research Department seminar paper; no. 5 LC Classification: HF1616.7 .O95 1998

Pacific rim development: integration and globalisation in the Asia-Pacific economy / edited by Peter J. Rimmer. Published/Created: Canberra, ACT: Allen & Unwin in association with the Dept. of International Relations and the Dept. of Human Geography, RSPAS, ANU, 1997. Related Names: Rimmer, Peter James. Australian National University. Dept. of International Relations. Australian National University. Research School of Pacific and Asian Studies. Dept. of Human Geography. Description: xiii, 294 p.: ill., maps; 22 cm. ISBN 1863739785 Notes: Original studies stemming from collaboration between the Dept. of

Geography, University of Sydney and the Dept. of Human Geography at the Research School of Pacific and Asian Studies-Australian National University, with assistance from the Dept. of International Relations at ANU. Includes bibliographical references and index. Subjects: Competition, International. Asia--Foreign economic relations. Asia--Economic integration. Pacific Area--Foreign economic relations. Pacific Area--Economic integration. Asia--Economic conditions--1945- Pacific Area--Economic conditions. Series: Studies in world affairs; 13 LC Classification: HF1583 .P334 1997 Dewey Class No.: 337.5 21

Page, Sheila. Some implications of Europe 1992 for developing countries / by Sheila Page. Published/Created: Paris: Organisation for Economic Co-operation and Development, 1992. Description: 58 p.; 30 cm. Notes: "Under the direction of Charles Oman. Produced as part of the Research Programme on Globalisation and Regionalisation." "General distribution OCDE/GD(92)61." Summary also in French. Includes bibliographical references (p. 57-58). Subjects: Europe 1992. European Economic Community countries--Economic conditions. Developing countries--Economic conditions. Series: Technical papers (Organisation for Economic Co-operation and Development. Development Centre); no. 60. LC Classification: HC241.2 .P285 1992

Pak, Kil-song. Segyehwa, chabon kwa munhwa ui kujo pyondong / Pak Kil-song cho. Published/Created: Soul: Sahoe Pip'yongsa, 1996. Description: 365 p.: ill.; 23 cm. ISBN 8930070566 Notes: Includes bibliographical references (p. 339-355) and indexes. Subjects: International economic relations--Social aspects. International relations--Social aspects.

Cultural relations. International finance--Social aspects. Globalization. Series: Sahoe pip`yong sinso; 56 LC Classification: HF1359 .P336 1996

Palmer, Richard, 1952- Historical patterns of globalization: the growth of outward linkages of Swedish long-standing transnational corporations, 1890s-1990s / Richard Palmer. Published/Created: Stockholm: Almqvist & Wiksell International, c2001. Description: xvi, 235 p.: ill.; 25 cm. ISBN 9197267457 Notes: Extra t.p. with thesis statement and abstract inserted. Thesis (doctoral)--Stockholms universitet, 2000. Includes bibliographical references (p. 215-222). Subjects: International business enterprises--Sweden. Globalization. Series: Acta Universitatis Stockholmiensis. Stockholm studies in economic history, 0346-8305; 33 LC Classification: HD2883 .P35 2001

Panchamukhi, Vadiraj Raghawendracharya, 1936- Globalisation, competition, and economic stability [microform] / V.R. Panchamukhi. Published/Created: New Delhi: Research and Information System for the Non-Aligned and Other Developing Countries, 1998. Description: 44, v p.; 22 cm. ISBN 8171220657 Notes: Includes bibliographical references (p. 43-44). Microfiche. New Delhi: Library of Congress Office; Washington, D.C.: Library of Congress Photoduplication Service, 1999. 1 microfiche. Master microform held by: DLC. Subjects: International economic relations. LC Classification: Microfiche 99/60307 (H)

Panitch, Leo. Renewing socialism: democracy, strategy, and imagination / Leo Panitch. Published/Created: Boulder, Colo.: Westview Press, c2001. Description: x, 238 p.; 23 cm. ISBN 0813398215 (alk. paper) Notes: Includes bibliographical references and index. Subjects: Socialism.

Democracy. Globalization. LC Classification: HX73 .P35 2001 Dewey Class No.: 320.53/1 21

Papers [microform] / organised by Asian Institute for Development Communication in collaboration with Konrad Adenauer Foundation, Germany. Published/Created: [Kuala Lumpur]: The Institute, [1997] Description: 1 v. (various foliations); 30 cm. Notes: Microfiche. Jakarta: Library of Congress Office; Washington, D.C.: Library of Congress Photoduplication Service, 1997. 2 microfiches; 11 x 15 cm. LC Classification: Microfiche 97/51675 (H)

Papers presented at the National Seminar on Globalisation and the Ageing: Implications for Gerontological Social Work [microform] / organised by Tata Institute of Social Sciences and Family Welfare Agency, Mumbai. Published/Created: [Bombay: The Institute, 1997] Related Names: Tata Institute of Social Sciences. Description: 1 v. (various pagings); 29 cm. Summary: With reference to India. Notes: Includes bibliographical references. Microfiche. New Delhi: Library of Congress Office; Washington, D.C.: Library of Congress Photoduplication Service, 1998. 5 microfiches. Master microform held by: DLC. Subjects: Aged--India--Congresses. Public health--India--Congresses. LC Classification: Microfiche 98/60248 (H)

Paquin, Stéphane. La revanche des petites nations: le Québec, l'Écosse et la Catalogne face à la mondialisation / Stéphane Paquin. Published/Created: Montréal: VLB éditeur, c2001. Description: 219 p.; 22 cm. ISBN 2890057755 Notes: Includes bibliographical references (p. [203]-219). Subjects: Nationalism. Nationalism--Québec (Province) Nationalism--Scotland. Nationalism--Spain--Catalonia. Pluralism

(Social sciences) Globalization. Series: Collection Partis pris actuels; 25 LC Classification: JC311 .P22 2001

Paratian, Rajendra. Bangladesh / Rajendra Paratian and Raymond Torres. Published/Created: Geneva: International Labour Office, 2001. Related Names: Torres, Raymond. Description: xiv, 87 p.: ill.; 24 ISBN 9221113914 Notes: Includes bibliographical references (p. 79-81) and index. Subjects: Foreign trade and employment--Bangladesh International economic integration--Social aspects Globalization--Social aspects. Bangladesh--Social conditions Series: Studies on the social dimensions of globalization LC Classification: HD5710.75.B3 P37 2001

Parenti, Michael, 1933- The terrorism trap: September 11 and beyond / Michael Parenti. Published/Created: San Francisco: City Lights Books, 2002. Description: p. cm. ISBN 0872864057 Notes: Includes bibliographical references. Subjects: Intervention (International law) September 11 Terrorist Attacks, 2001. War on Terrorism, 2001- Militarism--Political aspects--United States. Militarism--Economic aspects-- United States. Corporations--Social aspects--United States. Globalization-- Social aspects. United States--Foreign relations--1989- United States--Politics and government--1989- United States-- Military policy. LC Classification: E840 .P268 2002 Dewey Class No.: 973.931 21

Parsi, Vittorio Emanuele. Interesse nazionale e globalizzazione: i regimi democratici nelle trasformazioni del sistema post- westfaliano / Vittorio Emanuele Parsi. Edition Information: 1. ed. Published/Created: Milano: Jaca book, 1998. Description: 355 p.; 24 cm. ISBN 8816404612 Notes: Includes bibliographical references (p. 311-344)

and indexes. Subjects: International relations. Globalization. Nationalism. Series: Di fronte e attraverso; 461 LC Classification: JZ1318 .P37 1998 Dewey Class No.: 327.1 21

Pasar global agroindustri: prospek dan strategi / editor, M. Amin Aziz. Edition Information: Cet. 1. Published/Created: Cijantung, Jakarta: Bangkit, 1993. Related Names: Aziz, M. Amin. Lokakarya Strategi Operasional Investasi dan Perdagangan Subsektor Agroindustri Dalam Era Globalisasi (1993: Jakarta, Indonesia) Description: 1 v. (various pagings): ill.; 20 cm. Summary: Investment and trade in Indonesian agroindustry with respect to globalization; proceedings. Notes: Proceedings of: Lokakarya Strategi Operasional Investasi dan Perdagangan Subsektor Agroindustri Dalam Era Globalisasi. Includes bibliographical references. Subjects: International trade. International economic relations. Agricultural industries--Indonesia. Indonesia-- Economic policy. LC Classification: HF1372 .P37 1993

Passet, René. Eloge du mondialisme: Par un anti présumé / René Passet. Published/Created: Paris: Fayard, 2001. Description: 167 p.; cm. ISBN 2213609470 Subjects: Globalization.

Patomäki, Heikki. Democratizing globalization: the leverage of the Tobin tax / Heikki Patomaki. Published/Created: London New York: Zed Books: Distributed exclusively in the USA by Palgrave, a division of St Martin's Press, c2001. Description: xxiii, 260 p. 22 cm. ISBN 1856498700 (cased) 1856498719 (limp) Notes: Includes bibliographical references and index. Subjects: Foreign exchange futures--Taxation. Globalization. LC Classification: HG3853

.P385 2001 Dewey Class No.: 332.4/5 21

Pedersen, Poul O. The changing structure of transport under trade liberalisation and globalization and its impact on African development / Poul Ove Pedersen. Published/Created: Copenhagen, Denmark: Centre for Development Research, [2000] Description: 22 p. 30 cm. Subjects: Transportation--Africa. Free Trade--Africa. Globalization--Africa. Series: CDR working paper, 0904-4701; 00.1 Working paper subseries on globalisation and economic restructuring in Africa; no. 7 LC Classification: HD72 .C38 no. 00.1

Pedersen, Poul O. The changing structure of transport under trade liberalisation and globalization and its impact on African development / Poul Ove Pedersen. Published/Created: Copenhagen, Denmark: Centre for Development Research, [2000] Description: 22 p. 30 cm. Subjects: Transportation--Africa. Free Trade--Africa. Globalization--Africa. Series: CDR working paper, 0904-4701; 00.1 Working paper subseries on globalisation and economic restructuring in Africa; no. 7 LC Classification: HD72 .C38 no. 00.1

Pedersen, Poul O. The freight transport and logistical system of Ghana: / Poul Ove Pedersen. Published/Created: Copenhagen, Denmark: Centre for Development Research, [2001] Description: 64 p.; 30 cm. Subjects: Transportation--Ghana. Series: CDR working paper; 01.2. CDR working paper. Working paper subseries on globalisation and economic restructuring in Africa; no. 12. LC Classification: HD72 .C38 no. 01.2

Pedersen, Poul O. Trading agents and other producer services in African industrialisation and globalisation / Poul

Ove Pedersen. Published/Created: Copenhagen, Denmark: Centre for Development Research, c1998. Description: 17 p.; 30 cm. Notes: Includes bibliographical references. Subjects: Commercial agents--Africa. Series: CDR working paper, 0904-4701; 98.14 LC Classification: HD72 .C38 no. 98.14

Pemberton, Jo-Anne. Global metaphors: modernity and the quest for one world / Jo-Anne Pemberton. Published/Created: London; Sterling, Va.: Pluto Press, c2001. Description: p. cm. ISBN 0745316530 0745316549 (pbk.) Notes: Includes index. Subjects: Civilization, Modern--20th century. World politics--20th century. Globalization--History--20th century. Technology and civilization. Intellectual life--History--20th century. Rhetoric--Political aspects--History--20th century. Postmodernism. LC Classification: CB427 .P39 2001 Dewey Class No.: 909.8 21

Pérez Sáinz, Juan Pablo. Encuentros inciertos: globalización y territorios locales en Centroamérica / Juan Pablo Pérez Sáinz. Edition Information: 1a ed. Published/Created: San José: Facultad Latinoamericana de Ciencias Sociales (FLACSO), 2000. Description: 272 p.; cm. ISBN 9977681112 Summary: Five scholarly essays on globalization and territory in Central America, including regional analysis and case studies of Belen in Costa Rica and El Peten of Guatemala.

Pérez Sáinz, Juan Pablo. Globalización y comunidades en Centroamérica / Juan Pablo Pérez Sáinz ... [et al.]. Edition Information: 1a ed. Published/Created: San José: Facultad Latinoamericana de Ciencias Sociales (FLACSO), 2001. Description: 280 p.; cm. ISBN 9977681139 Summary: Four scholarly essays on globalization in Central

America: investment and tourism in La Fortuna de San Carlos, Costa Rica; the maquila industry in Zacatepéquez, Guatemala; the economy of Chalatenango, El Salvador and local dynamics in the entire region.

Perlas, Nicanor. Elite globalization and the attack on Christianity / Nicanor Perlas. Edition Information: 1st ed. Published/Created: Quezon City, Philippines: Center for Alternative Development Initiatives, [1998] Related Names: Center for Alternative Development Initiatives (Philippines) Description: 56 p.: ill. (some col.); 28 cm. Notes: "Easter 1998." Subjects: Catholic Church--Doctrines. Globalization--Religious aspects--Catholic Church. Series: CADI monograph LC Classification: BX1753 .P447 1998 Dewey Class No.: 261.8/5 21

Perlas, Nicanor. Shaping globalization: civil society, cultural power, and threefolding / Nicanor Perlas. Edition Information: 1st ed. Published/Created: Quezon City, Philippines: Center for Alternative Development Initiatives, 1999. Related Names: Center for Alternative Development Initiatives (Philippines) Description: 145 p.: ill.; 23 cm. Notes: Includes bibliographical references (p. 140-144). Subjects: Civil society. Globalization. LC Classification: JC337 .P47 1999 Dewey Class No.: 300 21

Perspectives on globalization and employment / Yilmaz Akyüz ... [et al.]; edited by Bibek Debroy. Published/Created: New York: United Nations Development Programme, Bureau for Development Policy, Office of Development Studies, c1998. Related Names: Akyüz, Yilmaz. Debroy, Bibek. United Nations Development Programme. Office of Development Studies Description: vii, 87 p.: ill.; 23 cm. Notes: "Responses to

Discussion paper 4: Rival States, Rival Firms, How Do People Fit In? The Global Unemployment Challenge by Isabelle Grunberg"--Cover. Includes bibliographical references. Subjects: Manpower policy. Unemployment. Economic policy. Globalization. Series: Discussion paper series (United Nations Development Programme. Office of Development Studies); 14. LC Classification: HD5713 .P47 1998

Perulli, Adalberto, 1961- Diritto del lavoro e globalizzazione: clausole sociali, codici di condotta e commercio internazionale / Adalberto Perulli. Published/Created: Padova: CEDAM, 1999. Description: xxvi, 361 p.; 25 cm. ISBN 881321832X Notes: Includes bibliographical references and indexes. Subjects: Labor laws and legislation, International. Globalization. Series: Collana del Dipartimento di scienze giuridiche, Università degli studi Ca' Foscari, Venezia; nuova ser., 5 LC Classification: K1705 .P+

Pessanha, Rodolfo Gomes. As forças armadas face à globalização: dois ensaios de urgência / Rodolfo Gomes Pessanha. Published/Created: Niterói, RJ: Muiraquitã, c1998. Description: 160 p.; 21 cm. ISBN 8585483571 Subjects: World politics--1989- Globalization. National characteristics, Brazilian. Brazil--Armed Forces. Brazil--Defenses. LC Classification: UA619 .P47 1998

Petras, James F., 1937- América Latina: de la globalización a la revolución / James Petras; [traducción, Arturo Firpo [y] Stephen Hasam]. Published/Created: Rosario: Homo Sapiens Ediciones, c1999. Description: 220 p.; 22 cm. ISBN 9508082593 Notes: Includes bibliographical references. Subjects: Globalization. Social movements--Latin America. Latin America--Economic policy. Latin America--Social conditions--

20th century. Latin America--Relations--
United States. United States--Relations--
Latin America. Series: Serie paradigmas y
debates LC Classification: HC125 .P463
1999

Petras, James F., 1937- Globalization
unmasked: imperialism in the 21st century
/ James Petras and Henry Veltmeyer.
Published/Created: New York: Zed
Books, 2001. Related Names: Veltmeyer,
Henry. Description: p. cm. ISBN
1856499383 (cased) 1856499391 Notes:
Includes bibliographical references and
index. Subjects: International economic
relations--Political aspects. International
business enterprises. Globalization--Moral
and ethical aspects. United States--
Foreign economic relations. LC
Classification: HF1455 .P476 2001
Dewey Class No.: 325/.32/0973 21

Petras, James F., 1937- Globaloney: la
globalización de la tontería: el lenguaje
imperial, los intelectuales y la izquierda /
James Petras; [prólogo de Eduardo
Pavlovsky]. Published/Created: Buenos
Aires: Editorial Antídoto, 2000. Related
Names: Pavlovsky, Eduardo A.
Description: 157 p.; 22 cm. ISBN
9879306082 Notes: "... parte del esfuerzo
editorial de la revista Herramienta ..."--
Back cover. Subjects: Globalization
Imperialism. Latin America--Foreign
economic relations. Series: Colección
Herramienta

Pettigrew, Pierre S., 1951- Pour une politique
de la confiance / Pierre S. Pettigrew.
Published/Created: [Montréal]: Boréal,
c1999. Description: 271 p.; 23 cm. ISBN
2890529398 Notes: Includes
bibliographical references (p. [235]-244)
and index. Subjects: Federal government--
Canada. Globalization. Relations
internationales. Mondialisation (Économie
politique) Fédéralisme--Canada. Canada--
Politics and government--1980- Canada--

Foreign relations--1945- Québec
(Province)--Politics and government--
1960- Québec (Province)--History--
Autonomy and independence movements.
Canada--Politique et gouvernement--
1993- Canada--Relations extérieures.
Québec (Province)--Politique et
gouvernement--1994- Québec (Province)-
-Histoire--Autonomie et mouvements
indépendantistes. LC Classification:
F1034.2 .P48 1999 Dewey Class No.:
971.064/8 21

Pettigrew, Pierre S., 1951- The new politics of
confidence / Pierre S. Pettigrew;
translated by Phyllis Aronoff and Howard
Scott. Published/Created: Toronto:
Stoddart, 1999. Related Names: Aronoff,
Phyllis, 1945- Scott, Howard, 1952-
Description: xix, 210 p.; 24 cm. ISBN
0773731806 (bound) Notes: Translation
of: Pour une politique de la confiance.
Includes bibliographical references and
index. Subjects: Globalization. Federal
government--Canada. Canada--Politics
and government--1980- Canada--Foreign
relations--1945- Québec (Province)--
Politics and government--1960- Québec
(Province)--History--Autonomy and
independence movements. LC
Classification: F1034.2 .P4813 1999
Dewey Class No.: 971.064/8 21

Phases of capitalist development: booms,
crises, and globalizations / edited by
Robert Albritton ... [et al.].
Published/Created: Houndmills,
Basingstoke, Hampshire; New York:
Palgrave, 2001. Related Names: Albritton,
Robert, 1941- Description: xiii, 352 p.:
ill.; 23 cm. ISBN 033375316X Notes:
Includes bibliographical references (p.
318-339) and indexes. Subjects:
Capitalism. Economic development.
Finanical crises. Globalization. LC
Classification: HB501 .P4175 2001
Dewey Class No.: 338.9 21

Places and politics in an age of globalization /
edited by Roxann Prazniak and Arif
Dirlik. Published/Created: Lanham, MD:
Rowman & Littlefield Publishers, c2001.
Related Names: Prazniak, Roxann. Dirlik,
Arif. Description: xiv, 329 p.; 24 cm.
ISBN 0742500381 074250039X (pbk.)
Notes: Includes bibliographical references
and index. Subjects: Group identity.
Globalization. LC Classification: HM753
.P53 2001 Dewey Class No.: 305.8 21

Planteamientos y debate: globalización,
descentralización y desarrollo local /
Marisela Benavides ... [et al.].
Published/Created: Lima: Escuela para el
Desarrollo, 2000. Related Names:
Benavides, Marisela. Description: 130 p.;
21 cm. ISBN 9972921123 Notes: Includes
bibliographical references. Subjects:
Globalization. International economic
relations. Decentralization in government.
Community development. Series: Aportes
para el desarrollo; 4

Plural globalities in multiple localities: new
world borders / edited by Martha W. Rees,
Josephine Smart. Published/Created:
Lanham, MD: University Press of
America, 2001. Related Names: Rees,
Martha W. Smart, Josephine. Description:
p. cm. ISBN 0761819665 (cloth: alk.
paper) 0761819673 (pbk.: alk. paper)
Notes: Includes bibliographical references
and index. Subjects: Economic
anthropology. Globalization. Series:
Monographs in economic anthropology;
no. 17 LC Classification: GN448 .P55
2001 Dewey Class No.: 306.3 21

Political culture and institutions for a world
community: 1998 Copenhagen Seminar
for Social Progress: report.
Published/Created: Copenhagen: Royal
Danish Ministry of Foreign Affairs,
[1999] Related Names: Denmark.
Udenrigsministeriet. Description: 78 p.;
24 cm. ISBN 8772656832 Notes: "August

1999"--Cover. Subjects: Globalization.
International organization. World
citizenship. International politics. Political
culture. Series: Issues in focus (Denmark.
Udenrigsministeriet) LC Classification:
JZ1318 .C+

Political economy and the changing global
order / edited by Richard Stubbs and
Geoffrey R.D. Underhill. Edition
Information: 2nd ed. Published/Created:
Don Mills, [North York] Ontario; New
York: Oxford University Press, 2000.
Related Names: Stubbs, Richard.
Underhill, Geoffrey R. D. Description: x,
422 p.: ill.; 23 cm. ISBN 0195414640
Notes: Includes bibliographical references
and index. Subjects: International
economic relations. World politics--1989-
Economic history--1990- Globalization.
LC Classification: HF1359 .P65 2000
Dewey Class No.: 337 21

Political space: frontiers of change and
governance in a globalizing world / edited
by Yale H. Ferguson and R.J. Barry Jones.
Published/Created: Albany: State
University of New York Press, 2002.
Related Names: Ferguson, Yale H. Jones,
R. J. Barry. Description: p. cm. ISBN
0791454592 (alk. paper) 0791454606
(pbk.: alk. paper) Notes: Includes
bibliographical references and index.
Subjects: Political geography.
International relations. Globalization.
Series: SUNY series in global politics LC
Classification: JC319 .P6 2002 Dewey
Class No.: 327.1/01 21

Politics and globalisation: knowledge, ethics,
and agency / edited by Martin Shaw.
Published/Created: London; New York:
Routledge, 1999. Related Names: Shaw,
Martin. Description: x, 229 p.; 25 cm.
ISBN 0415206987 Notes: Includes
bibliographical references (p. 202-225)
and index. Subjects: Globalization.
Political science. International relations.

Series: Routledge advances in international relations and politics; 8 LC Classification: JZ1318 .P65 1999 Dewey Class No.: 306 21

Politics and globalisation: knowledge, ethics, and agency / edited by Martin Shaw. Published/Created: London; New York: Routledge, 1999. Related Names: Shaw, Martin. Description: x, 229 p.; 25 cm. ISBN 0415206987 Notes: Includes bibliographical references (p. 202-225) and index. Subjects: Globalization. Political science. International relations. Series: Routledge advances in international relations and politics; 8 LC Classification: JZ1318 .P65 1999 Dewey Class No.: 306 21

Ponte, Stefano. The "latte revolution"?: winners and losers in the restructuring of the global coffee marketing chain / Stefano Ponte. Published/Created: Copenhagen, Denmark: Centre for Development Research, [2001] Description: 35 p.; 30 cm. Subjects: Coffee industry. Coffee--Marketing. Series: CDR working paper; 01.3. CDR working paper. Working paper subseries on globalisation and economic restructuring in Africa; no. 13. LC Classification: HD72 .C38 no. 01.3

Posse, Abel. Argentina: el gran viraje / Abel Posse. Edition Information: 1. ed. Published/Created: Buenos Aires, Argentina: Emecé Editores, c2000. Description: 204 p.; 22 cm. ISBN 9500421623 Subjects: Globalization. Argentina--Politics and government--1983- Argentina--Moral conditions. Argentina--Economic conditions. Series: Escritores argentinos (Emecé Editores) LC Classification: F2849.2 .P675 2000

Post, James E. Redefining the corporation: stakeholder management and organizational wealth / James E. Post, Lee

E. Preston, Sybille Sachs. Published/Created: Stanford, Calif.: Stanford University Press, 2002. Related Names: Preston, Lee E. Sauter-Sachs, Sybille. Description: p. cm. ISBN 0804743045 (alk. paper) Notes: Includes bibliographical references and index. Subjects: Corporate governance. Corporations--Investor relations International business enterprises. International trade. Globalization--Economic aspects. Corporations. LC Classification: HD2741 .P67 2002 Dewey Class No.: 658.4 21

Postsocialist transformations and civil society in a globalizing world / Hans-Peter Meier Dallach and Jakob Juchler, editors. Published/Created: Huntington, N.Y.: Nova Science Pub., 2001. Related Names: Meier-Dallach, Hans-Peter, 1944- Juchler, Jakob. Description: p. cm. ISBN 1590331389 Notes: Includes bibliographical references and index. Subjects: Civil society--Europe, Eastern. Globalization. LC Classification: JC599.E92 P67 2001 Dewey Class No.: 300/.947 21

Pot, Ferrie, 1969- Employment relations and national culture: continuity and change in the age of globalisation / Ferrie Pot. Published/Created: Cheltenham, UK; Northampton, Mass.: Edward Elgar Pub., c2000. Description: x, 231 p.: ill.; 24 cm. ISBN 1840642297 Notes: Includes bibliographical references (p. 202-222) and index. Subjects: Comparative industrial relations. Industrial relations--Cross-cultural studies. Foreign trade and employment. International trade--Social aspects. Industrial relations--United States--Case studies. Industrial relations--Netherlands--Case studies. Series: New horizons in institutional and evolutionary economics LC Classification: HD6971 .P67 2000 Dewey Class No.: 306.3/4 21

Pour une construction citoyenne du monde: Un an après Seattle. Rencontre internationale, grande halle de la Villette, 30 novembre - 1er et 2 décembre 2000 / actuel Marx, la Cimade, fondation Copernic, ... [et al.]. Published/Created: Paris: Syllepse, 2001. Description: 221 p.; cm. ISBN 291316563X Subjects: Globalization - Citizenship - Humanism. Series: Explorer, confronter, innover

Pour une mondialisation au service de l'homme: Actes de la session annuelle du 11 au 14 novembre 1999, organisée à Saint-Etienne au Palais des congrès / Association des amis de Pierre Teilhard de Chardin. Published/Created: Saint-Etienne: Saint-Aubin, 2000. Description: 180 p.; cm. ISBN 2910576361 Subjects: Globalization - Human Ethics. Series: Science et spiritualité avec Teilhard de Chardin

Poverty reduction: what role for the state in today's globalized economy? / edited by Francis Wilson, Nazneen Kanji, and Einar Braathen. Published/Created: Cape Town: NAEP; London; New York: Zed Books; New York: Distributed in the USA exclusively by Palgrave, 2001. Related Names: Wilson, Francis, 1939- Kanji, Nazneen. Braathen, Einar, 1957- Description: xvi, 372 p.: ill.; 23 cm. ISBN 1856499529 (cased) 1856499537 (limp) 1919876030 (South Africa) Notes: Includes bibliographical references and index. Subjects: Poverty--Government policy--Case studies. Poor--Case studies. Globalization. Series: CROP international studies in poverty research LC Classification: HC79.P6 P693 2001 Dewey Class No.: 362.5/5 21

Power in the global era: grounding globalization / edited by Theodore H. Cohn, Stephen McBride, and John Wiseman. Published/Created: New York: St. Martin's Press, 2000. Related Names:

Cohn, Theodore H., 1940- McBride, Stephen, 1947- Wiseman, John Richard, 1957- Description: x, 221 p.; 23 cm. ISBN 0312235623 Notes: Includes bibliographical references and index. Subjects: International business enterprises--Congresses. Globalization--Congresses. LC Classification: HD2755.5 .P68 2000 Dewey Class No.: 338.8/8 21

Power, politics, and geography: placing scale / edited by Andrew Herod and Melissa W. Wright. Published/Created: Oxford, UK; Malden, MA: Blackwell Publishers, 2002. Related Names: Herod, Andrew, 1964- Wright, Melissa W. Description: p. cm. ISBN 0631225579 (alk. paper) 0631225587 (alk. paper) Notes: Includes bibliographical references and index. Subjects: September 11 Terrorist Attacks, 2001. Terrorism--United States. Globalization. International relations. World politics--1995-2005. LC Classification: HV6432 .P68 2002 Dewey Class No.: 303.48/2 21

Pranarka, A. M. W. Arah sejarah, transformasi global, dan era kebangkitan nasional kedua / A.M.W. Pranarka. Published/Created: Yogyakarta: Yayasan Kebangkitan Nasional, 1993. Related Names: Yayasan Kebangkitan Nasional (Yogyakarta, Indonesia) Description: iv, 111 p.; 21 cm. Summary: Impact of globalization on Indonesian nationalism. Subjects: Indonesia--History--1945- Indonesia--Forecasting. LC Classification: DS644 .P68 1993

Prasetyantoko, A., 1973- Arsitektur baru ekonomi global: belajar dari keruntuhan ekonomi Asia Tenggara / A. Prasetyantoko. Published/Created: Jakarta: Elex Media Komputindo, 2001. Description: xxiv, 179 p.; 21 cm. ISBN 9792021744 Summary: Globalization and the economic crisis in Asia; collection of articles.

Progressive governance for the XXI century: conference proceedings, Florence, 20th and 21st November 1999. Published/Created: [Florence, Italy]: European University Institute; [New York]: New York University School of Law, [2000?]. Related Names: European University Institute. New York University. School of Law. Description: 213 p.; 24 cm. Partial Contents: Background papers prepared for the conference: Dmocratic global governance in the 21st century / Thomas Risse -- Five (hypo)theses on democracy and its future / Yves Mény -- The "not-a-cat" syndrome: rethinking human rights law to meet the needs of the twenty-first century / Philip Alston -- Building a sustainable welfare state: reconciling social justice and growth in the advanced economies / Maurizio Ferrera and Martin Rhodes -- Global markets, national law and the regulation of business: the new "international economic order" / Eleanor M. Fox -- Political organization and the future of democracy / Larry Kramer -- Global governance for sustainable development / Richard B. Stewart -- Does equality matter? / Ronald Dworkin. Notes: Features proceedings of a panel of world leaders including Tony Blair, Fernando H. Cardoso, William Jefferson Clinton, Massimo D'Alema, Lionel Joseph and Gerhard Schröder, and keynote speaches by Norman Dorsen, Yves Mény, Javier Solana and Juan Somavía Includes bibliographical references. Subjects: Democracy World politics--21st century Globalization International economic integration Human rights Social policy Economic development Europe--Politics and government Europe--Social policy Europe--Economic policy

Progressive politics in the global age / edited by Henry Tam. Published/Created:

Malden, Mass.: Polity Press, 2001. Related Names: Tam, Henry Benedict. Description: p. cm. ISBN 0745625789 0745625797 (pbk.) Notes: Includes bibliographical references and index. Subjects: Social justice. Social policy. Family policy. Democracy. Free enterprise. Globalization. LC Classification: HM671 .P76 2001 Dewey Class No.: 361.6/1 21

Questioning geopolitics: political projects in a changing world-system / edited by Georgi M. Derluguian and Scott L. Greer. Published/Created: Westport, Conn.: Greenwood Press, 2000. Related Names: Derluguian, Georgi M. Greer, Scott L. Description: vi, 249 p.: ill., 1 map; 24 cm. ISBN 0313310823 (alk. paper) Notes: Includes bibliographical references (p. [227]-242) and index. Subjects: Globalization. International relations. Series: Studies in the political economy of the world-system Contributions in economics and economic history, 0084-9235; no. 216 LC Classification: JZ1308 .D55 2000 Dewey Class No.: 327.1/01 21

Rachmat, Haikin. Pengembangan sistem kesehatan nasional dalam era globalisasi / oleh H. Haikin Rachmat. Published/Created: [Jakarta]: Departemen Pertahanan Keamanan RI, Lembaga Ketahanan Nasional, 1997. Description: v, 97, [2] leaves; 29 cm. Summary: Policy for developing Indonesian public health programs in the globalization era; paper. Notes: Cover title. Includes bibliographical references (leaves [98]-[99]). LC Classification: MLCME 97/00591 (R)

Raikes, Philip Lawrence. Global commodity chain analysis and the French filière approach: comparison and critique / Philip Raikes ... [et al.]. Published/Created: Copenhagen, Denmark: Centre for Development Research, [2000]

Description: 26 p. 30 cm. Subjects: Primary commodities. Series: CDR working paper, 0904-4701; 00.3 Working paper subseries on globalisation and economic restructuring in Africa; no. 9 LC Classification: HD72 .C38 no. 00.3

Raipuria, Kalyan. Human rights and globalisation: 'what-if' questions, expanding scope, and recent initiatives / Kalyan Raipuria. Published/Created: New Delhi: Rajiv Gandhi Institute for Contemporary Studies, [2000] Related Names: Rajiv Gandhi Institute for Contemporary Studies. Description: 17 p.; 22 cm. Series: RGICS working paper series; 2000, no. 16.

Ramonet, Ignacio. Marcos: la dignité rebelle: conversations avec le sous-commandant Marcos / Ignacio Ramonet; [les propos du sous-commandant Marcos ont été traduits de l'espagnol par Laurence Villaume]. Published/Created: Paris: Galilée, c2001. Related Names: Marcos, subcomandante. Description: 71 p.; 22 cm. ISBN 2718605650 Subjects: Marcos, subcomandante--Interviews. Indians of Mexico--Mexico--Chiapas--Social conditions. Globalization--Social aspects. Marginality, Social. Mexico--Politics and government--1988- Chiapas (Mexico)--History--Peasant Uprising, 1994- Series: Espace critique. LC Classification: F1236 .R363 2001 Dewey Class No.: 972/.750835 21

Randle, Patricio H. Soberanía global: adonde lleva el mundialismo / Patricio H. Randle. Published/Created: Buenos Aires: Ciudad Argentina, 1999. Description: 349 p.; 24 cm. ISBN 9875071706 Notes: Includes bibliographical references and index. Subjects: Globalization. Sovereignty. International relations. LC Classification: JZ1318 .R36 1999 Dewey Class No.: 327.1/01 21

Rao, P. Venkateshwar (Ponugoti Venkateshwar), 1950- Globalisation and the new regionalism in the Indian Ocean / P. Venkateshwar Rao. Published/Created: Colombo: Bandaranaike Centre for International Studies, S.W.R.D. Bandaranaike National Memorial Foundation, 1997. Related Names: Bandaranaike Centre for International Studies. Description: 55 p.; 31 cm. ISBN 9559147226 Notes: Includes bibliographical references. Subjects: International economic integration. Regionalism. LC Classification: MLCL 2000/00646 (H)

Rasjid, M. Ryaas. Nasionalisme dan demokrasi Indonesia: menghadapi tantangan globalisasi / Muhammad Ryaas Rasyid. Edition Information: Cet. 1. Published/Created: Jakarta: Diterbitkan untuk Masyarakat Ilmu Pemerintahan Indonesia (MIPI) [oleh] Yarsif Watampone, 1998. Description: xiii, 112 p.; 19 cm. ISBN 9798980069 Summary: Political and economic conditions in Indonesia and the challenge of globalization; paper. Notes: Includes bibliographical references (p. 111-112). Subjects: Nationalism--Indonesia. Indonesia--Politics and government--1998- Indonesia--Economic conditions--1945- LC Classification: DS644.4 .R39 1998

Regional cooperation in a global context / sous la direction de Raphael Bar-El, Ehud Menipaz, Gilbert Benhayoun. Published/Created: Paris: Harmattan, c2000. Related Names: Bar-El, Raphael. Menipaz, Ehud. Benhayoun, Gilbert. Description: 319 p.: ill.; 22 cm. ISBN 2738498493 Notes: Includes bibliographical references. Subjects: Regionalism--Middle East. Globalization--Economic aspects--Middle East. Middle East--Economic integration. Arab cooperation. Arab countries--Foreign economic relations--Israel. Israel--Foreign economic relations--Arab countries. Series: Emploi, industrie et territoire. LC Classification: HC415.15 .R438 2000 Dewey Class No.: 337.1/5 21

Regionalism and globalization: theory and practice / edited by Sajal Lahiri. Published/Created: New York: Routledge, 2001. Related Names: Lahiri, Sajal. Description: p. cm. ISBN 0415220750 (alk. paper) Notes: Includes bibliographical references and index. Subjects: International economic integration. International trade. Regionalism. Globalization. LC Classification: HF1418.5 .R4436 2001 Dewey Class No.: 337.1 21

Regions, globalization, and the knowledge-based economy / edited by John H. Dunning. Published/Created: Oxford; New York: Oxford University Press, 2000. Related Names: Dunning, John H. Description: xiv, 506 p.; 24 cm. ISBN 0198295367 Notes: Includes bibliographical references and index. Subjects: International business enterprises--Case studies. Regional economics--Case studies. Globalization. LC Classification: HD2755.5 .R426 2000 Dewey Class No.: 337 21

Reimagining the future: towards democratic governance: a report of the Global Governance Reform Project. Published/Created: Bundoora, VIC: Department of Politics, La Trobe University, 2000. Related Names: Malhotra, Kamal. Camilleri, J. A. (Joseph A.), 1944- Tehranian, Majid. La Trobe University. Dept. of Politics. Focus on the Global South. Toda Institute for Global Peace and Policy Research. Global Governance Reform Project. Description: xxiii, 101 p.; 23 cm. ISBN 0646399942 Notes: "Project directors and sponsoring institutions - Joseph A. Camilleri, The

Department of Politics, La Trobe University, Melbourne; Kamal Malhotra, Focus on the Global South, Bangkok; Majid Tehranian, The Toda Institute for Global Peace and Policy Research, Tokyo and Honolulu". Subjects: International organization. Globalization.

Reinventing Ireland: culture, society and the global economy / edited by Michael Cronin, Luke Gibbons, and Peadar Kirby. Published/Created: Sterling, Va.: Pluto Press, 2002. Related Names: Cronin, Michael, 1960- Gibbons, Luke. Kirby, Peadar. Description: p. cm. ISBN 0745318258 (hardback) 074531824X (pbk.) Subjects: Ireland--Civilization--20th century. Ireland--Social conditions--20th century. Ireland--Economic conditions--20th century. Series: Contemporary Irish studies LC Classification: DA959.1 .R45 2002 Dewey Class No.: 941.5082 21

Reinventing Ireland: culture, society, and the global economy / edited by Michael Cronin, Luke Gibbons and Peadar Kirby. Published/Created: London; Sterling, Va.: Pluto Press, 2002. Related Names: Cronin, Michael, 1960- Gibbons, Luke. Kirby, Peadar. Description: p. cm. ISBN 0745318258 (hardback) 074531824X (pbk.) Subjects: Ireland--Economic conditions--1949- Ireland--Social conditions. Series: Contemporary Irish studies LC Classification: HC260.5 .R44 2002 Dewey Class No.: 306/.09417 21

Religions/globalizations: theories and cases / edited by Dwight N. Hopkins ... [et al.]. Published/Created: Durham, NC: Duke University Press, 2001. Related Names: Hopkins, Dwight N. Description: p. cm. ISBN 0822327856 (cloth: alk. paper) 0822327953 (pbk.: alk. paper) Notes: Includes index. Subjects: Religion and culture. Globalization--Religious aspects. LC Classification: BL65.C8 R457 2001

Dewey Class No.: 291.1/7 21

Report on management: globalisation and change: ways to the future / edited by Bogdan Wawrzyniak. Published/Created: Warsaw: Leon Ko´zmi´nski Academy of Entrepreneurship and Management, 2000. Related Names: Wawrzyniak, Bogdan. Leon Ko´zmi´nski Academy of Entrepreneurship and Management. Polska Akademia Nauk. Komitet Nauk Organizacji i Zarzadzania. Lunds universitet. Institutet för ekonomisk forskning. Description: 485 p.: ill.; 25 cm. ISBN 8386846488 Subjects: Industrial management--Poland--Congresses. Industrial management--Sweden--Congresses. Organizational change--Poland--Congresses. Organizational change--Sweden--Congresses. Globalization--Economic aspects--Poland--Congresses. Globalization--Social aspects--Poland--Congresses. Globalization--Economic aspects--Sweden--Congresses. Globalization--Social aspects--Sweden--Congresses. International trade--Congresses. European Union--Poland--Congresses. LC Classification: HD70.P7 R47 2000

Report on management: globalisation and change: ways to the future / edited by Bogdan Wawrzyniak. Published/Created: Warsaw: Leon Ko´zmi´nski Academy of Entrepreneurship and Management, 2000. Related Names: Wawrzyniak, Bogdan. Leon Ko´zmi´nski Academy of Entrepreneurship and Management. Polska Akademia Nauk. Komitet Nauk Organizacji i Zarzadzania. Lunds universitet. Institutet för ekonomisk forskning. Description: 485 p.: ill.; 25 cm. ISBN 8386846488 Notes: At head of Leon Ko´zmi´nski Academy of Entrepreneurship and Management; Committee of Organization and Management, Polish Academy of Science; Institute of Economic Studies, Lund

University. Papers presented at the 4th annual conference, Report on management entitled" "Business and managers facing the challenges of the 21-st century." Includes bibliographical references. Subjects: Industrial management--Poland--Congresses. Industrial management--Sweden--Congresses. Organizational change--Poland--Congresses. Organizational change--Sweden--Congresses. Globalization--Economic aspects--Poland--Congresses. Globalization--Social aspects--Poland--Congresses. Globalization--Economic aspects--Sweden--Congresses. Globalization--Social aspects--Sweden--Congresses. International trade--Congresses. European Union--Poland--Congresses. LC Classification: HD70.P7 R47 2000

Republics of ideas: republicanism culture visual arts / edited by Brad Buckley and John Conomos. Published/Created: Annandale, N.S.W: Pluto Press Australia and Artspace Visual Arts Centre, 2001. Related Names: Buckley, Brad, 1952- Conomos, John. Description: 265 p.: ill.; 22 cm. ISBN 1864031859 1864031859: 1864031859 (pbk.) Notes: Includes index. Bibliography: p. 246-251. Subjects: Republicanism--Australia. Nationalism--Australia. National characteristics, Australian. Globalization. Art--Australia. Art, Australian. Australia--Social conditions.

Rethinking American history in a global age / edited by Thomas Bender. Published/Created: Berkeley, Calif.: University of California Press, c2001. Related Names: Bender, Thomas. Description: p. cm. ISBN 0520230574 (cloth: alk. paper) 0520230582 (paper: alk. paper) Contents: Part I. Historicizing the nation -- Transnationalism and the challenge to national histories / Prasenjit Duara -- Internationalizing international history / Akira Iriye -- Where in the world is America? The history of the United States in a global age / Charles Bright and Michael Geyer -- Part II. New historical geographies and temporalities -- International at the creation: early modern American history / Karen Ordahl Kupperman -- How the West was one: the African diaspora and the re-mapping of U.S. history / Robin D. Kelley -- Time and revolution in African America: temporality and the history of Atlantic slavery / Walter Johnson -- Beyond the view from Euro-America: environment, settler societies, and internationalization of American history / Ian Tyrrell -- Part III. Opening the frame -- From Euro- and Afro-Atlantic to Pacific migration system: a comparative migration approach to North American history / Dirk Hoerder -- Framing United States history: democracy, nationalism, and socialism / Robert Wiebe -- An age of social politics / Daniel T. Rodgers -- The age of global power / Marilyn B. Young -- American empire and cultural imperialism: a view from the receiving end / Rob Kroes -- Part IV. The constraints of practice -- Do American historical narratives travel? / François Weil -- The modernity of America and the practice of scholarship / Winfried Fluck -- The exhaustion of enclosures: a critique of internationalization / Ron Robin -- The historian's use of the United States and vice versa / David A. Hollinger. Notes: Includes index. Subjects: Globalization. United States--Historiography. United States--History--Philosophy. LC Classification: E175 .R48 2001 Dewey Class No.: 973/.07/2 21

Richardson, J. L. (James L.), 1933- Contending liberalisms in world politics: ideology and power / James L. Richardson. Published/Created: Boulder, Colo.: L. Rienner, 2001. Description: viii, 239 p.; 24 cm. ISBN 1555879152 (alk.

paper) 155587939X (pbk.) Notes: Includes bibliographical references (p. 211-229) and index. Subjects: Liberalism. Globalization. International relations. LC Classification: JC574 .R53 2001 Dewey Class No.: 327.1/01 21

Rionda Ramírez, Jorge Isauro. Prolegómenos en torno a la realidad social, política y económica de México / Jorge Isauro Rionda Ramírez. Edition Information: 1a ed. Published/Created: Guanajuato: Centro de Investigaciones Humanísticas, Universidad de Guanajuato, 2001. Description: 208 p.; cm. ISBN 9688642525 Summary: An analysis of socioeconomic conditions in contemporary Mexico, with focus on the impact of neoliberal policies and globalization in the areas of ethics, poverty, finances, state political policies, labor, corruption and participatory democracy.

Rivero B., Oswaldo de. The myth of development: non-viable economies and national survival in the 21st century / Oswaldo de Rivero; translated by Claaudia Encinas and Janet Herrick Encinas. Published/Created: New York: Zed Books, 2001. Description: p. cm. ISBN 1856499480 1856499499 Notes: Includes bibliographical references and index. Subjects: Globalization. Economic development. Developing countries-- Economic conditions. Developing countries--Social conditions. Series: Global issues series (New York, N.Y.: 1999) LC Classification: HC59.7 .R54 2001 Dewey Class No.: 330.9172/4 21

Rivero, José. Educación y exclusión en América Latina: reformas en tiempos de globalización / José Rivero. Edition Information: 1. ed. Published/Created: Lima: Tarea, 1999. Description: 436 p.; 25 cm. ISBN 9972618420 Notes: Includes bibliographical references (p. 419-436).

Subjects: Educational change--Latin America. Education--Social aspects--Latin America. Educational equalization--Latin America. Globalization. LC Classification: LA541 .R59 1999

Riviere d'Arc, Helene. Desarrollo y política en la frontera norte / Helene Riviere d'Arc ... [et al.]; coordinadores: Carlos Alba Vega y Alberto Aziz Nassif. Edition Information: 1a ed. Published/Created: México: Centro de Investigaciones y Estudios Superiores en Antropolgía Social / Universidad Autónoma Ciudad Juárez, 2000. Description: 218 p.; cm. ISBN 9684963947 Summary: Articles on the frontier between Chihuahua and the U.S., organized under the categories of local empresarios and political change, empresarios and globalization, empresarios and political culture, alternating political power and alternative structures. Series: Colección Antropologías

Robertson, Roland. Globalization: social theory and global culture / Roland Robertson. Published/Created: London: Sage, 1992. Description: x, 211 p.; 24 cm. ISBN 0803981864 (cased) 0803981872 (pbk) : Contents: Globalization as a problem -- The cultural turn -- Mapping the global condition -- World-systems theory, culture and images of world order -- Japanese globality and Japanese religion -- The universalism-particularism issue -- 'Civiliztion,' civility and the civilizing process -- Globalization theory and civilization analysis -- Globality, modernity and the issue of postmodernity -- Globalization and the nostalgic paradigm -- 'The search for fundamentals' in global perspective -- Concluding reflections. Notes: Includes index. Includes bibliographical references (p. [189]-203) and index. Bibliography: p. 189-203. Subjects: Culture. International relations. Cultural relations.

Globalization. Series: Theory, culture & society (Unnumbered) LC Classification: HM101 .R54 1992 Dewey Class No.: 306 20

Robertson, Susan L. A class act: changing teachers' work, the state, and globalisation / Susan L. Robertson. Published/Created: New York: Falmer Press, 2000. Description: xviii, 240 p.; 23 cm. ISBN 0815335768 (alk. paper) 0815335784 (pbk.: alk. paper) Notes: Includes bibliographical references (p. 215-231) and index. Subjects: Teaching--Political aspects. Teachers--Social conditions. Critical pedagogy. Education and state. Educational sociology. Series: Garland reference library of social science; v. 1465. Garland reference library of social science. Studies in education/politics; vol. 8. LC Classification: LB1775 .R565 2000 Dewey Class No.: 306.43 21

Roché, Sebastian. Sociologie politique de l'insécurité: violences urbaines, inégalités et globalisation / Sebastian Roché. Edition Information: 1. éd. Published/Created: Paris: Presses universitaires de France, 1998. Description: viii, 283 p.; 22 cm. ISBN 2130489869 Notes: Includes bibliographical references (p. [263]-283). Subjects: Fear--Social aspects. Security (Psychology) Interpersonal conflict. International economic integration--Social aspects. Social control. Series: Sociologie d'aujourd'hui LC Classification: HM291 .R57585 1998 Dewey Class No.: 302/.17 21

Rodemer, Horst. Globalisierung, europäische Integration und internationaler Standortwettbewerb / Horst Rodemer, Hartmut Dicke unter Mitarbeit von Michael Bauer und Uwe Geisel. Edition Information: 1. Aufl. Published/Created: Baden-Baden: Nomos, 2000. Related Names: Dicke, Hartmut. Description: 325 p.; 23 cm. ISBN 3789067679 (pbk.)

Notes: Includes bibliographical references (p. 308-325). Subjects: Competition, International. Globalization. Europe--Economic integration. LC Classification: HF1414 .R63 2000

Roldán, Martha. Globalización o mundialización?: teoría y práctica de procesos productivos y asimetrías de género: una interpelación desde las realidades de la organización del trabajo en el apogeo y crisis de una industria nacional autopartista (1960-1990) / Martha Roldán. Edition Information: 1. ed. Published/Created: [Buenos Aires]: Eudeba, 2000. Description: 347 p.; 24 cm. ISBN 9502310977 Notes: "Universidad Nacional de la Patagonia (SJB), Delegación Zonal Trelew. FLACSO." Includes bibliographical references (p. 339-347). Subjects: Argfilsa (Firm) Automobile supplies industry--Argentina. Women employees--Argentina. Globalization. Argentina--Economic conditions--1945- LC Classification: HD9710.3.A74 A77 2000

Room, Graham. Social exclusion, solidarity and the challenge of globalisation / Graham Room. Published/Created: Jerusalem: The Hebrew University of Jerusalem, The Paul Baerwald School of Social Work, 1998. Description: 22 p.; 25 cm.

Rosen, Ellen Israel. Making sweatshops: the globalization of the U.S. apparel industry / Ellen Israel Rosen. Published/Created: Berkeley, Calif.: University of California Press, c2002. Description: p. cm. ISBN 0520233360 (Cloth: alk. paper) 0520233379 (Paper: alk. paper) Notes: Includes bibliographical references and index. Subjects: Clothing trade--United States--History--20th century. Clothing trade--History--20th century.. Women clothing workers--United States . Globalization. LC Classification:

HD9940.U4 R666 2002 Dewey Class No.: 338.4/7687/0973 21

Roudometof, Victor, 1964- Nationalism, globalization, and orthodoxy: the social origins of ethnic conflict in the Balkans / Victor Roudometof; foreword by Roland Robertson. Published/Created: Westport, CT: Greenwood Press, 2001. Related Names: Robertson, Roland. Description: xvii, 304 p.: maps; 24 cm. ISBN 0313319499 (alk. paper) Notes: Includes bibliographical references (p. 246-285) and index. Subjects: Nationalism--Balkan Peninsula. Globalization. Balkan Peninsula--Ethnic relations--History. Balkan Peninsula--Ethnic relations--Social aspects. Ethnic relations--Religious aspects. Series: Contributions to the study of world history, 0885-9159; no. 89 LC Classification: DR24 .R68 2001 Dewey Class No.: 320.9496 21

Rouet, Albert. Faut-il avoir peur de la mondialisation: Enjeux spirituels et mission de l'Eglise / Albert Rouet; introduction de Pierre Vilain. Published/Created: Paris: Desclée de Brouwer, 2000. Description: 96 p.; cm. ISBN 2220047938 Subjects: Globalization.

Rowbotham, Michael. Goodbye America!: globalisation, debt and the dollar empire / Michael Rowbotham. Published/Created: Charlbury: J. Carpenter; Sydney: Envirobook; Concord, MA: Distributed in the USA and Canada by Paul and Company, 2000. Description: vi, 209 p.: ill.; 23 cm. ISBN 1897766564 (Jon Carpenter) 0858811774 (Envirobook) Notes: Includes bibliographical references (p. [204]-206) and index. Subjects: Debts, External--Developing countries. Debt cancellation--Developing countries. Developing countries--Economic policy. Developing countries--Foreign economic relations--United States. United States--

Foreign economic relations--Developing countries. LC Classification: HJ8899 .R69 2000

Roxborough, Ian. The Hart-Rudman Commission and the homeland defense / Ian Roxborough. Published/Created: Carlisle, PA: Strategic Studies Institute, U.S. Army War College: May be obtained from the Publications Office, [2001] Related Names: Army War College (U.S.). Strategic Studies Institute. Description: viii, 32 p.; 23 cm. ISBN 1584870656 Notes: Not distributed to depository libraries in a physical form. "September 2001." Includes bibliographical references (p. 28-32). Subjects: United States Commission on National Security/21st Century. National security--United States. Terrorism--United States--Forecasting. Globalization Political aspects. United States--Defenses. United States--Military policy. LC Classification: UA23 .R79 2001 Dewey Class No.: 355/.033073 21 Govt. Doc. No.: D 101.146:2001043684

Rubio, Enrique, 1943- La izquierda del futuro / Enrique Rubio. Published/Created: Montevideo, Uruguay: Biblioteca de Marcha, [1999] Description: 271 p.; 20 cm. Notes: Includes bibliographical references (p. 249-264). Subjects: Socialism. Globalization. LC Classification: HX44.5 .R83 1999

Rugman, Alan M. The end of globalization / Alan Rugman. Published/Created: London: Random House Business Books, 2000. Description: xv, 237 p.: ill.; 25 cm. ISBN 0712684751 Notes: Includes bibliographical references (p. [220]-226) and index. Subjects: World Trade Organization. International business enterprises--Management. Regionalism. Investments, Foreign. Foreign trade regulation. Free trade--Social aspects. Free trade--Environmental aspects.

Globalization. LC Classification: HD62.4 .R84 2000 Dewey Class No.: 658/.049 21

Rugman, Alan M. The end of globalization: why global strategy is a myth & how to profit from the realities of regional markets / Alan Rugman. Published/Created: New York: AMACOM, 2001. Description: xvi, 237 p.; 24 cm. ISBN 0814406386 Notes: The North American ed. has a new pref. and updated data. Includes bibliographical references (p. [220]-226) and index. Subjects: World Trade Organization. International business enterprises-- Management. Regionalism. Investments, Foreign. Foreign trade regulation. Free trade--Social aspects. Free trade-- Environmental aspects. Globalization. LC Classification: HD62.4 .R84 2001 Dewey Class No.: 658/.049 21

Rumford, Chris, 1958- The European Union: a political sociology / Chris Rumford. Published/Created: Oxford, UK; Malden, MA, USA: Blackwell Publishers, 2002. Description: p. cm. ISBN 0631226176 (alk. paper) 0631226184 (alk. paper) Notes: Includes bibliographical references and index. Subjects: European Union. Globalization. Civil society--European Union countries. European Union countries--Social conditions. LC Classification: JN30 .R87 2002 Dewey Class No.: 306.2/094 21

Rupert, Mark. Ideologies of globalization: contending visions of a new world order / Mark Rupert. Published/Created: London; New York: Routledge, 2000. Description: p. cm. ISBN 0415189241 041518925X (pbk.) Notes: Includes bibliographical references and index. Subjects: Free trade--United States. International economic relations--Political aspects. Globalization--Moral and ethical aspects. United States-- Foreign economic relations. LC Classification: HF1455 .R78 2000 Dewey

Class No.: 337.73 21

Ryner, J. Magnus. Capitalist restructuring, globalisation, and the third way / J. Magnus Ryner. Published/Created: New York: Routledge, 2002. Description: p. cm. ISBN 0415252946 Notes: Includes bibliographical references and index. Subjects: Socialism. Socialism--Sweden. Welfare state. Series: Routledge/RIPE studies in global political economy LC Classification: HX44.5 .R96 2002 Dewey Class No.: 330.9485 21

Saelan, H. Maulwi. Kiprah pendidikan Al-Azhar Kemang: pandangan cendekiawan Muslim mengantisipasi tantangan era globalisasi / H. Maulwi Saelan. Edition Information: Cet. 1. Published/Created: Jakarta: Yayasan Syifa Budi, 1993. Related Names: Al-Azhar Kemang Jakarta. Description: xvi, 244 p.: ill. (some col.); 21 cm. ISBN 9798379004 Summary: Role of Islamic religious educational school on anticipation of globalization; volume commemorating the 12th anniversary of Al-Azhar Kemang Jakarta; Islamic school in Jakarta. Notes: Includes bibliographical references (p. 241-244). Subjects: Al-Azhar Kemang Jakarta. Islamic religious education--Indonesia. LC Classification: BP10.A44 S24 1993

Salamé, Ghassane, 1951- Appels d'empire: ingérences et résistances à l'âge de la mondialisation / Ghassan Salamé. Published/Created: [Paris]: Fayard, 1996 Description: 351 p.; 24 cm. ISBN 2213595941 Notes: Includes bibliographical references (p. [335]-348). Subjects: Globalization--Social aspects. Geopolitics. International relations. National security. World politics. LC Classification: D2003 .S35 1996

Salmon, Jean Marc, 1943- Un monde à grande vitesse: globalisation, mode d'emploi /

Jean-Marc Salmon. Published/Created: Paris: Seuil, c2000. Description: 249 p.; 21 cm. ISBN 2020370611 Notes: Includes bibliographical references (p. 231-[237]) and indexes. Subjects: Globalization. Series: Essai/Seuil. LC Classification: JZ1318+

Salmon, Jean Marc, 1943- Un monde à grande vitesse: globalisation, mode d'emploi / Jean-Marc Salmon. Published/Created: Paris: Seuil, c2000. Description: 249 p.; 21 cm. ISBN 2020370611 Notes: Includes bibliographical references (p. 231-[237]) and indexes. Subjects: Globalization. Series: Essai/Seuil. LC Classification: JZ1318+

San, Gee. Taiwanese corporations in globalisation and regionalisation / by San Gee. Published/Created: Paris: Organisation for Economic Co-operation and Development, 1992. Related Names: Research Programme on Globalisation and Regionalisation. Description: 56 p.; 30 cm. Notes: "General distribution. OCDE/GD(92)62." "Under the direction of Charles Oman. Produced as part of the Research Programme on Globalisation and Regionalisation." Summary in French. Includes bibliographical refernces (p. 55-56). Subjects: Investments, Taiwan. International business enterprises--Taiwan. Investments--Government policy--Taiwan. Technology and state--Taiwan. Taiwan--Foreign economic relations. Series: Technical papers (Organisation for Economic Co-operation and Development. Development Centre); no. 61. LC Classification: HF1606 .S26 1992

Scheffler, Samuel, 1951- Boundaries and allegiances: problems of justice and responsibility in liberal thought / Samuel Scheffler. Published/Created: Oxford; New York: Oxford University Press, 2001. Description: 221 p.; 24 cm. ISBN 019924149X Notes: Includes bibliographical references and index. Subjects: Liberalism. Justice. Responsibility. Globalization. LC Classification: JC574 .S34 2001 Dewey Class No.: 320.51 21

Scherrer, Christoph. Globalisierung wider Willen?: die Durchsetzung liberaler Aussenwirtschaftspolitik in den USA / Christoph Scherrer. Published/Created: Berlin: Edition Sigma, c1999. Description: 397 p.: ill.; 21 cm. ISBN 3894044640 (pbk.) Notes: Slightly revised version of the author's Habilitationsschrift--Freie Universität Berlin, 1999, under the Weltmarkt als Projekt? Includes bibliographical references (p. 355-393). Subjects: United States--Foreign economic relations. Globalization. LC Classification: HF1455 .S339 1999

Scheve, Kenneth F. Globalization and the perceptions of American Workers / Kenneth F. Scheve and Matthew J. Slaughter. Published/Created: Washington, DC: Institute For International Economics, 2000. Related Names: Slaughter, Matthew J. (Matthew Jon) Description: p. cm. ISBN 0881322954 Notes: Includes bibliographical references and index. Subjects: Foreign trade and employment--United States. Globalization. Investments, Foreign, and employment--United States. LC Classification: HD5710.75.U6 S34 2000 Dewey Class No.: 331.1/0973 21

Schirm, Stefan A., 1963- Globalization and the new regionalism: global markets, domestic politics and regional co-operation / Stefan A. Schirm. Published/Created: Cambridge, UK: Polity Press in association with Blackwell Publishers, 2002. Description: p. cm. ISBN 0745629695 (hb) 0745629709 (pb) Contents: The weaknesses of regional integration theories -- The global markets approach in explaining cooperation -- Methodology and the empirical plausibility of the hypotheses -- Global financial markets -- Global production and foreign direct investment -- World trade -- Conclusion: crises, interests, and instruments -- Liberalization strategies in the single market project "1992" -- France -- Germany -- Great Britain -- The European level -- Liberalization strategies in the common market of the South -- Argentina -- Excursus: transnational banks and the international monetary fund -- Brazil -- Liberalization strategies in the North American Free Trade Agreement -- Mexico -- United States -- Empirical results: preference and the global markets approach -- Theoretical development of the global markets approach -- Implications for theories of regional integration and international relations. Subjects: International economic relations. International economic integration. Globalization. LC Classification: HF1359 .S354 2002 Dewey Class No.: 382/.9 21

Scholte, Jan Aart. Civil society and global finance / Jan Aart Scholte with Albrecht Schnabel. Published/Created: New York: Routledge, 2002. Related Names: Schnabel, Albrecht. Description: p. cm. ISBN 0415279356 0415279364 (pbk.) Notes: Includes bibliographical references and index. Subjects: International finance. Civil society. Globalization. Series: Warwick studies in globalisation LC Classification: HG3881 .S3744 2002 Dewey Class No.: 332/.042 21

Scholte, Jan Aart. Civil society and global finance / Jan Aart Scholte with Albrecht Schnabel. Published/Created: New York: Routledge, 2002. Related Names: Schnabel, Albrecht. Description: p. cm. ISBN 0415279356 0415279364 (pbk.) Notes: Includes bibliographical references and index. Subjects: International finance.

Civil society. Globalization. Series: Warwick studies in globalisation LC Classification: HG3881 .S3744 2002 Dewey Class No.: 332/.042 21

Scholte, Jan Aart. Globalization: a critical introduction / Jan Aart Scholte. Published/Created: New York: St. Martin's Press, 2000. Description: xix, 361 p.; 24 cm. ISBN 031223631X 0312236328 (paper) Notes: Includes bibliographical references and index. Subjects: Globalization. International relations. LC Classification: JZ1318 .S36 2000 Dewey Class No.: 303.4 21

Schoonmaker, Sara, 1956- High-tech trade wars: U.S.-Brazilian conflicts in the global economy / Sara Schoonmaker. Published/Created: Pittsburgh, Pa.: University of Pittsburgh Press, c2002. Description: p. cm. ISBN 0822941791 Contents: Globalization, neoliberalism, and the Brazilian informatics case -- Information trade politics: from telecommunications to trade policy -- Who's afraid of Brazilian informatics? -- The double desire: mediation and resistance through software policy -- From technological autonomy to neoliberalism: constructing an open market -- Incipient denationalization: Brazilian informatics in 2001 -- Neoliberal globalization and beyond: protest, celebration, and alternatives to development. Notes: Includes bibliographical references (p.) and index. Subjects: Computer software industry--Brazil. Computer industry--Brazil. Globalization. United States--Foreign economic relations--Brazil. Brazil--Foreign economic relations--United States. Series: Pitt Latin American series LC Classification: HD9696.63.B72 S36 2002 Dewey Class No.: 382/.45005/0981 21

Security and development in Southern Africa / edited by Nana Poku; foreword by Stephen Chan. Published/Created: Westport, Conn.: Praeger, 2001. Related Names: Poku, Nana, 1971- Description: xviii, 166 p.; 25 cm. ISBN 0275964000 (alk. paper) Notes: Includes bibliographical references and index. Subjects: Economic security--Africa, Southern. National security--Africa, Southern. Globalization. Africa, Southern--Economic integration. LC Classification: HC900 .S43 2001 Dewey Class No.: 337.68 21

Security in the new millennium: views from South Asia / editor Rajesh M. Basrur. Published/Created: New Delhi: India Research Press, 2001. Related Names: Basrur, Rajesh M. Regional Centre for Strategic Studies (Colombo, Sri Lanka) Description: 248 p.; 23 cm. ISBN 8187943157 Summary: Contributed articles. Contents: Towards a citizen-state: a view from Bangladesh / Amena Mohsin -- Expanded domain of security in the new millennium: a view from Nepal / Lok Raj Baral -- Ensuring whose security? the new millennium and nuclear weapons of India and Pakistan / Haider K. Nizamani -- Security's insecurity: South Asia's state, societies, and citizens in the age of globalisation / Jayadeva Uyangoda -- Human security, the state, and democracy in a globalising world / Rajesh M. Basrur -- South Asian security in the new millennium / Moonis Ahmar. Notes: "Regional Centre for Strategic Studies, Colombo." Includes bibliographical references.

Seeds of suicide: the ecological and human costs of globalisation of agriculture / Vandana Shiva ... [et al.]. Published/Created: New Delhi: Research Foundation for Science, Technology, and Ecology, c2000. Related Names: Shiva, Vandana. Research Foundation for Science, Technology, and Ecology (New Delhi, India) Description: 144 p.: ill.; 29

cm. Summary: With reference to India. Notes: Includes bibliographical references (p. 142-144).

Segesvary, Victor. From illusion to delusion: globalization and the contradictions of late modernity / Victor Segesvary. Published/Created: San Francisco, Calif.: International Scholars Publications, 1998. Description: p. cm. ISBN 157309322X (hardcover: alk. paper) Notes: Includes bibliographical references and index. Subjects: Civilization, Modern--1950- International relations and culture. International economic relations. Ethics. Acculturation. Globalization. LC Classification: CB430 .S44 1998 Dewey Class No.: 909.82/5 21

Segyehwa wa Han'guk sahoe ui mirae: sin chayujuuijok segyehwa wa Miguk, ku taean un omnun'ga / Kang Ch`i-won yokkum. Edition Information: Ch`op`an. Published/Created: Soul-si: Paegui, 2000. Related Names: Kang, Ch`i-won, 1953- Yoksa Munhwa Ak`ademi (Korea) Description: 445 p.: ill.; 23 cm. ISBN 8980260776 Notes: "Chiuni Yoksa Munhwa Ak`ademi"--Colophon. Includes bibliographical references. Subjects: Social integration. Globalization. Civilization, Modern. Social intergration-- Korea (South) Frontier thesis. LC Classification: HM683 .S45 2000

Sellers, Jefferey M. Governing from below: urban regions and the global economy / Jefferey M. Sellers. Published/Created: New York: Cambridge University Press, 2001. Description: p. cm. ISBN 0521651530 0521657075 (pbk.) Notes: Includes bibliographical references and index. Subjects: Metropolitan government. Urban economics. Regional economics. Globalization. Metropolitan areas--United States--Case studies. Metropolitan areas--France--Case studies. Metropolitan areas--Germany--Case

studies. Series: Cambridge studies in comparative politics LC Classification: JS241 .S45 2001 Dewey Class No.: 330.9173/2 21

Seminar Nasional Globalisasi Kebudayaan dan Ketahanan Ideologi, Yogyakarta, 16-17 November 1994 [microform]: [kertas kerja]. Published/Created: [Yogyakarta]: Forum Diskusi Filsafat, Universitas Gadjah Mada, [1994] Description: 1 v. (various pagings); 29 cm. Summary: Seminar on cultural globalization and ideological persistent of Pancasila, the state philosophy of Indonesia; papers of seminar. Notes: Microfiche. Jakarta: Library of Congress Office; Washington, D.C.: Library of Congress Photoduplication Service, 1998. 3 microfiches; 11 x 15 cm. In Indonesian, with one article in Malaysia. LC Classification: Microfiche 95/50562 (J)

Shaping a new international financial system: challenges of governance in a globalizing world / edited by Karl Kaiser, John J. Kirton, Joseph P. Daniels. Published/Created: Aldershot; Burlington, Vt.: Ashgate, c2000. Related Names: Kaiser, Karl. Kirton, John J. Daniels, Joseph P. Description: xvi, 280 p.; 23 cm. ISBN 0754614123 Notes: Includes bibliographical references and index. Subjects: Group of Eight (Organization) International finance. International economic relations. Series: The G8 and global governance series LC Classification: HF1359 .S542 2000 Dewey Class No.: 332/.042 21

Sharma, Brahm Dev, 1931- Globalisation, the tribal encounter / B.D. Sharma. Published/Created: New Delhi: Har- Anand Publications, c1995. Description: 143 p.; 22 cm. ISBN 8124103356 : Summary: With special reference to Bastar District in southern Madhya Pradesh of India on new economic policy.

Subjects: Bastar (India: District)--
Economic policy. Bastar (India: District)--
Social conditions. LC Classification:
HC435.2 .S478 1995

Shifting sands: women's lives and
globalization / edited by Centre for
Women's Development Studies.
Published/Created: Calcutta: Stree;
Mumbai: Distributed by Popular
Prakashan, 2000. Related Names: Centre
for Women's Development Studies (New
Delhi, India) Description: xiv, 326 p.; 23
cm. ISBN 8185604401 Summary:
Collection of articles with reference to the
Indian scene. Notes: Includes
bibliographical references (p. [295]-315)
and index. Subjects: Women--India--
Social conditions. Women's rights--India.
Globalization. Social change--India.
India--Economic policy--1980- LC
Classification: HQ1743 .S49 2000

Shiva, Vandana. Climate change,
deforestation, and the Orissa super
cyclone: ecological costs of globalisation /
Vandana Shiva, Ashok Emani.
Published/Created: New Delhi: Research
Foundation for Science Technology &
Ecology, 2000. Related Names: Emani,
Ashok. Research Foundation for Science,
Technology, and Ecology (New Delhi,
India) Description: 32 p.: ill., maps (some
col.); 29 cm. Notes: Includes
bibliographical references (p. 32).
Subjects: Cyclones--Environmental
aspects--India--Orissa. Climatic changes--
India--Orissa. Orissa (India)--
Environmental degradation. Series:
Research Foundation white papers on
globalisation; no. 2 LC Classification:
QC947 .S48 2000 Dewey Class No.:
551.55/2/095413 21

Shiva, Vandana. Ecological costs of economic
globalisation: the Indian experience /
Vandana Shiva, Afsar H. Jafri, Gitanjali
Bedi. Published/Created: New Delhi:

Research Foundation for Science,
Technology & Ecology, [1997] Related
Names: Jafri, Afsar H. Bedi, Gitanjali.
Research Foundation for Science,
Technology & Ecology (New Delhi,
India) Description: iv, 66 p.: ill.; 29 cm.
Notes: "Prepared for UN General
Assembly Special Session on Rio + 5
(UNGASS)." Subjects: Economic
development--Environmental aspects--
International cooperation. Economic
forecasting--Developing countries.
Developing countries--Economic policy.
LC Classification: HD77 .S45 1997

Shiva, Vandana. The beedi ban, tobacco
monopolies, and the myth of child labour:
deconstructing the politics of trade
sanctions / Vandana Shiva, Margaret
Antony. Published/Created: New Delhi:
Research Foundation for Science
Technology & Ecology, 2000. Related
Names: Antony, Margaret. Research
Foundation for Science, Technology, and
Ecology (New Delhi, India) Description:
33 p.: ill.; 29 cm. Summary: In the Indian
context. Notes: Includes bibliographical
references (p. 31-32). Subjects: Cigarette
industry--India. Tobacco industry--India.
Women tobacco workers--India. Child
labor--India. Series: Research Foundation
white papers on globalisation; no. 1 LC
Classification: HD9149.C43 I446 2000

Shiva, Vandana. Yoked to death: globalisation
and corporate control of agriculture /
Vandana Shiva. Published/Created: New
Delhi: Research Foundation for Science,
Technology, and Ecology, c2001. Related
Names: Research Foundation for Science,
Technology, and Ecology (New Delhi,
India) Description: 58 p.; 29 cm.
Summary: With reference to India. Notes:
Includes bibliographical references (p. 57-
58). Subjects: Agriculture--Economic
aspects--India. LC Classification:
HD2072 .S+

Sicherheit in der Welt heute: geschichtliche
    Entwicklung und Perspektiven:
    Atzelsberger Gespräche 2000: drei
    Vorträge / herausgegeben von Helmut
    Neuhaus. Published/Created: Erlangen:
    Universitätsbund Erlangen-Nürnberg:
    Universitätsbibliothek Erlangen
    [distributor], 2001. Related Names:
    Neuhaus, Helmut. Description: 77 p.: ill.;
    24 cm. ISBN 3930357437 Notes: Includes
    bibliographical references. Subjects:
    National security--Europe--Congresses.
    Globalization--Economic aspects--
    Congresses. Series: Erlanger
    Forschungen. Reihe A.,
    Geisteswissenschaften 0423-3433; Bd. 94
    LC Classification: UA646 .A89 2000
    Dewey Class No.: 355/.00304 21

Sindhwani, Trilok N., 1939- India's role in
    globalisation / T.N. Sindhwani. Edition
    Information: 1st ed. Published/Created:
    New Delhi: Capital Foundation Society,
    1992. Description: 138 p.; 22 cm. ISBN
    8185298025 : Subjects: International
    economic relations. India--Commercial
    policy. LC Classification: HF1589 .S56
    1992

Singaporeans exposed: navigating the ins and
    outs of globalisation / edited by Lee Geok
    Boi. Published/Created: Singapore:
    Landmark Books, c2001. Description: 230
    p.: ill.; 23 cm. ISBN 9813065559

Singh, Kavaljit. The globalisation of finance: a
    citizen's guide / Kavaljit Singh.
    Published/Created: London; New York:
    Zed Books, 1998. Description: p. cm.
    ISBN 1856496910 1856496929 (pbk.)
    Notes: Includes bibliographical references
    and index. Subjects: International finance.
    Capital movements. LC Classification:
    HG3881 .S537 1998 Dewey Class No.:
    332/.042 21

Sishankamrata (Indonesia) menghadapi era
    globalisasi [microform] / oleh kelompok

A. Published/Created: [Jakarta]: Markas
    Besar Angkatan Bersenjata, Republik
    Indonesia, Lembaga Pertahanan Nasional,
    [199-] Related Names: Lembaga
    Pertahanan Nasional (Indonesia)
    Description: 20 leaves; 28 cm. Summary:
    Improvement of the Indonesian people
    defence and security system towards the
    globalization era. Notes: Microfiche.
    Jakarta: Library of Congress Office;
    Washington, D.C.: Library of Congress
    Photoduplication Service, 1995. 1
    microfiche; 11 x 15 cm. LC
    Classification: Microfiche 93/50876 (U)

Situating globalization: views from Egypt /
    Cynthia Nelson, Shahnaz Rouse (eds.).
    Published/Created: Bielefeld: Transcript,
    c2000. Related Names: Nelson, Cynthia.
    Rouse, Shahnaz J. Description: 361 p.; 23
    cm. ISBN 3933127610 (pbk.) Contents:
    Globalization, Islam and the
    indigenization of knowledge / Philip
    Marfleet -- The islamization of knowledge
    between particularism and globalization,
    Malaysia and Egypt / Mona Abaza --
    Gendering globalization, alternative
    languages of modernity / Cynthia Nelson
    and Shahnaz Rouse -- Struggling and
    surviving, the trajectory of Sheikh
    Moubarak Abu Fadl / Didier Monciaud --
    Al-daght, pressures of modern life in
    Cairo / Mohammed Tabishat -- Creating
    bodies, organizing selves, planning the
    family in Egypt / Kamran Asdar Ali --
    Death of a midwife / Petra Kuppinger --
    Problematizing marriage, minding my
    manners in my husband's community /
    Anita Häusermann Fábos -- A tale of two
    contracts, towards a situated
    understanding of "women interests" in
    Egypt / Heba El-Kholy -- "We are not
    feminists!" / Nadje Al-Ali. Notes:
    Includes bibliographical references.
    Subjects: Globalization--Social aspects.
    Egypt--Economic conditions--1981-
    Egypt--Social conditions--1952- LC

Classification: HC830 .S566 2000

Small countries in a global economy: new challenges and opportunities / edited by Dominick Salvatore, Marjan Svetlicic, and Joze P. Damijan. Published/Created: Houndmills, Basingstoke, Hampshire; New York: Palgrave, 2001. Related Names: Salvatore, Dominick. Svetlicic, Marjan. Damijan, Joze P. (Joze Pavlic), 1967- Description: xii, 305 p.: ill.; 23 cm. ISBN 0333789849 Notes: Includes bibliographical references and index. Subjects: International economic integration. Structural adjustment (Economic policy)--Europe, Central. Structural adjustment (Economic policy)--Europe, Eastern. States, Small--Foreign economic relations. States, Small--Economic conditions. Globalization. Europe, Central--Foreign economic relations. Europe, Eastern--Foreign economic relations. LC Classification: HF1418.5 .S63 2001 Dewey Class No.: 337 21

Small economies' adjustment to global challenges / edited by Zoltán Bara and László Csaba. Published/Created: Budapest: Aula Pub. Co., c2000. Related Names: Bara, Zoltán. Csaba, László, 1954- Description: xiv, 430 p.: ill.; 24 cm. ISBN 9639215899 Notes: Papers selected from a workshop entitled: "Small economies' adjustment to global tendencies" in Budapest, Sept. 1999. Includes bibliographical references and indexes. Subjects: International economic integration--Congresses. States, Small--Economic integration--Congresses. Structural adjustment (Economic policy)--Congresses. Globalization--Congresses. Hungary--Economic integration--Congresses. LC Classification: HF1418.5 .S64 2001 Dewey Class No.: 337.1 21

Social democracy: global and national perspectives / edited by Luke Martell with Matthew Browne ... [et al.]. Published/Created: New York: Palgrave, 2001. Related Names: Martell, Luke. Description: p. cm. ISBN 0333804058 Notes: Includes bibliographical references and index. Subjects: Socialism--Europe. Socialist parties--Europe. Globalization. LC Classification: HX238.5 .S6 2001 Dewey Class No.: 335.5 21

Social exclusion and European policy / edited by David G. Mayes, Jos Berghman, Robert Salais. Published/Created: Northampton, MA: Edward Elgar, 2001. Related Names: Mayes, David G. Berghman, Jos. Salais, Robert. Description: p. cm. ISBN 1840646888 Notes: Includes bibliographical references and index. Subjects: Marginality, Social--European Union countries. European Union countries--Social policy. Series: Globalisation and welfare series LC Classification: HN380.Z9 M26685 2001 Dewey Class No.: 305.5/6/094 21

Social forces in the making of the new Europe: the restructuring of European social relations in the global political economy / edited by Andreas Bieler and Adam David Morton; foreword by Robert W. Cox. Published/Created: Basingstoke, Hampshire; New York: Palgrave, 2001. Related Names: Bieler, Andreas, 1967- Morton, Adam David, 1971- Description: xviii, 243 p.; 23 cm. ISBN 0333913213 0333920678 (pbk.) Notes: Includes bibliographical references (p. 218-238) and index. Subjects: Social change--Europe. Capitalism--Social aspects--Europe. Globalization. Europe--Economic integration--Social aspects. Series: Series in international political economy. LC Classification: HN377 .S63 2001 Dewey Class No.: 303.4/094 21

Social security in the global village / Roland Sigg and Christina Behrendt, editors. Published/Created: New Brunswick, NJ:

Transaction Publishers, 2002. Related Names: Sigg, Roland. Behrendt, Christina. Description: p. cm. ISBN 0765809303 (pbk.: alk. paper) Notes: Includes bibliographical references and index. Subjects: Social security. Globalization. Series: International social security series; v. 8 LC Classification: HD7091 .S6185 2002 Dewey Class No.: 362 21

South Africa and the non-aligned movement in an era of regionalisation and globalisation: proceedings of a preparatory workshop jointly organised by the Foundation for Global Dialogue and the South African Department of Foreign Affairs, Pretoria, 29-30 April 1998 / edited by Pieter Fourie & Riaan de Villiers. Published/Created: Braamfontein, South Africa: The Foundation, 1998. Related Names: Fourie, Pieter. De Villiers, Riaan. Foundation for Global Dialogue. South Africa. Dept. of Foreign Affairs. Description: iii, 112 p.; 30 cm. ISBN 1919697292 Notes: Includes bibliographical references. Subjects: Non-Aligned Movement--Congresses. Nonalignment--South Africa--Congresses. Globalization--Congresses. South Africa--Foreign relations--1994---Congresses. LC Classification: DT1971 .S68 1998

South Africa and the non-aligned movement in an era of regionalisation and globalisation: proceedings of a preparatory workshop jointly organised by the Foundation for Global Dialogue and the South African Department of Foreign Affairs, Pretoria, 29-30 April 1998 / edited by Pieter Fourie & Riaan de Villiers. Published/Created: Braamfontein, South Africa: The Foundation, 1998. Related Names: Fourie, Pieter. De Villiers, Riaan. Foundation for Global Dialogue. South Africa. Dept. of Foreign Affairs. Description: iii, 112 p.; 30 cm. ISBN 1919697292 Notes: Includes bibliographical references. Subjects: Non-Aligned Movement--Congresses.

Nonalignment--South Africa--Congresses. Globalization--Congresses. South Africa--Foreign relations--1994---Congresses. LC Classification: DT1971 .S68 1998

Southern California and the world / edited by Eric J. Heikkila and Rafael Pizarro. Published/Created: Westport, Conn.: Praeger, 2002. Related Names: Heikkila, Eric John. Pizarro, Rafael, 1958- Description: p. cm. ISBN 0275971120 (alk. paper) Notes: Includes bibliographical references and index. Subjects: Pluralism (Social sciences)--California, Southern. Globalization. Civilization, Modern--American influences. California, Southern--Civilization. California, Southern--Relations--Foreign countries. LC Classification: F867 .S697 2002 Dewey Class No.: 303.48/27949 21

Sozialstaat in der Globalisierung / herausgegeben von Diether Döring unter Mitarbeit von Erika Mezger. Edition Information: 1. Aufl. Published/Created: Frankfurt: Suhrkamp, 1999. Related Names: Döring, Diether, 1939- Mezger, Erika, 1957- Description: 202 p.: ill.; 18 cm. ISBN 3518120964 Notes: Includes bibliographical references. Subjects: Welfare state. International economic relations. Globalization. LC Classification: JC479 .S69 1999

State and society in Latin America: challenges of globalisation / edited by Abdul Nafey, Vishnu Priya, Dalbir Singh. Edition Information: 1st ed. Published/Created: New Delhi: Commonwealth Publishers, 2000. Related Names: Abdul Nafey, 1953- Priya, Vishnu. Dalbir Singh. Description: xii, 319 p.; 22 cm. ISBN 8171696244 Summary: Papers presented at various conferences. Notes: Includes bibliographical references (p. [296]-308) and index. Subjects: Democratization--Latin America. Latin America--Economic conditions--1982- LC Classification: JL966 .S73 2000 Dewey Class No.: 306/.098 21

Steinherr, Alfred. Derivatives: the wild beast of finance: a path to effective globalisation? / Alfred Steinherr. Edition Information: Rev. ed. Published/Created: Chichester, West Sussex, England; New York: John Wiley, 2000. Description: xx, 308 p.: ill.; 25 cm. ISBN 047182240X (pbk.: alk. paper) Notes: Includes bibliographical references (p. [294]-298) and index. Subjects: Derivative securities. LC Classification: HG6024.A3 S753 2000 Dewey Class No.: 332.64/5 21

Stevenson, Nick. The transformation of the media: globalisation, morality, and ethics / Nicholas Stevenson. Published/Created: London; New York: Longman, 1999. Description: p. cm. ISBN 0582292050 Notes: Includes bibliographical references and index. Subjects: Mass media--Moral and ethical aspects. Communication, International. Mass media and culture. LC Classification: P94 .S74 1999 Dewey Class No.: 175 21

Stopford, John M. Offensive and defensive responses by European multinationals to a world of trade blocs / by John M Stopford. Published/Created: Paris: Organisation for Economic Co-operation and Development, 1992. Related Names: Organisation for Economic Co-operation and Development. Development Centre. Description: 59 p.: ill., map; 30 cm. Notes: "Under the direction of Charles Oman. Produced as part of the research programme on Globalisation and regionalisation." "May 1992." "General distribution; OCDE/GD(92)78." Summary in French. Includes bibliographical references (p. 55-59). Subjects: Corporations, European--Management. International business enterprises--Management. Exports--Europe.

Competition--Europe. Europe--Commercial policy. Series: Technical papers (Organisation for Economic Co-operation and Development. Development Centre); no. 64. LC Classification: HD62.4 .S76 1992

Strachan, Graham L., 1941- Globalisation: demise of the Australian nation / Graham L. Strachan. Published/Created: Logan Village, Qld: Applause Press, c1998. Description: 176 p.; 21 cm. ISBN 0646361139 (pbk.) Notes: Includes bibliographical references. Subjects: Globalization. Australia--Economic conditions--1945- Australia--Economic policy. LC Classification: HC605 .S765 1998 Dewey Class No.: 338.994 21

Strange power: shaping the parameters of international relations and international political economy / edited by Thomas C. Lawton, James N. Rosenau, Amy C. Verdun. Published/Created: Aldershot; Burlington, Vt.: Ashgate, c2000. Related Names: Lawton, Thomas C. Rosenau, James N. Verdun, Amy, 1968- Description: xxii, 453 p.; 24 cm. ISBN 0754613240 (HB) Notes: Includes bibliographical references (p. 421-443) and index. Subjects: Strange, Susan, 1923- Retreat of the state. International economic relations--Political aspects. International relations. Globalization. World politics--1989- Power (Social sciences) LC Classification: HF1359 .S767 2000 Dewey Class No.: 337 21

Streeten, Paul. Globalisation: threat or opportunity? / Paul Streeten. Edition Information: 1. ed. Published/Created: Copenhagen; Herndon, VA: Copenhagen Business School Press, 2001. Description: 190 p.; 23 cm. ISBN 8716135245 Notes: Includes bibliographical references (p. [175]-183) and indexes. Subjects: International economic integration. International trade--Social aspects.

International trade--Political aspects.
Globalization--Economic aspects.
Globalization--Social aspects.
Globalization--Political aspects. LC
Classification: HF1418.5 .S77 2001
Dewey Class No.: 337 21

Studies on the social dimensions of
globalization. Published/Created: Geneva:
International Labour Office, < 2001- >
Related Names: Reinecke, Gerhard.
Torres, Raymond. Description: v. <2-4, 6-
7 >: ill.; 24 cm. ISBN 9221113922 (v. 2)
Notes: Includes bibliographical references
and indexes. Subjects: International
economic integration--Social aspects
International trade--Social aspects.
Foreign trade and employment.
Globalization--Social aspects.
Globalization--Economic aspects.
International economic relations. LC
Classification: HF1418.5 .S78 2001

Sustainable agriculture and environment:
globalisation and the impact of trade
liberalisation / edited by Andrew K.
Dragun and Clem Tisdell.
Published/Created: Cheltenham, UK;
Northampton, MA: Edward Elgar Pub.,
1999. Related Names: Dragun, Andrew K.
Tisdell, C. A. (Clement Allan)
Description: xxi, 308 p.: ill.; 25 cm. ISBN
184064172X Notes: "This book was
conceived following an international
workshop on Sustainable agriculture and
environment in Uppsala, Sweden, in May
of 1997"--Pref. Includes bibliographical
references (p. [304] and index. Subjects:
Agriculture--Environmental aspects--
Developing countries Congresses.
Sustainable agriculture--Developing
countries--Congresses. Agriculture and
state--Developing countries--Congresses.
International trade--Congresses. LC
Classification: S589.76.D44 S88 1999
Dewey Class No.: 333.76/15/091724 21

Swamy, Dalip Singh, 1934- The political
economy of industrialisation: from self-
reliance to globalisation / Dalip S.
Swamy. Published/Created: New Delhi,
India; Thousand Oaks, Calif.: Sage
Publications, 1994. Description: 292 p.;
22 cm. ISBN 0803994737 (US: hb)
0803991304 (US: pbk.) 8170363330
(India: hb) 817036356X (India: pb) Notes:
Includes bibliographical references (p.
[282]-288) and index. Subjects: Industrial
policy--India. India--Economic policy--
1947- India--Economic conditions--1947-
LC Classification: HD435.2 .S92 1994
Dewey Class No.: 338.954 20

Taiwan in the global economy: from an
agrarian economy to an exporter of high-
tech products / edited by Peter C.Y.
Chow; foreword by Kuang-Sheng Liao.
Published/Created: Westport, Conn.:
Praeger, 2002. Related Names: Chow,
Peter C. Y. Description: p. cm. ISBN
0275970795 (alk. paper) Notes: Includes
bibliographical references and index.
Subjects: Globalization. Taiwan--
Economic conditions--1975- Taiwan--
Foreign economic relations. LC
Classification: HC430.5 .T296 2002
Dewey Class No.: 337.5124/9 21

Technological globalisation: the end of the
nation state? / edited by Daniele
Archibugi and Jonathan Michie.
Published/Created: New York: Cambridge
University Press, 1997. Related Names:
Archibugi, Daniele. Michie, Jonathan.
Description: p. cm. ISBN 052155392X
(hardback) Notes: Includes index.
Subjects: Technological innovations--
Economic aspects. Technology and state.
Competition, International. National state.
LC Classification: HC79.T4 T4312 1997
Dewey Class No.: 338/.064 20

Technology, development, and democracy:
international conflict and cooperation in
the information age / edited by Juliann

Emmons Allison. Published/Created: Albany: State University of New York Press, c2002. Related Names: Allison, Juliann Emmons, 1965- Description: p. cm. ISBN 0791452131 (alk. paper) 079145214X (pbk. alk. paper) Notes: Includes bibliographical references and index. Subjects: Information society. Information society--Political aspects. Globalization. Series: SUNY series in global politics LC Classification: HM851 .T45 2002 Dewey Class No.: 303.48/33 21

Television in contemporary Asia / edited by David French and Michael Richards. Published/Created: New Delhi; Thousand Oaks: Sage Publications, 2000. Related Names: French, David, 1946- Richards, Michael, 1945- Description: 457 p.; 23 cm. ISBN 0761994696 (US HB) 8170369444 (India HB) Notes: Includes bibliographical references and index. Subjects: Television broadcasting--Asia--Cross-cultural studies. Television broadcasting--Asia--Influence. Globalization. LC Classification: HE8700.9.A78 T45 2000 Dewey Class No.: 384.55/095 21

The American century?: in retrospect and prospect / edited by Roberto Rabel. Published/Created: Westport, Conn.: Praeger, c2002. Related Names: Rabel, Roberto Giorgio, 1955- Otago Foreign Policy School (35th: 2000) Description: p. cm. ISBN 0275976726 (alk. paper) Notes: "This book draws on revised conference papers first presented at the 35th University of Otago Foreign Policy School in Dunedin, New Zealand"-- Introd. Includes bibliographical references and index. Subjects: Globalization--Social aspects--Congresses. Globalization--Forecasting--Congresses. United States--Foreign relations--20th century Congresses. United States--Foreign relations--2001---Forecasting Congresses.

LC Classification: E744 .A53 2002 Dewey Class No.: 327.73 21

The anthropology of globalization: a reader / edited by Jonathan Xavier Inda and Renato Rosaldo. Published/Created: Malden, MA: Blackwell Publishers, 2001. Related Names: Inda, Jonathan Xavier. Rosaldo, Renato. Description: p. cm. ISBN 0631222324 (alk. paper) 0631222332 (alk. paper) Subjects: Anthropology. Globalization. Series: Blackwell readers in anthropology; 1 LC Classification: GN27 .A673 2001 Dewey Class No.: 306 21

The Bulgarian village and globalisation processes: XVII Congress of the European Society of Rural Sociology / edited by Veska Kozhuharova. Edition Information: 1. izd. Published/Created: Sofiia: Alja, 1997. Related Names: Kozhuharova, Veska. Description: 99 p.; 20 cm. ISBN 9548465299 Notes: "Local responses to global integration"--Extended t.p. At head of Bulgarian Society of Rural Sociology. Institut of Sociology. Includes bibliographical references. Subjects: Villages--Bulgaria--Congresses. Sociology, Rural--Bulgaria--Congresses. Agriculture--Social aspects--Bulgaria--Congresses. Bulgaria--Rural conditions--Congresses. Series: Bulgaria rusticana LC Classification: HN623.5 .E87 1997 Dewey Class No.: 307.76/2/09499 21

The challenge to Africa of globalization and the information age: proceedings of African Development Forum, 1999. Published/Created: Addis Ababa: United Nations Economic Commission for Africa, [2000] Description: ii, 132 p.: ill.; 29 cm. Notes: "August 2000." Subjects: Information technology--Africa--Congresses. Globalization--Congresses. LC Classification: HC800.Z9 I5533 1999

The contemporary Giddens: social theory in a globalizing age / edited by Christopher G.A. Bryant and David Jary; foreword by Will Hutton. Published/Created: Houndmills, Basingstoke, Hampshire; New York, N.Y.: PALGRAVE, 2001. Related Names: Bryant, Christopher G. A. Jary, David. Description: xviii, 331 p.: ill.; 23 cm. ISBN 0333779045 Notes: Includes bibliographical references (p. 271-320) and index. Subjects: Giddens, Anthony. Sociology. Globalization. Capitalism. Structuralism. International economic relations. LC Classification: HM585 .C655 2001 Dewey Class No.: 301 21

The creative society of the 21st century. Published/Created: Paris: Organisation for Economic Co-operation and Development, c2000. Related Names: OECD Forum for the Future, Organisation for Economic Co-operation and Development. Description: 197 p.: ill. (some col.); 23 cm. ISBN 9264171967 Notes: Papers from a conference held in Berlin, Germany, Dec. 6-7, 1999. "OECD Forum for the Future"--P. 3. Includes bibliographical references. Subjects: Social history--21st century--Congresses. Civilization, Modern--21st century--Congresses. Economic development--Social aspects--Congresses. Technology and civilization--Congresses. Series: Future studies LC Classification: HN3 .C74 2000 Dewey Class No.: 306/.09/05 21

The economic and financial imperatives of globalisation: an Islamic response / edited by Nik Mustapha Nik Hassan, Mazilan Musa. Published/Created: Kuala Lumpur: Institute of Islamic Understanding, Malaysia, 2000. Related Names: Mustapha bin Hj. Nik Hasan, Nik. Mazilan Musa. Institut Kefahaman Islam, Malaysia. Description: xii, 403 p.; 24 cm. ISBN 983909971X Notes: Includes bibliographical references and index.

Subjects: Globalization--Economic aspects--Islamic countries. Economics--Religious aspects--Islam. International economic relations. Islamic countries--Foreign economic relations. LC Classification: HF1610.5 .E36 2000 Dewey Class No.: 337/.0917/671 21

The economic and financial imperatives of globalisation: an Islamic response / edited by Nik Mustapha Nik Hassan, Mazilan Musa. Published/Created: Kuala Lumpur: Institute of Islamic Understanding, Malaysia, 2000. Related Names: Mustapha bin Hj. Nik Hasan, Nik. Mazilan Musa. Institut Kefahaman Islam, Malaysia. Description: xii, 403 p.; 24 cm. ISBN 983909971X Notes: Includes bibliographical references and index. Subjects: Globalization--Economic aspects--Islamic countries. Economics--Religious aspects--Islam. International economic relations. Islamic countries--Foreign economic relations. LC Classification: HF1610.5 .E36 2000 Dewey Class No.: 337/.0917/671 21

The economic geography reader: producing and consuming global capitalism / edited by John Bryson ... [et al.]. Published/Created: Chichester; New York: Wiley, 1999. Related Names: Bryson, J. R., 1963- Description: xii, 481 p.: ill.; 26 cm. ISBN 0471985279 (hardback) 0471985285 (paperback) Notes: Includes bibliographical references (p. [441]-469) and index. Subjects: Economic geography. Production (Economic theory) Consumption (Economics) Foreign trade and employment. Capitalism. Globalization. LC Classification: HF1025 .E192 1999 Dewey Class No.: 330.9 21

The ends of globalization: bringing society back in / edited by Don Kalb ... [et al.]. Published/Created: Lanham, MD: Rowman & Littlefield Publishers, c2000.

Related Names: Kalb, Don, 1959-
Description: vii, 403 p.; 24 cm. ISBN
084769884X (cloth: alk. paper)
0847698858 (paper: alk. paper) Notes:
Includes bibliographical references and
index. Subjects: International cooperation.
International relations. Globalization.
Global governance LC Classification:
JZ1318 .E53 2000 Dewey Class No.:
327.1/7 21

The future of the automotive industry:
challenges and concepts for the 21st
century: updated translation / edited by
Ralf Landmann ... [et al.].
Published/Created: Warrendale, Pa.:
Society of Automotive Engineers, c2001.
Related Names: Landmann, Ralf.
Description: v, 256 p.: ill.; 23 cm. ISBN
0768006880 (pbk.) Notes: Includes
bibliographical references. Subjects:
Automobile industry and trade.
Automobile industry and trade--
International cooperation. Joint ventures.
Globalization. LC Classification:
HD9710.A2 Z8513 2001 Dewey Class
No.: 338.4/76292 21

The global agenda: issues and perspectives /
edited by Charles W. Kegley, Jr., Eugene
R. Wittkopf. Edition Information: 6th ed.
Published/Created: Boston: McGraw-Hill,
c2001. Related Names: Kegley, Charles
W. Wittkopf, Eugene R., 1943-
Description: xiv, 503 p.; 23 cm. ISBN
0072322691 (acid-free paper) Notes:
Includes bibliographical references.
Subjects: International relations.
International economic relations.
Globalization. World politics--1989- LC
Classification: JZ1242 .G56 2001 Dewey
Class No.: 327.1/01 21

The global century: globalization and national
security / edited by Richard L. Kugler and
Ellen L. Frost. Published/Created:
Washington, D.C.: National Defense
University Press, 2001. Related Names:

Kugler, Richard L. Frost, Ellen L.
Description: 2 v. (xvii, 1125 p.); 26 cm.
ISBN 1579060536 (pbk.) Notes: Includes
bibliographical references (p. 1093-1124).
Subjects: Globalization. Security,
International. National security--United
States. United States--Foreign relations--
1993-2001. LC Classification: JZ1318
.G556 2001 Dewey Class No.: 327.73 21

The global challenge to industrial districts:
small and medium sized enterprises in
Italy and Taiwan / edited by Paolo
Guerrieri, Simona Iammarino, Carolo
Pietrobelli. Published/Created:
Northampton, MA: Edward Elgar Pub.,
2001. Related Names: Guerrieri, Paolo,
1947- Iammarino, Simona Pietrobelli,
Carlo, 1959- Description: p. cm. ISBN
1840646985 Notes: Includes
bibliographical references and index.
Subjects: Industrial districts--Italy.
Industrial districts--Taiwan. Competition,
International. Globalization--Economic
aspects. LC Classification: HC310.D5
G56 2001 Dewey Class No.:
338.6/42/0945 21

The global economy: changing politics,
family, and society / edited by Lee
Edwards. Published/Created: St. Paul,
Minn.: Professors World Peace Academy,
c2001. Related Names: Edwards, Lee.
Description: vi, 345 p.: ill.; 23 cm. ISBN
1885118139 (alk. paper) Notes: Includes
bibliographical references and index.
Subjects: International economic
relations. Globalization--Economic
aspects. Globalization--Social aspects. LC
Classification: HF1359 .G5725 2001
Dewey Class No.: 337 21

The global third way debate / edited by
Anthony Giddens. Published/Created:
Malden, Mass.: Polity Press, 2001.
Related Names: Giddens, Anthony.
Description: p. cm. ISBN 0745627412
0745627420 (pbk.) Notes: Includes index.

Subjects: Post-communism. Mixed economy. Globalization. Welfare state. Democracy. Right and left (Political science) LC Classification: HX73 .G59 2001 Dewey Class No.: 337 21

The globalization of financial services / edited by Mervyn K. Lewis. Published/Created: Cheltenham, UK; Northampton, MA, USA: Edward Elgar Publishing, c1999. Related Names: Lewis, Mervyn. Description: xxxiv, 637 p.: ill.; 25 cm. ISBN 1858988934 Notes: Includes bibliographical references and index. Subjects: Financial services industry. Banks and banking, International. International finance. Globalization. Series: The globalization of the world economy; 7 An Elgar reference collection LC Classification: HG173 .G639 1999 Dewey Class No.: 332.1/5 21

The globalization of U.S.-Latin American relations: democracy, intervention, and human rights / edited by Virginia M. Bouvier. Published/Created: Westport, Conn.: Praeger, 2002. Related Names: Bouvier, Virginia Marie, 1958- Description: p. cm. ISBN 027597250X (alk. paper) Notes: Includes bibliographical references and index. Subjects: Globalization. Democracy. Human rights. Latin America--Foreign relations--United States. United States--Foreign relations--Latin America. United States--Foreign relations--20th century. United States--Military relations--Latin America. Latin America--Military relations--United States. LC Classification: F1418 .G58 2002 Dewey Class No.: 327.7308 21

The globalization of world politics: an introduction to international relations / edited by John Baylis and Steve Smith. Edition Information: 2nd ed. Published/Created: Oxford; New York: Oxford University Press, 2001. Related Names: Baylis, John, 1946- Smith, Steve, 1952- Description: xxx, 690 p.: ill.; 25 cm. ISBN 0198782632 Notes: Includes bibliographical references and index. Subjects: International relations. Globalization. World politics--1989- LC Classification: JZ1242 .G58 2001 Dewey Class No.: 327.1/01 21

The globalization of world politics: an introduction to international relations / edited by John Baylis and Steve Smith. Published/Created: New York: Oxford University Press, 1997. Related Names: Baylis, John, 1946- Smith, Steve, 1952- Description: xxviii, 526 p.: ill., map; 25 cm. ISBN 0198781083 (acid-free paper) 0198781091 (pbk.) Notes: Includes bibliographical references (p. 498-513) and index. Subjects: International relations. Globalization. LC Classification: JZ1242 .G58 1997 Dewey Class No.: 327.1/01 21

The globalizing learning economy / edited by Daniele Archibugi and Bengt-Åke Lundvall. Published/Created: New York: Oxford University Press, 2001. Related Names: Archibugi, Daniele. Lundvall, Bengt-Åke, 1941- European Socio-Economic Research Conference (1999: Brussels, Belgium) Description: xvii, 307 p.; 24 cm. ISBN 0199241090 Notes: A collection of 15 revised papers first presented at the "European Socio-Economic Research Conference," and held in Brussels on 28-30 April 1999 to present results of studies promoted by the European Commission. Includes bibliographical references and index. Subjects: Organizational learning--Europe--Congresses. Technological innovations--Economic aspects--Europe Congresses. Globalization--Congresses. LC Classification: HD58.82 .G55 2001 Dewey Class No.: 338/.064 21

The hidden assembly line: gender dynamics of subcontracted work in a global economy / edited by Radhika Balakrishnan. Published/Created: Bloomfield, Conn.: Kumarian Press, 2002. Related Names: Balakrishnan, Radhika. Description: viii, 154 p.; 23 cm. ISBN 1565491394 (pbk.: alk. paper) 1565491408 (cloth: alk. paper) Notes: Includes bibliographical references and index. Subjects: Subcontracting--Asia--Case studies. Women--Employment--Asia--Case studies. Home labor--Asia--Case studies. Globalization--Case studies. LC Classification: HD2385.A77 H53 2002 Dewey Class No.: 338.4/76928/095 21

The Impact of globalisation on Europe's firms and industries / edited by Marc Humbert. Published/Created: London: Pinter Publishers; New York: Distributed in the United States and Canada by St. Martin's Press, 1993. Related Names: Humbert, Marc. Description: xv, 266 p.: ill.; 24 cm. ISBN 1855671131 Notes: Includes bibliographical references (p. [238]-258) and index. Subjects: International business enterprises--Europe. Competition, International. Investments, Foreign--Europe. LC Classification: HD2844 .I55 1993 Dewey Class No.: 338.8/894 20

The limits of globalization: cases and arguments / edited by Alan Scott. Published/Created: London; New York: Routledge, 1997. Related Names: Scott, Alan, 1956- Description: xi, 359 p.: ill.; 24 cm. ISBN 041510565X (hbk.) 0415105668 (pbk.) Notes: Includes bibliographical references (p. 327-349) and index. Subjects: International economic relations--Social aspects. International relations--Social aspects. Cultural relations. Intercultural communication. Internationalism. International economic relations--Case studies. Globalization. Series: International library of sociology LC Classification: HF1359 .L548 1997

The Mediterranean response to globalization before 1950 / edited by Sevket Pamuk and Jeffrey G. Williamson. Published/Created: London; New York: Routledge, 2000. Related Names: Pamuk, Sevket. Williamson, Jeffrey G., 1935- Description: xvi, 430 p.: ill.; 24 cm. ISBN 041522425X (alk. paper) Notes: Includes bibliographical references (p. [381]-416) and index. Subjects: Globalization. International trade. Mediterranean Region--Economic conditions. Mediterranean Region--Economic policy. Series: Routledge explorations in economic history; 18 LC Classification: HC244.5 .M413 2000 Dewey Class No.: 338.91/09182/2 21

The modern/colonial capitalist world-system in the twentieth century: global processes, antisystemic movements, and the geopolitics of knowledge / edited by Ramon Grosfoguel and Ana Margarita Cervantes-Rodríguez. Published/Created: Westport, CT: Greenwood Press, 2002. Related Names: Grosfoguel, Ramón. Cervantes-Rodríguez, Ana Margarita. Description: p. cm. ISBN 0313318042 (alk. paper) Notes: Includes index. Subjects: Social systems. Economic development--Social aspects. Globalization. Series: Contributions in economics and economic history, 0084-9235; no. 227 LC Classification: HM701 .M63 2002 Dewey Class No.: 306 21

The nation state in a global/information era: policy challenges: proceedings of a conference held at Queens University 14-15 November 1996 / Thomas J. Courchene, editor. Published/Created: Kingston, Ont.: John Deutsch Institute for the Study of Economic Policy, Queen's University, [1997] Related Names: Courchene, Thomas J. John Deutsch Institute for the Study of Economic

Policy. Description: vii, 349 p.: ill.; 24 cm. ISBN 0889117667 (bound) 0889117705 (pbk.) Notes: Includes bibliographical references. Subjects: National state--Congresses. International relations--Congresses. International economic relations--Congresses. Globalization--Congresses. Information society--Congresses. Series: The Bell Canada papers on economic and public policy; 5 LC Classification: JZ1316 .N+

The new economy of oil: impacts on business, geopolitics, and society / John Mitchell ... [et al.]. Published/Created: London: Royal Institute of International Affaurs, Energy and Environment Programme: Earthscan, 2001. Related Names: Mitchell, John V. Description: xiii, 286 p.: ill.; 22 cm. ISBN 1853837458 Notes: Includes bibliographical references and index. Subjects: Petroleum industry and trade--Political aspects. Energy industries--Political aspects. Capital movements--Political aspects. Globalization. Security, International. LC Classification: HD9560.6 .N48 2001

The new millennium: challenges and strategies for a globalizing world / edited by Sai Felicia Krishna-Hensel. Published/Created: Aldershot, Hampshire, England; Burlington, Vt., USA: Ashgate, c2000. Related Names: Krishna-Hensel, Sai Felicia. Description: xiv, 329 p.: ill.; 23 cm. ISBN 0754613917 Notes: "Most of these papers were presented at the CISS/ISA Paris conference, which was held on August 9-10, 1999"-- Introd. Includes bibliographical references. Subjects: Globalization--Congresses. International cooperation--Congresses. International economic relations--Congresses. World politics--1989---Congresses. Human rights--Congresses. Series: Global interdisciplinary studies series LC Classification: JZ1318 .N487

2000 Dewey Class No.: 327.1 21

The new political economy of globalisation / edited by Richard Higgott and Anthony Payne. Published/Created: Cheltenham, UK Northampton, MA: Edward Elgar Pub., c2000. Related Names: Higgott, Richard A. Payne, Anthony. Description: 2 v.; 25 cm. ISBN 1840640561 (2 volume set) Notes: Includes bibliographical references and indexes. Subjects: International economic relations. International economic integration. Globalization--Economic aspects. Globalization--Social aspects. LC Classification: HF1359 .N482 2000 Dewey Class No.: 337 21

The new political economy of globalisation / edited by Richard Higgott and Anthony Payne. Published/Created: Cheltenham, UK Northampton, MA: Edward Elgar Pub., c2000. Related Names: Higgott, Richard A. Payne, Anthony. Description: 2 v.; 25 cm. ISBN 1840640561 (2 volume set) Notes: Includes bibliographical references and indexes. Subjects: International economic relations. International economic integration. Globalization--Economic aspects. Globalization--Social aspects. LC Classification: HF1359 .N482 2000 Dewey Class No.: 337 21

The OECD guidelines in a globalisation world. Published/Created: Paris: OECD, 1999. Description: 13 p. Series: OECD working papers, 1022-2227; . 7 no. 66

The OECD, globalisation, and education policy / Miriam Henry ... [et al.]. Edition Information: 1st ed. Published/Created: Amsterdam; New York: Published for IAU Press, Pergamon, 2001. Related Names: Henry, Miriam. Description: xiii, 197 p.; 24 cm. ISBN 0080434495 (hardcover) Notes: Includes bibliographical references (p. 177-187) and index. Subjects: Organisation for Economic Co-operation and Development. Higher education and state--Cross-cultural studies. Globalization--Cross-cultural studies. Series: Issues in higher education (Oxford, England) LC Classification: LC171 .O43 2001

The OECD, globalisation, and education policy / Miriam Henry ... [et al.]. Edition Information: 1st ed. Published/Created: Amsterdam; New York: Published for IAU Press, Pergamon, 2001. Related Names: Henry, Miriam. Description: xiii, 197 p.; 24 cm. ISBN 0080434495 (hardcover) Notes: Includes bibliographical references (p. 177-187) and index. Subjects: Organisation for Economic Co-operation and Development. Higher education and state--Cross-cultural studies. Globalization--Cross-cultural studies. Series: Issues in higher education (Oxford, England) LC Classification: LC171 .O43 2001

The other Davos summit: the globalization of resistance to the world economic system / edited by Francois Houtart and Francois Polet. Published/Created: London; New York: Zed Books, 2001. Related Names: Houtart, François, 1925- Polet, François. Description: p. cm. ISBN 1856499871 (case) 185649988X Notes: Includes bibliographical references and index. Subjects: World Economic Forum International economic relations. International economic integration. Globalization. Capitalism. LC Classification: HF1411 .A9813 2001 Dewey Class No.: 337 21

The political economy of globalization / edited by Satya Dev Gupta. Published/Created: Boston: Kluwer Academic Publishers, c1997. Related Names: Gupta, Satya Dev. Description: 344 p.: ill.; 25 cm. ISBN 079239903X (acid-free paper) Notes: Includes bibliographical references and

index. Subjects: International economic relations. International economic integration. International economic relations--Social aspects. International relations. International cooperation. Globalization. Series: Recent economic thought series; 55. LC Classification: HF1359 .P654 1997 Dewey Class No.: 337 21

The political economy of Japanese globalization / edited by Glenn D. Hook and Hasegawa Harukiyo. Published/Created: London; New York: Routledge, 2001. Related Names: Hook, Glenn D. Hasegawa, Harukiyo, 1943- University of Sheffield. Centre of Japanese Studies. Kokusai Nihon Bunka Kenkyu Senta. Description: p. cm. ISBN 0415232864 (alk. paper) Notes: Papers presented at an international symposium sponsored by the Centre for Japanese Studies at the University of Sheffield in collaboration with the International Research Center for Japanese Studies in Kyoto held from 20-22 March 1998. Includes bibliographical references and index. Subjects: Globalization--Economic aspects--Japan--Congresses. Globalization--Social aspects--Japan--Congresses. Japan--Foreign economic relations--Congresses. Series: Sheffield Centre for Japanese Studies/Routledge series LC Classification: HF1601 .P654 2001 Dewey Class No.: 337.52 21

The politics of change: globalization, ideology, and critique / edited by Werner Bonefeld, Kosmas Psychopedis. Published/Created: Houndmills, Basingstoke, Hampshire; New York: Palgrave, 2000. Related Names: Bonefeld, Werner, 1960- Psychopedis, Kosmas. Description: vii, 212 p.; 23 cm. ISBN 0312235593 (cloth) Notes: Includes bibliographical references and index. Subjects: Habermas, Jürgen. Social

change. Globalization. Socialism. LC
Classification: HM831 .P65 2000 Dewey
Class No.: 303.4 21

The politics of labor in a global age: continuity
and change in late-industralizing and post-
socialist economies / Christopher
Candland and Rudra Sil [editors].
Published/Created: New York: Oxford
University Press, 2001. Related Names:
Candland, Christopher. Sil, Rudra, 1967-
Description: p. cm. ISBN 0199240817
Notes: Includes bibliographical references
and index. Subjects: Comparative
industrial relations. Industrial relations--
Developing countries--Case studies. Post-
communism. Globalization--Economic
aspects. Foreign trade and employment.
LC Classification: HD6971 .P55 2001
Dewey Class No.: 331/.09172/4 21

The role of product design in post-industrial
society / edited by Tevfik Balcioglu;
contributors Victor Margolin ... [et al.].
Published/Created: Ankara: Middle East
Technical University, Faculty of
Architecture Press; Rochester, Kent: Kent
Institute of Art & Design, 1998. Related
Names: Balcioglu, Tevfik. Orta Dogu
Teknik Üniversitesi (Ankara, Turkey).
Faculty of Architecture Press. Kent
Institute of Art & Design. Chartered
Society of Designers. Courtauld Institute
of Art. Description: vii, 113 p.: ill. (some
col.), map. ISBN 9754291225 (METU,
FoA) 1870522303 (Kent Inst.) Partial
Contents: Design and the world situation /
Victor Margolin -- The responsibility of
design in the future / Dieter Rams --
Products in a period of transition:
products, services and interactions for a
sustainable society / Ezio Manzini --
Things to enjoy: reassessing craft and
design objects in an age of technology /
Jeremy Myerson -- The economic role of
industrial design / John Heskett -- Beyond
the dogma of globalisation / James
Woudhuysen. Notes: This book is based

on papers presented at a conference
organized by the Kent Institute of Art &
Design with the support of the Chartered
Society of Designers, held on 7th July
1995 at the Courtauld Institute in London.
Includes bibliographical references.
Subjects: Design, Industrial--Social
aspects. Design, Industrial--
Environmental aspects. LC Classification:
TS171.4 .R65 1998 Dewey Class No.:
745.2 21

The role of the World Trade Organization in
global governance / edited by Gary P.
Sampson. Published/Created: Tokyo; New
York: United Nations University Press,
c2001. Related Names: Sampson, Gary P.
Description: x, 298 p.; 23 cm. ISBN
9280810553 (pbk.) Notes: Includes
bibliographical references and indexes.
Subjects: World Trade Organization.
World Trade Organization--Developing
countries. Foreign trade regulation.
Commercial policy. Free trade--
Environmental aspects. Free trade--Social
aspects. International economic relations.
Globalization. LC Classification: HF1385
.R65 2001 Dewey Class No.: 382/.92 21

The technology revolution: nations in the age
of computers / Scott Barbour, book editor.
Published/Created: San Diego, CA:
Greenhaven Press, 2002. Related Names:
Barbour, Scott, 1963- Description: p. cm.
ISBN 0737707054 (pbk.) 0737707062
(lib.) Notes: Includes bibliographical
references and index. Subjects: World
politics--1989- Technology--Social
aspects. National security. Globalization.
Terrorism. Computers--Social aspects.
Series: World history by era; v. 10 LC
Classification: D860 .T363 2002 Dewey
Class No.: 909.82/5 21

The third force: the rise of transnational civil
society / Ann M. Florini, editor.
Published/Created: Tokyo: Japan Center
for International Exchange; Washington,

D.C.: Carnegie Endowment for International Peace: Brookings Institution Press [distributor], c2000. Related Names: Florini, Ann Description: viii, 295 p.; 23 cm. ISBN 0870031791 (pbk.: acid-free paper) 0870031805 (cloth: acid-free paper) Notes: Includes bibliographical references and index. Subjects: Civil society. Globalization. LC Classification: JC337 .T45 2000 Dewey Class No.: 322.4 21

There is an alternative: subsistence and world-wide resistance to corporate globalization / edited by Veronika Bennholdt-Thomsen, Nicholas Faraclas, Claudia von Werlhof. Published/Created: New York: Zed Books, 2001. Related Names: Bennholdt-Thomsen, Veronika. Faraclas, Nicholas. Werlhof, Claudia von, 1943- Description: p. cm. ISBN 1842770055 (cased) 1842770063 (limp) Notes: Includes bibliographical references and index. Subjects: International business enterprises--Social aspects. Globalization--Social aspects. Globalization--Economic aspects. Subsistence economy. Sustainable development. Subsistence economy--Developing countries. Sustainable development--Developing countries. Developing countries--Economic conditions LC Classification: HD2755.5 .T55 2001 Dewey Class No.: 338.9/27/091724 21

Tourism in the age of globalisation / edited by Salah Wahab and Chris Cooper. Published/Created: New York: Routledge, 2001. Related Names: Wahab, Salah. Cooper, Christopher P. Description: p. cm. ISBN 0415213169 (hb) Notes: Includes bibliographical references (p.). Subjects: Tourism. Globalization. LC Classification: G155.A1 T59215 2001 Dewey Class No.: 338.4/791 21

Tourism in the age of globalisation / edited by Salah Wahab and Chris Cooper.

Published/Created: New York: Routledge, 2001. Related Names: Wahab, Salah. Cooper, Christopher P. Description: p. cm. ISBN 0415213169 (hb) Notes: Includes bibliographical references (p.). Subjects: Tourism. Globalization. LC Classification: G155.A1 T59215 2001 Dewey Class No.: 338.4/791 21

Trade and investment in a globalising world: essays in honour of H. Peter Gray / edited by Rajneesh Narula. Edition Information: 1st ed. Published/Created: Amsterdam; New York: Pergamon, 2001. Related Names: Gray, H. Peter. Narula, Rajneesh, 1963- Description: xiii, 242 p.: ill.; 24 cm. ISBN 0080438911 (alk. paper) Notes: Includes bibliographical references and indexes. Subjects: International trade. Investments, Foreign. International finance. International business enterprises. International economic relations. Globalization. Series: Series in international business and economics LC Classification: HF1379 .T696 2001 Dewey Class No.: 337 21

Trade and investment: issues in the Indian Ocean rim / edited by J. Mahender Reddy. Published/Created: New Delhi: Sterling Publishers, c2000. Related Names: Mahender Reddy, J., 1942- Seminar on "Trade and Investment Issues in the Indian Ocean Rim Association for Regional Cooperation" (1999: Maputo, Mozambique) Description: xii, 500 p.: ill., map; 22 cm. ISBN 8120722868 Summary: Proceedings of the Seminar on "Trade and Investment Issues in the Indian Ocean Rim Association for Regional Cooperation" held in Maputo on March 26-27, 1999. Notes: Includes statistical tables. Includes bibliographical references. Subjects: International trade--Congresses. Investments, Foreign--Congresses. Globalization--Congresses. LC Classification: HF1372 .T735 2000

Trade in the global economy / Samuel Edwards, editor. Published/Created: Huntington, NY: Nova Science Publishers, c2001. Related Names: Edwards, Samuel. Description: 229 p.: ill.; 27 cm. ISBN 1560729481 Notes: Includes bibliographical references and index. Subjects: Free trade. International trade. Globalization--Economic aspects. LC Classification: HF1713 .T693 2001 Dewey Class No.: 382 21

Trading services in the global economy / edited by Juan R. Cuadrado Roura, Luis Rubalcaba Bermejo, J.R. Bryson. Published/Created: Northampton, MA: E. Elgar, 2002. Related Names: Cuadrado Roura, Juan R. Rubalcaba-Bermejo, Luis. Bryson, J. R., 1963- RESER Congress (9th: 1999: Universidad de Alcalá de Henares) Description: p. cm. ISBN 1840646101 Notes: Selected papers presented at the 9th RESER Congress, held at University of Alcalá in October 1999. Includes index. Subjects: Service industries--Congresses. International trade--Congresses. Globalization--Congresses. LC Classification: HD9980.5 .T733 2002 Dewey Class No.: 382/.45 21

Transatlantic governance in the global economy / edited by Mark A. Pollack and Gregory C. Shaffer. Published/Created: Lanham, Md.: Rowman & Littlefield, c2001. Related Names: Pollack, Mark A., 1966- Shaffer, Gregory C., 1958- Description: xi, 354 p.; 24 cm. ISBN 0742509311 (alk. paper) 074250932X (pbk.: alk. paper) Notes: Includes bibliographical references (p. 307-330) and index. Subjects: International economic relations. Globalization. Series: Governance in Europe LC Classification: HF1359 .P656 2001 Dewey Class No.: 337 21

Transatlantic studies / [edited by] Will Kaufman, Heidi Slettedahl Macpherson. Published/Created: Lanham, Md.: University Press of America, c2000. Related Names: Kaufman, Will. Macpherson, Heidi Slettedahl. Description: xxiii, 273 p.; 24 cm. ISBN 0761817891 (cloth: alk. paper) 0761817905 (pbk.: alk. paper) Notes: Essays based on on-going discussions at the Maastricht Center for Transatlantic Studies. Includes bibliographical references (p. [259]-266) and index. Subjects: Globalization. Citizenship--Cross-cultural studies. Aliens--Cross-cultural studies. Human rights--Cross-cultural studies. Popular culture--Cross-cultural studies. Europe--Relations--America. America--Relations--Europe. LC Classification: D1065.A4 T73 2000 Dewey Class No.: 303.48/2407 21

Transfer of technology: information for development / edited by Robert Haas and Khairul Bashar. Published/Created: Kuala Lumpur: Friedrich Naumann Foundation: Asian Institute for Development Communication, c1993. Related Names: Haas, Robert, Dr. Khairul Bashar. Friedrich-Naumann-Stiftung. Asian Institute for Development Communication. Description: 86 p.: ill.; 23 cm. ISBN 9839981706 Contents: Technological competition / Hans-Peter Brunner -- The globalisation of the word / Zoran Jasic -- Technology transfer on company basis / Klaus Obermeier -- Technology transfer / Gunther Illek -- Human development imperatives and implications for the media towards 2020 / Sulaiman M. Yassin -- The socio-cultural impact and the role of the mass media in technology transfer / Thilla Chelliah -- Technology development and transfer / P.C. Shivadas -- Technology policy and the mass media / Rozali bin Mohamed Ali -- Technology information transfer and exchange in the national development / Abdullah Zawawi Ali and Nor Tashid Ismail -- Application of information technology (IT) in decentralised management / Syed Abdus Samad. Notes: Includes bibliographical references. Subjects: Technology transfer--Malaysia. Technology and state--Malaysia. LC Classification: T174.3 .T672 1993 Dewey Class No.: 338.9/26 20

Transitions in a globalising world / editors, Pim Martens & Jan Rotmans. Published/Created: Lisse, [Netherlands]; Exton, Pa.: Swets & Zeitlinger, 2001. Related Names: Martens, Willem Jozef Meine, 1968- Rotmans, Jan, 1961- Description: p. cm. ISBN 9026519214 Notes: Includes bibliographical references and index. Subjects: Social change. Globalization--Social aspects. Globalization--Environmental aspects. Globalization--Health aspects. Human ecology. Sustainable development. Series: Integrated assessment studies, 1569- 299X; v. 1 LC Classification: HM831 .T73 2001 Dewey Class No.: 303.4 21

Treaty-making and Australia: globalisation versus sovereignty? / edited by Philip Alston and Madelaine Chiam. Published/Created: Annandale, NSW: Federation Press, in association with the Centre for International and Public Law, Faculty of Law, Australian National University, 1995. Related Names: Alston, Philip. Chiam, Madelaine. Australian National University. Centre for International and Public Law. Description: x, 309 p.; 22 cm. ISBN 1862871957 Notes: Includes bibliographical references (p. 292-294) and index. Subjects: Treaty-making power--Australia. Australia--Foreign relations--Treaties. Australia--Politics and government--1945- LC Classification: KU2224 .T73 1995

Twenty-first century world order and the Asia Pacific: value change, exigencies, and power realignment / edited by James C. Hsiung. Edition Information: 1st ed.

Published/Created: New York: Palgrave, 2001. Related Names: Hsiung, James Chieh, 1935- Description: x, 390 p.; 22 cm. ISBN 0312238797 (hbk.) Notes: Includes bibliographical references and index. Subjects: World politics--21st century. National security--Asia. Security, International. Globalization. Asia--Politics and government--21st century. LC Classification: DS35.2 .T86 2001 Dewey Class No.: 327/.095 21

Twining, William L. Globalisation and legal theory / William Twining. Published/Created: Evanston, Ill.: Northwestern University Press, 2001. Description: p. cm. ISBN 0810119048 (pbk.: alk. paper) Notes: Originally published: London: Butterworths, 2000. (Law in context). Includes bibliographical references and index. Subjects: Globalization. Legal positivism. Jurisprudence. Law--Philosophy. LC Classification: JZ1318 .T858 2001 Dewey Class No.: 340 21

Twining, William L. Globalisation and legal theory / William Twining. Published/Created: London: Butterworths, 2000. Description: xii, 279 p.; 22 cm. ISBN 0406913595 Notes: Includes bibliographical references and index. Subjects: Globalization. Legal positivism. Jurisprudence. Law--Philosophy. Series: Law in context LC Classification: JZ1318 .T858 2000

Tyabji, Nasir. Globalisation in a uni-polar world [microform]: five case studies of the corporate sector in India under deregulation / by Nasir Tyabji. Published/Created: New Delhi: Centre for Contemporary Studies, Nehru Memorial Museum and Library, 1998. Related Names: Nehru Memorial Museum and Library. Centre for Contemporary Studies. Description: 85 p.; 27 cm. Notes: Includes bibliographical references (p. 71-85).

Microfiche. New Delhi: Library of Congress Office; Washington, D.C.: Library of Congress Photoduplication Service, 1999. 2 microfiches. Master microform held by: DLC. Subjects: Organization--Deregulation--India. Series: Occasional papers on perspectives in Indian development; no. 57. LC Classification: Microfiche 99/60140 (H)

Unconventional wisdom: alternative perspectives on the new economy / Jeff Madrick, editor. Published/Created: New York: Century Foundation Press, 2000. Related Names: Madrick, Jeffrey G. Description: vi, 376 p.: ill.; 23 cm. ISBN 0870784447 Notes: Includes bibliographical references (p. 321-354) and index. Subjects: Economic forecasting--United States. Social prediction--United States. Globalization. United States--Economic policy--1993-2001. United States--Social policy--1993- United States--Foreign economic relations. LC Classification: HC106.82 .U53 2000 Dewey Class No.: 330.973 21

Understanding the impact of global networks on local social, political and cultural values: first symposium of the German American Academic Council's project ..., Dresden, February 18-20, 1999 / Christoph Engel, Kenneth H. Keller (eds.). Published/Created: Baden-Baden: Nomos, c2000. Related Names: Engel, Christoph, 1957- ed. Keller, Kenneth H. ed. German-American Academic Council Foundation. Description: 298 p.: ill.; 23 cm. ISBN 3789063894 Notes: Includes bibliographical references. Subjects: Computer networks--Social aspects. Computer networks--Political aspects. Computer networks--Economic aspects. Globalization. Series: Law and economics of international telecommunications, 0935-0624; v. 42. LC Classification: HM567 .U53 2000 Dewey Class No.:

303.48/33 21

Unions in a globalized environment: changing borders, organizational boundaries, and social roles / edited by Bruce Nissen. Published/Created: Armonk, N.Y.: M.E. Sharpe, 2002. Related Names: Nissen, Bruce, 1948- Description: p. cm. ISBN 0765608693 (alk. paper) Notes: Includes bibliographical references and index. Subjects: Labor unions. Foreign trade and employment. Globalization--Economic aspects. LC Classification: HD6483 .U66 2002 Dewey Class No.: 331.88/091 21

Urban movements in a globalising world / edited by Pierre Hamel, Henri Lustiger-Thaler, and Margit Mayer. Published/Created: New York: Routledge, 2001. Related Names: Hamel, Pierre, 1947- Lustiger-Thaler, Henri, 1951- Mayer, Margit. Description: p. cm. ISBN 0415244250 Notes: Includes bibliographical references and index. Subjects: Sociology, Urban. Social movements. Globalization. LC Classification: HT119 .U695 2001 Dewey Class No.: 307.76 21

Views from the South: the effects of globalization and the WTO on Third World countries / edited by Sarah Anderson; foreword by Jerry Mander; afterword by Anuradha Mittal. Published/Created: Oakland, CA: Food First Books, 2000. Related Names: Anderson, Sarah (Sarah Denny) International Forum on Globalization. Description: p. cm. ISBN 093502882X Notes: "In conjunction with International Forum on Globalization." Includes bibliographical references and index. Subjects: World Trade Organization--Developing countries. Globalization--Economic aspects--Developing countries. Globalization--Social aspects--Developing countries. Globalization--Environmental aspects--Developing countries.

International trade. International finance. Developing countries--Foreign economic relations. LC Classification: HF1413 .V53 2000 Dewey Class No.: 330.9172/4 21

Virtual globalization: virtual spaces/tourist spaces / David Holmes. Published/Created: New York: Routledge, 2001. Related Names: Holmes, David, 1962- Description: p. cm. ISBN 0415236738 Notes: Includes bibliographical references and index. Subjects: Information society. Information technology--Social aspects. Globalization. Tourism. Virtual reality. LC Classification: HM851 .V57 2001 Dewey Class No.: 303.48/33 21

Vom ewigen Frieden und vom Wohlstand der Nationen: Dieter Senghaas zum 60. Geburtstag / herausgegeben von Ulrich Menzel. Edition Information: 1. Aufl. Published/Created: Frankfurt am Main: Suhrkamp, 2000. Related Names: Senghaas, Dieter, 1940- Menzel, Ulrich. Description: 629 p.; 18 cm. ISBN 3518121731 (pbk.) Notes: Includes bibliographical references (623-[626]). Subjects: Peace. Globalization. International relations. LC Classification: JZ5538+

Washington, Sally. Globalisation: what challenges and opportunities for governments? / [prepared by Sally Washington]. Published/Created: Paris: OECD, 1996. Related Names: Organisation for Economic Co-operation and Development. Description: 18 p.; 30 cm. Notes: Cover title. Includes bibliographical references (p. 17-18). Subjects: International economic relations. OECD countries--Foreign relations administration. Series: OECD working papers; v. 4, no. 28. LC Classification: HD72 .O38 vol. 4, no. 28

Webster, Thomas, D. Ed. Globalisation of education policies: the extent of external influences on contemporary universal primary education policies in Papua New Guinea / by Thomas Webster. Published/Created: Port Moresby: University of Papua New Guinea Press, 2000. Description: 111 p.: ill.; 30 cm. Notes: Based on research work submitted for the Degree of Doctor of Education of Bristol University. Includes bibliographical references (p. 96-111). Subjects: Education and state--Papua New Guinea. Education, Elementary--Papua New Guinea. Educational assistance--Papua New Guinea. LC Classification: LC94.P26 W43 2000

Wege zur Globalisierung des Rechts: Festschrift für Rolf A. Schütze zum 65. Geburtstag / herausgegeben von Reinhold Geimer. Published/Created: München: Beck, 1999. Related Names: Geimer, Reinhold. Schütze, Rolf A. Description: xvii, 1017 p.; 23 cm. ISBN 3406455131 Notes: 60 German, 7 English contributions. Includes bibliographical references (p. [1011]-1017). Subjects: Schütze, Rolf A. Globalization. International law.

Went, Robert, 1955- Globalization: neoliberal challenge, radical responses / Robert Went; translated by Peter Drucker, foreword by Tony Smith. Published/Created: London; Sterling, Va.: Pluto Press with the International Institute for Research and Education (IIRE), 2000. Description: xii, 170 p.: ill.; 22 cm. ISBN 0745314279 Contents: Globalisation: what's new about it? -- Globalisation: a product of technological change? -- Long waves of capitalist development -- Stagnation and restructuring: towards a new expansion? Notes: Includes bibliographical references (p. [155]-163) and index. Subjects: International economic relations. International business enterprises. Capitalism. Socialism. Globalization. Developing countries--Foreign economic relations. LC Classification: HF1359 .W46 2000 Dewey Class No.: 337 21

Westward dharma: Buddhism beyond Asia / edited by Martin Baumann, Charles Prebish. Published/Created: Berkeley: University of California Press, 2002. Related Names: Prebish, Charles S. Baumann, Martin, 1960- Description: p. cm. ISBN 0520226259 (Cloth: alk. paper) 0520234901 (Paper: alk. paper) Notes: Includes bibliographical references and index. Subjects: Buddhism--Missions--History. Buddhism--20th century--History. Globalization--Religious aspects--Buddhism. LC Classification: BQ5925 .W47 2002 Dewey Class No.: 294.3/09 21

What global economic crisis? / edited by Philip Arestis, Michelle Baddeley, and John McCombie. Published/Created: Houndmills, Basingstoke, Hampshire; New York: Palgrave, 2001. Related Names: Arestis, Philip, 1941- Baddeley, Michelle, 1965- McCombie, J. S. L. Description: xviii, 258 p.: ill.; 23 cm. ISBN 0333800176 Notes: "The papers in this book were presented at a conference on Global financial crisis, held in Gonville and Caius College, Cambridge, UK, in early September 1999"--Introd. Includes bibliographical references and index. Subjects: Financial crises--Congresses. International finance--Congresses. Globalization--Congresses. LC Classification: HB3722 .W49 2001 Dewey Class No.: 332/.042 21

Which "global village"?: societies, cultures, and political-economic systems in a Euro-Atlantic perspective / edited by Valeria Gennaro Lerda. Published/Created: Westport, Conn.: Praeger, 2002. Related Names: Gennaro Lerda, Valeria. Università di Genova. Center for Euro-

Atlantic Studies. International Conference (2nd: 1998 Genoa, Italy) Description: p. cm. ISBN 0275973905 (alk. paper) Subjects: Globalization--Congresses. LC Classification: JZ1318 .W48 2002 Dewey Class No.: 303.48/2 21

Wieviel Globalisierung verträgt unser Land?: Zwänge und Alternativen / herausgegeben von Hans Sallmutter; Redaktion, Patrizia Reidl und Tom Schmid. Published/Created: Wien: Verlag des Österreichischen Gewerkschaftsbundes, c1998. Related Names: Sallmutter, Hans. Reidl, Patrizia. Schmid, Tom. Description: 288 p.: ill.; 24 cm. ISBN 3703507187 Notes: Includes bibliographical references. Subjects: International economic relations. Globalization. International relations. Austria--Economic conditions--1945- LC Classification: HC265 .W52 1998

Will Europe work?: integration, employment and the social order / edited by Martin Kohli and Mojca Novak. Published/Created: New York: Routledge, 2001. Related Names: Kohli, Martin. Novak, Mojca, 1948- Description: p. cm. ISBN 0415260221 Notes: Includes bibliographical references and index. Subjects: Globalization. Europe--Economic integration. Europe--Economic policy. Europe--Social policy. LC Classification: HC240 .W48 2001 Dewey Class No.: 337.1/4 21

Wiseman, John Richard, 1957- Global nation?: Australia and the politics of globalisation / John Wiseman. Published/Created: Cambridge, UK; New York: Cambridge University Press, 1998. Description: viii, 202 p.; 24 cm. ISBN 0521592275 0521597552 (pbk.) Notes: Includes bibliographical references (p. 152-196) and index. Subjects: International economic relations. Australia--Foreign economic relations. LC Classification:

HF1359 .W57 1998 Dewey Class No.: 337.94 21

Women and globalisation: reflections, options, and stragegies / edited by Pam Rajput & Hem Lata Swarup. Published/Created: New Delhi, India: Ashish Pub. House, 1994. Related Names: Rajput, Pam, 1942- Swarup, Hem Lata, 1929- Description: xxiv, 393 p.: ill.; 23 cm. ISBN 8170246695 : Summary: Contributed articles on the loans provided by the international organizations to developing countries and its consequences on women and the poor. Notes: Includes bibliographical referernces. Subjects: Women--Government policy--Developing countries. Women--Employment--Developing countries. Women--Developing countries--Social conditions. LC Classification: HQ1236.5.D44 W66 1994 Dewey Class No.: 362.83/098172/4 20

Women in Asia: tradition, modernity, and globalisation / edited by Louise Edwards & Mina Roces. Published/Created: Ann Arbor: University of Michigan Press, c2000. Related Names: Edwards, Louise P. Roces, Mina, 1959- Description: 327 p.; 22 cm. ISBN 0472087517 (pbk.) Notes: Includes bibliographical references and index. Subjects: Women in development--Asia. Women--Asia--Social conditions. Women--Asia--Economic conditions. Feminism--Asia. Sex role--Asia. LC Classification: HQ1240.5.A78 W63 2000 Dewey Class No.: 305.42/095 21

Women resist globalisation: mobilising for livelihood and rights / Sheila Rowbotham and Stephanie Linkogle (eds.). Published/Created: New York: Zed Books, 2001. Related Names: Rowbotham, Sheila. Linkogle, Stephanie. Description: p. cm. ISBN 185649876X (cased) 1856498778 (limp) Notes:

Includes bibliographical references and index. Subjects: Women's rights. Women political activists. Women social reformers. Globalization. LC Classification: HQ1236 .W6423 2001 Dewey Class No.: 305.42 21

Women resist globalisation: mobilising for livelihood and rights / Sheila Rowbotham and Stephanie Linkogle (eds.). Published/Created: New York: Zed Books, 2001. Related Names: Rowbotham, Sheila. Linkogle, Stephanie. Description: p. cm. ISBN 185649876X (cased) 1856498778 (limp) Notes: Includes bibliographical references and index. Subjects: Women's rights. Women political activists. Women social reformers. Globalization. LC Classification: HQ1236 .W6423 2001 Dewey Class No.: 305.42 21

Women, citizenship and difference / edited by Nira Yuval-Davis and Pnina Werbner. Published/Created: London; New York: Zed; New York: Distributed in the USA exclusively by St. Martin's Press, 1999. Related Names: Werbner, Pnina. Yuval-Davis, Nira. Description: xii, 271 p.; 23 cm. ISBN 1856496457 1856496465 (pbk.) Notes: Includes bibliographical references and index. Subjects: Citizenship. Women's rights. Citizenship. Women's rights. Series: Postcolonial encounters LC Classification: JF801 .W66 1999 Dewey Class No.: 323.6/082 21

Women,men,globalisation & trade liberalisation. Published/Created: Fiji: UNIFEM, 1997. Description: 30 p.

Women's activism and globalization: linking local struggles and transnational politics / edited by Nancy A. Naples and Manisha Desai. Published/Created: New York: Routledge, 2002. Related Names: Naples, Nancy A. Desai, Manisha. Description: p. cm. ISBN 0415931444 0415931452 (pbk.) Notes: Includes bibliographical references and index. Subjects: Women social reformers. Women political activists. Globalization. LC Classification: HQ1236 .W596 2002 Dewey Class No.: 303.48/4 21

Woodiwiss, Anthony. Globalisation, human rights and labour law in Pacific Asia/ Anthony Woodiwiss. Published/Created: Cambridge, U.K.; New York, N.Y.: Cambridge University Press, c1998. Description: xii, 316 p.: ill.; 24 cm. ISBN 0521621445 0521628830 (pbk.) Notes: Includes bibliographical references (p. 270-303) and index. Subjects: Human rights--Asia, Southeastern. Social values--Asia, Southeastern. Labor laws and legislation--Asia, Southeastern. Series: Cambridge studies in law and society LC Classification: JC599.A785 W66 1998 Dewey Class No.: 303.3/72/095 21

Work motivation in the context of a globalizing economy / edited by Miriam Erez, Uwe Kleinbeck, Henk Thierry. Published/Created: Mahwah, N.J.: L. Erlbaum Associates, 2001. Related Names: Erez, Miriam. Kleinbeck, Uwe. Thierry, Henk. Description: x, 439 p.: ill.; 24 cm. ISBN 0805828141 (cloth: alk. paper) 080582815X (pbk.: alk. paper) Notes: Includes bibliographical references and index. Subjects: Employee motivation. Organizational commitment. Globalization. LC Classification: HF5549.5.M63 W3728 2001 Dewey Class No.: 658.3/14 21

World development: an introduction / edited by Prodromos Panayiotopoulos and Gavin Capps. Published/Created: London; Sterling, Va.: Pluto Press, 2001. Related Names: Capps, Gavin. Panayiotopoulos, Prodromos. Description: xxiv, 289 p.; 22 cm. ISBN 0745314074 0745314023 (pbk.) Notes: Includes bibliographical references (p. 254-271) and index.

Subjects: Economic development. Economic history. Globalization. Developing countries--Economic conditions. LC Classification: HD75 .W667 2001

World investment prospects: comparing business environments across the globe Edition Information: 1st ed. Published/Created: London, U.K.; New York: Economic Intelligence Unit, c2001. Related Names: Franklin, Daniel. Economist Intelligence Unit (Great Britain) Description: vi, 259 p.: ill.; 27 cm. ISBN 0862181453 Contents: World investment prospects -- Introduction -- The case for globalisation -- Comparing investment conditions around the globe -- Forecasting foreign direct investment -- Recent trends in foreign direct investment and international business activity -- The changing shape of the multinational enterprise -- Select market and foreign investment data -- World classification -- Business environment rankings methodology -- Business rankings questionnaire -- Country profiles. Notes: Edited by Daniel Franklin and others. "Comparing business environments across the globe"--Cover. Includes index bibliographical references. Subjects: Investments, Foreign. Globalization. International business enterprises. Series: Research report (Economist Intelligence Unit (Great Britain)); IBP 115. LC Classification: HG4538 .W672 2001 Dewey Class No.: 332.67/3 21

World investment prospects: comparing business environments across the globe Edition Information: 1st ed. Published/Created: London, U.K.; New York: Economic Intelligence Unit, c2001. Related Names: Franklin, Daniel. Economist Intelligence Unit (Great Britain) Description: vi, 259 p.: ill.; 27 cm. ISBN 0862181453 Notes: Edited by Daniel Franklin and others. "Comparing business environments across the globe"--Cover. Includes index bibliographical references. Subjects: Investments, Foreign. Globalization. International business enterprises. Series: Research report (Economist Intelligence Unit (Great Britain)); IBP 115. LC Classification: HG4538 .W672 2001 Dewey Class No.: 332.67/3 21

World wide workers: twelve contributions to a global trade union strategy / [authors, Sergio D'Antoni ... et al.]. Published/Created: Stockholm: Brevskolan, 1998. Related Names: D'Antoni, Sergio. Description: 189 p.: ports; 20 cm. ISBN 9157453950 Subjects: International labor activities. Labor unions. Labor laws and legislation, International. Labor movement--International cooperation. Globalization--Social aspects. LC Classification: HD6475.A1 W67 1998 Dewey Class No.: 331 21

Wright, Shelley. International human rights, decolonisation and globalisation: becoming human / Shelley Wright. Published/Created: London; New York: Routledge, 2001. Description: p. cm. ISBN 0415259517 (alk. paper) Notes: Includes bibliographical references and index. Subjects: Human rights. Human rights--Case studies. Decolonization--Case studies. Postcolonialism--Case studies. Globalization. LC Classification: JC571 .W954 2001 Dewey Class No.: 323 21

WTO, globalization, and Nepal / editor, Ananda P. Srestha. Edition Information: 1st ed. Published/Created: Kathmandu: Nepal Foundation for Advanced Studies: United States Embassy, 2001. Related

Names: Shrestha, Ananda P. Nepal Foundation for Advanced Studies. United States. Embassy (Nepal) NEFAS/NUSACCI Seminar on WTO, Globalization, and Nepal (2000: Kathmandu, Nepal) Description: 125 p.; 22 cm. ISBN 9993333034 Notes: Includes bibliographical references.

Zampetti, Americo Beviglia. Globalisation of industrial activities: a case study of the consumer electronics sector. Published/Created: Paris: OECD, 1994. Related Names: Organisation for Economic Co-operation and Development. Description: 53 p.: ill.; 30 cm. Notes: "Prepared by Americo Beviglia Zampetti'--P. [1]. Includes bibliographical references (p. 27-28). Subjects: Electronic industries--Case studies. International division of labor--Case studies. International business enterprises--Case studies. Series: OECD working papers; v. 2, no. 44. LC Classification: HD72 .O38 vol. 2, no. 44

Zukunftsverantwortung in der Marktwirtschaft / Thomas Bausch .. [et al.] (Hrsg.); Redaktion , Micha H. Werner. Published/Created: Münster: Lit, [2000] Related Names: Bausch, Thomas. Jonas, Hans, 1903- Description: 531 p.: ill.; 24 cm. ISBN 3894736798 Notes: "In memoriam Hans Jonas"--Cover. Includes bibliographical references (p. [491]-520). Subjects: Economic policy--Moral and ethical aspects. Economic development--Moral and ethical aspects. Globalization--Moral and ethical aspects. Environmental policy--Moral and ethical aspects. Social ethics. Series: Ethik und Wirtschaft im Dialog; Bd. 3 LC Classification: HD87.5 .Z85 2000 Dewey Class No.: 174/.4 21

Author Index

C

TITLE INDEX

E

Early globalization and the economic development of the United States and Brazil, 37

East Asia and globalization, 41

East Asian democratization: impact of globalization, culture, and economy, 29

Ecological costs of economic globalisation: the Indian experience, 152

EcoNews. U. S. farmland preservation [and] Global sustainable development, 41

Economía global, política y medios de comunicación, 30

Economic development: a global perspective, 8

Economic globalisation and the environment, 41, 105

Economic integration in the Pacific region, 39

Economic regionalisation and intra-industry trade: Pacific-Asian perspectives, 51

Economic structure-functionalism in European unification and globalization of the economies, 101

Economic transition in the Middle East: global challenges and adjustment strategies, 41

Economics for business: competition, macro-stability, and globalisation, 114

Educación y exclusión en América Latina: reformas en tiempos de globalización, 144

Educational restructuring in the context of globalization and national policy, 42

Educational traditions compared: content, teaching, and learning in industrialised countries, 115

Egalitarian politics in the age of globalization, 42

El desencuentro americano: México y Estados Unidos en la globalización, 124

El fraude de la tercera vía, 6

El nihilismo al desnudo: los tiempos de la globalizació´n, 89

Elect the ambassador!: building democracy in a globalised world, 99

Elite globalization and the attack on Christianity, 135

Eloge du mondialisme: Par un anti présumé, 133

Employment relations and national culture: continuity and change in the age of globalisation, 138

En el alba del milenio: globalización y medios de comunicación en América Latina, 130

Encuentros inciertos: globalización y territorios locales en Centroamérica, 134

Ensayando a ensayar: ensayos académicos universitarios, 110

Entrepreneurs and the transformation of the global economy, 42

Entrepreneurship, strategic management, and globalization, 43

Environment and global modernity, 43

Environmental regulation in the new global economy, 43

Erasmus: revista para el diálogo intercultural., 44

Essays in economic globalization, transnational policies, and vulnerability, 44

Estado, política y recomposición institucional en el sector rural en América Latina, 44

Estructura económica y comercio mundial, 12

Ethics and the future of capitalism, 45

Ethnicity and globalization: from migrant worker to transnational citizen, 21

Europe 2020: adapting to a changing world, 45

European integration and the postmodern condition: governance, democracy, identity, 86

European Union and new regionalism: regional actors and global governance in a post-hegemonic era, 45

Exploring the gaps: vital links between trade, environment, and culture, 107

External and internal constraints on policy making: how autonomous are the states?, 46

External liberalization, economic performance, and social policy, 46

Eyes of the heart: seeking a path for the poor in the age of globalization, 8

F

Facets of Globalization: international and local dimensions of development, 46

Familiar medicine: everyday health knowledge and practice in today's Vietnam, 31

Faut-il avoir peur de la mondialisation: Enjeux spirituels et mission de l'Eglise, 146

FERA, Indian reforms, globalisation (FIRG), 117

Fighting the wrong enemy: antiglobal activists and multinational enterprises, 84

Financial crises in emerging markets: an essay on financial globalisation and fragility, 105

Financial services without borders: how to succeed in professional financial services, 46

Five days that shook the world: Seattle and beyond, 26

Fragmentation: new production patterns in the world economy, 48

H

I

M

N

O

P

T

Z

Subject Index